2010 BPM

and

Workflow

Handbook

2010 BPM and Workflow Handbook

Methods, Concepts, Case Studies and Standards in Business Process Management and Workflow

Spotlight on Business Intelligence

Published in association with the
Workflow Management Coalition

Workflow Management Coalition

WfM
C

16 Years of Thought-Process Leadership

Edited by

Layna Fischer

Future Strategies Inc., Book Division

Lighthouse Point, Florida

2010 BPM and Workflow Handbook

Copyright © 2010 by Future Strategies Inc.

ISBN-13: 9780981987057

Published by Future Strategies Inc., Book Division

3640-B3 North Federal Highway #421
Lighthouse Point FL 33064 USA
954.782.3376 fax 954.719.3746
www.FutStrat.com; books@FutStrat.com

Cover by STUDIO H Advertising & Design

Publisher's Cataloging-in-Publication Data

Library of Congress Catalog Card LCCN No. 2010928398

2010 BPM and Workflow Handbook:
/Layna Fischer (editor)

p. cm.

Includes bibliographical references, appendices and index.

ISBN 978-0-9819870-5-7

1. Business Process Management. 2. Workflow Management. 3. Technological Innovation. 4. Business Intelligence. 5. Business Process Technology. 6. Organizational Change 7. Management Information Systems. 8. Office Practice Automation. 9. Business Process Technology. 10. Electronic Commerce. 11. Process Analysis

Fischer, Layna (editor)

Table of Contents

Foreword

It is my pleasure to introduce to you WfMC's tenth annual BPM and Workflow Handbook, rounding out a complete decade of this important reference work. Throughout the decade, led by Layna Fischer, the Handbooks have consistently focused on the leading trends and advancements in the process technology marketplace.

Year 2009 was a real turning point in the process technology space. It was a year where a number of key pure-play business process management suite (BPMS) vendors were acquired, and are now incorporated into the stacks of large technology vendors. Many analysts responded asking the question whether we were seeing the end of BPM, but such a shopping spree should be viewed instead of the ultimate complete legitimization of BPM. The consolidation of the industry indicates that it has become mainstream. A budget item for BPM technology is no longer exotic and hard to justify, but instead a normal and frequently required part of IT spending. It seems that BPM has come of age.

Looking over the decade, we have seen both the introduction and the maturation of an area of technology known as business process management (BPM). Back at the time of the first Handbook, in 2001, the acronym BPM would have been unfamiliar to all but a few people. This handbook in 2001 was called simply the "Workflow Handbook." It is interesting to see the introduction of the term *BPM* at about that time, later to rise and completely eclipse the use of the term *workflow*. BPM promised many different things to different people: in fact even today, there are two different personalities of BPM. BPM means two distinct things to two different sets of people.

To some in the information technology sector, BPM means essentially a way to develop solutions that integrate information from many separate applications across the enterprise. This kind of BPM is an extension of the Enterprise Application Integration (EAI) field. As applications gain the ability to deliver raw information to remote requesters, they have become services which play a part in a Service Oriented Architecture (SOA). To these people BPM has represented the ability to orchestrate web services (using BPEL), and to make composite applications by integrating the results from many separate application.

To others, BPM represented the idea that management would represent the work of the organization as business processes, and they then manage these processes over the long term. This approach is completely separate from the technology (we are talking about processes, which, in many cases involve humans) but still technology was developed to help in the describing of processes, and the facilitation of the work to manage and maintain the processes. The end goal is the same; better support for the business. Proponents in this group will sometimes vigorously protest that BPEL and the integration technology are not central to the management aspect of BPM.

This bifurcation into two personalities of BPM still exists. What is interesting about the consolidation of 2009 was that companies in the integration space were acquiring companies in the management space. This allows the key vendors to offer the entire range from low level IT integration to higher level organizational management of processes.

While BPM crosses the gap into the mainstream, those who chase the cutting edge are asking "what is next?" The first half of 2010 was filled with soul searching for a "new definition" of BPM. Is it going to be Social BPM? Dynamic BPM? Consider that BPM is built on the concepts of Scientific Management, and idea that perfecting a process to be repeatable and efficient is the best way to get work done. The main push behind BPM in recent years has been toward making more and more elaborate process definitions with increasing capabilities for handling information flow. Notation, such as BPMN, has been elaborated toward the precise definition of information flow, and it is now seen as primarily a programming tool for process specialists. The idea of mass production of processes, done thousands of times in exactly the same way, achieving the benefits of scalability, has clearly been shown not only possible, but readily available. What is next?

Many analysts noted the rising importance of "Case Management" in the latter half of 2009 and early 2010. Case Management represents the antithesis of scientific management. Case Management is founded on the idea that getting the work done is more important than perfecting the process. It goes further than this, in saying that the details of the case are so overwhelmingly responsible for the plan of attack, that it is not useful to isolate the plan from the case itself. A large investment in creating a plan is not justified when the plan is used only once. Each case must be handled by an intelligent human being who can take in the situation, bring to bear experience and knowledge gained from earlier cases, and synthesize for this particular case the process necessary. It is the opposite of BPM because instead of trying to find one single "best" process, Case Management is oriented toward finding a different and unique process for every different situation, and tools that support custom on-the-fly elaboration of processes.

The process community is having a hard time understanding the difference that case management brings, because after a decade of struggle to get people to view all work as a process, it is hard then to see another view. Because the case manager is not a programmer, it can't be exclusively a paradigm around programming the integration. Forrester has talked about Dynamic Case Management, IBM announces Advanced Case Management, and the WfMC has been active in trying to refine the concepts under the term Adaptive Case Management (ACM). It seems that while BPM is an approach that works well for predictable processes, Case Management is a separate approach that works for unpredictable, emergent processes. Interestingly, some of the same technology underlies both of these approaches.

The Workflow Management Coalition continues to push forward on standards to enable process model interchange, working directly with the BPMN finalization task force, as well as with other efforts to define conformance classes to allow for distinct levels of interoperability. WfMC remains the only standards organization focused exclusively on process technology.

Which brings us to the reason to focus this volume on Business Process Intelligence. Regardless of whether you design a fixed definition in advance for a predictable process, or whether a case manager extends the plan for an unpredictable process while working, the results can be analyzed with process intelligence technology. Retrospective analysis can tell us if the processes are going according to plan, and can tell us if the plan itself is a good idea. In cases where work was performed without the guidance of a process, process mining, also known as automatic process discovery, can tell us what the process has actually been without having to involve people in lengthy, and error prone, interviews. Process mining can tell us what is efficient and inefficient about an existing work pattern, and it can give us a jump-start on new BPM implementation efforts when no previous process definition exists. Business (Process) Intelligence is a field that is just beginning to show very promising results. Eleven independent authors bring us views of this topic. After all, in the end, it is process analytics that keeps us all honest. Because it can measure performance, Business Process Intelligence is a critical part of delivering on the promise of improving performance of the business.

While the next decade remains unpredictable, it is only through the careful consideration of current trends, and maintaining an ability to respond with agility, that one can hope to navigate successfully. Representing the membership of the Workflow Management Coalition, I hope you find these articles helpful in your efforts to keep up to date on the current trends in the process technology community.

Keith D. Swenson, Fujitsu America, USA and
Chair WfMC Technical Committee

Introduction

Layna Fischer, Future Strategies Inc. USA

Welcome to the *2010 BPM and Workflow Handbook*. This edition marks the 10th year of publication and each year, in collaboration with the WfMC, we have produced a valuable handbook capturing state-of-the-art in workflow practices and for the past few years we expanded our focus to include articles on BPM along with spotlights on industry niches such as Healthcare, Human Workflow and Government.

This year we focus on *Business Intelligence* to illustrate how Business Process Management and Business Intelligence are increasingly intertwined. Linking business intelligence and business process management creates stronger operational business intelligence. Users seek more intelligent business process capabilities in order to remain competitive within their fields and industries. BPM vendors realize they need to improve their business processes, rules and event management offerings with greater intelligence or analytics capabilities.

This is a book for business people who just want to understand the how and why of process automation and integration in simple non-jargon terms. It is also for the technical practitioner looking for the latest insights into where BPM standards are heading, how others are managing implementations and more.

Throughout the book international industry experts and thought leaders present significant new ideas and concepts to help you plan a successful future for your organization.

- SECTION 1: SPOTLIGHT ON BUSINESS INTELLIGENCE covers a wide spectrum of viewpoints and discussions by experts in their respective fields. Papers range from an examination of the *Knowledge Work and Unpredictable Processes* through to Using *BPM to Drive Clinical Intelligence* and *Predictive BPM*.
- SECTION 2—THE BUSINESS VALUE OF BPM AND WORKFLOW introduces new key concepts and sets out the business case for workflow technology and BPM. This perspective is covered by papers that provide practical information on BPM (including case studies) designed for an audience of business users.
- SECTION 3—STANDARDS AND TECHNOLOGY. BPM standards have evolved from technical nuance to a business imperative. This perspective is covered by papers on system structure and values, operation and scalability issues, written for an audience of Information Technology (IT) professionals.
- SECTION 4—DIRECTORY AND APPENDICES offers an explanation of the structure of the Workflow Management Coalition and references comprise the last section including a membership directory.

SECTION 1—SPOTLIGHT ON BUSINESS INTELLIGENCE

BUSINESS PROCESS INTELLIGENCE: BEYOND THE CONVERGENCE OF BPM AND BI   19

Linus Chow, Manoj Das and Peter Bostrom, Oracle Corp, USA

The use of BPM and BI together is not a new concept. Business Process Intelligence (BPI) takes on new meaning and importance as organizations become process-centric and standards and technologies mature and converge. This chapter brings discusses key trends of where organizations are moving toward bringing together products and methodology to improve business performance beyond BPM and BI: Combining the 4 Bs: Business Design + Business Process + Business Intelligence + Business Rules, Event Driven Process Intelligence, and BPI as a Cloud or Appliance.

Keith D. Swenson, Fujitsu America, USA, and Vice Chair, Workflow Management Coalition
What is the next thing beyond Business Process Management (BPM)? To many this is an unexpected question. Is there anything wrong with BPM? Any reason it seems to be flagging? Over the course of 2009 there were a number of high profile acquisitions of BPM companies and many say this as an indication of the end of BPM. Others, however, see this as an indication that BPM is mature, solid, and relatively well-defined, and a natural occurrence of a maturing technology area. Either way, it prompts people to wonder what is going to be next.

Patrick Beaucamp, BPM-Conseil/Vanilla, France
Over the past few years, the Business Intelligence (BI) and Business Process software market has given new opportunities and challenges to software startup companies. An opportunity exists for those market segments to progress and make significant contribution to IT. Both evolve in a situation that is now comparable to what existed in other market segments (such as databases or servers) and are in a position to challenge existing commercial products.

Francesco BATTISTA, Respondo, Italy and Gianpiero BONGALLINO, Italy
A future, but shortly-forthcoming, scenario is going to change the approach to process management: semantic techniques and automatic tools (based on Artificial Intelligence) will guide and support humans in designing and implementing process centric solutions.
This article explores this pioneering frontier made of an added-value mix of Business Process Management systems and Artificial Intelligence.

Dr. Setrag Khoshafian, Pegasystems Inc., USA
Most businesses today engage in "predictions." Will a customer agree to upgrade a purchase based on an array of offers? What is the likelihood that a customer within a cluster of similar customers will default on a loan? How much more effective will a targeted marketing campaign be, compared to a random sampling? How can the churn rate of subscribers be improved? What is the likelihood that a particular financial transaction is fraudulent? These are some questions that could utilize prediction with concrete and tangible business benefits.

James Taylor, Decision Management Solutions, USA
The challenge of putting BI to work in business processes is that reports and dashboards only work in manual processes. If the process is automated, if straight through processing is called for, then the analytics required are different. Embedding these analytics in rules-based decisions is the ideal way to analytically enhance these processes and build intelligent, automated processes.

Juan J. Moreno, Marcelo Cordini, Cristian Mastrantono, INTEGRADOC, Uruguay and Martín Palatnik, Universidad Católic, Uruguay
Business Process Management (BPM) discipline has allowed organizations to considerably optimize their business processes, by including within some products the functionality required to assign work items to participants in an efficient way. However, nowadays these solutions do not consider user's "busy-ness" level (meaning how busy the user is) neither participant's efficiency when work items are assigned; this constitutes a major optimization and improvement opportunity for these tools.
This work presents the unified results of three researches with a common objective: provide a complete model to represent and predict user's busyness, in order to optimize work items assignment in a BPM environment. The methodology included a comprehensive analysis of

the state of the art. Subsequently, a team of several researchers developed the solution for the problem. This work has had several validation and verification stages to prove its feasibility and effectiveness, including a prototype developed using a world-class open source BPM tool, and standard programming languages.

American Recovery and Reinvestment Act (ARRA) of 2009 and Joint Commission/Centers for Medicare & Medicaid Services (CMS) core measures specifications.

SECTION 2—THE BUSINESS VALUE OF BPM AND WORKFLOW 131

BPM-ON-DEMAND: FANTASY OR FAST TRACK TO AGILITY? 133
Jon Pyke, WfMC Chair, United Kingdom
The automation of processes is a key enabler of the Cloud phenomena—without *process*, the Cloud remains a passive environment that undoubtedly saves you money and removes some of the operational headaches, but does little else. The Cloud without process cannot deliver on the promise of Business Technology or the Service-Oriented Enterprise. All of the thoughts and ideas around assembling applications quickly to support a business imperative simply won't happen without process technology. However we need to be very clear; process management in the Cloud is not just about BPM Suites-on-Demand. Indeed, the term BPM-on-Demand is beginning to take on a new meaning when used in conjunction with cloud computing.

A GENERIC FRAMEWORK FOR BUSINESS PROCESS MANAGEMENT 137
Philippe Declercq and Vincent Fauliot, CNAMTS, France
This article introduces a generic framework for business process management. It is largely inspired from BPM and other new IT standards. Functional architecture is used as a link between process definition and implementation of IT new standards, such as BPM, BI, BAM or BRMS technologies. This framework demonstrates how BPM solutions can bring added value to business users, and allows IT professionals to quickly deliver applications corresponding to business and users needs. This article is illustrated with real case studies, issued from our experience in the French National Healthcare Insurance. This efficient way for designing business processes and implementing them is now successfully used in some of our main projects.

ENTERPRISE PROCESS AUTOMATION–PROVIDING THE GIFT OF TIME 149
Roy Altman, Peopleserv Inc., USA
I recently embarked on a project to improve Human Resources processes for a client. My methodology was to interview stakeholders from various points of view, from line-level managers through executives, globally. From their feedback, it became clear that if we could eliminate the work that can be effectively automated, it would have the effect of creating more time, and the added benefit of being able to use that time for tasks more enjoyable for the worker, and more of a value-add for the company. I called the resulting action plan: *"Enterprise Process Automation."*

TRANSFORMING SECURITY THROUGH ENTERPRISE ARCHITECTURE AND BPM 159
Christine Robinson, Christine Robinson & Associates, LLC and Daniel Turissini, Operational Research Consultants, USA
This unified Enterprise Architecture (EA), Business Process Management (BPM), and security approach offers the potential to radically transform security on all levels, providing leadership and practitioners alike the tools to benefit from a strategic to a granular level. Security often suffers from cultural barriers, inadequate funding, insufficient attention, bolting it on the back end, lack of understanding, lack of uniformity, and many more ills. This approach enables organizations to plan and implement security throughout an enterprise and beyond through harnessing EA frameworks and integrated business process management (BPM) software to enable the EA.

CUSTOMER EXPERIENCE TRANSFORMATION—A FRAMEWORK TO ACHIEVE MEASURABLE RESULTS 179
Vinaykumar S Mummigatti, Virtusa, USA
IThe era of extreme competition is creating immense importance for customer experience and how companies manage their customers' expectations. The ability to successfully manage the customer value chain across the life cycle of a customer is the key to the survival of any company today. Most companies realize this but are struggling to measure and influence the customer experience. This paper is an attempt to look at various facets of custom-

er experience and how to transform customer experience to achieve measurable business goals. Business Process Management and the convergence of technologies *(such as Portals, web 2.0, BI, Content Management)* are two key elements of this transformation and hence we will focus on how the convergence of various technologies led by BPM will help achieve the business goals around Customer Experience Transformation (CET).

SECTION 3—STANDARDS AND TECHNOLOGY · 189

HOW TO OPTIMIZE CAPABILITY-CENTERED ENTERPRISE INTEGRATION · 191
Nathaniel Palmer and Jason Adolf, SRA International, Inc., VA, USA
Increasingly, COTS BPM and SOA platforms are leveraged as the bones of architecture and approach, allowing for the maximum amount of flexibility while reducing the need for tenuous custom coding. Yet the 'Integration-centric' approach most commonly followed obviates the inherent benefits offered by BPM, notably the ability to deliver business capabilities, rather application functionality.

Taking a capability-centered approach to extracting and exposing existing application functionality, while mapping these to new processes and interaction models, allows organizations to realize optimal value from current generation COTS BPM and SOA platforms. This approach begins with modeling business concepts as addressable capabilities, and then extending these into specific deployment models which leverage BPM and SOA for capability-centered business integration. This chapter gives step-by-step instructions on optimizing this capability.

XPDL 2.2: INCORPORATING BPMN 2.0 PROCESS MODELING EXTENSIONS · 203
Robert M. Shapiro, Global 360, USA
In June 2009 the OMG voted to adopt the BPMN 2.0 specification which then entered the Finalization Task Force (FTF) phase. At that time the WfMC initiated work revising XPDL2.1. The new version, XPDL2.2, is described in this paper.

XPDL2.2 is intended as a preliminary release which supports the graphical extensions to process modeling contained in BPMN2.0. In fact, the BPMN specification addresses four different areas of modeling, referred to as:

- Process Modeling
- Process Execution
- BPEL Process Execution
- Choreography Modeling

We focus only on Process Modeling. Within that we define several sub-classes to support process interchange between tools. This is discussed in a later section of this paper.

WORKFLOW CONTROL-PATH INTELLIGENCE AND ITS IMPLICATIONS · 217
Haksung Kim, Dongnam Health University and Kwanghoon Kim, Kyonggi Univ., Rep. of Korea
In this paper, we describe the basic concept of workflow control-path intelligence and its implications on the arena of business process analysis, prediction and optimization. That is, we introduce a series of models, algorithms and frameworks for analyzing, predicting, optimizing and rediscovering the control-path intelligence from a workflow model. Conclusively, we strongly believe that the workflow control-path intelligence must be an essential factor for improving the quality of workflow model itself as well as a pioneering research issue in extracting other workflow-related knowledge and intelligence to rapidly and reliably deliver agile services to businesses and IT customers.

WORKFLOW DESIGN PATTERNS FOR DEVELOPING AND MAINTAINING E-BUSINESS WORKFLOW SYSTEMS · 232
Farhi Marir and John Ndeta, Knowledge Management Research Centre, Faculty of Computing, London Metropolitan University, UK
Designing an e-business workflow system for your organisation using a traditional framework is not appropriate as it ignores the human dimension of organisational knowledge creation and the dynamic situations encountered in organisations collaborative work processes in the new e-business environment. As a result e-business workflows systems

developed using this framework are less capable in dealing with the new e-business era which is characterised by an increasing pace of radical, discontinuous and unforeseen change in e-business processes.

This paper highlights the limitation of this traditional framework and presents an alternative framework for designing flexible and dynamic e-business workflow management systems that respond to the continual changes of e-business processes.

UTILIZING PROCESS DEFINITIONS FOR PROCESS AUTOMATION: A COMPARATIVE STUDY   247

Filiz Çelik Yeşildoruk and Onur Demirörs, Middle East Technical University, Informatics Institute, Turkey

Process modeling offers a very effective means for understanding and analyzing what needs to be improved. Process models are also used for many other purposes such as process automation, which increases the effectiveness of process improvement especially when organizations need to react quickly. Although there are numerous studies on various approaches to be separately applied to process modeling and process automation, the relationship and dynamics between the two still remains undiscovered. This paper presents the results of an exploratory study on the usability of process models developed for process improvement to be applied to the automation of processes with selected Business Process Management (BPM) tools.

The case study covers two processes in a software development unit of a large organization. The extended Event Driven Process Chain (eEPC) notation was utilized for process modeling and BizAgi, WebMethods and Intalio BPM suites for automation. A comparison was made concerning time spent to carry out the modeling and automation and the effectiveness of the BPM tools was analyzed.

SECTION 4—DIRECTORIES AND APPENDICES   257

Section 1

Business Intelligence

Business Process Intelligence: Beyond the Convergence of BPM and BI

Linus Chow, Manoj Das and Peter Bostrom, Oracle Corp, USA

ABSTRACT

The use of BPM and BI together is not a new concept. Business Process Intelligence (BPI) takes on new meaning and importance as organizations become process-centric and standards and technologies mature and converge. This chapter brings discusses key trends of where organizations moving toward bringing together products and methodology to improve business performance beyond BPM and BI: Combining the 4 Bs: Business Design + Business Process + Business Intelligence + Business Rules, Event Driven Process Intelligence, and BPI as a Cloud or Appliance.

INTRODUCTION: THE START OF A DECADE OF CONVERGENCE?

Successful Information Technology (IT) Capabilities are driven by customer requirements and adoption of new methodologies. In turn methodologies are driven by the maturation of Technologies and the introduction of new tools. Mission stakeholders demand has driven IT to produce technology enabled solutions more and more aligned to the way the Enterprise really runs. With each business cycle, and disruptive event (e.g. new technologies, market forces, government regulations) Technology Tools and associated methodologies are created and evolved. Combining technology tools is obviously not a new concept; almost all functional enterprises use multiple technologies to manage processes and reporting in some fashion.

What we are currently on the cusp of could either be a "blurring of the boundaries" or a "systematic convergence" of IT tools and methodologies that will reshape how business and IT interact. This confluence of events has built a growing consensus of thought leaders in the industry that Business Process Management is the epicenter of far reaching change. Why is this? BPM itself was the market driven convergence of EAI and workflow (and later BAM) and is a driving factor behind giving Business (Mission) stakeholders more control and understanding of how IT actually functions. The game-changing event that is further propelling this convergence and BPM leadership is the new BPMN 2.0 standard. BPMN 2.0 is unique in that it is the first step in allowing non-IT experts of the business to create standards-based processes that don't get radically transformed when executed. This breaks down several barriers:

- Between Mission and IT (What you see is what you get)
- Design-Time vs Run-Time (Train like you Fight)
- EA and SOA (Potential Bridge Between DoDAF / TOGAF and SOA)
- Cloud-Enabled IT Assets (Share SOA Assets with a comprehensible standard)
- Technology Tool Convergence (Forcing Tool Vendors to a Common Standard both for BPA and BPM)

- Drives the Value of BI (No more Garbage In/Out. BPM collects real data points through end-to-end process automation)
- Appliance Enabler (Adds Flexibility to Appliances to be modified)

Across the industry and customers BPM is increasingly seen as both the technology and methodology to build a more agile Enterprise. Analysts like Forrester to Gartner, System Integrators, and Customer CIOs are realizing the convergence of these technologies and expanding where the boundaries of BPM are (see Figure 1 below).

BPM ECOSYSTEM: BLURRING BOUNDARIES OR SYSTEMATIC CONVERGENCE?

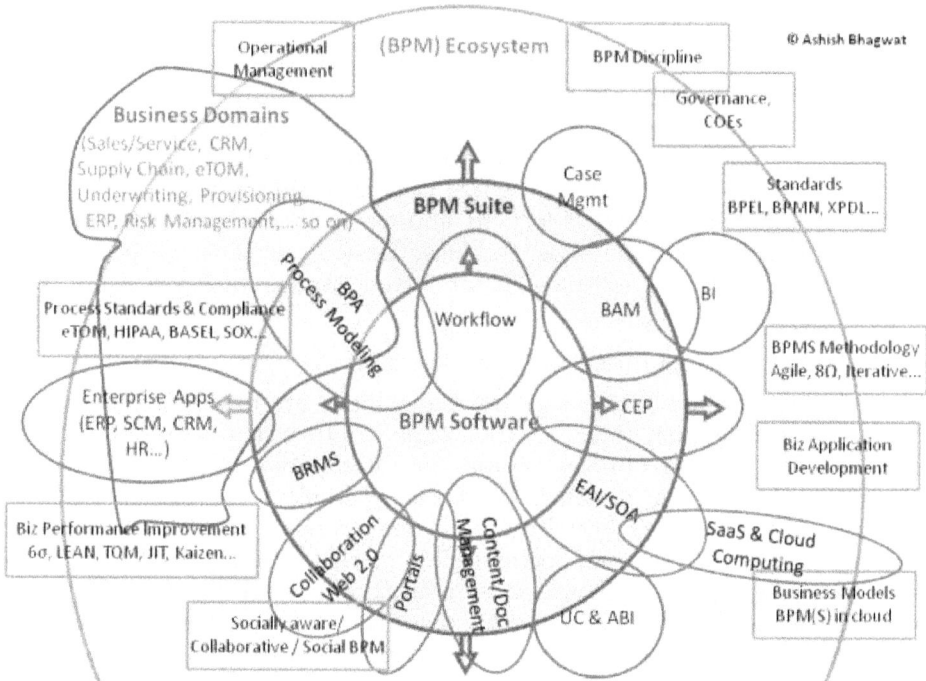

Figure 1: Blurring Boundaries or Systematic Convergence?

So what is happening? Both is the answer. IT vendors are being driven by the market demand (which is blurring the boundaries); at the same time IT vendors are reacting by systematically converging and integrating their technologies. This theory is supported by the recent marketing driven acquisitions that started when Oracle bought BEA, Haley and Hyperion over the last couple of years. This trend accelerated very recently with IBM buying Lombardi, Software AG buying IDS Sheer, and Progress acquiring Savvion. The other data point is that BPM tools continue to maintain its market value and functional strengths against Open Source capabilities. Clearly, this proves that the sums of the parts are worth more than the individual components and that BPM is the glue that is bringing them together.

How did we get here? It is important to understand how BPM and the convergence of the 4 Bs came to pass. The evolutionary history of this convergence has been a road traveled by IT and business together (see Figure 2 below).

A Historical Perspective

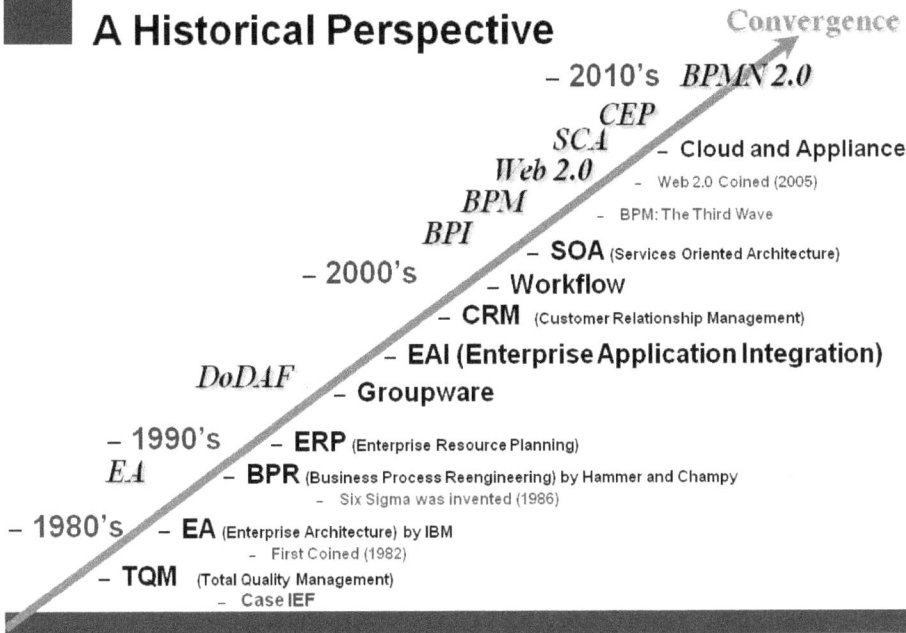

Convergence

– 2010's *BPMN 2.0*

CEP

SCA – Cloud and Appliance

Web 2.0 – Web 2.0 Coined (2005)

BPM – BPM: The Third Wave

BPI – SOA (Services Oriented Architecture)

– 2000's – Workflow

– CRM (Customer Relationship Management)

– EAI (Enterprise Application Integration)

DoDAF – Groupware

– 1990's – ERP (Enterprise Resource Planning)

EA – BPR (Business Process Reengineering) by Hammer and Champy

– Six Sigma was invented (1986)

– 1980's – EA (Enterprise Architecture) by IBM

– First Coined (1982)

– TQM (Total Quality Management)

– Case IEF

Figure 2: History of Business Driven IT Evolution

This historical evolution is important in that the underpinnings of any future converged / combined technologies and methodologies are based on sound experience (both trials and tribulations).

COMBINING THE 4 BS: BUSINESS DESIGN + BUSINESS PROCESS + BUSINESS INTELLIGENCE + BUSINESS RULES

The pressure for an organization to be more Agile, Efficient, and Effective is always present. At certain times those pressures are heightened due to market, political, and business forces. We are again at that cross-road in history, where we have to adapt rapidly to events that quickly ripple across the globe, while dealing with unprecedented challenges. Examples of what we are facing:

- The US is engaged in (and trying to disengage with) two wars
- The US has first African-American President elected on "Change"
- The US has a huge (and increasing) debt burden while still recovering from a recession
- The EU just had to bail out Greece and injected $1 Trillion to support the Euro
- Largest deep water oil spill in history occurred in the Gulf of Mexico (and as, of this writing, we still don't know how to stop the leak.)
- Stock Markets world-wide are going through wild gyrations (and we don't yet know all the causes)
- Ash clouds from an erupting Icelandic volcano shut down air-space for days over Britain and Europe with resultant travel chaos and billions of dollars loss to airlines and industry.

These forces are driving both Commercial and Government Enterprises to improve their operation by increasing capabilities while cutting costs. An example would be US Secretary of Defense Gates' directive to cut Pentagon bureaucracy. Note that this is not just about cost-cutting. For example, cost-cutting without improving capability plays a part in our inability to date to contain the oil spill in the Gulf of Mexico. IT is key to enabling better mission/business performance, but the challenge is that our legacy investments have created a business as usual infrastructure (see Figure 3 below)

The Challenge

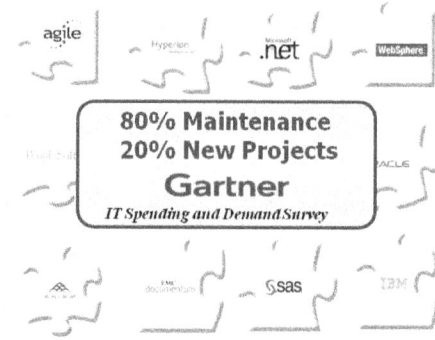

How to....?

• ... orchestrate multi-channel constituent interactions?

• ...automate processes across applications?

• ...easily modify such processes?

• ...make relevant business insight available to the masses?

• ... make upgrade safe customization to applications?

Figure 3: Challenge of IT Agility

If 80 cents of every dollar you spend goes just to sustaining what you have, this does not bode well for Agility. The result of this is a Business Execution Gap between what the Mission requires and what the IT platform can deliver (see Figure 4 below).

The Result

When mission conditions evolve faster than the Enterprise's ability to change and respond...

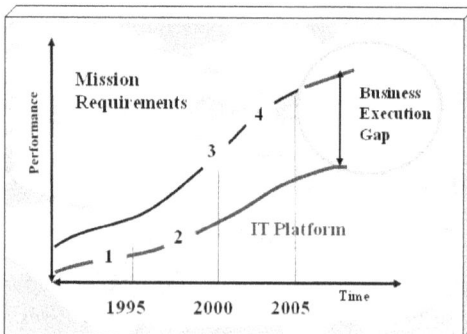

1 ERP Deployment

2 CRM Deployment

3 Internet Explosion

4 Mission Change

... business performance suffers

Figure 4: Resulting Business Execution Gap

The solution is bringing IT capabilities together to leverage the strengths of each component, reuse as much capabilities as possible across the Enterprise, while abstracting capabilities for each stakeholder so they can focus on their tasks. Seems simple enough right? But this also means that each part of the Enterprise Architecture (EA) isn't just integrated but also must somehow understand the context of its use and alignment to overall organizational goals and objectives. This is what is driving the convergences of the 4Bs. The end result is an Agile, SOA enabled Enterprise (see Figure 5 below)

The Solution

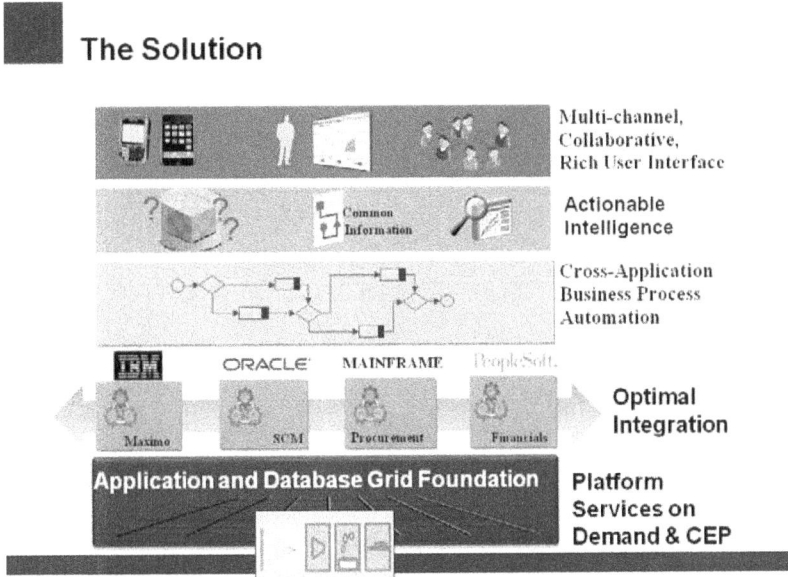

Figure 5: Solution: Agile & SOA Enabled Enterprise

BPM provides the capability to visually connect the user focused capabilities with the technical capabilities. That is its core strength across the Application Development Lifecycle (see Figure 6 below).

Complete - Full Lifecycle Support
Rich and Easy-to-Use Tools for Every Persona

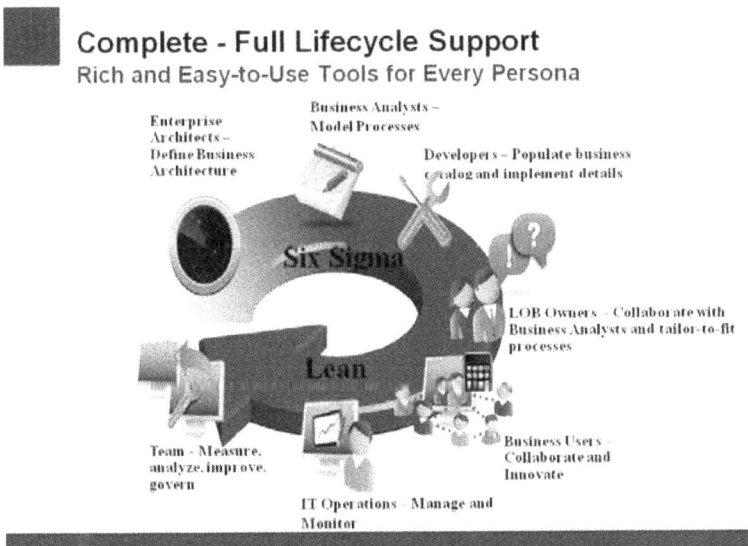

Figure 6: BPM Spans the Complete Lifecycle

This is driving BPM Suites to include and/or connect to the other 4Bs (Business Design, Business Intelligence, and Business Rules) as well as SOA (see Figure 7 below)

Example BPM Architecture

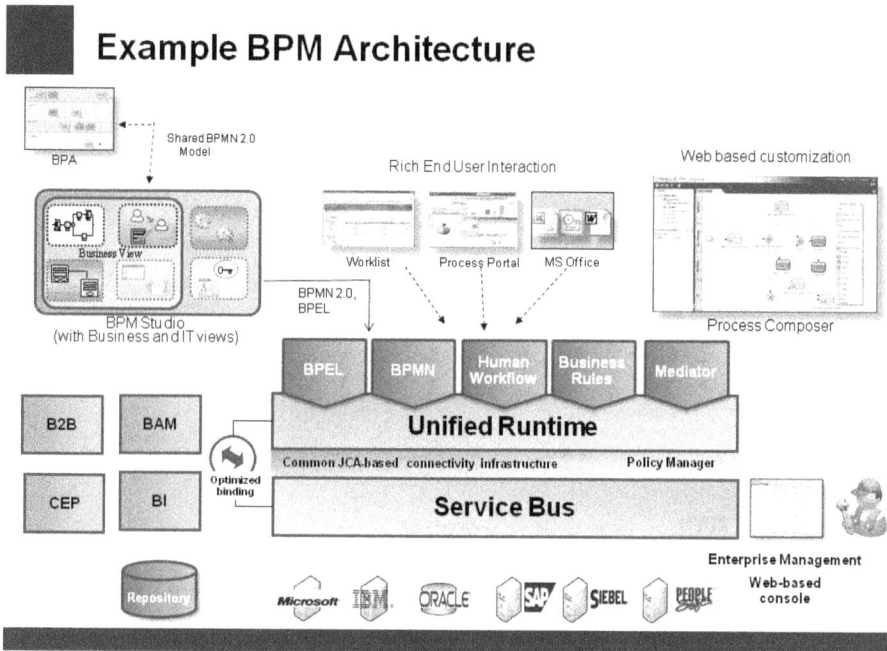

Figure 7: Example BPM Architecture

Enterprises, such as the US Department of Defense, are taking advantage of this maturing and convergence of the 4Bs and specifically BPMN 2.0's ability to bridge the design-time /run-time gap. DoDAF is the US Department of Defense Architectural Frameworkto. There are current initiatives to bring BPMN 2.0 process models, Business Intelligence and Business Rules in alignment to its Business/Mission Design (see Figure 8 below)

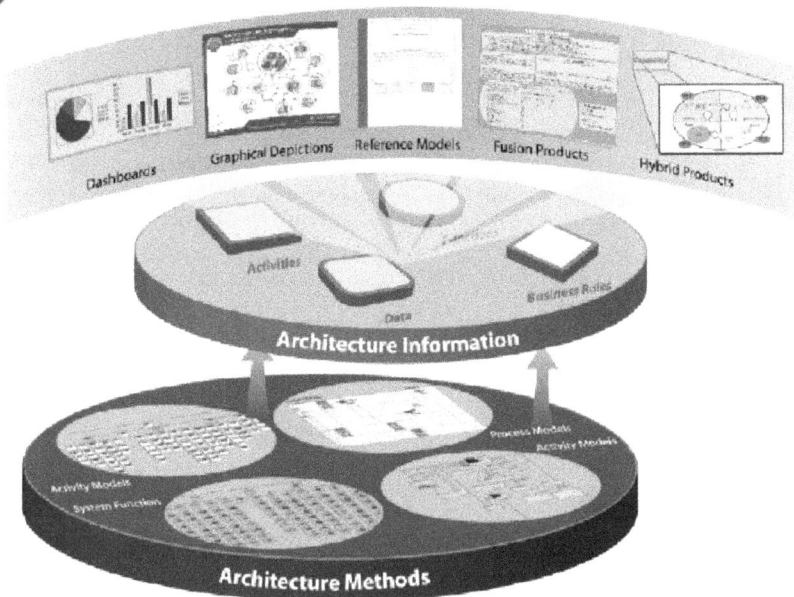

Figure 8: Aligning the 4Bs with DoDAF5

Combining both technologies and methodologies is no easy task, but the end result will enable a true Enterprise view of the organization that is actually based on how it is running versus assumed data points.

Additionally, another relatively new specification is Service Component Architecture (SCA) and was first published as a 0.9 version in November 2005. SCA provides a programming model for building applications and systems based on a Service Oriented Architecture. It is based on the idea that business function is provided as a series of services, which are assembled together to create solutions that serve a particular business need. These composite applications can contain both new services created specifically for the application and also business function from existing systems and applications, reused as part of the composition. SCA provides a model both for the composition of services and for the creation of service components, including the reuse of existing application function within SCA compositions.

SCA is a model that aims to encompass a wide range of technologies for service components and for the access methods which are used to connect them. For components, this includes not only different programming languages, but also frameworks and environments commonly used with those languages (including BPMN 2.0, BPEL, and Business Rules). See Figure 9a and 9b below.

BPM and SCA Views

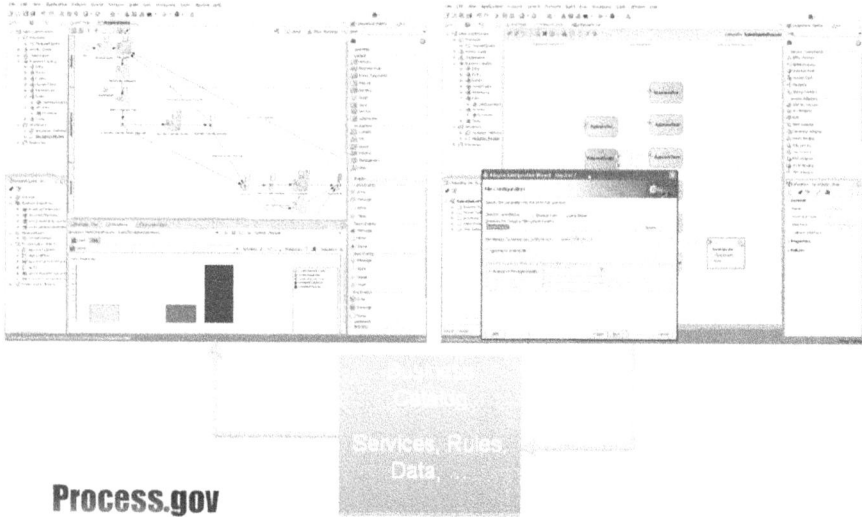

Figure 9a: BPM and SCA

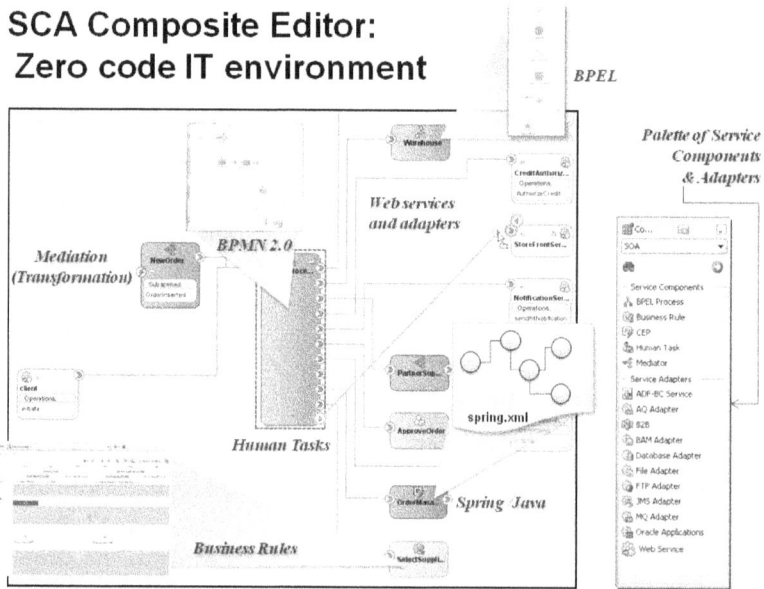

Figure 9b: BPM and SCA

EVENT DRIVEN PROCESS INTELLIGENCE

Enabling Actionable Process Intelligence can bring together BPM, BI and Business Rules. It can also extend to Complex Event Processing technologies as well. The basics behind the interaction between BPM and BI are symbiotic. Automated Business Process collect real life data points across processes in the enterprise providing BI with the data it requires to meet the stakeholders need to correctly track how the organization is running. Those reports and dashboards on KPIs and SLAs allow those stakeholders to make business decisions that drive process or rule changes (see Figure 10 below).

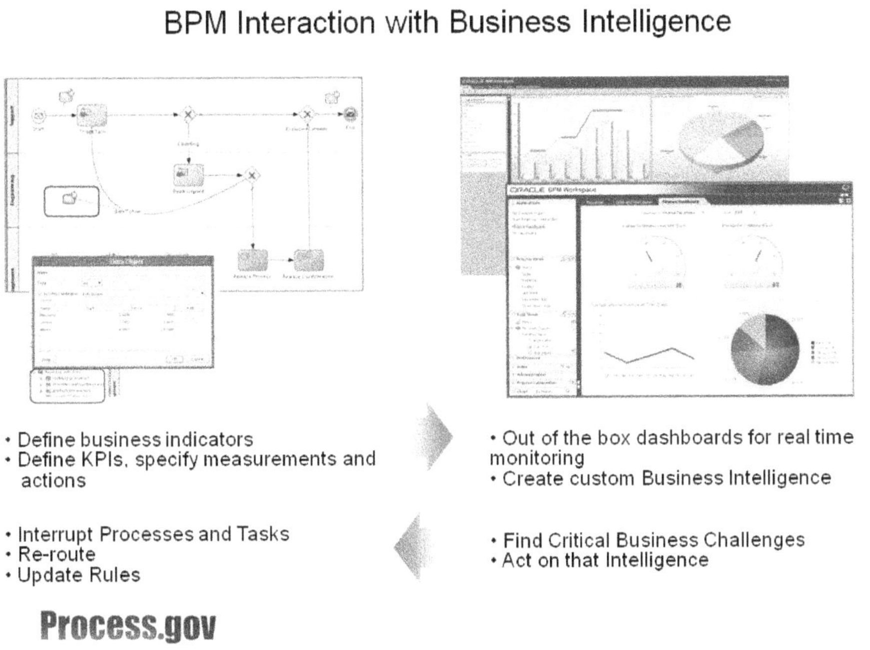
BPM Interaction with Business Intelligence
• Define business indicators
• Define KPIs, specify measurements and actions
• Out of the box dashboards for real time monitoring
• Create custom Business Intelligence
• Interrupt Processes and Tasks
• Re-route
• Update Rules
• Find Critical Business Challenges
• Act on that Intelligence
Process.gov

Figure 10: BPM and Business Intelligence

An example of BPM and BI working together can be seen by the Award Winning implementation done by San Joaquin County for its Integrated Justice System (see Figure 11 below).

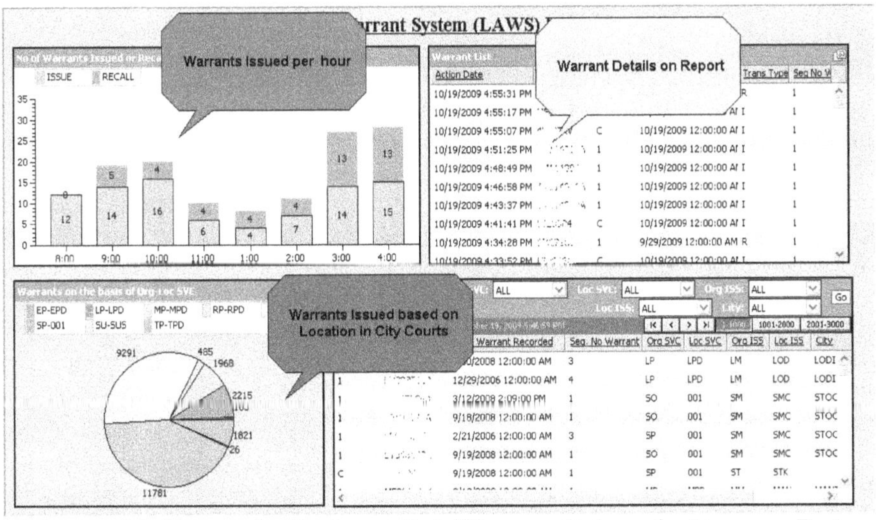
Warrants Issued per hour
Warrant Details on Report
Warrants Issued based on Location in City Courts

Figure 11: Example Business Intelligence Driven by Process Data

Combining BPM and Business Rules allows the abstraction of complex rules that could change from processes. What this allows is for the different stakeholders to have the most impact on aligning processes to the business in real-time without the complexity of a tightly coupled approach. For example a policy might change every month based on the business while the process itself stays relatively constant. The Policy Rule can by changed (or set effective dates) by Policy Managers without affecting the Business Process (and all the turmoil that might entail both from a technical and business standpoint). See Figure 12 below

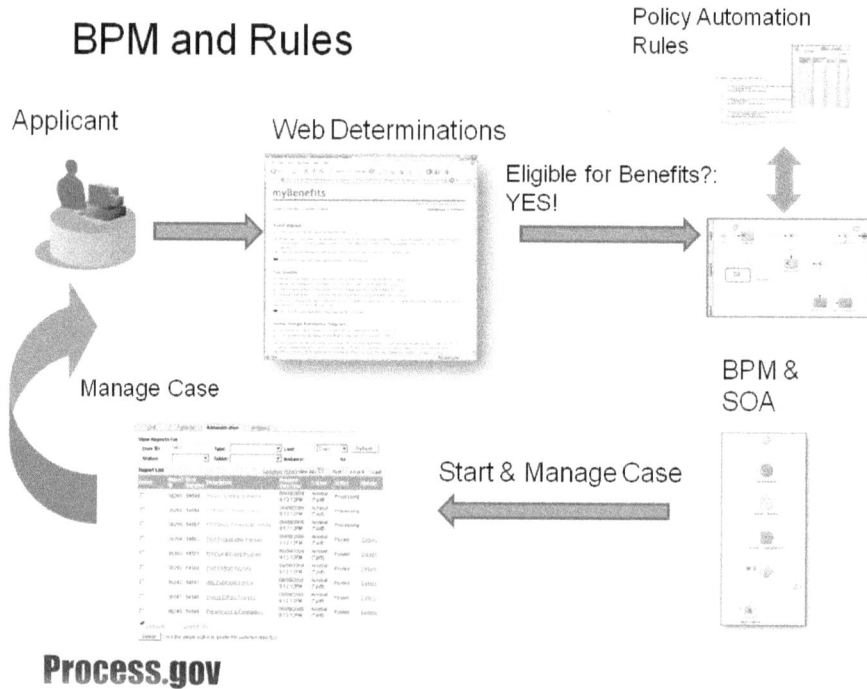

Figure 12: BPM and Business Rules

Real-time Complex Event Management is a new up-and-coming technology filling a huge requirement to detect and analysis patterns from multiple data sources near instantaneously. Currently, Defense and Intelligence capabilities are being stretched to the limit to keep us safe. The challenge is the vast amount of data from multiple sources that need to be tracked and analyzed when seconds count. While Improved Command & Control, Intelligence, surveillance, and reconnaissance (iC2ISR) is a clear application of CEP, also consider other applications, such as the recent stock market turmoil where, partly due to automated systems, it plunged almost 1,000 points in 30 minutes and then recovered most of its value and shaking investor confidence. Financial regulators are still trying to find out how it happened.

What CEP and BPM enables is a way for a business process (such as an exception or KPI) to trigger a real-time complex event engine to gather data from a multitude of sources to detect and analyze patterns. This allows the capability for potential self-corrections and/or call-backs to the process for human intervention with relevant data. This provides Actionable Intelligence (see Figure 13 below)

BPM and CEP

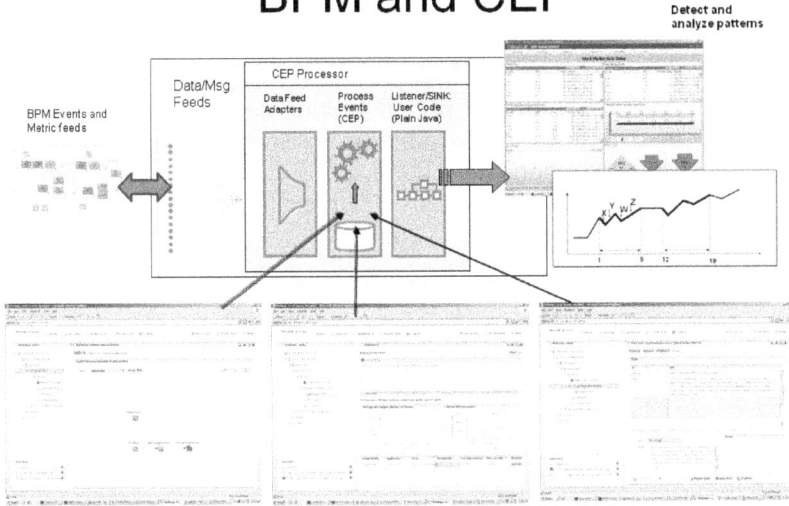

Figure 13: BPM and CEP "Actionable Intelligence"

An example application of this capability was recently done for the Air Force in cooperation with MITRE during a seven-month effort in support of the iC2ISR initiative. The scenario was based on tracking terrorist activities from multiple data sources (UAVs, Predators, etc.), visualizing this with mapping technologies, establishing areas of interest and how the data relates to those areas to provide actionable intelligence (see Figure 14 below)

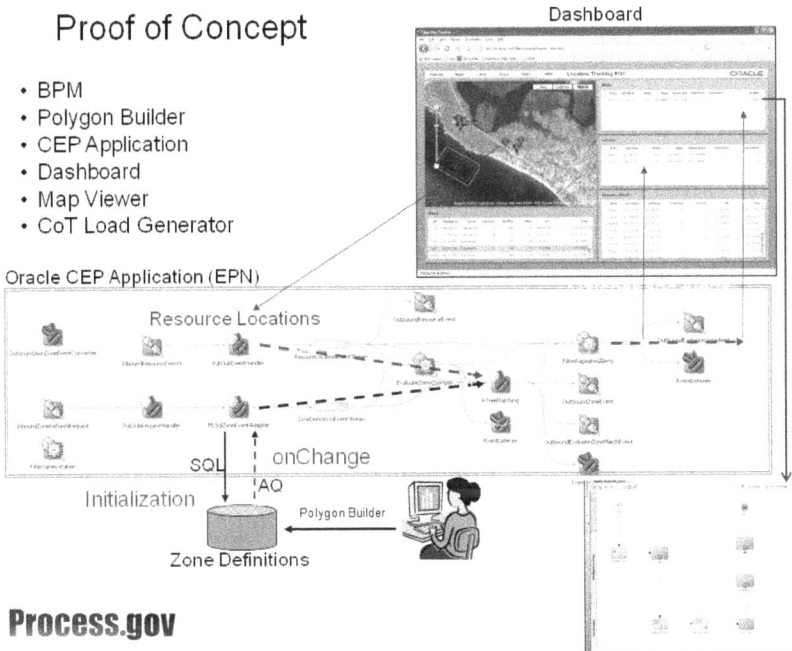

Figure 14: Actionable Intelligence for iC2ISR

Event-Driven Process Intelligences is a new and growing technology capability driven by both market demand and the evolution of technology. This extends BPM and BI to real-time mission critical scenarios.

BPI AS A CLOUD OR APPLIANCE

The concepts of Cloud Computing and Solutions as an Appliance are relatively new and driven by a need to further abstract business capabilities from the underlying IT infrastructure. Notionally there are 3 categories of Cloud Computing: Software as a Service (Saas), Platform as a Service (PaaS), and Infrastructure as a Service (IaaS) see Figure 15 below.

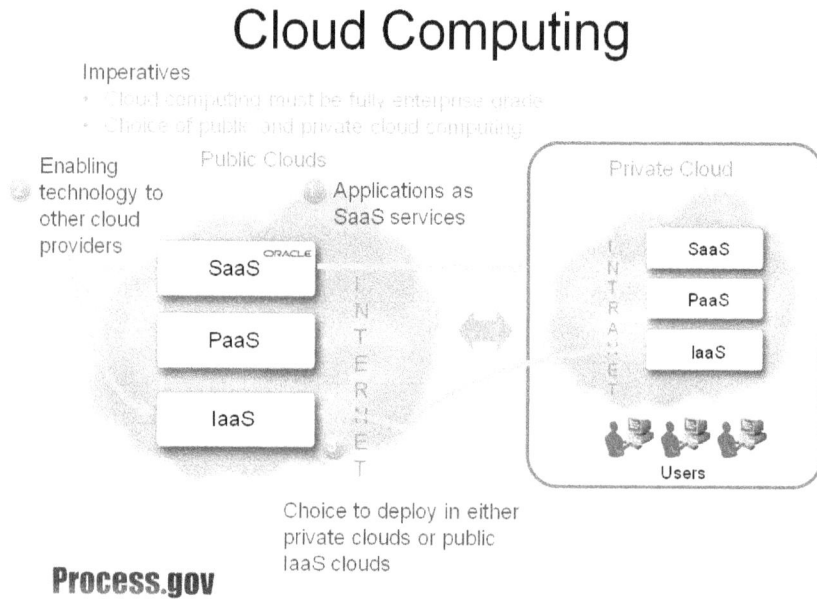

Figure 15: Cloud Computing

The idea of an Appliance is also about abstraction whereby a customer can choose a boxed solution that is pre-built to order. This has been done for consumers for some time now. If you have ordered a computer on-line and were satisfied with it when you received it in the mail, then in a way you have been successfully served an Appliance. However, Enterprise Application/Software Appliances are more complicated to deliver in the component parts are potentially an order of magnitude greater (we aren't talking about word processing software anymore). The challenge to both Cloud Computing and Appliances is tied to its value of Abstraction. How do you *Abstract* the IT Infrastructure while still allowing the Enterprise consumer to both understand what they are buying and tweak the capabilities to best fit their business? BPM (especially the advent of BPMN 2.0) facilitates the move to Cloud Computing and Appliances allowing a common standards based way to both understand and share within the Enterprise and a way to Collaborate with External Stakeholders (see Figure 16 below).

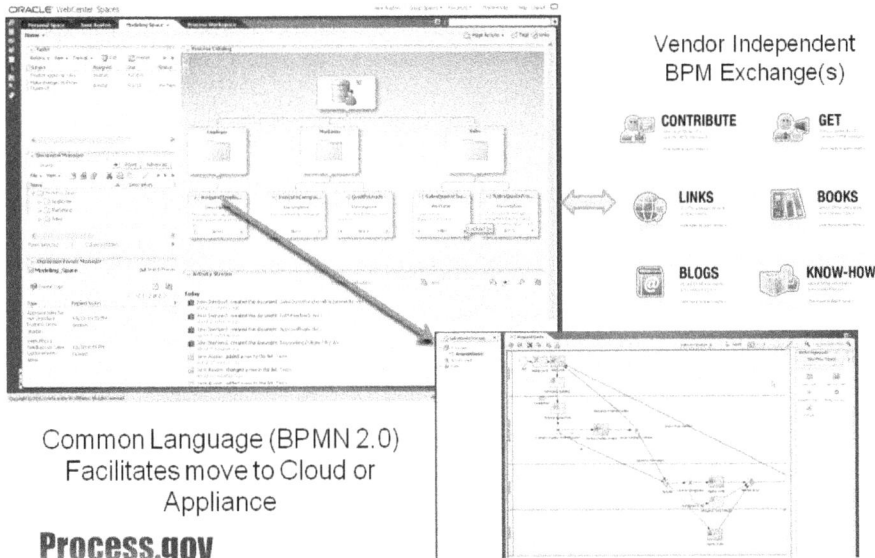

Figure 16: BPM in Cloud and/or Appliance

CONCLUSION

We are on the cusp of a decade of Change and Convergence driven by economic, social, government, technology and security forces. Our maturing methodologies and technologies are being combined in new ways that are driving the evolutionary cycle of between Business and IT. Because BPM is used by both Business and IT, it bridges the Design-Time/Run-Time divide and because it is so symbiotic to many other technologies, it is at the epicenter of this change.

REFERENCES

Process.gov 2010; March 13-14 2010, Reston VA.

http://www.futstrat.com/download_oracle.php; BPM Related White Papers and Case Studies; Various, Future Strategies

http://ashishbhagwat.wordpress.com/2010/03/16/bpm-ecosystem-blurring-boundaries-or-systematic-convergence; Ashish Bhagwat, Wipro Consulting, March 16, 2010

Enterprise Architecture based on Design Primitives and Patterns Guidelines for the Design of Business Process Models (DoDAF OV-6c) using BPM, March 3 2009, Business Transformation Agency

Lexicon/Primitives IPR; Michael zur Muehlen, James Kindrick; DWiz DCMO/BMA CTO/CA Briefing; April 14, 2009

The New Decade of Advanced Analytics: Roll Over Rocket Scientists!; James Kobielus' Blog, January 5, 2010

Gartner Reveals Five Business Intelligence Predictions for 2009 and Beyond, Gartner January 15, 2009

Gartner Reveals Five Business Process Management Predictions for 2010 and Beyond; Business Process Management Summit 2010, 1-2 March in London and 22-24 March in Las Vegas

http://www.intelligententerprise.com//021205/601feat2_1.jhtml, Mark Smith, December 5, 2002, Intelligent Enterprise

http://www.ebizq.net/blogs/nari/2008/09/business_process_intelligence.php

http://www.mitre.org/news/digest/defense_intelligence/07_09/warfighters.html; iC2ISR, Ray Modeen, MITRE Proof of Concept, 2009

Improving Business Process Quality through Exception Understanding, Prediction, and Prevention; Daniela Grigori, Fabio Casati, Umesh Dayal, Ming-Chien Shan, Proceedings of the 27th VLDB Conference, Roma, Italy, 2001

2009 WfMC Award Submission for San Joaquin County, Linus Chow, 2009

http://www.mitre.org/work/tech_papers/tech_papers_08/08_0750/08_075 0.pdf; Air Force SOA Enterprise Service Bus Study Using Business Process Management Workflow Orchestration for C4I Systems Integration, MITRE, 2008, Case Number 08-0750; ©2008 The MITRE Corporation

http://blogs.oracle.com/enterprise20/2010/04/aiim_best_practice_awards_to_t. html; AIIM 2010 Awards, Charles Town Police

Knowledge Work and Unpredictable Processes

Keith D. Swenson, Fujitsu America, USA, and Vice Chair, Workflow Management Coalition

INTRODUCTION

What is the next thing beyond Business Process Management (BPM)? To many this is an unexpected question. Is there anything wrong with BPM? Any reason it seems to be flagging? Over the course of 2009 there were a number of high profile acquisitions of BPM companies, and many say this as an indication of the end of BPM. Others, however, see this as an indication that BPM is mature, solid, and relatively well-defined, and a natural occurrence of a maturing technology area. Either way, it prompts people to wonder what is going to be next.

According to Forrester, we saw in 2009 a surge of interest in case management, so much so, that in December Craig Le Clair and Connie Moore released a white paper on Dynamic Case Management (Moore 2009). A number of companies, including IBM, announced in April 2010 a new offering in Case Management above and beyond their extensive BPM presence.

Ironically, it is precisely the success of BPM that leaves us looking for what is next. BPM has slowly but profoundly affected our business culture to the point that BPM is being used in almost all organizations to support routine work processes. This is not yet the case with *all* routine processes—there are still many more to be implemented—but BPM has freed a lot of people from routine tasks, allowing them to focus more on the harder-to-automate knowledge work tasks. Our working population is about 40 percent knowledge workers, and this percentage is growing steadily.

Can we use BPM to support knowledge work? The answer is "no." I will give a number of reasons for this below. This is a highly charged question, which I expect to be subject to quite a bit of debate.

This answer is not lightly given.

Before explaining the answer fully, we need to understand what knowledge work is, then the qualities of BPM. To support knowledge work, I will propose that a new kind of technology will be needed: Adaptive Case Management (ACM) (Swenson 2010).

WHAT IS KNOWLEDGE WORK?

Don't think of knowledge work as the manipulation of large amounts of information. The term "knowledge worker" tends to connote someone who is unusually knowledgeable or manages a large volume of information like a professor or a librarian. It is true that a professor does research, and a librarian categorizes books. These tasks are knowledge work. However other tasks of managing a library, such as the routine storing, filing, and managing of books should not be considered knowledge work because they are routine tasks. While professors and librarians can be considered knowledge workers, they are really not very typical examples. Most knowledge workers are not so explicitly tied to large volumes of information.

A knowledge worker is anyone who draws upon tacit knowledge, evaluating input from many very widely disbursed and rapidly fluctuating sources. Knowledge workers must figure out what to do next as they are working. An excellent example of a knowledge worker is a search and rescue worker. Often, the information on the rescue is not very well known when they start out, and they have to gather it as they proceed. Based on information they gather, they need to make decisions about what is to happen next.

It is probably not surprising that doctors and nurses practice knowledge work when they determine the course of treatment for a patient, always gathering more information, and always tweaking the treatment in light of what they have discovered.

Lawyers and judges are knowledge workers not only because they bring a lot of knowledge to their work, but that the case unfolds in response to what new things are uncovered, and that there are many unpredictable decisions to be made along the way. Designers are knowledge workers. Executives are knowledge workers. Project managers are knowledge workers. Customer support is mainly knowledge work. Product research and development is knowledge work. Knowledge work requires one to think in order to do the job. It is that thinking that separates it from routine work, not just thinking about a result, but thinking about the way the work needs to proceed along the way.

While routine work can be predicted, knowledge work is unpredictable. Knowledge work does not look like a traditional business process where work is performed according to a detailed plan prepared in advance. Knowledge work involves what are called "emergent processes." In an emergent process, the sequence of actions depends strongly upon the specifics of the situation. An initial plan is drawn up with whatever information is available at the time. It may incorporate elements of prepared procedures. The plan may draw upon roles that individuals have been trained to play. The specifics of the situation will drive a unique plan with a unique collection of individuals to meet the needs of a particular case.

The initial plan is not enough. As the situation changes, often the original plan has to be discarded and a new plan drawn up. This is the nature of knowledge work: as the situational information changes, so too must the plan. It is not simply a matter of assess, plan, then execute—it is an ongoing activity of continuous assessment, continuous planning, and continuous execution. No plan is ever final until the goal is achieved.

Like rescue workers, fire fighters "figure out" what they have to do as they go along. Forest fires are increasingly battled using IT resources (Gogek 2007). Satellite pictures are requested and then analyzed with increasing sophistication to produce an accurate outline of the area on fire. Sophisticated models are used to project the position of the front of the fire. Databases of toxic hazards are accessed and symbols are overlaid onto maps warning workers of dangers. This knowledge helps fire fighters deploy resources as effectively and safely as possible. Detailed instructions flow to the people in the field and detailed status information, including GPS coordinates, come back in near real time.

While rescue and fire workers are dramatic, many more knowledge workers spend their days in the office working for businesses. Consider how often business people describe their day as having been spent "solving problems." Workers who leverage knowledge and make course-of-action decisions account for 25 percent to 50 percent of the workforce (Davenport 2005). A stock trader goes to work without a predefined script for the day, instead, news from many sources will guide the actions of that stock trader on that day. A medical doctor does not usually have a complete script for the treatment of all patients, but instead, must follow the progression and make decisions about patient care at many points along the way. A social worker does not have a prescribed way to handle all cases but must make decisions along the way to decide what to do next. If you look past the special skills required for a particular line of work, many jobs consist of being prepared for and handling emergencies.

QUALITIES OF KNOWLEDGE WORK

Non-repeated

Knowledge work is rarely, if ever, repeated the same way many times in a row. In some cases, it is not possible to do the same work in the same manner twice, such as the negotiation of a merger of two companies. In other cases, it is simply unnecessary, such as the discovery of a new product idea.

There are always elements of similarity. For example, all news reporters might submit articles by a particular time of the day to make it into that day's newspaper. But the journalists' work over the entire life of the article—what is done, who is contacted, and where information is gathered—will have elements that are unique for any given article. A merger of two companies may follow a very familiar pattern: initial contact, hypothetical probing conversations, a getting-to-know-each-other phase, a proposal, a due diligence phase, agreement, and follow-through. This high-level pattern does not say anything specific about what a given individual would be doing at a particular time. A stock trader goes to work every day and buys and sells stocks, but that does not mean that the same work is repeated every day; quite the contrary, the actual trading patterns are adjusted over the course of the day in response to many factors.

Routine work cases may be very similar, but the cases are not entirely identical. A bank may open fifty accounts today with each account for a different person with different personal data. One might argue that every new account opening is unique, since it is for a different customer. These differences, such as the name and background of the customer, do not materially affect the course of actions that the bank must go through. There may be variants of the process, such as loans for high-income applicants might follow a different path than loans for low-income applicants. A loan application process is often visualized as having branches for treating cases differently. But even with the branches, the process can still be thought of as highly repeatable.

The key is the degree of repeatability: routine work will be repeatable enough that it might benefit from a formal description of the process to take. Whereas, knowledge work is not repeatable enough, and a formal description of the process tends to cost more than it would benefit.

Unpredictable

Routine work is predictable; knowledge work is unpredictable. When talking about unpredictable, we need to be clear about the level of unpredictability. A bank branch manager may not know who is going to walk into the branch in a given day to sign up for a new account, but the process of signing a given person up is predictable and repeatable. A checkout clerk will not know ahead of time what items will be scanned, but the task of scanning the barcodes of all of the goods being bought and totaling the amount is very predictable.

We need not be concerned about unpredictability at the micro scale. A checkout clerk will not know exactly which items, or even how many items will be scanned in a particular sale, but it is unimportant to know that level of detail in advance.

When we talk about the course of events being unpredictable, we mean that the sequence of significant human acts is not knowable in advance, and the course may vary greatly from case to case. The course will depend greatly on the details of the situation itself, and the details themselves may change before the work is finished. We will see examples below of a hospital which will start with the relatively routine task of admitting a patient, but what happens next is entirely unpredictable. The care may involve a single procedure taking one hour, or it may involve hundreds of procedures taking many months.

Prediction of the course of events must be based on actual information that the organization has at the time. Omniscience might make knowledge work predictable, but we cannot claim omniscience. For example, care must be provided for a patient that arrives unconscious, without identification, and without retrievable medical history.

Emergent

Stories told about knowledge work have the quality of "unfolding" as they go along. As a knowledge-work scenario unfolds, an early step may yield some knowledge, and that discovered knowledge determines the next step to be taken. The second step yields more knowledge, which in turn determines the third step to be taken, and so on. This iterative unfolding aspect is what makes knowledge work so unpredictable.

If I were to ask you to run to the store and bring back a box of mints, I could probably generate a plan of how to accomplish this to an annoying level of detail. I could predict fairly accurately the route to walk and the number of paces to the car, the route to drive, the approximate place to park, the number of paces to the store, the aisle to visit, the location of the product, the approximate location of the cash register, the amount to pay, and similar details for the return trip. This is because the entire task can be known as a whole and, given sufficiently detailed information, the entire plan can be laid out. In execution, problems may arise—such as needing to detour because a particular road is blocked or having to park farther away because the parking lot is full—but these unpredictable changes cause very little structural change in the overall plan. They remain minor perturbations from the original plan.

Investigation of a crime, which is knowledge work, has a completely different nature. One clue leads to the questioning of one individual. This in turn yields a clue that leads to another investigation and more clues. This may lead to a laboratory test that yields more clues. The details of the case exert a strong influence on the course of events for that case. A good detective will apply heuristics persistently in the hope that, eventually, enough clues will be discovered to solve the case, but at no point can the detective confidently map more than a few steps into the future. Often, there is a breakthrough that allows the next few steps to become clear—this is also known as an "ah ha!" moment. This sudden realization may change the current course of subsequent action. In knowledge work, even the concept of a plan has a special meaning, since plans are always tentative, contingent upon the next piece of knowledge uncovered. The hallmark of knowledge work is the mention of "Plan B," as this implies the very unpredictability of the situation.

This sort of work is not exclusively the domain of Sherlock Holmes, but it appears in many lines of work: for example, working together with a customer to find a new product direction, coming up with a new advertisement campaign, increasing the quality of a production line, and finding a source of funding for a public works project.

Robustness in the face of Varying Conditions

One of the most non-intuitive aspects of knowledge work is reliability and robustness in the face of variable conditions. Organizations that need a very high level of reliability make use of knowledge work techniques to ensure that.

The U.S. Marines train their soldiers to know that decisions are made "on the front line." Marines are not sent into the field with immutable instructions detailed to the finest level, but instead, they have the flexibility to adapt the plan as the situation evolves. This is not meant to imply that they act "willy-nilly" in any regard, nor do they modify the goals of the mission. The original orders represent the strict goals to be achieved, and there exist well-defined regulations on how they can be carried out. But the generals know that they don't have perfect knowledge of the situation the soldiers will face, and they must count on the behavior of intelligent adaptation as necessary to the specific situation as it unfolds. From the general's position, the exact details are not entirely predictable, but the goals can be achieved reliably.

This is counterintuitive because we normally think of machines as precise and reliable, while humans are error prone. Some might think that jobs left to the knowledge of the worker would be erratically implemented and error ridden. That is possible, but not usually the case.

Consider instead the reliability of an extremely rigid automated process. By defining the exact process too thoroughly, you can end up with a fragile process that breaks upon encountering the first exceptional situation. Realize that in any formalized work process, there is an assumed amount of knowledge work going on around it, either to handle the exceptional cases or to analyze and improve the process plan itself. Knowledge work exists outside of and all around the more routine practices making sure that cases that fall out of the routine course are picked back up and put back on track.

There are also cases where very well-defined, high-risk tasks are made considerably more reliable by layering knowledge work on top of the routine work. The U.S. Navy nuclear program has an unblemished record because of a practice of engaging every participant in the constant practice of looking for unexpected situations and continually suggesting improvements to the process (Spear 2009). Similarly, Toyota practices the same strategy with their Lean TPS (Toyota production system) method of developing cars. The knowledge work of suggesting improvements is unpredictable, but it serves to make the routine work processes more reliable.

WHAT ARE THE REQUIREMENTS TO SUPPORT KNOWLEDGE WORK?

Given the qualities of knowledge work, we can then propose that Adaptive Case Management, the category of tools that support knowledge workers, must have the following capabilities (Swenson 2010):

1. Explicit representation of goals and sub goals. While the process is not predictable, the goal is well known, and can be used to drive the work to a successful completion.
2. Rich data model. The various entities are represented directly and often remain behind as a permanent record.
3. Ability to task people directly to do a thing, without needing it to be part of a pre-defined process.
4. Ability to support a process (a sequence of tasks) when custom or law requires a specific sequence of tasks to be done.
5. Collaboration support that allows for threaded discussions among the participants involved in a case, without that communication being tied to a particular action. Some call this "social network" capability.
6. Rich access control model. Many BPM systems control access mainly by controlling who is assigned at a particular time.
7. History of all actions is kept, even meta-actions such as giving access to someone, or revoking access permissions.
8. Ability to start with a blank slate and build everything as you go without any preparation needed. There is no distinction between design time and run time. There is no development lifecycle where processes are developed and then deployed.
9. Case templates which are collections of elements that the case manager can use at run time to compose the case itself.

The above capabilities are tuned to the way that knowledge work presents itself: unpredictable, non-repeating, and yet still very important.

CAN KNOWLEDGE WORK BE SUPPORTED BY BPM?

When you have a hammer, all the problems start to look like nails. What is happening is that we are, at last, realizing that while there are many nails, there are also many non-nails that cannot be solved with a hammer.

Those who worry about the end of BPM are not looking at the entire picture, and are not seeing the real trend that is emerging. Understand that there have been many different meanings for BPM. Many have promoted it vigorously, claiming that it would solve every organizational woe. In many senses, BPM was the answer to everything, or so it would seem. All you need is BPM, and your organization will be transformed into a global front runner.

BPM (like many other high tech topics) has been overhyped, and proponents have said that it will be useful for things that we are now seeing. This just ain't so. There were many people promising that BPMN would be used directly by business people, but what we see is not only that business people shun such diagramming, but that tool vendors make their modeling tools more and more for trained specialists. Even the BPMN 2.0 standard committee is pushing it to be more and more oriented toward a language you build systems with.

When a "hammer user" encounters a screw for the first time, it appears to be a nail with a very inconvenient edge wrapped around it. After pounding a few in, they conclude it is a very inferior sort of nail.

When we encounter something new, we evaluate it and judge it in terms of what we already know. It is very hard to escape the context bias. Knowledge work is really quite different from routine work, and requires a different approach.

Many people define work as that activity which is done for a purpose, and is repeatable, and produces a measurable result in a fixed amount of time. Work is what laborers do, not what executives do. It is very hard to observe exactly what an executive produces, and hard to define the process they use to achieve it. Many people consider that type of knowledge work non-work: for example, have you heard someone say "I didn't get anything done today because I spent the whole time putting out fires." Unless that person is actually a fireman, they probably meant that they spent their time solving problems, making decisions, and otherwise taking care of things that had to be done, but which they did not consider to be work. Part of the problem is that when a person says that BPM can handle all kinds of work, they are often excluding any consideration for handling knowledge work.

When a process automation expert looks around to find work that might be automated, the work of an executive is never considered, for obvious reasons: it is not predictable or repeatable. The job of a facilitator is never considered for BPM support. And so it is with all knowledge work. The question we face today, and increasingly over the next decade, will be how to support knowledge work.

Many BPM defenders will then jump in and say "but our BPM system is flexible and can be used by an executive for knowledge work just as well as routine work." I have an answer for this, but let's start by clarifying two key points.

First, I am not asking if a particular product might or might not support knowledge work. Many products go beyond BPM, and I am not in the position to judge particular products. Instead, this statement is based on the most common definition of BPM and what must logically follow from that.

Second, I do not want to get into a lengthy discussion of the definition of BPM. There are many contradictory opinions on exactly what constitutes BPM. Ignoring the exotic definitions, BPM is clearly about "management" of "business processes," and without any doubt the process is the central concept which is to be managed. Most descriptions of BPM include the idea that a representation of the process (a process definition) becomes an important organizational asset which is improved over time. The purpose of BPM is to collect a library of best practice process definitions, which are optimized either through analytics or simulation.

It follows logically that in order to have a representation of the process, then you must be able to predict the process. But emergent processes such as you see in knowledge work are not predictable, and therefore are not representable as a process definition. In order to support knowledge work, we must use something other than a process definition. For this reason I believe it is clear and unequivocal that BPM, because of its focus on process is inappropriate for knowledge work. There are three responses you might en-counter.

First, some vendors are sure to say "Our system is so flexible that you can support work without having a pre-defined process definition." That is great. Yet this capability goes beyond the definition of BPM. This non-BPM capabil-ity may be useful for knowledge work. I am not trying to argue that none of the BPMS products can handle knowledge work, but that BPM by its defini-tion is not appropriate for knowledge work and emergent processes.

Second, some may claim that knowledge work is a simple fixed process: (1) figure out what to do, and (2) do it. This extremely generic two-step fixed process is the simplest possible, and more elaborate 3-, 4- or more step ge-neric processes have been suggested. The problem with these generic processes is that the history that results is generic and meaningless. Seeing that 1000 people figured out 5000 generic things to do and did 4000 generic things today is not useful to the organization. To track what knowledge workers are accomplishing, the activities need to be specific, not generic.

Third, some have technology that allows what is needed, and argue that it should still be called BPM because the knowledge worker is directly and in-dividually involved in the management of those business processes. While they don't start with a pre-defined process definition, within the scope of a single case, they define and improve the process. With this narrow interpre-tation of the terms, the technology that supports knowledge workers might be called BPM, but doing so would do violence to many of the other aspects of BPM that are normally assumed, such as cyclical improvement of processes and finding best practices.

A DIFFERENT STYLE OF MODELING

In the end, if one insists that the technology that supports knowledge work-ers be called a BPMS, then so be it, but there is a serious danger in doing this. Almost all BPM systems existing today are designed to separate the role of process definers from the end users. This happens from the desire to make the most faithful representation of the process possible. To make a process that runs accurately 1000 times, you need a specialized skill and a complex language. For a process that is created on the fly by the case man-ager, and then discarded, the requirements on the language are very differ-ent.

Consider the restaurant analogy with two kinds of restaurants: a sit-down restaurant and a self-serve buffet. The final dinner plate is analogous to the process. In a sit-down restaurant, you order a meal, and it is delivered com-pletely prepared on the plate, ready to eat. This is like BPM where the end user chooses a process definition and runs it. In a buffet the diner starts with an empty plate. From the buffet table, the diner selects and combines the selected food on the plate, ultimately ending up with a meal to eat. The buffet table does not consist of prepared plates, but instead food in a differ-ent form ready for the diner to select from. In ACM, the end user (the case manager) composes the process from parts that are made available in the template.

In BPM, the process is designed by a specialist, and is meant to be used by a user without the user having to compose anything. This makes the processes more elaborate, complex, and fully defined. In ACM, the case manager com-poses the process while the work is going on. This means that the processes have to be much less complex, much less complete, but much easier to manipulate. It would be a grave mistake to assume that one style of process modeling will be the same for both domains.

There is quite of a bit of interest in presenting a simple checklist representation of the model to a case manager (Swenson 2001). While a linear checklist does not contain the fine details that would be necessary to have a single process definition run for thousands of cases, it is however convenient when the task list is needed only for a single case. An elaborate diagram using BPMN would be too much trouble for a process will be run only once. Also, the checklist metaphor is easy to all people to understand. Adding a task into a list of tasks is uncomplicated. It is possible that for one-off process definitions, a checklist approach may be the best.

A DIFFERENT METHOD OF IMPLEMENTATION

When implementing a BPM solution, the first step is "process discovery" where one attempts to write down the process, either by interviewing the participants, or by mining the log files of what has occurred in the past. This process definition becomes the core of the new solution.

Adaptive Case Management does not start this way. The first thing you do is define the entities involved. For a medical case template, you start with a representation of a patient, including medical history. You might define some roles to represent different kinds of interactions that might be allowed, and access control to that information. There is no necessity to define a process, but often a collection of pre-defined activities is included in the template so that the case manager can bring them in with minimal trouble. You may also have a collection of process fragments which can be brought in after the case has started. A case instance can be started almost completely blank and nothing more than a case file to place things.

CONCLUSIONS

In order to summarize what has been presented, we see that knowledge work is widespread (40 percent of the workforce) but is unpredictable. The four main characteristics of knowledge work are given. Because it is unpredictable, BPM, which is based on defining a process definition ahead of time does not work. Instead, a different approach is needed, called Adaptive Case Management (ACM). ACM has a different way of modeling processes from BPM, and is used as part of a different methodology. It is possible that a single product may contain technology that can support both predictable and unpredictable process support, you should approach such claims skeptically because of the way that knowledge work falls outside of the expectation of what is normally considered "work."

Twelve experts in this space came together to collaborate on a book called "Mastering the Unpredictable" (Swenson 2010) that focuses on the need to support work which is not predictable. Some of this article contains excerpts from that book, mixed with additional information uncovered during the launch discussions. Mastering the Unpredictable continues to provide 350 pages of description and discussion on how Adaptive Case Management might be used to support unpredictable work. Find out more at http://www.MasteringTheUnpredictable.com/

ACKNOWLEDGEMENT

The author gratefully acknowledges the support of Fujitsu America, Inc. for the research on these topics. Fujitsu produces the Interstage family of middleware products, including Interstage Business Process Manager a full featured BPM Suite supporting server to server integration, human routine process automation, dynamic process capability and collaboration platform for knowledge workers. The suite is rounded out with a process analytics server, and a unique Automated Process Discovery capability which can mine the process out of existing application log files to be exported onto the suite platform to streamline and automate the business processes. Visit http://www.fujitsu.com/interstage for more information.

REFERENCES

(Davenport 2005) Thomas H. Davenport. Thinking for a Living: How to Get Better Performances and Results from Knowledge Workers. Boston: Harvard Business School Publishing, 2005.

(Gogek 2007) Jim Gogek. University of California, San Diego, "UC San Diego's High-tech Tools Helped Combat Wildfires: Emergency Advancements Can Aid Disaster Worldwide," News Release, November 5, 2007. http://ucsdnews.ucsd.edu/newsrel/general/11-07HighTechToolsCombatFiresJG-L.asp/.

(Moore 2009) Connie Moore and Craig Le Clair. "Dynamic Case Management—An Old Idea Catches New Fire." Forrester Research (December 28, 2009). http://www.forrester.com/rb/Research/dynamic_case_management_%26%238212%3B_old_idea_catches/q/id/55755/t/2/.

(Spear 2009) Steven J. Spear. Chasing the Rabbit: How Market Leaders Outdistance the Competition and How Great Companies Can Catch Up and Win. New York: McGraw-Hill, 2009.

(Swenson 2001) Keith D. Swenson. "Workflow for the Information Worker," in Workflow Handbook 2001, edited by Layna Fischer, 39–49. Lighthouse Point, FL: Future Strategies, 2000. http://kswenson.workcast.org/2001/Workflow for the InformationWorker.pdf/.

(Swenson 2010) Keith D. Swenson. Mastering The Unpredictable: How Adaptive Case Management Will Revolutionize The Way that Knowledge Workers Get Things Done. Meghan-Kiffer Press, 2010.

Open Source Business Intelligence and Business Process Platform

Patrick Beaucamp, BPM-Conseil/Vanilla, France

Over the past few years, the Business Intelligence (BI) and Business Process software market has given new opportunities and challenges to software startup companies. An opportunity exists for those market segments to progress and make significant contribution to IT. Both evolve in a situation that is now comparable to what existed in other market segments (such as databases or servers) and are in a position to challenge existing commercial products.

First and foremost, the new competition has brought a steady decline in overall cost, most notably with the introduction of pricing "by server" instead of the habitual pricing "by user".

Most of those new offers and challengers are recent and come from the Open Source world. The first professional BI offers came from Pentaho in 2006, followed by JasperSoft in 2007 and Vanilla in 2008. For the Business Process offers, except from a long standing one from Shark, new blood appeared with Intalio in 2006, while RedHat launched its JBPM platform in 2007 and Bonita in 2009 (as a spin-off of Bull).

Most of those new competitors and offers were heavily fueled by Venture Capital money before the financial dry-up of late 2008.

Since this crisis, money has become dearer and harder to raise, and some of the mentioned companies encountered difficulties closing financing rounds, leaving direct impacts on their overall strategy and product quality and features. Some of that easy money created the same effect as the last dot-com burst, enticing companies to oversell their offers, investing too much effort in marketing and sales instead of providing "production-ready" software at company-wide levels.

Even though those professional Open Source projects are recent and may lack certain features available in long-established products, they offer key advantages for new projects in both small and big companies. Most notably is price, but are definitely not reduced to low-cost and low quality offerings. They are catching on fast to existing commercial offers by providing new and missing features, being more reactive and offering faster response times.

Professionalism of the services and of the products is also an important point as it is now well underway in BI as it once was in other IT areas (Operating Systems, Databases, etc...).

In addition, Open Source is a domain where people and products can easily meet to give birth to new developments in a short time, or add missing features by leveraging another Open Source product feature. Business Intelligence and Business Process platforms have complementary needs which makes sense to have a cross association of features and products:

- Both are missing from "enterprise" features in their first level offers that the other platform can provide easily. Just as a simple example, early BI platforms were missing Business Process features to manage BI processes running in production environment, and BPM platforms were missing professional Business Activity Monitoring Dashboard along with multidimensional OLAP (Online Analytical Processing) log analysis of the Business Process deployed in production.

- Both may have a few dependencies of other Open Source platforms, such as Open Source ERP (OpenErp, Erp5 ....), a CRM platform (SugarCrm, Vtiger) , or an ECM/portal platform (Nuxeo, Drupal, ExoPlatform, Liferay or Alfresco) while those projects would gladly include more professional BI and BPM features, while at the same time opening new markets for Open Source BI and BPM platforms.

In the following article we will describe the current situation in both the BI and BPM world and will argue for the possible synergies between them.

THE LAUNCH OF OPEN SOURCE BI

In a very short time-span—less than 3 years—Open Source has developed, prospered and obtained recognition from key IT actors such as editors, integrators and corporations. The Open Source BI has also created or at least addressed a new market in the form of large Internet BI deployments, applications that were not viable until recently due to the inherent costs of licenses and deploying commercial.

The arrival of Open Source in BI has induced a healthy drop in price and a steep increase in competition.

Simple isolated offers existed for OLAP – Online Analytical Processing, multidimensional view of data - (Mondrian), Reporting (Ireport, Birt) and ETL - Extraction/Transformation/Loading (designer and engine that take in charge data transfert between databases) - (CloverETL and Enhydra). (Extract, transform, and load (ETL) is a process in database usage and especially in data warehousing.) But they did not provide a common and consistent framework to make the transition towards "production ready".

We have the example of Dashboards where offers of components existed (a dashboard is an aggregate workspace for reports and OLAP documents) but they was no offer of a complete set in the Open Source landscape.

Pentaho, JasperSoft and Vanilla have all provided global consistent platform in a short time, with basic services such as reporting, OLAP, dashboard or ETL. Every strategy is different, and purpose of this paragraph is not to comment the strategy, but only to give indication to readers to help them understand the consequence of each choice :

In a short time Pentaho, JasperSoft, and Vanilla all provided a common and consistent framework to integrate basic BI features (reporting, OLAP, dashboards, ETL, etc...). Each with a different strategy and aim:

- Pentaho bought existing products and tried integrating them, the same thing happened to Mondrian (OLAP), Jfree (reporting) and Kettle (ETL), leading sometimes to confusion in term of global appearance of its software
- Jaspersoft built its offer around Ireport (renamed since JasperReport) and has signed OEM agreements with French Open Source company Talend for an ETL (renamed since TalendEtl) and others for a BPM platform with eBuilder.
- Vanilla choose to do it from the ground up and developed every component over a common and secured Metadata, so that different modules can

talk and interact with each other. With the exception of BIRT which is leveraged and for which a plugin to access the metadata was developed.

While the growth of OpenSource BI has mainly been due to its own merits, the failure of the existing commercial offering of the major players (Hyperion, Cognos, Business Objects) to keep up to their promises of providing an Internet-Ready BI Platform in a reasonable time and for a reasonable price has also helped the development of an alternative. Major buy-outs also somewhat destabilized the sector (Hyperion was bought by Oracle, Cognos by IBM, and Business Objects by SAP). This state was also beneficial to existing commercial platforms such a QlikView.

So despite the fact that the initial batch of Open Source BI platforms offerings were incomplete and not fully integrated, they have been changed, replaced, and improved in most cases. They are now able to compete with and provide comparable solutions to the existing commercial offers. This is a nice progression from PDF mail-sending robots.

OPEN SOURCE BUSINESS INTELLIGENCE AND LARGE PROJECTS

The spread of "rich" Internet applications has made reporting and dashboard features a "must" for every project and those components a necessary commodity.

Real life uses of reporting and dashboards has made the rest of the BI toolbox increasingly necessary to process data while at the same time forcing Open Source BI towards more professional methods, processes, services and development.

An ETL to move and analyze data is now mandatory for any large BI deployments. And so are many more Open Source components such as column-oriented database or data quality / data management platforms. Each product line and niche has been occupied by reactive startup companies such as Vertica, Infobirght, GreenPlum or ParAccel (database), Talend, Apatar, Xaware and CloverEtl (ETL).

When it comes to large deployments, all Open Source BI editors have faced the same challenges, such as :

- how to manage the development cycle, and how to move application from development to production
- how to manage data flow between large databases
- how to ensure good response time when dealing with large database available through Ad-Hoc Web Reporting services modules
- how to automate processes such as data transformation, load of BI databases or report production & delivery
- how to have a global orchestration of a BI application, along with management tools for administrators

BI is the showcase of any reporting projects but deploying and managing a large BI project is not possible without the use of other additional tools such as fast databases, ETL and BPM platforms. it appeared with Open Source BI platforms. This was before the appearance of Open Source BI, but as soon as it appeared it became a key player in innovation and in driving the general trends and especially in making Internet BI deployments.

A NEW MARKET FOR OPEN SOURCE BUSINESS PROCESS MANAGEMENT PLATFORMS

Business Process has moved beyond IT and just Process Management and is now a refined art. Business Process Management platforms have addressed large and various problems, and leaders (Lombardi, Ids Scheer) have been specialized in the major vertical integrations of the past century (in Banking and Trading for example.)

Having a "de facto" monopoly on their customers along with their strong business knowledge has enabled them to have both powerful solutions and a captive market. But these solutions are neither viable nor affordable for most middle sized companies. This is an opportunity for small and reactive startups and especially Open Source new comers.

It is a very big niche market but history has also shown time and again that a market is often conquered from the low end as currently happening in the database industry, with MySql and PostGreSql, but also with Jboss which took BEA and IBM WebSphere out of the market.

Those successes happened because of the strategy and pricing that made those products accessible to the mass market and not only high-end companies.

We believe it is now on the verge of happening in the BI world which has already experienced some turmoil in recent years.

Business Process has seen a rapid emergence of reliable offers from companies like Intalio, BonitaSoft, long established Enhydra/Shark or Jboss/Jbpm (a de facto standard).

The new BPM platforms have yet to achieve global recognition and still have progress to make but akin to BI Platforms, have the potential to break through.

With the notable exception of Intalio which provides a comprehensive platform with many development toolkits and templates, Shark and Bonita seemed to be more centered and positioned on the Business Process Engine segment, providing easily embeddable software for any framework. This industry segment has yet to achieve standardization though with competing standards (BPEL for Intalio, XPDL for Shark and Bonita, and JBoss and Jbpm also having its own).

Contrary to Open Source BI, Open Source Business Platforms have yet to be adopted from specialized BPM System Integrators, most notably because of the lack of features in the available Open Source Process Designers, and the absence of integration with external products such as Form Designers. Again, Intalio strikes out, providing a rich platform to develop and deploy Business Process applications.

Maybe more so than others, those Open Source companies need to sign agreements with other editors and collaborate with existing Platforms (BI, ERP, CRM, ECM...) to accelerate their adoption amongst large companies. This situation is more or less the same for fast column database platforms or ETL platforms: customers are looking for a global offer. They don't want to deploy ten different applications and integrate those.

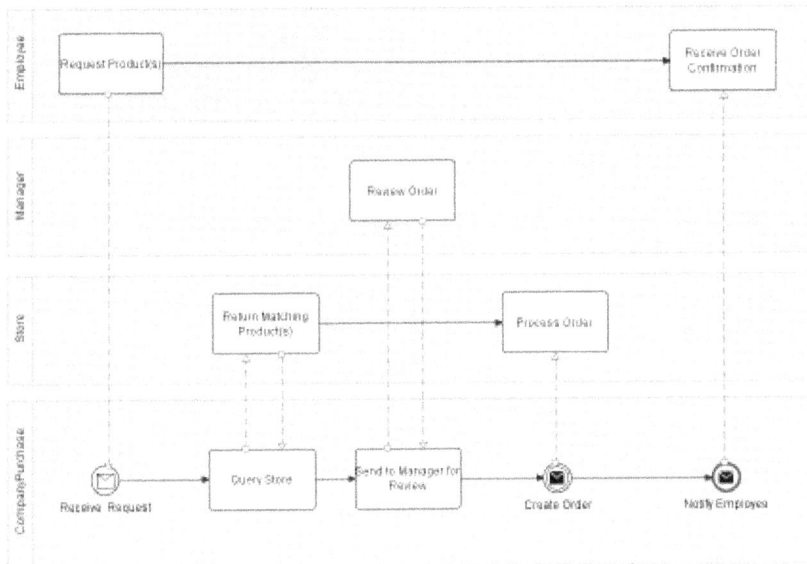

Intalio Visual Designer Interface

HELP WANTED : OPEN SOURCE BI IS LOOKING FOR OPEN SOURCE BPM PLATFORMS

Open Source is a philosophy, but is now also an economic activity and a new paradigm that follows rules, both in term of product development and integration.

One of the most important things in Open Source, as in any other industry is the adoption of standards for development, document storage, and integration in general. Some companies believe that controlling the standards is of key business importance, and compete on imposing those standards. They forget that standards are beneficial to everyone and recent history is full of "Davids" reusing a "goliath's" standard and overturning it. Possession and control of standard is not the key.

Until recently, even commercial BI platforms were not providing any Business Process components, simply because BI applications were running on separate servers, with a single entry point: the data warehouse database model. Open Source BI platform have broken this barrier, by grabbing data from anywhere in the enterprise, and even through Internet portals. Shifting the paradigm and allowing more user interaction.

Open Source BI platforms need features such as process orchestration (for example: loading data in database, checking some key performance indicator (KPI) values, building reports and sending those reports along with KPI alerts to top management), along with management tools for administrators (process administration, process monitoring and global enterprise process management) and tools to manage development cycle (for example, tools to help developers and administrators to move applications from development to production). Those features are available in some Open Source BPM platform leading to a natural association between the two kinds of software.

This integration between Open Source platforms was possible, because of the nature of the platforms, the availability of the code and respect of Open Source standards. Notable integrations from Pentaho (Shark) and Vanilla (Bonita) are already available, with slight difference between the two projects: Pentaho provides a technical Eclipse PlugIn editor for some of its products (reporting and OLAP) along with another workflow designer for its ETL, Vanilla on the other hand provides a global Eclipse product—Vanilla BIWorkflow—for all its components (reporting, ETL, OLAP and KPI), along with integration of Form Designers such as Orbeon, FreeDashboard or GoogleForms and an integration of Vanilla Authentication providers (pools)

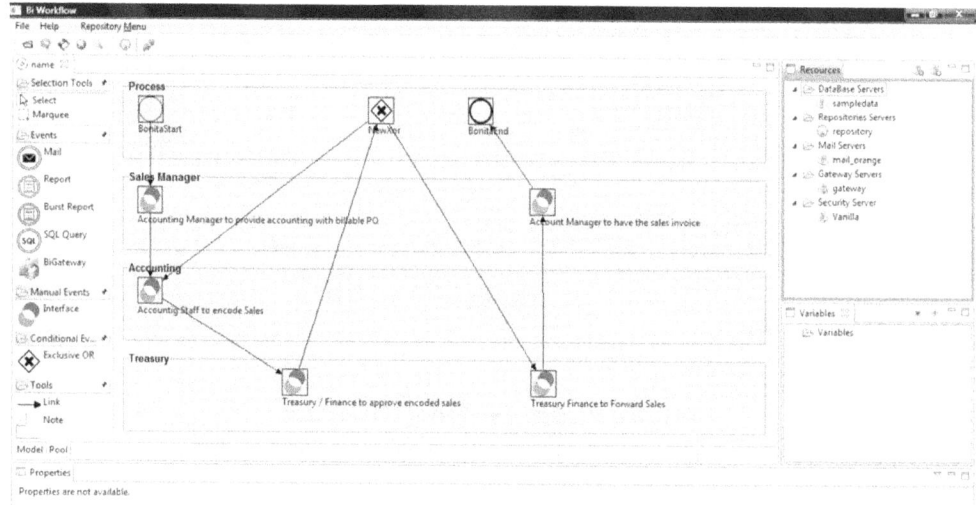

Vanilla BI Workflow Designer – Secured Pool Visual presentation

JasperSoft kept the same policy of signed agreements with other companies to provide BPM features, such as the recent announcement with eBuilder. It's difficult to understand the level of integration when it comes to subjects such as access to a BI Document—the location and sharing of security, both for Repositories and for Databases. Difficulties can arise with choice of scheduler to run the Business Processes.

To complete the situation, we can add that another agreement has been reached between Talend (ETL) and BonitaSoft which could lead to strange situations when we remember that JasperSoft uses OEM Talend for its ETL module.

A notable agreement is the one between Intalio and Informatica, where Informatica decided to use Intalio as its BPM platform. It was one of the first most important agreements between companies coming from both the Open Source and commercial market.

The need is not unidirectional though, BPM platforms are also in need of BI features such as global standard dashboard, Business Activity Monitoring, reporting, OLAP analysis, etc. This need might be less evident than for integration of BPM in BI partly of the limited wide-scale deployments of Open Source BI Solutions.

WHAT ABOUT THE FUTURE?

Companies' situation and position

The market's situation is still very fluid and moving fast due to recent acquisitions and expansions. Consolidation is underway but new-comers could still appear over the next few months, as could existing players be bought. Difficulties to raise money will still impact and reduce movements of certain players, reducing their abilities to fund development and strategies.

Platform Architecture

In recent years, vaporware fueled by marketing announcements have become the norm, but they do have a tendency to become solid "out of the box" products and we should not dismiss new trends as fads. "Agile", "Cloud-ready" and other SAAS/PAAS/IAAS are the new fashion and we strongly believe that Open Source BI and BPM will be in better position for those segments. Integration of the two would be a major business shift. The ubiquity of today's information and data favors integration of BI and BPM, and provide readily available solutions to customers needs: collecting, managing and displaying data flows. Future is bright for "BI/ BPM in the cloud" and "BI/ BPM as a service".

Integration with other Platforms

Integrations with other platform may also go to the next level. On one hand ERPs (OpenErp, Erp5, OpenBravo, Compiere), CRM solutions (Vtiger or SugarCrm) and ECM portal solutions (ExoPlatform, Nuxo, Liferay or Alfresco) and on the other more technical platforms such as ETLs (Talend, Apatar, Xaware, CloverETL) or Fast Database platforms (ParAccel, Infobright, Vertica) have an interest in integration and formulating common standards. Those solutions could represent an alternative to major players.

Standard and product Evolution

The BPMN 2.0 notation with its extensions for BI could be something that can accelerate the adoption of global BI-BPM Platforms and push interoperability among editors. As always, those kinds of standard notation have to come from existing development (Vanilla/Bonita has set an interesting set of standards for BI+BPM actions and events), and a new kind of visual BI/ BPM editor will be soon available to help BI developers to draw BI Process & Workflow.

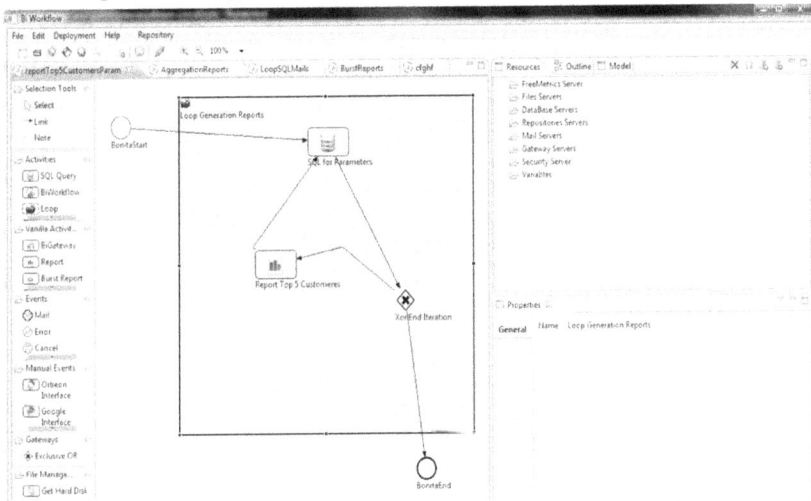

Vanilla BI Workflow Designer with support for BI documents

Conclusion

Open Source BI and BPM platforms have many things to share and can help each other in order to bring business application to the next level of quality in terms of integration and management. This integration is already available at engine level, because both kind of platform follow standards such as XML, Java libraries, Web Services and Service-Oriented Architecture (SOA) technologies. Visual modelers for developer are still missing to design BI workflow (notable exception is Vanilla BI Workflow)

Open Source BI and BPM platforms should soon be bundle as Business Intelligence and Business Process Platform (known as "BPI Platform"), available as services in any kind of Application Server (such as Jboss), because developers and customers don't want to have to manage multi-editor products, especially when those products are new. As a simple bundle service, we can expect a global adoption in a short period of time.

REFERENCES

Open Source BI companies / Platforms

Pentaho : www.pentaho.com

JasperSoft : www.jaspersoft.com

 BPM-Conseil / Vanilla: www.bpm-conseil.com

Open Source ETL companies

Talend : www.talend.com

Xaware : www.xaware.com

Apatar : www.apatar.com

CloverETL : www.cloveretl.com

Open Source BPM companies / products

Intalio : www.intalio.com

Bonita : www.bonitasoft.com

Vertical & column database / Datawarehouse database companies

Vertica : www.vertica.com

Infobright : www.infobright.com

GreenPlum : www.greenplum.com

ParAccel : www.paraccel.com

Artificial Intelligence and the Future of BPM: Semantic Process Automation

Francesco BATTISTA, Respondo, Italy and Gianpiero BONGALLINO, Italy

A future, but shortly-forthcoming, scenario is going to change the approach to process management: semantic techniques and automatic tools (based on Artificial Intelligence) will guide and support humans in designing and implementing process centric solutions.

This article explores this pioneering frontier made of an added-value mix of Business Process Management systems and Artificial Intelligence.

INTRODUCTION

In many branches of computer science, Artificial Intelligence (AI) demonstrated its ability to successfully reproduce, in specific scenarios, typical human behaviors: deduction, automation, optimization, control and many others.

Even working in a Business Process Management (BPM) context, from processes early definition to their final streamlined shape, AI techniques and tools already provide important and sometimes unique advantages. The richer the experience knowledge base and the more focused the involved business domain, the more efficient those techniques and tools.

A wider AI-based support for business process lifecycle management is not far. It will allow analysts to speed-up process definition, mapping and tagging, developers to find quickly and automatically appropriate reusable sub-processes and managers to continuously improve their own processes and their process management skills.

As a challenging future frontier, an AI injection might also allow processes themselves to autonomously solve issues and automatically change single process instance flows.

AI EVOLUTION

Some people believe that AI will allow incredible things like producing intelligent robots capable of learning, moving, taking decisions, replicating almost identically human behaviors, some others think AI is just science fiction.

What is clear today, in daily life, is that AI-based methods, algorithms and technologies are already widely used (camera autofocus systems, washing machine automatic settings, mobile phones voice-recognition functions, etc.) and when AI is properly adopted in the appropriate content, results may actually appear incredible.

Extending history chronology (1760, 1st industrial revolution—steam engine, 1870, 2nd industrial revolution—electricity, 1970, 3rd industrial revolution—electronic and computer science) more AI enthusiasts are sure that the 4th industrial revolution will occur around 2070 as a consequence of AI and nanotechnology maturity.

This may or may not be the case, but for sure AI is already there: AI has added, is adding and can add a great value in many contexts and should always be taken into account in scientific and technological research and development.

Some AI techniques (e.g. Soft Computing) allow us to deliver intelligent software applications to classify, predict, schedule, control and take decisions within an uncertain scope: all very useful features within a process management context.

Other AI techniques (e.g. automatic reasoning) are evolving very fast demonstrating to be very useful for searching information and orchestrating software services. Many of these AI reasoning mechanisms are based on the so-called ontologies, sets of concepts within a specific domain enriched with relationships between those concepts that are used to formally represent knowledge within a specific domain.

In this article we will present AI-based tools and technologies, already available and capable of adding value and supporting humans during the execution of BPM lifecycle phases.

We will see that AI may be very useful in performing repetitive activities (transcriptions, recognitions, searches, etc.), reusing knowledge (processes, resources, services, etc.) and generating data based logical models otherwise hardly manageable for humans (automatic optimizations, cause-effect relations, model extraction from data, etc.).

BPM LIFECYCLE PHASES

In order to present AI benefits for BPM, we will refer to the following classical set of BPM lifecycle phases.

Design

Identify *AS IS* processes and design *TO BE* processes. This phase includes the representation of process flows, their actors, alerts and notifications, Service Level Agreements, etc.

Modeling

From the theoretical design of the preceding Design phase, it introduces combinations of variables (to evaluate how the process might operate under different circumstances) and also includes processes "what-if analysis".

Execution

A process engine enables the full business process (as developed in the Design phase and refined in the Modeling phase) to be executed as software by a computer. It will either use services in applications to perform business operations or, when needed, ask for human inputs. This approach allows easier management and a more agile improvement of business processes.

Monitoring

Track execution of individual process instances, producing clear and detailed data about their state and history, along with performance aggregated real-time statistics.

Optimization

Analyze and elaborate process performance information coming from previous phases, potential or actual bottlenecks are identified along with opportunities for cost savings and other kind of improvements.

While in this article we will concentrate on deepening AI innovation within Design, Execution and Optimization phases, it has to be clearly underlined that relevant examples of AI-based useful tools exist for each BPM lifecycle phase.

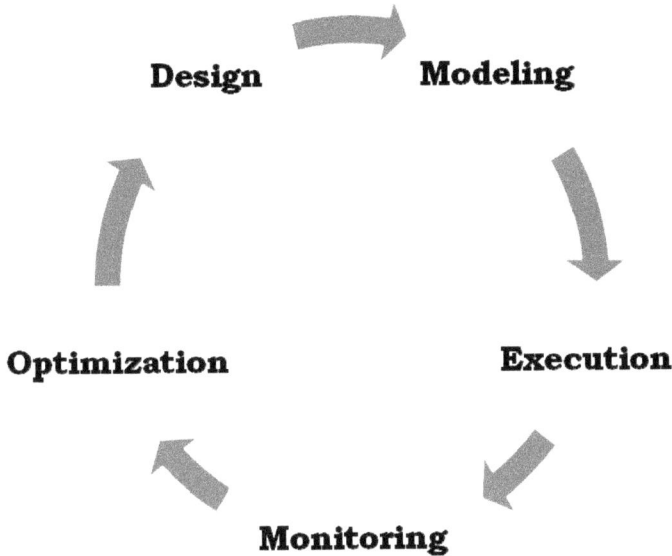

Design   **Modeling**

Optimization   **Execution**

Monitoring

Figure 1: BPM lifecycle

DESIGN IN BPM LIFECYCLE

Process Design includes both the identification of existing AS IS processes and the design of TO BE processes. This phase focuses on the representation of how an organization actually works, detailing not only process flows but also their actors, alerts and notifications, documents, Service Level Agreements, Standard Operating Procedures, etc.

For every organization, the Design phase is the base to create a clear and shared map of business processes, providing a fundamental reference for their management. The quality of the Design phase outcome, being the base for each subsequent decision, will have a very strong impact on process efficiency and performances.

Design activities may refer and map all possible kind of flows, including: human-to-human, system-to-system and mixed human-to-system-to-human ones.

Design and AI

AI may have a very strong impact on the Design phase of a BPM project: a couple of relevant example are Process model automatic composition (the opportunity to automatically create the shape of a process model from existing knowledge and data) and Process model reuse (when whole processes or parts of them, single activities, organizational elements, forms, documents, functions, etc. are efficiently recycled).

Process model automatic composition

In the Design phase, the business analyst usually interviews company employees and managers and then reviews existing business knowledge made of guideline documents and data available in transactional systems (ERP, CRM, etc.).

Proceeding with this activity of collection, business analysts are able to understand, streamline and clearly model the way an organization (or part of it) is actually managed, mapping AS IS processes.

Unfortunately all above-mentioned activities are extremely time-consuming, challenging and strictly dependent from employees and business analyst experience, communication and investigation skills.

AI-based software tools support the business analyst as they are able to automatically generate an AS IS process model, simply analyzing and elaborating historical data available from transactional systems.

This elaboration, made of cycles of automatic iteration on transactional data, will start providing a rough initial process map then generating in the end, after repeated refinement cycles, a well structured and reliable AS IS process model. Even if the obtained process model may need further improvements and reviews by the business analyst to be completed, advantages brought by AI in this case may be measured in terms of time and cost orders of magnitude.

Process model reuse

During employees and managers interviews in the Design phase, the business analyst is used to search into her own process knowledge repository (made of paper, digital data and neurons) looking for past experiences. When her search is successful, she can reuse a previously mapped process to fulfill organization needs, may be adapting or changing it, but not re-building it from scratch.

According to specific needs, a business analyst may reuse (or recycle) and adapt a whole process, part of it, single activities, organizational elements, forms, documents, functions like local or remote services, etc.

But this reuse practice is possible if and only if business analyst has a deep knowledge and experience of concepts and processes of the specific business domain (e.g. banking, finance, telecommunication, chemical, etc.). Moreover, this reuse practice may be automated if and only if there's a formal, clear and structured representation of entities and relations connecting them, within a specific business domain.

Such a formal representation is called "ontology" and is the basic element for the automation of process reuse during the Design phase of BPM lifecycle.

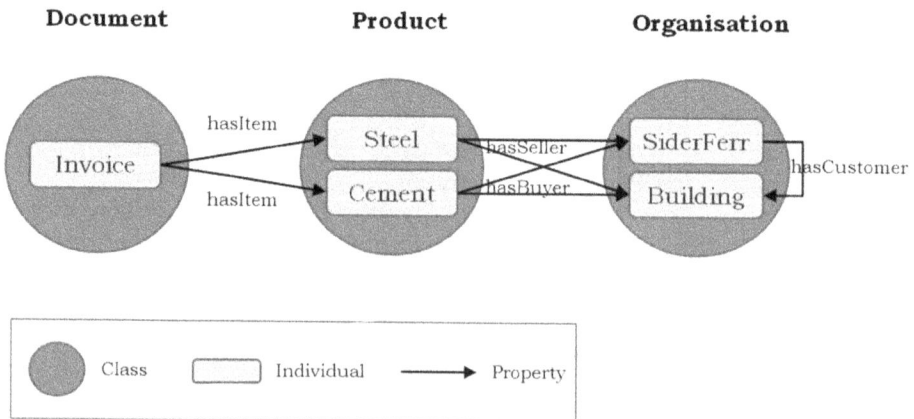

Figure 2: an ontology example (OWL Ontology)

To have an idea of how an ontology looks like, we propose an example (Ontology Web Language, OWL) based on concepts like classes, properties and individuals.

Classes are hierarchy concepts at the base of a specific domain, while individuals are class instances and properties represent relationships between individuals or types of data.

As each ontology is a semantic formal representation, when Web Services are associated with existing ontologies, they are defined Semantic Web Services (SWS).

The combination of BPM and SWS allows business analysts to:

- identify a service, or a composition of services, functionally equivalent to an existing one we need or want to replace (e.g. travel booking service substituted by another single service or by a set of services grouped in one transaction like flight booking, plus hotel booking, plus car rental booking, etc.)
- identify activity sets matching process definition needs (e.g. identify a subpart of a process to manage invoice approval for payment)

In daily practice, when a business analyst has to define or modify processes, she can use those sophisticated semantic AI-based tools to search for processes, services and resources, getting suggestions and/or automatic completion of process models (IntelliSense-like) while she's mapping them.

But to fully take advantage of the reuse semantic AI-based functionalities just mentioned, the intervention of a professional profile, in addition to the business analyst, is needed. Knowledge engineer work is to fully understand a specific business domain and model it to define appropriate ontologies.

In order to facilitate ontologies description and use, structured architecture have been defined for ontologies and one of them is the Business Management Ontology (BMO by Jenz and Partner GmbH). BMO is a structured architecture for ontologies, presenting three different levels: Core-Business, Industry-Specific and Organization-Specific.

Starting from Core-Business level, ontologies are then specialized into Industry-Specific business domains and then further refined into Organization-Specific details. This approach allows to provide ontologies users with at least part of the job done, encouraging the reuse of ontology fragments coming from different sources.

Some initiatives (Super Integrated Project [1]) have already defined and collected a relevant number of ontologies and other semantic tools capable of supporting BPM lifecycle phases.

While more abstract ontology level (Core-Business) is already mature, Industry-Specific still needs to be enriched and completed, while Organization-Specific has largely to be defined from scratch.

Once knowledge engineers have defined appropriate ontologies, the only thing a business analyst will have to do is assign those ontologies to the components of the process she's designing.

To associate an ontology with a process activity, the business analyst will have to define:

- activity goal: the objective she wants to reach through the activity (Validation, Archiving, Notification, etc.)
- activity business function: functionalities the activity has to perform (Verify Customer, Transform Document, etc.)

- domain: the object of the business function, selected in a collection of conceptually related categories (Customer, Product, Market Sales, etc.)

All defined associations with ontologies provide a great support to business analysts in many scenarios:

- process model definition: search, auto-completion, correctness check
- process implementation: automatic selection of resources and services
- process execution: run-time substitution of services and organizational elements

Moreover, when a process model has been assigned to a defined and specific ontology and each process activity has been properly assigned to the ontology itself, whole process implementation may be completed without human intervention. This means that rules definition, services selection, input/output adaptation, activity participants' declaration, electronic form definition, etc., may be performed automatically according to the semantic content of associate ontologies.

EXECUTION IN BPM LIFECYCLE

Only using BPM systems, full business processes (as defined in the process Design phase) may be directly executed as software by a computer.

In order to perform process models execution, BPM systems will either use services of connected applications (to complete some business operations, for instance, calculating a repayment plan for a loan) or ask for human intervention (when a process step is too complex to be completely automated).

The BPM approach not only gives great advantages while defining and executing a new process model for the first time, but most of all keeping its maintenance and update flexible and simple.

Execution and AI

The execution phase of a process is the one in which operations move in real-life environments and actual issues may occur, highlighting malfunctioning in the logic of the process itself or part of it.

When a business analyst is in charge of taking care of mission-critical processes, she should always adopt "compensations" (as defined in Business Process Management Notation). That simply means that she should manage error cases, setting up automatic actions to alert related process owner/responsible and/or reiterate operations or re-execute a process transaction.

Even if a "compensation" policy may solve a relevant set of problems, in other cases the process owner/responsible intervention is requested. Her authority may allow her to bypass any possible roadblock in the process flow execution or modify the process instance in order to solve any issue occurred.

As BPM systems are more and more based on services, malfunctioning cases may often be caused by the unavailability of such a service (or sets of services) or bad service performances impacting the whole process instance quality. Of course, in those cases, enterprise architecture should take those issues into account and prevent low performances adopting redundancy and load balancing policies.

But with growing offering of Software as a Service (SaaS), it may happen that the unavailable service is a remote one. This may occur for many different reasons: end of a contract, end of the credit, hacker attack, power cut, etc. Moreover, remote services could not only include automatic activities, but also human ones (*WS-HumanTask*).

In order to solve this class of issues and easily replace each unavailable service (or set of unavailable services) business analysts have to plan specific substitutions rules. This task consists of business analyst manual search to identify, for each service, an alternative service or composition of services with exactly the same functionalities. Moreover, again for each service, the business analyst will also have to define how to manage Input/Output structure with the replacing service and process execution restart point in case the service eventually gets blocked.

AI supports those manual service substitution practices by transforming them into automatic ones. Such a relevant result is obtained levering semantic associated to services that is, managing Semantic Web Services (SWS).

Semantic Web Services

To allow automatic substitution of a selected service, taking advantage of semantic associated with it, some key elements have to be defined:

- Functional features: Input, output and related bonds that have to be satisfied to invoke and use a specified service
- Non Functional features: service category, costs and quality
- Service provider info: provider name and address
- Task or Goal info: what the service is supposed to do

While many BPM system vendors already adopt standard (non-semantic) engines (*WS-BPEL)* to execute Business Process services orchestration, the same functionality may also be performed referring to semantics (*SWS Invoker*).

In this area some researcher (Super Integrated Project) have introduced conservative extensions to standard service engines (BPEL4SWS [2]), allowing SWS reference within a business process description. This extension allows a standard service engine to interact with ontologies: the first to assign activities to the execution flow and the second is used to perform the data transformations on behalf of the assigned activities (semantic data mediation).

Most developers used to deal with services using a standard service language (Web Service Description Language, WSDL): its logic is to explicitly specify all information needed to invoke a specific service.

But in order to make an additional step and add semantic information for service managing, allowing semantic service discovery, a standard service language extension has been created (SA-WSDL [3]).

As regards ontologies, in order to solve one of the most difficult issue related to their very complex and time consuming definition, some researcher have proposed an alternative route. Adopt a service semantic classification directly defined by services users: a service folksonomy, a taxonomy built up by folks (users) by properly tagging ontology elements [4].

This innovative approach provides a multiple service classification that evolves each time a service is adopted and integrated in a new application. This scenario is much more valid if we consider SaaS applications, that is, when the same single service is invoked and used by many different users.

OPTIMIZATION IN BPM LIFECYCLE

Optimization uses information obtained during the monitoring phase, identifying the potential or actual bottlenecks and the potential opportunities for cost savings or other improvements. In fact, very often not only the representation made during the Design phase doesn't catch all details to get perfectly streamlined process, but also simulations performed during the Modeling phase don't always consider actual time and cost of each activity.

Applying Enhancements identified during Optimization phase are then applied in the re-design of the process and this creates greater business value.

Most important steps in the Optimization phase are:

- Collect process instances data
- Display data of business processes and activities, discover bottlenecks and possible improvements
- Modify process flows and redistribute resources proposing differently balanced combinations
- Collect simulation data and compare them with other simulations or actual process instance data

Optimization and AI

All these steps can be supported through the use of AI-based and Data Mining techniques. This approach is particularly useful within BPM system, when process representation is needed, taking the name of Process Mining [5].

Process Mining is a science that starting from process data (process statuses, organizational model, event logs, etc.) allows to investigate, simulate and improve business processes.

Specifically, Process Mining allows us to answer the following questions:

- What is really happening? (Process discovery)
- Do we do what was agreed upon? (Conformance checking)
- Where are the bottlenecks? (Performance analysis)
- Will this case be late? (Process prediction)
- How to redesign this process? (Process improvement)

Process Mining software allows to automatically identify process models actually executed in a company and not managed by BPM system, but through transactional systems (ERP, CRM, etc.) or any kind of system able to produce event logs. Moreover such generated process models may be compared with quality manual processes or with any other *a priori* or theoretical map of a process.

In case process instances data is available, Process Mining software is able to detect which process branches are more frequently executed.

In order to support process Optimization phase (discovery, visualization, simulation, improvement) many complementary tools are available. Examples listed here below are some of the most well-known with corresponding main features:

- YAWL [6]
  - Create and execute process models
  - Maintain organizational models
  - Extract functionalities for event logs, organizational models and current state of the workflow system
- ProM [7]
  - Translate and integrate all the components into a Petri Nets model
  - Analyze event logs and simulation logs
- CPN Tools [8]
  - Run simulation experiments
  - Incorporate current state of workflows
  - Generate simulation logs

Other AI-based Utilities in the BPM Context

On top of the support AI provides within each single phase of BPM lifecycle, there are some other cross contexts where it is widely used, specifically in automatic recognition (levering neural networks, fuzzy logic and other AI elements).

During BPMS lifecycle phases, humans often have to identify, recognize, classify and store data and all those actions are time-consuming, repetitive, cause of errors and may become bottlenecks and generate corporate costs.

Automation provided by those AI-based recognizers not only allows us to save time and money in operations, but also to extract data and patterns often very difficult to capture or even invisible for humans.

Here follows some of the most common AI-based recognizers, now mature and widely used in BPM and document management.

Barcode recognition applied to documents, images or products, allows us to quickly identify and classify document and objects.

In document-oriented business processes automatic barcode recognition activities are very useful as they allow to elaborate even large sets of documents splitting each into the appropriate process path. In production–oriented business processes, barcode are used to manage logistics, sales and marketing processes, monitoring products cycles.

Optical Character Recognition (OCR) allows us to convert the image of scanned text into machine-encoded text. Even if the recognition result could be used for text to speech and text mining, OCR is mostly used to index documents to associate metadata and allow data searching.

Intelligent Character Recognition (ICR) allows us to convert hand written text into machine-encoded text. It is widely used especially for document-centric processes related to Form Recognition, that is, to recognize hand-written characters entered while filling-up a form, along with check boxes and producing a database data as a result.

Speech Recognition allows us to convert an audio speech into machine-encoded text. It could be useful for a business analyst to interview key users and process owners automatically obtaining interviews transcriptions.

Computer Vision allows us to extract information from images such as video clips, views from different cameras, or multidimensional data taken from medical scanners. Again, there are many applications in that area, and specifically in the BPM context, that allow us to generate events or support medical or general control activities.

Conclusions

Process design, modeling, execution, monitoring and optimization: the whole BPM lifecycle may take (and is already taking) great automation advantage from using AI technologies.

Machines able to learn, generalize, recognize, etc., are already available today and provide good performances, even if operating into limited (but growing) contexts AI-based tools must still be "taught and guided" within a specific domain to become a good alternative to humans, but in many cases they provide results that seem very close to science fiction for quality and timing.

AI may give a very important contribution in streamlining and accelerating BPM systems evolution into a daily, widely used tool for Line of Business managers, process owners and key users.

REFERENCES

1. Super Integrated Project, Semantics Utilised for Process Management within and between Enterprises
   www.ip-super.org
2. BPEL4SWS, BPEL for Semantic Web Services, Process Ontology Language and Operational Semantics for Semantic Business Processes
   www.ip-super.org/res/Deliverables/D1.3.pdf
3. SA-WSDL, Semantic Annotations for WSDL and XML Schema
   www.w3.org/2002/ws/sawsdl
4. Harald Meyer and Mathias Weske, Light-Weight Semantic Service Annotations through Tagging
   bpt.hpi.uni-potsdam.de/pub/Public/HaraldMeyer/tagging.pdf
5. Process Mining: research, tools, applications
   prom.win.tue.nl/research/wiki
6. YAWL – Yet Another Workflow Language
   www.yawlfoundation.org
7. ProM - the leading process mining toolkit
   prom.win.tue.nl/tools/prom
8. CPN Tools – Coloured Petri Nets Tools
   wiki.daimi.au.dk/cpntools/cpntools.wiki

Predictive BPM

Dr. Setrag Khoshafian, Pegasystems Inc., USA

Most businesses today engage in "predictions." Will a customer agree to upgrade a purchase based on an array of offers? What is the likelihood that a customer within a cluster of similar customers will default on a loan? How much more effective will a targeted marketing campaign be, compared to a random sampling? How can the churn rate of subscribers be improved? What is the likelihood that a particular financial transaction is fraudulent? These are some questions that could utilize prediction with concrete and tangible business benefits.

A "business" is a collection of policies and procedures. Almost every business policy or procedure has some aspect of prediction in it. Most of the time, policy and procedure requirements are based on intuition, best guesses, or business experience. Too frequently, no one in the organization can remember why certain policies were ever created in the first place.

There are actually several sources of policies and procedures that guide business operations. Here are some of them:

- *Policy and Procedure Manuals:* These reveal how things get done in the organization. You have manuals for handling customer interactions, for building products, for HR, for services, and more. Often, new employees are trained on these manuals; their jobs entail understanding and implementation of procedures and enforcement of policies.
- *People's Heads:* Almost invariably, there are designated "knowledge workers" who know how to get things done. They know the written, and often unwritten, policies and procedures and have these in their heads. These are the go-to people for specific tasks or procedures, and every organization has them. Equally important, they know which policies or procedures can be ignored— those little workarounds that technically break the rules but actually get things done. These people are also often the source of innovation—either of new products and services or process innovation. Their understanding of the organization puts them in a unique position to be able to identify how the organization could work better.
- *ERP and Point Solutions:* ERP solutions contain embedded business process logic. The customizations and configuration are based on an understanding of the policies and procedures at the time the system was implemented. However, because these business rules and processes are embedded within the solutions, they are not easy to extend and so become "ossified" and difficult to change.
- *Legacy or Custom Code:* Policies and procedures can also be implemented in homegrown legacy code. This code spans proprietary extensions of ERP solutions, such as ABAP, as well as programs in languages such as COBOL, Java, or C/C++/C#. In fact, the majority of legacy code is in COBOL. Sometimes millions of lines of code have been written to accommodate stakeholder requirements. This code is very difficult to maintain and change, and it is increasingly becoming a serious impediment to agility and change.
- *Automated Models:* This is the newest and most important category. Here, policies and procedures are directly captured through the business process management (BPM) suite and automated for execution in solutions that are

easy to change. BPM suites can allow business stakeholders to directly capture their requirements in the tool itself.

But there is another—perhaps less obvious and often less direct—source for both policies and procedures: *data*. There are many sources of data, including the following:

- *Operational* or transactional data from legacy, point-solution, or ERP applications
- Process instance and *case data* from BPM suites
- Data from *external sources* including, but not limited to, public and census data
- *Data warehouses* and/or data marts that aggregate databases (mostly relational) from a plethora of sources, including transactional, operational, or BPM databases

The volume, variation, and sources of data are exploding. The "data" here is, by and large, raw data that is not analyzed. For reporting, analytics, or predictive discovery the raw data needs to be extracted, cleaned, and transformed. Data warehouses/data marts are populated from operational databases, external sources, and BPM case and work data. The whole notion of *data mining* is one of detecting patterns—often operational behavioral patterns—in data. These patterns could be used to forecast future behavior. The detected patterns (called "models" in predictive analytics lingo) could become "operationalized" to help determine business responses. Predictive analytics is a scientific discipline within data mining that uses measurable *predictors* to assess probable outcomes of specific events. Predictive analytics can help the organization continually monitor and adapt operations—especially those realized through BPM suites—for anticipated future behavior. Predictive models often combine historical and operational data from the business to identify the risk or opportunity associated with a specific customer or transaction.

The essence of predictive BPM is the execution of discovered models that predict future behavior, in the context of automated BPM solutions. BPM suites are the platforms that automate policies and procedures. Thus, in predictive BPM there is a close affinity between what is discovered and its execution. For instance, scoring a potential customer for credit risk could involve simple aggregation of data or information about the customer and application of a weighted formula to score the risk. The decision of what to do with a specific score, or a detected pattern in general, is the policy—the decision logic. The policy itself is executed in the context of a process or case, automated through the BPM suite (e.g., the credit application).

From any of the aforementioned data sources and even combining multiple data sources, predictive analysts aggregate and mine historic enterprise operational data (and sometimes publicly available data) in order to detect patterns (models). These patterns can then be used to make predictions about the behavior of future instances. Predictive models deliver segmentation and scoring. For example, depending upon geographical location, demographics, age group, and/or purchasing power of a customer, you can score the likelihood of a customer responding to a marketing offer. Or given the transaction history and types of activities across claims, you can determine the likelihood of fraud. The predictive models can be captured in BPM suites through declarative expressions, properties, situational rules, flows, decision tables, and decision trees.

Predictive analytics is widely used in many industries. There are also applications of predicative analytics such as customer relationship management (CRM) that could be used across many industries.

Here are some examples:

- *Insurance:* In the insurance industry, companies frequently model the risk of insurance applications based on the factors they identify as indicators of future accidents, health risks, and premature deaths. These factors include attributes such as age, body mass index, lifestyle activities, and accident record. These predictive factors are what the insurance companies use to rate insurance applicants so as to create the right balance in their risk portfolios, and help determine what premium each applicant should pay to offset that risk.
- *Financial Services:* Credit scoring in consumer finance can be used to predict the likelihood of timely payments. Predictive modeling can also be used to assess the risk of fraud.
- *Telecommunications:* Customer churn (losing customers who switch to an alternative provider) is one of the most critical challenges in some industries—especially in telecom. Customer data could be used to analyze and predict potential customer churn—through better understanding of customer preferences and behavior and emerging trends.
- *Customer Experience and Marketing:* Marketing campaigns and customer relationships is another major area of predictive analytics that has applicability across many vertical industries. For example, in many industries there is a need to predict whether a prospect will respond favorably to a specific marketing or promotional offer.

Predictive models can greatly enhance the efficiency of processes, improve the customer experience, and reduce potential risks. The following figure illustrates the taxonomy of the type of knowledge or insight we can get from data, and the corresponding business value.

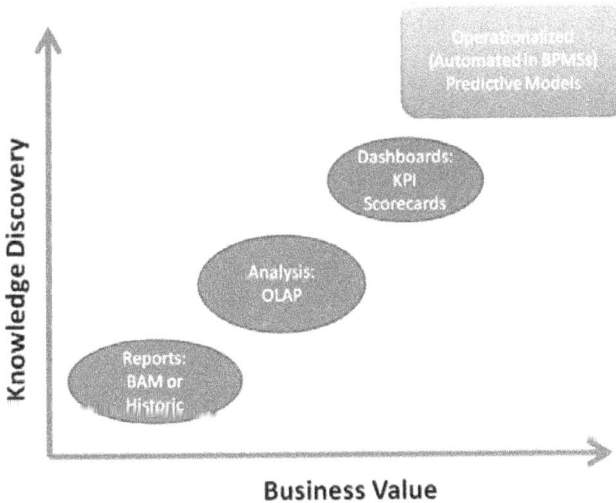

Figure 1: Knowledge Discovery vs. Business Value

Reports can be sourced from real-time business activity monitoring or data warehouses that contain historical data, potentially from multiple sources. BPM suites are increasingly becoming a key source of data for both business activity monitoring (BAM) and data warehouses. Reports are useful for understanding what happened (historic) or what is happening now (BAM).

Analysis goes further in data insight and attempts to "slice and dice" the data along different dimensions and perspectives. It attempts to discover trends and glean insight from aggregated data.

Dashboards allow business stakeholders to have a role-specific, strategic key-performance perspective on their operations. The users can drill down and potentially act on detected bottlenecks.

Predictive modeling and *automation* of decisions provides the greatest business value. Here models that are discovered from historic data are used not only to predict future behavior but to actually *enact the predictive decision in an executing process at the point of execution*. In other words, the current process instance or case provides a context in which the predictive models are operationalized.

The tools and techniques used in predictive modeling, in general, are more complex than reporting, Online Analytical Processing (OLAP), or dashboard tools. But at the same time, since the models are applied to pragmatic business questions, their recommendations have tremendous business value.

Many applications can benefit from automating predictive models. A TDWI[1] survey discovered "Cross-sell/up-sell" to be the top application of predictive analysis. Other top contenders included "Campaign management," "Customer acquisition," and "Retention." If and when these models are enacted and executed in the context of BPM-centric next-generation customer relationship management solutions, application of the predictive model will be executed at the point of interaction with the customer. For instance, if a call center receives a call from a customer following up on a complaint case (automated in the BPM suite), the customer provides additional information about his/her situation. If the enacted predictive model indicates a high likelihood that the customer will switch to another provider, an automated BPM policy could kick in and make an attractive offer to the customer—potentially avoiding the churn. The key value proposition of predictive BPM is the execution of the deepest data knowledge or insight, through BPM suite applications or solutions. The discovered decision is executed in BPM suite solutions.

THE TWO BPMS AND THE EMERGENCE OF PBPM

Predictive BPM is an emerging enterprise solution that aligns business processes with business intelligence. Two interrelated "BPM" acronyms enable predictive business processes. One designates the modeling and automation of processes (business *process* management). The other focuses on monitoring key performance indicators and managing the performance of the business (business *performance* management). BPM suites allow you to model and execute your policies and procedures or flows. They include human workflow, enterprise application integration, business to business choreographies, business rules, collaboration, and solution frameworks. Business process management suites typically support business activity monitoring and process performance capabilities. The other BPM—business performance management—includes monitoring and analysis of applications from a variety of sources: business processes, enterprise resource planning applications, customer relationship management systems, or any com-

---

[1] From www.tdwi.org, research report "Predictive Analytics Extending the Value of Your Data Warehousing Investment," by Wayne W. Eckerson, January 2007. Or see http://www.bi-bestpractices.com/view-articles/5642

mercial or homegrown applications. Business performance management supports strategic methodologies, analysis of ROI, key performance indicator measures, robust performance reporting and portals, data warehousing, OLAP, and business intelligence and data mining with predictive analysis.

We are witnessing the amalgamation of these two disciplines into Predictive BPM (PBPM): business process management and business performance management, especially business intelligence (BI). The dynamic combination of BI and BPM will enable you to monitor, report, analyze, learn, make changes, and improve your business processes in real time. The ultimate objective is to declare your desired performances (KPIs) and let the PBPM system figure out the best way to realize the objective, through predictive analytics, dynamic learning from data, and BPM case automation. This is a tall order. However, it is definitely the trend and becoming a reality.

Many technologies are involved in round-trip improvement life cycles, from strategic measures to underlying operational process applications that increasingly are becoming the main source of data for analysis and predictive modeling. We believe there are huge opportunities with enterprise architectures that clearly delineate and at the same time aggregate the functions of process and performance management. PBPM means that the event dimensions that are used to model, analyze, and extract predictive models from data warehouses are enacted in business process applications. It also means that business process management suites are the main, if not the sole, source of data for information warehouses. PBPM also implies the connection of high-level KPI measures to the execution of policies and processes. Monitored performance metrics such as KPIs in various perspectives are predictive: Stakeholders can take action *in the context of operational processes and policies.* Within PBPM frameworks, continuous improvement life cycles, with *performance* and *analytics*, are key functions in the round-trip improvement of process applications.

The following figure illustrates the continuous improvement life cycle with predictive BPM:

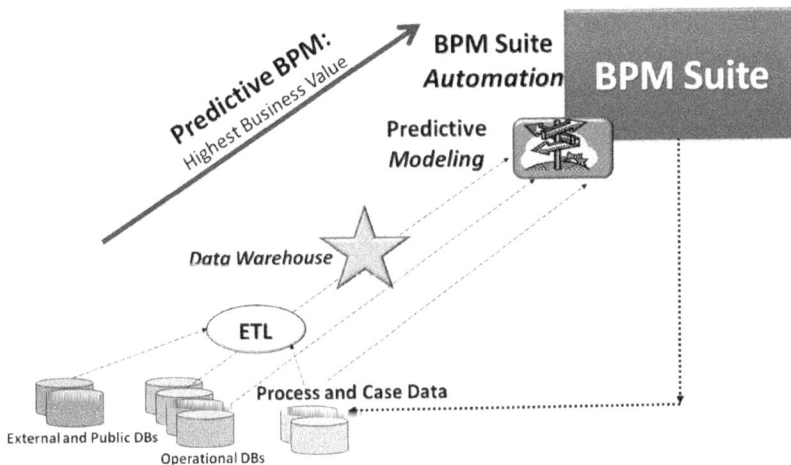

Figure 2: Continuous Improvement Cycle

Enterprise solutions typically have real-time reporting capabilities. BPM suites include BAM portals that allow business managers to run reports, analyze performance, and take action to remediate potential operational process bottlenecks.

BAM can also provide monitoring, reporting, and analysis from multiple enterprise solutions or operations.

Data warehouses can have several sources of external or operational data. These may involve mainframe applications, ERP applications, CRM tools, message queues, and most important, BPM process and case data.

The key observation here—and the focus of this paper—is that there are interesting patterns in the data. These patterns could be mined and subsequently operationalized. How? Through predictive modeling.

As discussed in the next section, there are different types of predictive models: clustering, associations, regression, trees, and more advanced models such as neural networks or Bayesian probabilistic models. All the data sources—BPM case data, operational databases, external databases, data warehouses, etc.— could be used to create predictive models. Predictive modeling could itself be part of the Predictive BPM tooling in a cohesive, unified PBPM platform.[2] Alternatively, predictive models can be imported from other analytical tools.[3] This is similar to importing business rules or process models that are defined in, say, XML or Visio. The main point is that the discovered predictive decision logic is deployed and executed in the context of automated BPM solutions. The operationalization and automation of the models is the key value proposition of PBPM.

Execution of the processes with all the business rules and decision logic continuously generates new case data. Potentially, there could be changes in the patterns or customer behaviors. Similar changes could be reflected in operational databases or external data sources. Data is never static. Thus, new patterns and behavior could be detected. The discovered predictive models can then introduce change to the PBPM. The continuous improvement cycle thus continues, with the PBPM keeping pace with newly discovered models.

BPM suites provide many advantages for business stakeholders. An understanding of the performance of operational processes and the automatic triggering of actions through changes in process states are key measurable benefits. These benefits bridge the gaps between the goals and objectives of the business stakeholders and the underlying IT systems that address these goals and objectives. Capturing and acting on business rules and business processes is the core value proposition in predictive BPM.

PREDICTIVE MODELING

Prediction is ubiquitous. Almost every business flow or business rule has some element of prediction in it. Most of the time requirements arise from intuition, history, experience, or ad hoc mechanisms to capture policies and procedures. Sometimes the original reasons for enacting these policies have long been obsolete. In contrast, predictive modeling is a scientific discipline within data mining that uses measurable *predictors* to predict the behavior of customers. These predictors can be an ordinal or numerical value that can be predicted from other variable values. Historical data is analyzed and modeled to predict future behavior.

---

[2] The discovery and deployment of models is itself a process with concrete phases and steps. This process has been standardized by an industry- and tool-neutral organization: CRISP-DM.org. CRISP stands for CRoss Industry Standard Process—Data Mining. See http://www.crisp-dm.org/.

[3] The Predictive Model Markup Language (PMML) is defined by the Data Mining Group (DMG). PMML is the Predictive Analytics XML standard to exchange predictive models between tools. See http://www.dmg.org/.

Examples of predictors include purchasing preferences, geographical location, age, income, and properties pertaining to the history of activities.

Several predictive models can be discovered from either operational or historic data. The latter is often managed through data warehouses and data marts. Here are some of the categories of predictive models:

- *Classification Models:* In classification one or more variables classify objects (e.g., customers). Then, given a new instance, the class of the instance can be determined from the classification models. *Tree models* are perhaps the most popular type of classification model. In tree models you partition the data by input variables. At each level of the tree you will typically use a different partitioning variable. Then, at the leaves of the tree, you will have the conclusions—namely the class. Through manual, semi-automated, or automated algorithms, the decision tree can be built by "predicting" the outcome of one or more predictable properties (attributes, or variables) based on other input properties. For instance, a model might predict customer buying patterns by partitioning on the customer's age, household size, geographical location (east, west, central, etc.), income, and purchase history. Each of these "features" will be used to provide the branches of the tree. Tree modeling algorithms will systematically partition the data. For new customer interactions, traversing the tree for specific values—the age, the household size, etc.—and reaching a leaf will predict the potential behavior of the customer: "will probably buy" or "will probably not buy." Thus, once the tree model is constructed and validated, it can be used as a predictor.

- *Regression Models:* There are different types of regression models (linear, nonlinear, multiple, logistic, etc.). Linear regression is probably the most popular of the regression models. Here the idea is to find the best-fit linear model $(Y = a*X)$ of a dependent variable Y. For example, a linear regression predictive model can predict *TotalSales* as a linear function of investment in *MarketingAndAdvertising*: *TotalSales = C1 + C2*MarketingAndAdvertising*. The predictive model will attempt to best fit the linear model, discovering the values for *C1* and *C2*.

- *Clustering Models:* Here you can have clusters or segments of your data or records. For instance, you might have a cluster based on the type of customer and his or her geographical location. Then the behavior of clusters could be different. For instance, you might determine that customers in cluster C1 might be quite different in their purchasing practices or their responses to, say, marketing campaigns than customers in cluster C2.

- *Advanced Models:* Predictive modeling can be very complex. The aforementioned models have many variations. Furthermore, there are more complex models—such as neural networks and Bayesian probabilistic models—that could be more appropriate in situations where there are complex or unknown relationship dependencies between variables.

The list here is by no means exhaustive. Some simple algorithms—such as binning—can provide amazingly good results in the prediction of future behavior. So the main philosophy of predictive models is to aggregate and mine historic operational data (and sometimes publicly available data) in order to make predictions about behaviors, within operations automated through BPM solutions.

REALIZING PREDICTIVE BPM

The previous section provided an overview of the relationship between predictive model discovery and BPM suites. This section further expands upon the robust requirements or capabilities in a BPM suite that are essential for predictive BPM. The three fundamental characteristics of PBPM can be summarized as follows:

- *Rich Collection of Rule Types*: Predictive models are usually captured in decision rules. The BPM suite needs to support a rich collection of rule types to handle the discovered models and operationalize them (i.e., automate or execute the predictive model in the context of an automated process application). A BPM suite cohesively integrates business rules, which can include decision-making criteria, evaluation of conformance, risk assessments, expressions, event rules (including event correlation, triggers, etc.) time constraints, task reassignment decisions, or decisions on quality. These business rules need to be captured and executed in the context of process flows. Behind every decision, service level, task assignment, calculation, constraint, integration, and user interaction, there are rules. The rules then drive the processes. The following figure illustrates business rules, including expressions, decision rules, integration rules (for just-in-time information from ERP or other legacy systems), UI rules, constraints, and event rules. The process is represented through the familiar swim-lane diagram. But what is interesting is the fact that behind every task assignment, link, decision, etc., there are business rules that are driving the processes—very similar to the way the nervous system directs the movement of the muscles.

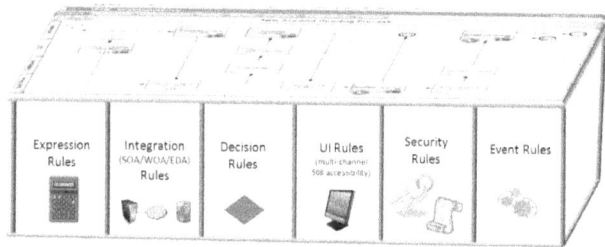

Figure 3: Business Rules Driving the Business Process

- *Circumstances and Situational Execution of Rules:* The assets here are the BPM assets for execution: processes, decision rules, constraints, event rules, UI, integration, information models, security, organization models, etc.

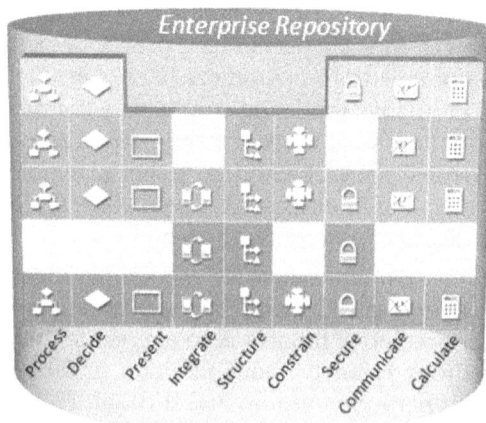

Figure 4: Dynamic Multidimensional Enterprise Repository

The BPM assets need to be organized in a dynamic multidimensional repository. Its dimensions include temporal versioning, but other dimensions are equally important. The repository will support central models and constrained customization for branches or departments, or geographical locations or offices. There can be a dimension that addresses the type of customer—the case subject. Access control/security is another dimension. This multidimensional repository provides a framework to organize, change, deploy, and execute the assets. With PBPM it offers a powerful multi-dimensional organization of the assets to reflect different segments or clusters, associating different business rules for each cluster. The PBPM engine can situationally determine which policy to apply, for a given context. The context is determined through values along the dimensions of the repository: the geographical location of the customer, time, type of service or issue, channel, type of customer, etc.

- *Ad hoc, Smart, and Dynamic Case Management:* A case is the collaboration of multiple tasks for a business objective. Case management brings together multiple related transactions to give a business person a complete picture of what is actually going on. Cases involve multiple flows, tasks, and content. Smart and dynamic case management involves ad hoc processing. This means that at case execution or processing time you can add new tasks, execute additional flow fragments, add content, or create sub-cases—all on an ad hoc basis. In smart case management, knowledge workers can discover policies and procedures (business or decision rules) and immediately automate them in the case management solution. Predictive analytics can dynamically discover models that need to be leveraged in the context of the case. Smart and dynamic case management also provides support for selection of the most appropriate UI, decision logic, flow fragment, or integration, depending upon the context, at case execution time. Dynamic situational selection can reflect the predictive behavior discovered in clusters depending upon the geographical location (where, what language), the time (when), the type of the customer (who), or the purpose (why) of the case.

Cases are event-driven: they generate and respond to events. Event management—including complex event processing—and case management are joined at the hip. A case event is an occurrence that pertains to any aspect of the case's life cycle, content, interactions, or associations. Events consist of a source, priority, time stamp, and data. Events are ubiquitous; in fact, many components of a business application deal with events. All the changes that a case undergoes throughout its life cycle are events. There are also events that pertain to the case subject: for instance, the case subject moves to another state. Then there are the external events (external to the case) that need to be processed. Events could be generated by people, devices, cases, or circumstances.

CONCLUSION

Data mining, and especially predictive modeling techniques, can be used to detect business patterns and then invoke or operationalize the discovered rules in the context of BPM solutions. This is the essence of predictive BPM. The predictive models are deployed and empower BPM solutions. For instance, consider a process that deals with transaction disputes (e.g., purchases, credit cards, etc.). After executing repeatedly and keeping track of the process data, the data mining discovers that, almost always, when the customer has made total purchases in excess of $1,000 and the disputed amount is less than $50, the decision was to write it off. Now this pattern is captured in a rule that automates the decision log-ic of a write-off dispute process. It could be "mined" from the process data. The rule can then be associated with a decision point within an automated process. After the customer dispute information is collected, the BPM suite can automati-cally decide to write off—essentially executing the rule—without human interven-tion. As this example illustrates, the mining of the rule also involved the aggregate history of customer transactions.

Predictive BPM is quite compelling. In BPM suites, the focus is on the operational execution of the processes and the goal-driven policies that support the business rules. In predictive analytics, the focus is on analyzing the historic data and dis-covering related patterns or models that incorporate the statistical relationships uncovered in the historical data. These analysis tools are not designed to execute the models in the context of business processes. Best practice in the industry in-volves an intense amount of rekeying, and translation of the predictive model for operational code. These translations slow the process of making the models ex-ecutable and introduce the potential for error. BPM suites eliminate this manual translation and offer an exponential increase in bandwidth to accommodate new and varied predictive models. BPM suites allow you to directly capture and ex-ecute your predictive models.

With PBPM, you can mine and discover rules or processes from your process da-ta, your data warehouse, or other operational data sources. The discovered rules or processes can then be automated. The new rules will be executed in the con-text of processes and generate new process data. As the behavior of various users in a process application changes (due to competition, customer behavior, or mar-ket pressures, for example), new process data will be generated. The discovery cycle continues, and the data mining will discover the new rules and redeploy them to the BPM execution environment.

It is this ability not only to discover but to automate and execute the processes that delivers the greatest business value. Before the dawn of business process management suites—with their strong support of process flows and business rules—BI applications focused on different types of reporting and analysis. Data warehouses provide some value in aggregating historical data from a variety of sources, but mining and exploring the data provides greater value. Users can run reports and better understand and employ the patterns in the data warehouse. Predictive models go a step further and discover models and patterns that are not obvious or at all evident through simple exploration and analysis of the data in the warehouse. But the ultimate business value emanates from the operational execution of the new policies discovered by predictive modeling.

Intelligent, Automated Processes: Embedding Analytics in Decisions

James Taylor, Decision Management Solutions, USA

The challenge of putting BI to work in business processes is that reports and dashboards only work in manual processes. If the process is automated, if straight through processing is called for, then the analytics required are different. Embedding these analytics in rules-based decisions is the ideal way to analytically enhance these processes and build intelligent, automated processes.

BUSINESS INTELLIGENCE AND BUSINESS PROCESS

There is a clear and obvious synergy between Business Intelligence (BI) and Business Process Management (BPM).

BI can use BPM

BI helps us understand what is happening in our business, what our results are, how well we are doing. If we are using BPM to define and manage our business processes then clearly information about our processes should be included in this analysis. We can consider the number of times a process executes, which steps are involved in each execution and how long things take—all of these are data about how our business is operating.

BPM can use BI

BPM helps us structure and manage the work that must be performed in our business. Often the tasks we need to perform, or how those tasks are carried out, are dependent on the current state of the business. The analysis of the state of our business using BI can and should be an input to these tasks. For instance, information about past customer orders or the frequency with which a particular supplier misses deadlines drives behavior in specific tasks.

BI is particularly helpful for Decisions

BI is particularly helpful to a certain subset of the tasks within our business processes-decisions. When we must decide how to treat a customer, what the risk of a particular supplier being late or how likely a particular approach is to work for a particular transaction, BI provides insight and information to help us do that.

BI and BPM can and do complement each other and organizations that adopt both approaches and technologies and use them together can gain significantly from the synergies inherent in these two closely related areas.

THE CHALLENGES OF AUTOMATED PROCESSES

When it comes to automated processes, however, there are challenges in combining BI and BPM. In an automated process, where the objective is straight through processing, the tasks or activities in our process are handled by computers, by systems, not by people. Herein lies the challenge as BI products and approaches focus on the presentation of information to people so they can use that information effectively. A dashboard, for instance, that allows a manager to see the status of their department or a report detailing last month's sales for a sales manager. With no people involved, automated processes have no obvious home for BI. There is no-one to watch the dashboard, no-one to read the report.

Automated processes need insight too

Yet the need for applying insight about our business is real and compelling. Just as people add intelligence to a manual process by using information to make better, more intelligent, decisions so an automated process must be informed by what we know. We need to take what we know about how our business operates, by what has worked or not worked in the past and the current state of the business and apply this business insight in the context of our automated processes.

To do this we must address three critical issues:

1. We must understand exactly what decisions are being made in our process.
    Computers are much more literal than people so much greater precision in definition is essential

2. We must be able to turn our data into insight that can be consumed by a computer.
    Traditional BI representations are aimed at people so something different is required.

3. We must be able to define the actions to be taken, and the constraints on those actions, so that the computer can act not just "understand." We need the process to keep moving, it cannot wait for a person to take action, so the computer must be able to act on its own.

DECISIONS AND PROCESSES

Building intelligent, automated processes requires that we understand the decisions in our processes. These decisions give us the points of control that we need and the places where insight might make a difference.

What is a decision?

Whether made by a person or a computer, a decision is a selection, a choice, made from a range of possible options. It might be a selection from Yes/No, from a list of products or even from a numeric range. A decision also involves taking action not just adding to what is known. It is not enough to find out something new or to create new knowledge; we must act on it if what we are doing is to be considered a decision. Decisions are also typically made after some consideration, after some analysis. Making a decision is a task, an activity within our process not just a branch or gateway within it.

Different types of decisions

Decisions are embedded in every kind of process and can be strategic, tactical or operational. Strategic decisions are the responsibility of the executive suite and are typically one-off decisions that make a significant difference to the overall direction of the organization. Tactical decisions are about managerial control, setting short term and local policies within a strategic framework. It is the last group —operational decisions—that is critical when it comes to automated processes.

> ✓ *Understand the decisions that matter to your business. Consider a decision audit to see what strategic, tactical and operational decisions you have that make a difference to your business processes. A broad but shallow understanding of your decisions will help you focus your effort.*

Automated processes are operational

Automated processes are high volume, high throughput processes or those requiring very fast turnaround times. Most organizations do not automate processes otherwise. While high performance, high volume processes may be constrained by tactical decisions or re-designed due to strategic ones, it is *operational* decisions that are embedded in them.

Little decisions add up

Operational decisions are low value, high volume decisions each of which impacts a single customer, a single transaction, a single instance of the process of which they are part. Just as an operational process can be automated by defining a standard way to execute the process and then doing so repeatedly, so can an operational decision be defined in a standard way and executed repeatedly in the context of such a process. While these decisions are individually low value, their cumulative value can be significant. For instance the individual decision about how to price a particular insurance policy might have a modest value but even a small insurance company makes many such decisions, ensuring that the overall value of the way we make the underwriting decision is significant.

Insight-driven operational decisions

Not every operational decision requires insight to make correctly or effectively. Deciding if a customer is eligible for a product, for instance, or deciding what the right discount is for a particular customer are operational decisions but they may be driven by a fixed set of business rules (of which more later). Two main categories of operational decisions do, however, require insight and these can be described as risk-based and opportunity-based operational decisions.

Risk-based operational decisions

In risk-based operational decisions, insight is required as to the risk of this particular transaction, this particular customer. For instance, an assessment of how likely this transaction is to be fraudulent given the history of other fraudulent transactions. This kind of decision includes decisions about fraud, about credit or perhaps about deliveries or suppliers where there is a risk of a negative outcome. Without insight, information, as to the likelihood of that negative outcome it is hard to make a good decision.

Opportunity-based operational decisions

Opportunity based decisions do not have a bad outcome but require that a choice is made between different degrees of opportunity. For instance, in marketing decisions, the wrong offer represents a lesser opportunity than the right offer. Insight into which choice will offer the greatest opportunity is not critical but will maximize the value of the decision being made.

> ✓ *Understand the link to performance management and metrics/KPIs*
> *One of the critical success factors for effective management of decisions, and effective use of analytic insight in decision making, is the linkage of decisions to the metrics and KPIs they impact. Without this understanding it is hard to tell a good decision from a bad one and hard therefore to determine what insight will help you make a good decision.*

Decision Services

To embed decisions in business processes we must develop decision services. A decision service is a service that answers business questions for other services, a service that makes decisions. Such a service should generally be stateless and have no side-effects (such as emails sent or databases being updated) so that any process that relies on the decision can use the decision service without fear of unintended consequences. Decision services have simple interfaces, allowing data to be passed in and returning simple information about the decision made and perhaps the way in which the decision was made.

EMBEDDING ANALYTICS IN DECISIONS

Once we have identified a risk-based or opportunity-based operational decision that we plan to implement as a decision service, we must determine how analytic insight can help us and what kind of analytic insight we need. Clearly visualizations, reports and dashboards are not going to be helpful to delivering insights to a decision service in an automated process. There are, after all, no eyes to look at these things. Instead we must develop the insight we need as something executable, something our automated process can use.

Different kinds of analytic insight

Analytics, analytic insight, covers a wide range of possible meanings. One of the simplest definitions of analytics is:

> Analytics simplify data to amplify its meaning.

This clearly states the purpose of analytics—to make it easier to get value, meaning, from data—but also covers a wide range of techniques and technologies. In particular it includes a range of analytics from business intelligence to descriptive analytics, predictive analytics and even optimization. It can be helpful to consider these different techniques as points on a spectrum, as shown in Figure 1 below.

As we move from left to right—from business intelligence to optimization—we increase the sophistication of the analytics involved. Descriptive analytic techniques or data mining creates segmentation, clustering, rules based on what happened or what worked (and did not work) in the past. Predictive analytic techniques turn uncertainty about the future into usable probabilities, giving us propensities or likelihoods for future behavior on the part of customers, parts, suppliers etc. Optimization and simulation help us manage the complex tradeoffs of a business, finding the most profitable or most effective scenario.

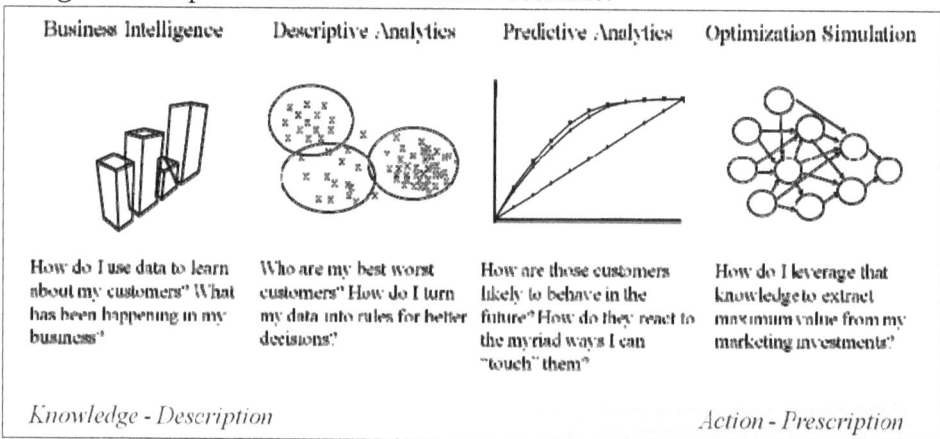

Figure 1: Increasingly sophisticated analytics

Embeddable analytics

More important for the creation of intelligent, automated processes than the increasing sophistication of these analytics techniques, is their embeddability. While business intelligence can be embedded into a process, as in-process dashboards or reports, business intelligence cannot be embedded into *automated* processes. As noted above, there is no-one to look at dashboards, no-one to interpret reports. What we need are techniques that allow someone to develop insight about our data outside a particular process instance and then embed that insight into an operational decision so that every process instance has access to it.

Instead of relying on the analytic skills of a dashboard or report user, we must create insight that can be used in an operational decision. The results of descriptive analytic techniques can often be embedded represented as a set of business rules or an equation. Predictive analytic models can be described using calculated attributes or equations. Optimization models can be represented as code also and can also drive operational decisions but this is less common in practice. The key tools and techniques for embedding analytics in decisions, and thus automated processes, are therefore those related to descriptive and predictive analytics.

Descriptive analytics

For example, consider data mining or descriptive analytic techniques that result in customer segments or clusters. The classic approach is to take information about customers, including something desirable such as profitability or loyalty, and see which properties of a customer (number of products purchased, time as customer, age etc) divide customers up into groups with a similar profitability or loyalty. Clustering or segmentation techniques create different groups and this can be visualized in a BI tool. But it can also be turned into a set of rules—customers with a specified combination of properties/values fall into this segment while customers with a different combination fall into this other segment. These rules can be executed by a decision service so that the decision itself—which customers to retain and how, for instance—can use the segmentation as part of its decision making process.

Predictive analytics

Predictive analytic techniques are also embeddable. Using predictive modeling techniques one can create a formula that predicts how likely something is to be true—how likely a customer is to churn, for instance, or how likely they are to accept a particular offer. These formulae or equations are hard to develop (at least they are hard to develop if we want them to be usefully predictive) but they are easy to express once developed. They also typically calculate a value, a score, representing how likely something is to be true.

Such an equation can be used to populate a field in a database so it can be used as part of a record. For instance, a predictive model of credit risk can be executed against every customer record, populating a column in the database called "risk score." However, this makes the value static in between updates.

Alternatively a decision service itself can execute the formula or equation, calculating the predictive "score" as it is called and making that available as part of the decision making process. For instance, the decision service can make a different decision for those customers who are more loyal than those who are less so.

By adopting these analytic techniques, we can turn the data we have into insight that can be consumed by automated decision services.

BUSINESS RULES AND ACTIONS

The third issue with intelligent, automated processes is the need for them to keep moving: for them to make decisions take actions and proceed without waiting for human intervention. We may not manage this 100 percent of the time, but we want our processes to move on without intervention as often as possible. Even if we turn the data we have and our understanding of our business into executable insight, we must still act on that insight. A prediction about a customer is not a decision, it is just a prediction. A description of our customer is *part* of what we need to decide but it is unlikely to be *everything* we need to decide. We must be able to define the actions we take as a consequence, and the action we take must be legal and appropriate.

Decisions need more than analytics

Take an example. We have a process for onboarding customers that needs to support kiosks and website signups—so it needs to be automated. During this process we want to make a decision about cross-sell, up-sell or down-sell—we want to make sure the customer has the right product(s). In particularly we want to drive a decision that will maximize loyalty.

We can build a set of predictive models that allow us to see how likely it is that someone will be a loyal customer for each of our base products. In other words, we can build a model to calculate the likelihood that a specific customer (with these characteristics) will be loyal if he or she buys a specific product. To make the decision about recommending an alternative product, however, we need to be able to take those different values, see if the product the customer is trying to buy is the best choice and, if it is not, decide if the "best" choice is more or less profitable. If it less profitable but boosts the potential loyalty of this customer enough and if we can deliver that product to that customer (perhaps there is a capacity limit on our products), then we may decide to make alternative offer.

To keep the process moving it is not enough to calculate the propensities for this customer, we must be able to act on them. We must be able to define the business rules that determine which action(s) to take.

Don't code decisions

While we could just write code to do this, that would be a mistake. Decisions are often high-change components of a process with many factors causing the rules to change. For example new regulations can be issued or we can change our policy. Delay in being able to change our decisions to reflect such changes may result in lost business or fines.

In addition the logic of a business decision is very much under the control of the business, not of IT. Writing code to implement these rules will make it hard to change them quickly and hard to bring the business into the ownership role for the decision. Instead of writing code we can and should use a Business Rules Management System or BRMS to manage Business Rules explicitly.

Business rules

Business Rules in this context are logical, atomic statements of what can and should be done in different circumstances. Each business rules is independent and can be written, assessed and changed independently. A BRMS can manage all the rules that go into our operational decisions and make it possible for the business to "own" them while still ensuring that IT can manage them. A BRMS is an effective way to automate decisions while remaining understandable by the business. Modern Business Process Management Systems are increasingly delivering an integrated BRMS or providing interfaces to make integration with one straightforward.

In addition to this business control and agility, decision making logic in a BRMS is now explicit. When the decision service makes a decision it is possible to log exactly how it did so—which rules fired, what analytic insight was applied. Not only is this helpful for regulatory compliance, it is also a new source of insight into how our business operates.

More than just analytic rules

While some of the rules in a decision might be derived analytically as discussed above, business rules can also be derived from regulations, policy or experience. Regulations impose restrictions on what is allowed and insist on certain actions being taken in certain circumstances. Similarly company policy or expertise can lead to rules that constrain or drive actions.

Many decisions require a mix of all these kinds of rules. For instance, a loan pricing decision requires rules set by the lender based on its policy and experience, additional rules set by State and Federal regulations, rules about what can and cannot be effectively sold on the secondary market and rules derived from analysis of the current loan portfolio to characterize the proposed loan in terms of likelihood of pre-payment or default. A good decision will use all these rules.

INTELLIGENT, AUTOMATED PROCESSES

Using embeddable analytic techniques, both descriptive and predictive, in combination with business rules allows you to effectively automate operational decisions so they can be embedded in automated processes.

Decision services in the technology stack

As Figure 2 below shows, the technologies required to build decision services fit inside a standard service-oriented architecture. Controlled by a business process management environment and taking full advantage of data and performance management infrastructure, a Decision Service contains the right mix of business rules, descriptive and predictive analytics, and optimization to make the decision for which it is designed.

Adaptive control is an additional step for organizations with more complex decisions to make using decision services. Adaptive control uses test and learn or champion/challenger approaches to constantly test new rules and analytic models against the current approach to see if better approaches are possible. For more details, see Taylor & Raden, 2007[1].

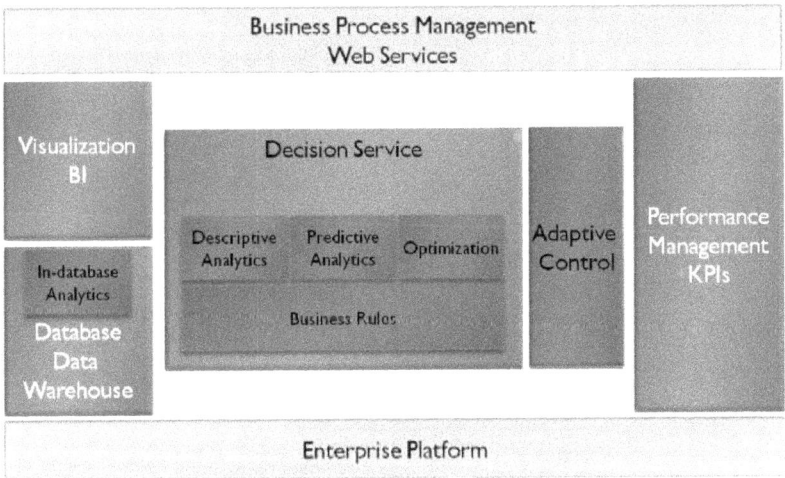

Figure 2: Technology for Analytics in Operational Systems

---

[1] Taylor, James and Raden, Neil. *Smart (Enough) Systems: How to Deliver Competitive Advantage by Automating Hidden Decisions.* New York. Prentice Hall, 2007.

Getting started

To get started with the approach, we begin by identifying the decisions that will make a difference to our processes and by understanding how they relate to our KPIs. We need to understand the decisions within and about our processes, we need to classify them and we need to put them in context.

When it comes to automating them we must begin with the decision and we must keep it in mind. We will develop analytics that will help with the decision or make it more accurate, we will find the rules that apply to the decision. We will use these analytics and rules to determine the data we need and then integrate and cleanse that data.

✓ *Consider business rules and analytics as linked decision-making technologies. There are problems that can be solved by one or the other but the combination is more powerful.*

✓ *Always begin with the decision in mind. There is a temptation to create infrastructure across all processes and this should be resisted. Focus on the decisions and drive infrastructure from the needs of those decisions.*

Intelligent, automated processes are not the stuff of science fiction. They can be developed by automating the decisions that are embedded in our operational processes.

Assigning Work Items More Efficiently Using Business Intelligence Tools

Juan J. Moreno, Marcelo Cordini, Cristian Mastrantono, INTEGRADOC and Universidad Católica, Uruguay; Martín Palatnik, Universidad Católica, Uruguay

ABSTRACT

Business Process Management (BPM) discipline has allowed organizations to considerably optimize their business processes, by including within some products the functionality required to assign work items to participants in an efficient way. However, nowadays these solutions do not consider user's "busy-ness" level (meaning how busy the user is) neither participant's efficiency when work items are assigned; this constitutes a major optimization and improvement opportunity for these tools.

This work presents the unified results of three researches with a common objective: provide a complete model to represent and predict user's busyness, in order to optimize work items assignment in a BPM environment. The methodology included a comprehensive analysis of the state of the art. Subsequently, a team of several researchers developed the solution for the problem. This work has had several validation and verification stages to prove its feasibility and effectiveness, including a prototype developed using a world-class open source BPM tool, and standard programming languages.

INTRODUCTION

Research about human participation in automated processes through BPMS has been relegated in recent years, focusing particularly in Enterprise Application Integration (EAI) and processes itself. "Processes don't do work, people do" says John Seely in his article "People Are the Company" (Seely, 2007) which highlights the importance of human beings in organizations, and emphasizes that informal methods, improvisation and inspiration of people may solve problems that formal processes cannot predict.

In a BPM application it is quite usual that a work item or document, in any step of the process, can be assigned to more than one potential participant. If it is desired for this assignation to be made to the person who can pay attention as soon as possible—and not to someone who is overloaded—it would be necessary to determine and use the busyness level of each user. This mechanism may also be useful to avoid interrupting a busy user, affecting even more his work and behavior.

Many elements can be considered to define user's busyness level; some of them are included in the BPMS and others are related to extra activities the user could be performing (e.g. work items assigned to each user, number of operations performed in a period of time, number of activities assigned in a timeframe, number of keystrokes per minute in an office application, number of visited web sites, running applications or number of received calls).

To distinguish the concept of "being busy" from "not being busy" metrics were defined. These metrics allow the comparison of busyness levels among different users and for the same user at different moments.

The first problems to solve are those of acquiring workload information inside and outside the BPMS, store it, analyze the collected data, infer new information, and make predictions. The second problems to face are the usage of workload information previously stored, information inferred and predictions to take smarter assignment decisions.

These problems were addressed by the team in the several investigations, finding innovative and comprehensive solutions, which are summarized and presented in this chapter. This work will also cover the obstacles found, their partial solutions, and the validation and verification mechanisms. Finally, conclusions and future work are presented.

PROBLEM DEFINITION

The problem to be solved is: detecting user's busyness automatically in a BPMS, in order to make a more efficient work item assignment.

PROPOSED SOLUTION

The main problem is divided into three sub problems, which are solved in separate—but interconnected—modules. The first module takes information about users and their activities in a BPMS. It is called **"Detection Module"** and also contains functions for extracting information about the several actions that users could be performing in the computer ("Workstation Detection"). The second module called **"Calculation and Transmission Module"** gets information from the Detection Module, calculates user's busyness level and transmits it to the third module: **"Assignment Module".** This last module is responsible for deciding how work items are assigned in the BPMS (see Figure 1).

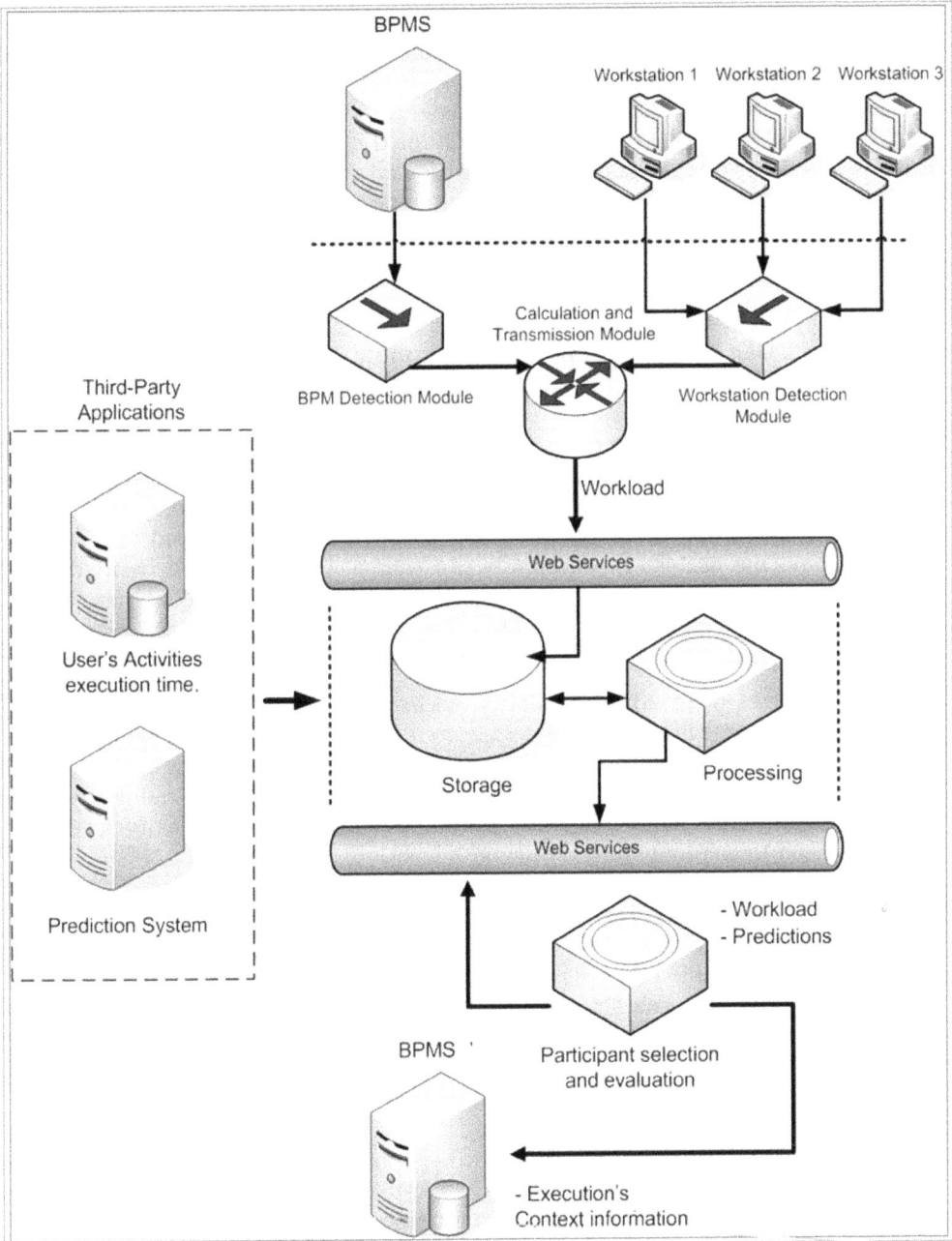

Figure 1 General Architecture

DETECTION MODULE

This module queries the BPMS and the Workstation Detection Module for information about participants' activities, in order to calculate their busyness level.

A participant's busyness will depend on the number of work items assigned by the BPMS and activities being performed at that time in his workstation. From these indicators, a busyness level could be calculated and subsequently assigned.

From this point, some problems arise. For example, it is not possible to match a number of assigned work items with a busyness level, because in different organizations activities are not equally complex. Consequently, the model has to consider a number of pending work items as normal in some organizations, while the same number could be too high in others. To solve this, a specific Comparison Number was used for each organization, defined by an expert or automatically calculated. For example, a simple approach for the last case is to get the number of work items assigned in a given moment for all the users, calculate an average and compare it to the assigned work items of a single user.

The model should be able to discriminate activities by its costs, in order to calculate user's busyness considering not only the number of assigned work items, but also its complexity.

In (Aldaz, 2004), it is described how to **recommend** which decisions to make in a BPMS. Aldaz' solution use Case Based Reasoning (CBR) in a BPMS environment, taking a process instance as the origin case, and a pattern as destination. He used a similarity function to compare the most interesting variables of each one. In each pattern, there are featured variables with values that are compared to the process' instance featured variables. From this point, when a process instance is evaluated, it is compared to the available patterns and it is linked to the most likely option. This pattern recommends two things: the decision to be made and the most suitable user to deal with the process instance. This mechanism avoids comparing the process instance against the whole base case (every process instance) situation that would not be suitable for a production environment.

This solution has been adapted to this research in a particular way; instead of using rankings for future decisions, the complexity of performing an activity is determined for each pattern. In this way, when a user has a pending activity of any process instance, the mechanism will associate it to a pattern using the similarity function. This pattern would "know" the activity's complexity level and would be used to calculate user's busyness level.

Load Calculation on BPM

The BPM Detection Module sends to the CBR component the pending users' activities and process' instances of each activity collected from the BPM System. The CBR, fed by BPM patterns activities, sends the cost of each of the activities that users have pending to the "Load Calculation on BPM" component. Once the total cost from each user is obtained, an average of all the users is calculated in order to establish the relationship with the Comparison Number.

Load Calculation on Workstations

An alternative to calculate the load on workstations is to analyze the activities performed on the computer, which when represented as human interactions with the computer generates events that can be studied at different levels of abstraction. These UI events are of importance because they provide useful information about user behavior and are very easy to catch and analyze (Hilbert, 1999). These events can also be captured in various ways and used to infer the activities that users are performing. For example, sequence detection's techniques look for predefined sequences of events in the UI events generated by users; when a sequence is detected, a higher-level event is determined, like the fulfillment of an activity or a goal. Therefore, analyzing the UI events generated by the user could be another way to detect the busyness of it since it is possible to infer which activity is performing. There are several projects (e.g., Dragunov, 2005; Rath, 2008) in which the interactions between the user and the computer allow to identify the activities that they are performing.

The application of the methodologies used in the projects mentioned above, may allow to obtain the information captured in a way in which it is possible to detect the activity that the user is performing, at a level of abstraction similar to the BPM solution (i.e. by activities). This allows us to apply the same methodology used in "Load Calculation on BPM": the use of patterns to return a cost for the activity, and the implementation of a Comparison Number to measure with the current activities of other users in the organization.

When a request of user's busyness occurs, the system will consult the events generated by the user lately and infer from them the activities that he is performing. Then, the CBR evaluation function will be applied to the activities obtained, to determine the corresponding pattern for those, and thus the cost of performing the whole activity. After that, an average of costs of all users it is calculated in order to get a Comparison Number (similar to the one described in Load Calculation on BPM), and finally it is used to calculate workstation's workload.

BPM Detection Module

This component aims to solve the problem of acquiring relevant information from the activities and actions of users in a BPM System. The first major question to define is where to obtain the necessary information about user's activities, and which technique to use.

The BPMS stores process' information, specified routes, user's data, roles, activities and permissions, all of these in its own databases. It is also obtained information from various process instances and user's pending activities. From all of this, information about the activities that the user has assigned will be collected. This type of solution is completely independent of the BPMS and there is no need of any special configuration.

Workstation Detection Module

Each Workstation must store the events produced. When the busyness of a particular user is requested, the module would request to the corresponding workstation the interaction events that have occurred. In an environment with a large number of workstations, this solution may not be appropriate if all of them broadcast simultaneously to the same point. It is proposed to establish a hierarchy for the transmission of data at levels of "Chiefs", shown in Figure 2.

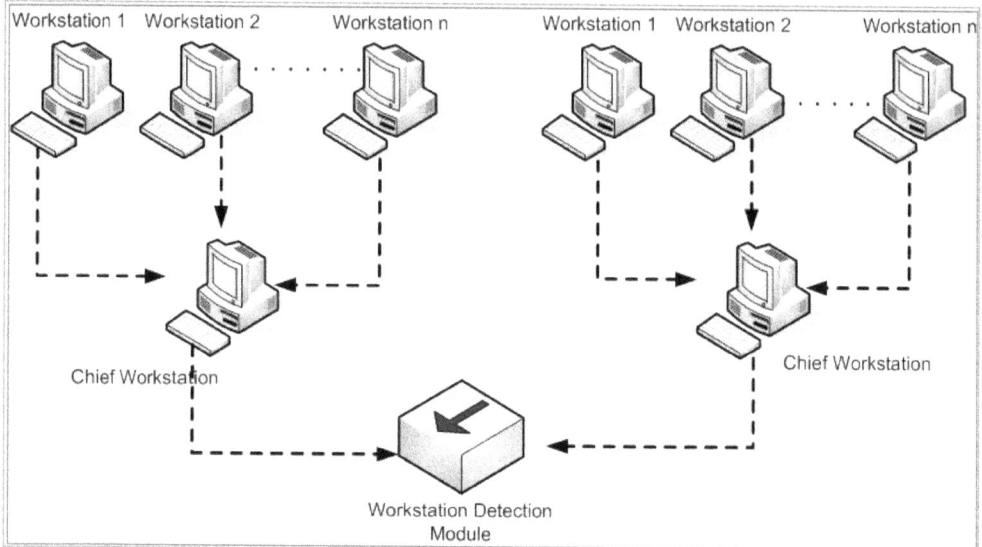

Figure 2 - Nested Detections in Workstations

Stations transmit their information to a "Chief" station, and this one transmits to the Detection Module (Figure 2). The number of levels of "Chiefs" will vary depending on the size of the organization. Controlling the transmission's load generated, will make possible to detect choke points from which to make groups or distribute in levels to solve it.

TRANSMISSION AND CALCULATION MODULE

The goal of this module is developing a model to represent the workload of users in a BPM System, in order to make predictions. It should also store information about execution time of activities, to also make predictions about it.

The solution for this module consists of four components: modeling, prediction, processing and communication. Regarding the first component, the information to be "modeled" comes from two heterogeneous data sources. First, there is the information about the workload of participants (estimated in the Detection Module) which is used in real time and also in the Prediction Module. Secondly, there is the information about execution time of activities per user, which is provided by a third-party application system and only necessary to make certain predictions.

Modeling Component

The proposed approach is designing a temporary database to store daily information of workload (which is going to be used in real time), and a Data Warehouse for the historical information on which to make predictions (Figure 3).

For the temporal information storage model, it was chosen a Star schema. While the resulting model consists of a fact table and only one dimension's table for the information of participants, this solution ensures a high level of flexibility, an appropriate design for quick queries, and better performance than other schemas (Browning, 2001; Broda, 2007).

For the storage of historical information the best approach was the design, development and implementation of a Data Warehouse, made up using open technologies, to make it easier the task of storing and retrieving relevant data about workload and execution time of activities.

Data Warehouses are optimized to deal with load of information at large scales, and they are capable also to execute complex, extensive and unpredictable queries that may access many rows per table (Browning, 2001). Another interesting fact is the possibility that they offer to maintain historical information in order to make comparisons and analysis, and also the ability to collect data from different systems under different schemas or different sources that perhaps are not being considered, and could be potentially useful (Jansen, 2006 and Sugandhi, 2004).

Prediction Component

For the "Workload Prediction component" and the "Execution Time of Activities per User component," the best approach is to define an interface through which a predictive expert system can reach the historical data stored in the model. This ensures a high degree of accuracy in predictions made, and delegating this task to a specialized software component designed for this purpose.

Based on this decision—and given the model defined to store historical data—it is a good choice to take advantage of the fact that historical data is stored in a Data Warehouse. Thus and making use of the mechanisms of removal and exposure of data that it provides (e.g. cubes OLAP—Online Analytical Processing), the interconnection with the prediction system becomes trivial.

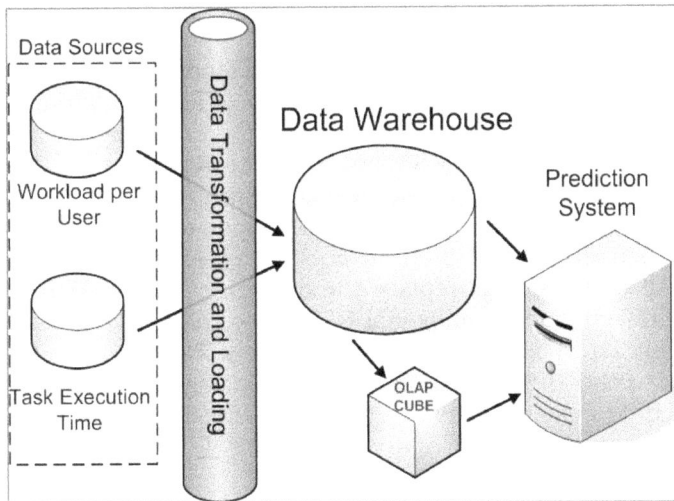

Figure 3 Data Warehouse model used.

Communication Component

Regarding the communication component, which is responsible for monitoring this process to proceed smoothly and flow between the modules of the solution, the best approach is implementing an open and synchronous communication mechanism: Web Services. Thus, the solution is decoupled from other systems and modules, and provide an open communication channel which is the standard used for communications of such characteristics over the Internet. In addition, there were also defined certain communication primitives necessary to allow the interaction and cooperation between the modules of the solution's model themselves. This primitives use a specific kind of messages to complete the communication process successfully. The messages mentioned above were defined using XML (eXtensible Markup Language) and are exchanged between the primitives defined at invocation-time.

Processing Component

Finally, the Processing component must respond on time and accurately to the requests received from other modules, and here is where the logic of the solution for this module is located. It also invokes the corresponding Data Warehouse's service for extracting data from the temporary database and third-party application systems make requests of predictions to the corresponding expert system and queries for additional information to the Detection Module if necessary. Furthermore, this component redefines the concept of busyness, synthesizing the workload of participants in a way that greatly resembles the real workload, and is adapted to the context, the environment of the problem, and the Assignment Module' needs. While the Detection Module mentioned above sends values about participants' busyness periodically, this information is a snapshot of their status at a time "t", and does not consider situations in which – for example – the participant is really busy but in the moment of calculating their busyness for some reason it results low, so it could return a wrong result.

ASSIGNMENT MODULE

To optimize the assignment of work items in the BPM System, a generic solution model was obtained. This model allows the optimization of job assignment in BPM Systems. To ensure a proper automation, the model takes into account factors such as user confidence and system awareness.

In the last years several researches have led to models of intelligent assignment of work items in BPM environments. In (Kumar et al., 2002), (Veloso and Macêdo, 2007; Veloso, 2006) and (Shen et al., 2003) there are several approaches based on scores computed from BPMS parameters. In (Reijers et al., 2007) a swarm intelligence approach is used for the distribution of work. Moreover, in (Ha et al., 2006) queuing theory is used to predict the workload and decide the assignments. Finally, in (Geppert et al., 1998) an auction approach is used to distribute the workload. All these models replace the assignment model based on roles. This creates a problem since commercial BPMS use roles for the assignment of work items. In contrast, the model presented in this work, optimizes the assignment of work items in the BPMS while it continues using the role-based model widely adopted in BPM Systems. The solution of this module is divided into three components: integration, evaluation, and storage.

Integration Component

This component is responsible for integrating the solution with the BPMS, enabling the solution to be completely independent from the BPMS and totally reusable. This part is integrated with the prediction and modeling component of the solution.

Evaluation Component

This is the part of the solution that incorporates the *intelligence*, dealing with the work distribution process' logic. Given an assignment event, the evaluation and participant selection process starts. First it uses roles to filter the participants who are able to take the work item and then it uses a computed score to determine who is in a better condition.

Storage Component

Store the logs related to the solution which are essential for a proper automation.

Score Computation

The system computes a score defining the assignment to be made based on the following parameters received from the other components: workload, execution time estimation and average workload on the estimated running time of activities. Each parameter is uniformed in a 1 to 10 (best) scale.

Linear Scoring Function

The linear scoring function takes three parameters and assigns a coefficient to each according to its importance. Currently there are several methods (Reijers et al., 2007; Veloso and Macêdo, 2007; Kumar et al., 2002) that use this approach but with different parameters.

$$Totalscore(p) = loadscore(p) * a + productivityscore(p) * b + averageloadscore(p) * c$$

These coefficients (a, b and c) are dependent on the organization where this solution is implemented. However, they are predefined here in terms of the importance to the authors. The coefficients are used in such a way that $a + b + c = 10$ and that consequently the total score is in the range 1 to 100.

For the first coefficient (a) a relatively high value in relation to the rest is taken. The reason, as described in a previous section, is that workload is an accurate data that represents the reality of the system. In some way it is a snapshot of the reality at some point in time. It is therefore assigned a value of 5.

The second coefficient (b) takes an intermediate value in relation to the rest. The value is lower than the workload coefficient because the productivity is calculated based on predictions. However, it is higher than the average workload coefficient because the productivity is a very important participant's value and will provide more information for an efficient assignment that the average workload. Therefore it is assigned a value of 3.

Base on the previous definition the third coefficient (c) is assigned a value of 2 obtaining the following function:

$$Totalscore(p) = workloadscore(p) * 5 + productivityscore(p) * 3 + averageworkloadscore(p) * 2$$

Fuzzy Logic Scoring Function

Based on (Shen et al., 2003) and considering that fuzzy logic can help the expert of the company to describe the assignment rules, it was decided to include a fuzzy logic alternative. Using a scoring function with the same parameters: workload, productivity and average workload an output overall score is obtained. The difference is that instead of rely on coefficients, a set of fuzzy rules are used.

Note that as in the previous scoring function the fuzzy system was defined with fuzzy sets and rules specific to the authors need, but it is expected that these rules are tailored to each organization.

For each input variable (score), three fuzzy sets (high, low and medium) and three output sets (for the output variable): high, low and medium were defined. The following rules were also established:

Table 1: Fuzzy Logic Scoring Function Rules

Premises	Conclusions
If load = high and (productivity >= medium or average Load >= medium)	assignment = high
If load = low	assignment = low
If load = medium and productivity <= medium and average Load <=medium	assignment = low
If load = medium and (productivity = high or average Load = high)	assignment = medium

In this alternative the workload score was prioritized again. Unlike the previous scoring function a greater expressiveness is found here. For instance, the second rule stating that with a low workload score the assignment chance is going to be low, it is easy understandable for a non technical person.

CONCLUSION

An innovative solution to the work item assignment problem in BPM Systems was proposed. This alternative is based not only on internal BPMS workload but also on external user workload, taking into account factors like future workload and participants' productivity. Some innovation was also introduced facing the problem from a human-computer interaction point of view, defining aspects of the solution for a proper automation in order to increase user confidence on the system.

Secondly, an unexplored type of solution was described. This approach tries to exploit the current characteristics of BPMS, supporting and not replacing the role-based assignment mechanisms that commercial BPMS use. Unlike other alternatives this work proposes an open and modifiable solution according to the current needs of organizations. In turn, it was introduced a scalable solution that can respond to requests quickly, efficiently and safely.

Thirdly, a prototype of the solution was implemented in a commercial and widely adopted BPMS, JBoss jBPM. The implementation process was successful showing that the solution is valid and can be implemented in BPMS available in the marketplace.

Some experiments were conducted to validate the solution. The data collection's time to calculate the busyness of users was measured to test if it was optimized. The prediction model's safety was measured by a statistical sample. Also, it was found that both the fuzzy logic-based implementation and the linear function implementation greatly reduce running times in relation to a random selection implementation. It was found that the solution based on the linear function is slightly better at run-time than the function based on fuzzy logic, which is not conclusive, but suggest that both have acceptable behavior. Finally, it was observed that the assignments made by the solution are very similar to the ones made by human, suggesting similar decision criteria.

FUTURE WORK

It is proposed to complete the resources allocation optimization process by objectively measuring the results using BAM (Business Activity Monitoring) and BI tools integrated into the BPMS.

Regarding the busyness detection, it is proposed to perform an in-depth research in data analysis techniques in the BPI (Business Process Intelligence) area. Another research area covers the relationship between the activities that a participant does in the workstation and the ones assigned in the BPMS. It would be interesting to determine if this relationship exists and how it can affect the computation of busyness.

In relation to the modeling and prediction, it is intended to improve the prediction mechanism in use. The present research has made use of an expert system that works properly on a generic environment. However, to improve the quality of the predictions it would be ideal to take into account BPMS' inherent factors. Referring to the effective allocation of work items proposed in the solution, it would be interesting to add more features such as activity priority and similar activities detection. Secondly, it is proposed to use reinforcement learning mechanisms to optimize the parameters of the linear and fuzzy scoring functions.

In this research, we could not find any product which implements the concepts described. After the successful implementation of the prototype, it is expected that they will exist soon.

REFERENCES

Seely, John; Estee Solomon Gray: The People Are The Company, http://www.fastcompany.com/magazine/01/people.html, [Checked: 07/04/2009]

Hilbert, David (1999). "Extracting Usability Information from User Interface Events" Department of Information and Computer Science, University of California, Irvine, CA.

Aldaz, Guillermo (2004). "Knowledge extraction algorithms for automated processes" *Thesis' Work, FIT, Univesidad Católica del Uruguay (UCUDAL)*.

Dragunov, Anton (2005). "Tasktracer: A Desktop Environment To Support Multitasking Knowledge Workers" *In IUI '05: Proceedings of the 10th international conference on Intelligent user interfaces*.

Rath, Andreas S. (2008). "Context-aware Knowledge Services, Personal Information Management" *PIM 2008, CHI 2008 Workshop, April 5-6, 2008, Florence, Italy*.

Browning, Dave; Mundy, Joy. Microsoft Corporation (2001). "Data Warehouse Design Considerations" *Microsoft® SQL Server™ 2000 Resource Kit*

Broda, Tal; Clugage, Kevin (2007) "Improving Business Operations With Real-Time Information: How to Successfully Implement a BAM Solution" *BPM.com* http://www.bpm.com/improving-business-operations-with-real-time-information-how-to-successfully-implement-a-bam-solution.html [Checked: 07/04/2010]

Jansen, Michel (2006) "Building data warehouses using open source technologies" *Draft version 197*.

Sugandhi, Abhishek (2004) "Data Warehouse Design Considerations". Course Seminar Report, Submitted in partial fulfillment of the requirements for the degree of Master of Technology - Department of Computer Science and Engineering, Indian Institute of Technology, Bombay, Mumbai.

Lechtenbörger, Jens (2001) "Data Warehouse Schema Design". Dept. of Information Systems, University of Münster, Leonardo - Campus 3, D-48149 M"unster, Germany - Berlin.

Kumar, Akhil; van der Aalst, Wil & Weske, Eric (2002) Dynamic Work Distribution in Workflow Management Systems: How to Balance Quality and Performance. *Journal of Management Information Systems,* 18, 157-193.

Geppert, Andreas; Kradolfer, Markus & Tombros, Dimitrios (1998) Market-Based Workflow Management. *IJCIS,* 7, 297-314.

Ha, Byung-Hyun; Bae, Joonsoo; Tae Park, Yong & Kang, Suk-Ho (2006) Development of process execution rules for workload balancing on agents. *Data & Knowledge Engineering,* 56, 64-84.

Reijers, Hajo; Jansen-Vullers, Monique; Zur Muehlen, Michael & Appl, Winfried (2007) Workflow Management Systems+ Swarm Intelligence= Dynamic Task Assignment for Emergency Management Applications. *Lectures Notes in Computer Science,* 4714, 125-140.

Shen, Mixin; Tzeng, Gwo-Hshiung & Liu, Duen-Ren (2003) Multi-criteria task assignment in workflow management systems. *Proceedings of the 36th Annual Hawaii International Conference on System Sciences.,* 9.

Rodrigues Veloso, Rêne (2006) Distribuicao de Tarefas em Sistemas de Workflow com Base na Aptidao dos Recursos. In: Universidade Federal de Uberlandia.

Rodrigues Veloso, Rêne & Macêdo, Autran (2007) Balancing Quality and Performance of Task Distribution in Workflow Based on Resource Aptitude. *Lectures Notes in Computer Science,* 4489, 281.

Staying Ahead of the Curve with Decision-Centric Business Intelligence

Sheila Donohue, CRIF Decision Solutions, Italy

INTRODUCTION

Customer-related decision points which impact a financial services firm's performance are spread across the customer lifecycle, from acquisition through portfolio management and collections. These decision points which involve risk taking have traditionally been focused on credit risk management, while, as more recently seen from the financial crisis, are taking a more holistic view considering also operational risk requirements which emphasize the importance of more control and to quickly respond to market events and compliance demands. Having more information easily at your fingertips to monitor, measure and analyze performance in business processes which manage these points of risk taking decisions is essential to responding quickly and deftly to competitive and regulatory pressures.

Business process, rules management and analytics are tools well suited to assess and manage the risk and opportunity at these decision points. However, without fully integrated business intelligence tools, the firm is missing an opportunity to continuously improve their business and risk performance, finding themselves scrambling when an executive, compliance officer or customer demands information on-the-fly.

THE ESSENTIALS

Financial decision-making processes, such as loan approval and origination, portfolio monitoring and debt management, require a financial institution to have an organizational commitment to formalize, document and monitor risk processes.

This discipline involves:
- Following a structured and consistent process to identify and assess risks,
- Applying the optimal set of controls and track the relevant data,
- Monitoring the results, through a set of pre-configured reports plus the capability to design one's own reports, however, without having an underlying toolset which embraces these fundamentals, financial decision-making processes can become cumbersome and expensive to manage.

In order to support these principles and allow financial institutions to master the balance of achieving high performance results, control and agility in their financial decision-making processes, integrated solutions with the following components are needed:

Business Process Management software focused on financial decision-making which offers:
- A workflow engine which executes and tracks all process steps, both manual as well as automatic, including automatic document generation;

- An integrated case management web front end to handle exceptions and necessary manual tasks, tracing all activity details and allowing for electronic document filing;
- A graphical designer tool for a business analyst to define the process flow, activity details, data, organization and role authorities logic;
- Authentication and authorization to control permissions of persons and systems allowed to access the process and system components;
- Framework to allow for ease of integration with required data sources, application systems, third party organizations and systems;
- Data retrieval, validation and storage to verify and save all pertinent data that the process and underlying engine(s) collect, calculate and transform.

Integrated Business Rules Platform specialized in financial risk evaluation which has:

- a rules engine to make automatic decisions which incorporate risk strategies that include analytical model calculations to give more confidence to the decision;
- a graphical tool to define the decision process logic which will include analytical scoring ;
- means to integrate easily with the Business Process software component.

Integrated Business Intelligence comes into play when, upon having a streamlined, automated workflow process based on the above components, a financial institution realizes it is sitting on a goldmine of data which can be used to help monitor, improve and better control the underlying the business process and automated risk based policies and decisioning logic. Without a Business Intelligence component, the institution is by-passing a critical opportunity to leverage their decision making solution investments to stay one step ahead of their market, customer and compliance demands.

An integrated Business Intelligence solution provides the following:

- A graphical tool to easily extract data from the Business Process Management software, not only when having just implemented a new business process, but also to introduce new or different data as the business process evolves; this tool should also allow a business user to define the underlying reporting data repositories which are relational and multidimensional data layers. With such capability, a business user without technical skills can define and modify the data to report on without needing to involve IT thus empowering them to respond to business demands as they arise;
- A turn-key extraction, transform and load (ETL) procedures which start from the extraction logic that the business person defined and automatically load the reporting database;
- Front end, preferably web based, to view pre-defined reports and to easily create new and modify existing reports.

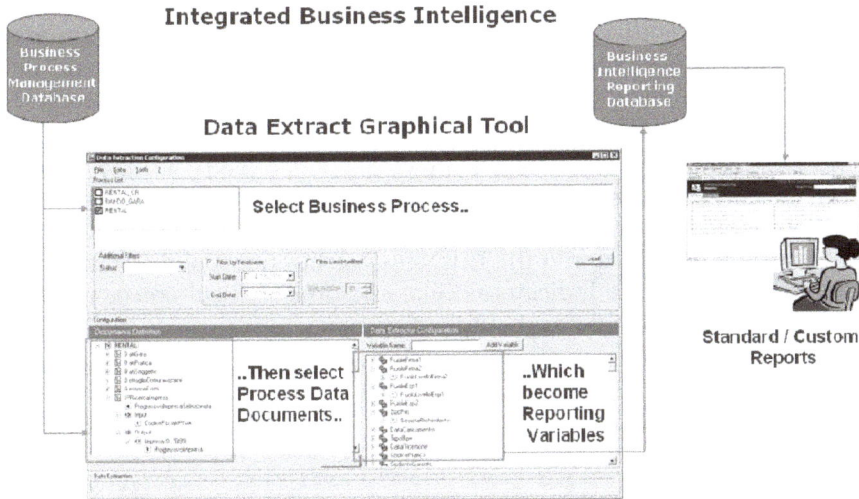

Figure 1: Business Intelligence Integrated with Business Process Management

In summary, Integrated Business Intelligence provides business users with the tools they need to extract and report on the process and performance information they need in a manner which is fully integrated with the Business Process Management and Business Rules components.

What follows are real examples of financial services institutions which were driven by competition, compliance and control to choose a business intelligence solution fully integrated with their financial decision making processes so to achieve improved process, business and risk performance.

CASE STUDY: FIAT AUTO FINANCIAL SERVICES

FIAT Auto Financial Services (FGA Capital) is the financial services arm of the Fiat group operating in 15 countries throughout Europe through various separate companies which manage all the financing activities to support automobile sales of major manufacturers by providing financing via manufacturers' networks and private channels, leasing services as well as small and medium sized business and fleet rentals.

The FIAT financial unit, having already utilized a business rules platform, for automatic scoring and decisioning of their Auto Retail loans and leases and being satisfied with its effectiveness and robustness, realized that they needed a more complete solution to fulfil the needs of their small business and corporate clientele. With non-standardized, stand-alone processes and decision making between the group companies, they realized a strong need to unify and streamline the rental application process between business units. As part of this, their priorities were to minimize manual processing, have a quick time-to-market solution implementation and have operations and risk measurements readily available for business, shareholder and regulatory reporting purposes.

To move forward, FGA Capital chose an integrated Business Process, Business Rules and Business Intelligence platform and proceeded to standardize the lending processes between the Group's companies which specialize in financing and long term rental services by re-engineering the underlying organizational model, and therefore the whole production chain, to obtain the most efficient coordination of the processes between the various group companies. The FGA Capital rental management process, implemented as illustrated in figure 2, performs automatic retrieval and validation of applicant and application information via both internal and external data sources, advanced scoring model and decision rule automation, notification to decision makers and presenting all results, to arrive at a final financing decision.

Once having defined the process, FGA Capital identified the key elements to measure performance, such as turn around times, automatic decisions and scores, types of applicants, geographic areas, types of rentals and channels, which were then extracted into the Business Intelligence tool that creates reports showing Key Performance Indicators (KPIs) and other critical process and risk information for distribution throughout the Group.

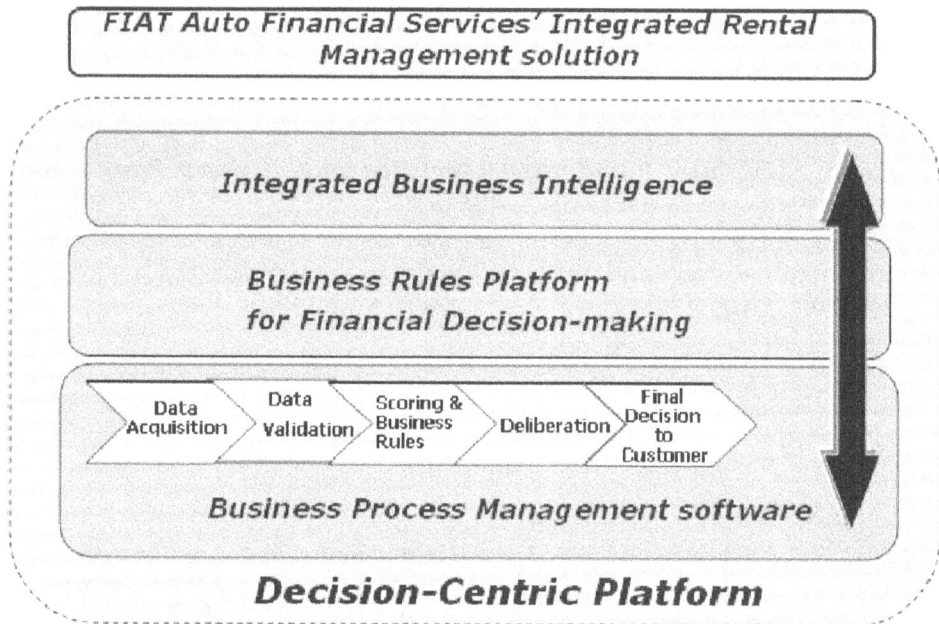

Figure 2: FIAT Auto Financial Services' integrated Rental Management solution components

Having an end-to-end solution in only four months, FGA Capital immediately began to reap the benefits of an integrated decision making process platform:

- With an automated business process, manual effort has been greatly reduced, resulting in lower costs and quicker end-to-end response;
- Processing more applications in a consistent and efficient manner between the business units;
- Credit granting policy and methodology is easily modifiable by the business user to keep in line with credit compliance requirements and credit performance evolutions;
- Easy access to information about processes helps to integrate the entire Group and allows for better communication with the customer;
- Compliance with shareholder and regulatory reporting requirements by providing timely visibility of key operating and risk measurements.

Using the platform's integrated Business Intelligence features, FGA Capital has the tools to continually monitor the process and risk performance, to identify *early* the areas of improvement by having quick, online access to information, such as the turn around times for critical process activities as shown in this report:

Activity (duration format dd:hh:mm:ss)	Instances	Average	Minimum	Maximum	Applications	Rate
Application Summary	24	00:03:/2:68	00:04:14:30	00:34:18:23	24	1
CheckList	14	00:03:20:19	00:04:14:32	00:34:13:31	14	1
Credit Analyst Outcome	11	00:03:29:27	00:04:14:42	00:34:19:29	7	1.57
Disbursement	10	00:04:14:42	00:04:14:32	00:34:15:06	10	1
Documents	19	00:03:21:54	00:04:14:29	00:34:13:41	19	1
Insert Main Applicant	46	00:02:29:32	00:04:14:28	00:34:17:16	18	2.56
Internal verification outcome	15	00:03:31:16	00:04:14:29	00:36:05:46	15	1
Product Data	28	00:03:11:01	00:04:14:28	00:34:15:16	15	1.87
Sociological	14	00:03:20:35	00:04:14:46	00:34:17:48	14	1
Total	181	00:03:13:38	00:04:14:28	00:36:05:46	136	1.33

Figure 3: Sample Activity Duration report

CASE STUDY: THE FINANCIAL INTERMEDIARY OF A LARGE ENERGY GROUP

Responsible for managing payment systems (electronic banking, clearing and settlement, transactional services, e-business services, cards) for its entire group, this financial intermediary of large energy group needed a platform to issue and monitor purchasing cards which allow cardholders to pay for fuel and related products and services for its clients performing professional and commercial transportation throughout Europe.

Besides needing a paperless loan origination and monitoring processes integrated with the group's internal systems as well as external data sources and to make the organization more efficient, such as by removing redundant operations and having tools to help identify process bottlenecks and setbacks, the firm was driven by the central bank's compliance requirements regarding credit and control policy rules.

Having first chosen Business Process Management and Business Rules Platform products to perform the issuing and portfolio monitoring of its purchasing cards for its Small and Medium Business and Corporate segments, this firm realized the need for credit risk and business operations business intelligence tools, taking advantage of the historical archive of application and credit data already available in the existing platform. Selecting Business Intelligence tools already integrated with the Business Process Management and Business Rules components, this firm now has improved process and risk operation through the introduction of tracking, monitoring and performance measurement tools.

For example, this Risk Class Distribution report is displaying the risk class as calculated by the Business Rules Platform showing trends of how the risk groupings change from month to month. Reports parameters can be easily changed so to analyze different aspects of the portfolio and drill down to necessary details:

Risk Class

(#clients/Risk Class)

RiskClass / Month	2008-01		2008-02		2008-03	
	# Clients	%	# Clients	%	# Clients	%
High		0 %		0 %	4	5 %
Low	6	8 %	12	16 %	18	24 %
Medium-High	2	3 %	4	5 %	4	5 %
Medium-Low	6	8 %	6	8 %	4	5 %
TOTAL	14	19 %	22	30 %	30	41 %

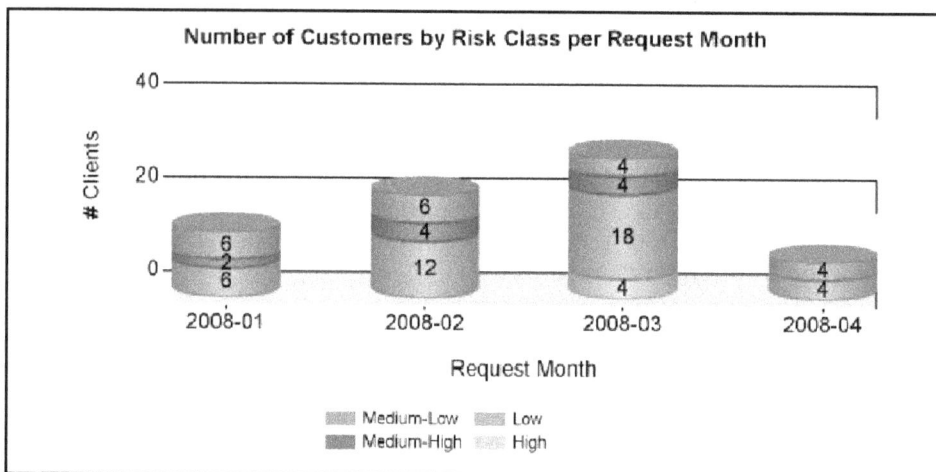

Figure 4: Example of a Risk Class Distribution Report

CASE STUDY: MEDIUM – LARGE ITALIAN BANK

This bank, with more than 250 branches across Italy, is seeking to improve the quality of its consumer and small business credit portfolio at a time when the financial crisis is putting pressure on margins and the Central Bank is requiring increased monitoring and control of portfolio credit quality and effectiveness of the bank's policies.

With non-standardized credit policy enforcement and unstructured monitoring due to lack of sufficient tools, this bank decided to proceed with an implementation using a Business Rules Platform and integrated Business Intelligence component, so to reduce underwriting and financial offer response times, while reducing risk and subsequently increasing the quality of its credit portfolio. Besides improving credit granting during the loan origination phase, this bank is focused on its existing customer portfolio, so to proactive identify the risks and opportunities within.

Using the Business Intelligence solution, the bank's portfolio is being monitored to identify deviations and analyze the cause(s) in order to define the necessary corrective measures to be taken such as to adjust scoring models, policy rules and credit decisioning methodology.

This sample report is comparing the decision made at application time to the current customer payment performance to see if the decisioning methodology is aligned with expectations or in need of adjustment:

Current Performance of Installment applications

Strategy / Sys Decision Grp /Risk Class			Delinquency Class			
			Bad		Good	Indeterminate
			Serious delinquency	Write off	No delinquency	Mild delinquency
Personal_Loans	AP-Approve	Low	1636	90	34064	1117
	RFP-Policy Reject	?	255	2	1102	32
		High	1			12
		Low	13		26	
		Medium	27		38	
	RF-Reject	High	1073	98	46115	1256
	RV-Refer	Medium	93		1345	18
		Total	3098	190	82690	2435

Comparison Delincuency Class

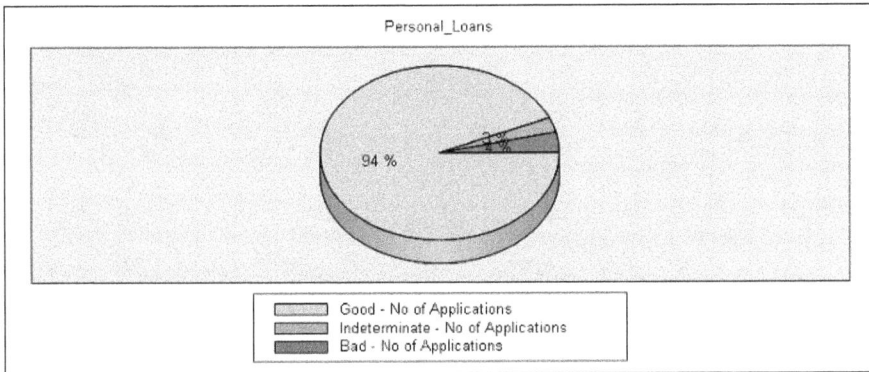

Figure 5: Application Performance Report

CONCLUSIONS

Business Intelligence tools that are integrated with the financial decision-making applications already used by the firm help to empower the business users to focus on their knowledge worker core competency and respond timely and effectively to ever evolving business and compliance demands. With these tools, whether in a risk, operations or business management role, leveraging your existing data assets to make better decisions and respond to business and compliance demands is a worthwhile investment to stay ahead of the curve.

ABOUT CRIF DECISION SOLUTIONS

CRIF Decision Solutions, part of the CRIF Group (www.crif.com), provides consulting, analytics and solutions which help financial institutions to be more efficient and innovative in their procedures and processes, from customer targeting and acquisition to portfolio management, debt collection and fraud management.

Combining Knowledge, Process and BI to Deliver Agility in a Collaborative Environment

Marinela MIRCEA, Bogdan GHILIC-MICU, and Marian STOICA, Academy of Economic Studies, Bucharest, Romania

In a collaborative environment, agility represents an objective for any organization, given the fact that all organizations must face complex interaction between agents, must quickly adapt to frequent market changes and be innovative. In this context, organizations have to continually change their business strategy in order to be able to use the market opportunities and cope with the pressure of an uncertain business environment. As a result, Business Process Management (BPM), Case Management, and other instruments and solutions have been adapted/built in order to respond to the current demands of the organizations in the field of modelling of collaborative processes.

As a response to the complex interactions between partners, integration of knowledge and business processes represents an important step in improving the agility of the organization. For intensive knowledge based processes Case Management may be used, which provides a real time image on the current events and generates a rapid response to the organization's internal and external events. Business Intelligence (BI) is used at the present for performance management within business processes, helping the organization to automatically detect the problems/opportunities and to initiate corrective actions and/or change business rules in order to optimise processes. The paper provides an approach on the way in which knowledge may be combined with processes and Business Intelligence in order to achieve agility within the collaborative environment.

1. BUSINESS PROCESS MANAGEMENT AND BUSINESS INTELLIGENCE

Participation in the collaborative environment helps organizations in the collaborative environment to combine processes and intelligence, first of all in processes that are intensively based on decisions and operational BI. By the use of BPM and of BI instruments, the organization gains not only a view on what is achieved, but also an image of the means to achieve the next level of development and of the changes that have to be made [1]. In order for the final objective of BP, that is Business Performance Management, to be achieved, organizations need BI capabilities (such as key performance indicators and advanced analyses) to analyze the process data. They will provide to the managers information on ways of improving workflows and on the execution of business processes. At the same time, BPM allows BI instruments to respond to business events through business processes and to measure and monitor the business. As a result, the relation between BPM and BI is bidirectional, the main source of information for BI being the inputs and outputs of BPM. At the same time, the output offered by BI represent inputs for grounding the decisions related to BPM processes.

BPM entails automation and/or streamlining processes, tasks and results in order to reach the business objectives [2] by simplifying and accelerating the workflows within the organization and at the global level. This is considered to be a proactive instrument, allowing the organization to measure performance and make the necessary adjustments. Also, BPM facilitates the gathering, simulation, and optimization of the knowledge on how people work and integrate them into the organization, putting intelligence into practice [3]. Although it provides numerous advantages, BPM is a complex process, related to the frequent changes of business and the complex interaction with the organization's systems and stakeholders.

In order to increase the efficiency of business processes, the users have to be able to understand processes, be aware of the factors influencing them, and the ways they may act in order to improve them. The main source of the information needed in making the decisions for streamlining of business processes, as well as the possibility of making simulations and analyses (measurement, evaluation and control of business processes) are provided by BI instruments, considered critical for BPM. In order to achieve the business objectives, BI has to be included in each stage of the life cycle of business processes.

For this purpose, a data-centred approach of BI represents only a part of the business image. For many years, BI has been oriented on relevant information of the organization and on the people, providing support for managers in making decisions to use opportunities or avoid risks. The main goal of BI was to transform data into intelligence; but, most of the time this intelligence could not be put into practice. Most organizations that used BI solutions did not achieved an improvement of business due to three main motives [3]: most owners did not know details on the daily business processes; the BI measures and analyses were not practical; the applications following the working processes were not in accord with the ways of working of the employees.

The process-oriented BI provides a complete image of the business processes and IT infrastructure, analyses and metrics on historical business processes, business plans, previsions and budgets, data from external events in the form of key performance indicators, of alerts, reports, and recommendations for adjustments. Process-oriented BI combines BPM and BI [1] and is subordinated to upper management. It provides the input data for business decisions that execute the organization's strategy, improve performance and in the end give the best results [2], applying intelligence into practice. The process-oriented BI is implemented in the entire organization, being used in business planning and in business development (tactic and operational BI) and providing information for strategic, tactic and operational decisions. At the same time, it represents a proactive instrument, offering recommendations and actions based on key performance indicators and metrics. Being process-oriented, BI analyzes the exceptions, responds to events and generates alerts, working with both structures and unstructured data.

In order to achieve success within the organization, strategic maps of business processes must be created, must be set goals and objectives for processes, and must be achieved their evaluation and control through the proper means. The combination between BPM and BI provides many benefits, leading to simplified, efficient and agile processes, but does not solve all problems that confront the organizations within a collaborative environment. Integration of BPM with BI capabilities entails many challenges, from choice of cost-efficiency and problems of systems' integration to difficulties of use. Also, within the collaborative environment, the instruments have to allow integration of systems, business partners and business users and respond to external events (system and transaction events) and internal events (generated by agents and internal systems) which lead to frequent changes in the organization.

In response to these challenges, the tendency of the instruments (e.g., Event-driven BPM, Event-based BI) is to provide cooperation capabilities (e.g., discovery, modelling, and optimization of processes) and dynamic capabilities (e.g., process flows and dynamic services led by business rules) within flexible business processes. The dynamic capabilities provide agility through detection of patterns and rapid adjustment of business processes to events and agents (clients, businessmen, analysts and programmers, process architects and analysts).

An independent, parallel system may be used for the analysis of events. CEP (Complex Event Processing) processes complex events and provide simple business events that may be easily manipulated by BPM, BI, SOA (Service Oriented Architecture) and other instruments existing within the organization. At the same time, it provides a mechanism for the easy description of events and identification of specific patterns for complex events of the real world. Two types of decisions to be made based on events are discernable in the context provided by CEP, namely manual and automated decisions. CEP solutions generally provide mechanisms to maintain decisions as rules that allow substantiation based on patterns of events. Combination between BPM, BI and CEP provides a complete solution that involves processes, intelligence, events and services which provide adaptability, rapid response and flexibility for the organization (figure 1).

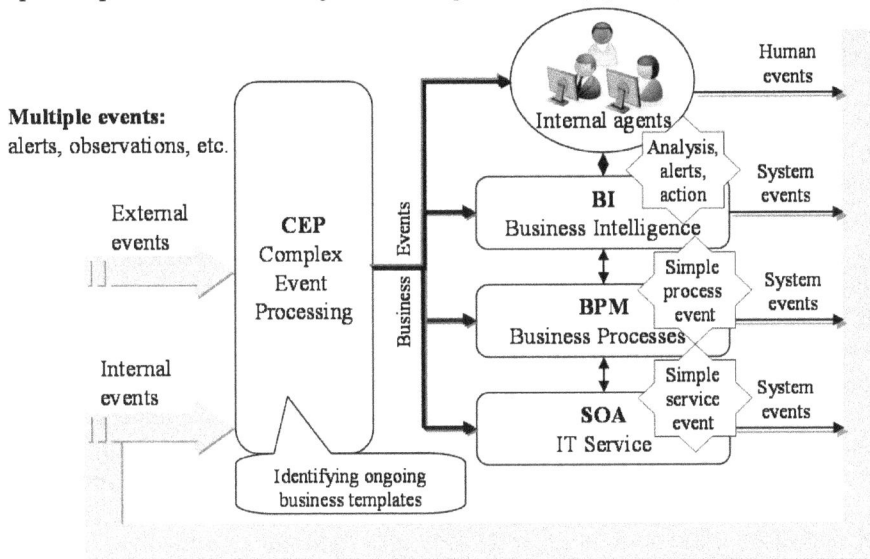

Figure 1: Event-based BI and BPM

In order for adoption of BI and BPM technologies to be accelerated, which involves rather high costs for the organization (especially for small and middle-sized enterprises) the Cloud Computing approach may be used, which is considered to be a cheaper solution for providing intelligence and for the management of business processes. Cloud Computing is considered to be the next step in the evolution of the Internet, providing means for the organization, against payment, to use IT services, from infrastructure and capacities of calculation, applications and business processes to personalized collaboration [4]. Because they are complex platforms, it should be said that the agility of these solutions is difficult to test and validate.

BPM combined with Cloud Computing technology may coordinate web services between users, information and systems, within/between organizations, the administration of business rules, real-time feedback in order to achieve tasks progress. It also may monitor results in relation to performance targets and may allow refining and permanent adjustment of flows for performance optimization [5]. The combination allows agile processes that may confront the complex events that exist in the collaboration context. Also, in the context of recession, the combination between Cloud Computing technology and BI provides new ways of management of analytical data and business opportunities. Cloud Computing will streamline BI, providing the necessary hardware, networks, security and software in order to create databases based upon request and different approaches related to the price of licensing and use. Integration of a BI system with a Cloud Computing service is not simple, because undertaking resources with the help of BI elements based on Cloud Computing involves activities of decision support systems, interrogations and reports, statistical analyses, previsions, data mining, OLAP and so forth.

2. KNOWLEDGE AND CASE MANAGEMENT

The knowledge determines the performance on the market of each organization and is present in all business processes, from the processes of production/service provision to attracting new clients and relational management with the stakeholders [6]. Management of knowledge involves the management of content (data and information), people (communities of interest), processes (procedures and workflows) and technology [7], providing correct information to the person having the right to access at the proper moment [8]. Knowledge workers attract more and more the attention of managers because their percentage in the organizations is increasing (between 25 percent and 50 percent [7]), and their wages are high. Peter Drucker considers the productivity of knowledge workers as the greatest management challenge of the 21st century.

Existence of processes highly based on knowledge (especially decision processes) entails that only a subset of activities within certain processes may be automated. Also, existence of collaborative processes, involving complex interactions between participants (who often work at the same time) and the need for the use of knowledge lead to a complexity that most BPM systems can not sustain (figure 2). BPM involves mainly prediction and definition of a set objective and implementation of an automated process [7]. Existence of the collaborative environment and of processes that involve human judgment and knowledge for execution imposes the need for a different type of approach, such as Case Management. Structured processes (BPM) are rigid compared to the needs of dynamic organizations.

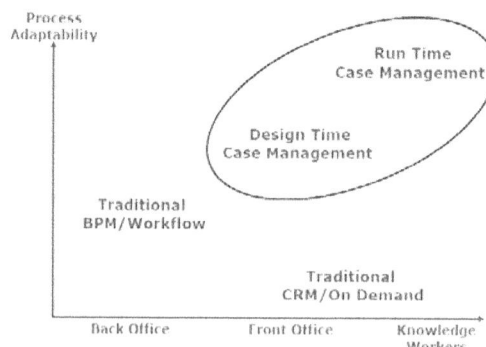

Figure 2: Adaptability vs. complexity [9]

In the specialized literature there is no universally accepted definition of Case Management. It was often described as a type of document management, management of particularized knowledge, (with the advantage of having an already-defined structure) or management of the relation with the customers. The main feature of Case Management is the unstructured progression of a case during its execution, from the initial stage to the final stage determined by human judgment, the external events and the business rules (figure 3). A case is a component of a business process that contains a collection of activities or tasks that cannot be set according to rules or patterns and that are determined at the moment of execution.

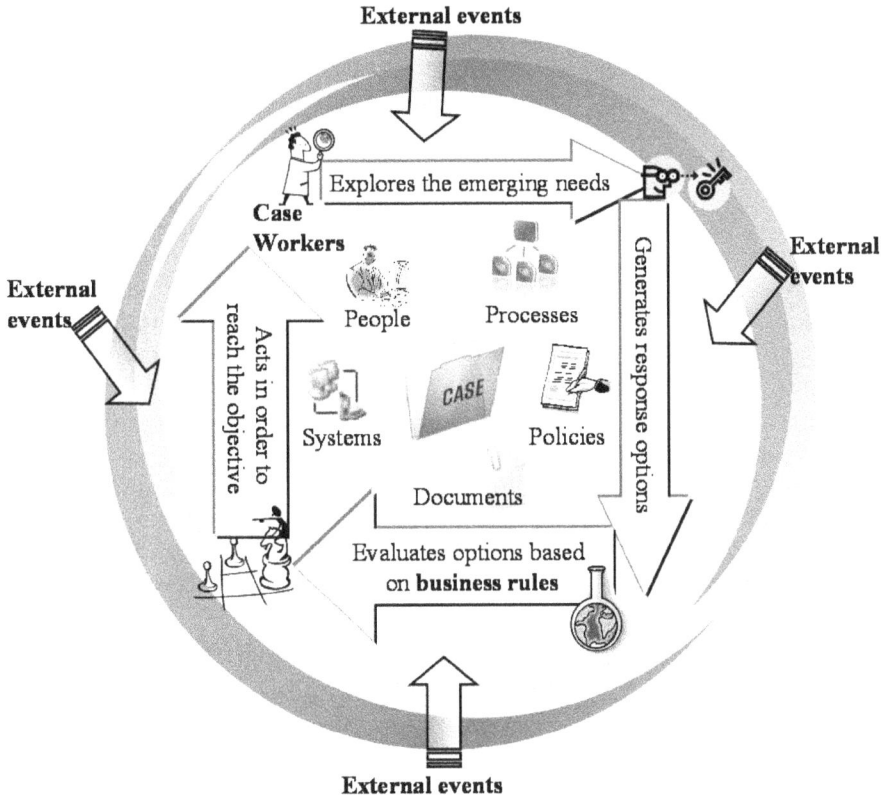

Figure 3: Case Management – instrument of collaboration and communication

Case Management is considered an often-used BPM pattern. Like BPM, it has important components, such as documents, elements of decision making in collaboration environments and interaction with customers. Therefore, a distinction should be made between Case Management and other instruments of modelling. Case Management is putting accent on customer orientation and at the present is used successfully in the fields of medicine, law, the public sector, financial services and telecommunications (figure 4). Case Management has the capacity of unify and administer clients and information, making possible to streamline the activities of an organization. In other words, Case Management is focused more on an organization policy of efficient use of resources and less on attraction and retention of the most profitable clients [10].

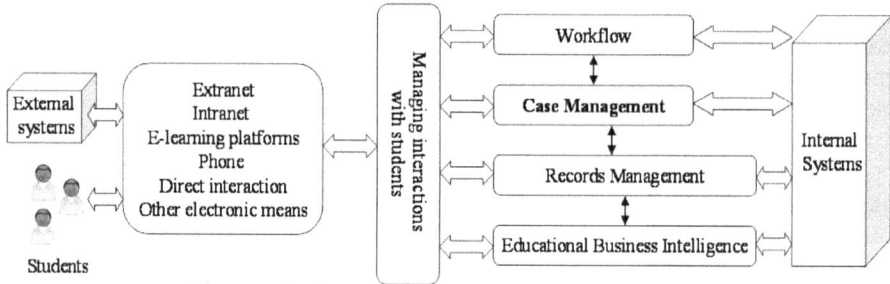

Figure 4: Case Management in Education

While Case Management provides many of the benefits of BPM, it is destined to a different category of problems, namely to processes that take place ad hoc, are dynamic, unstructured [11], non-repeatable, unpredictable, emergent, robust in confronting variable conditions [7], with collaboration and unique content management capacities. Beside processes, content, audit, workflow between processes, Case Management solutions also include the ability to learn and structure in time the business processes that are highly based on knowledge. Therefore, within the Case Management solution, two categories of processes may be found: structured processes controlled by the system and unstructured processes controlled by knowledge workers. Unstructured processes involve knowledge-based work, in which many important steps are executed individually or in collaboration, leading to processes that are highly based on knowledge, are difficult to analyze and structure [12].

Case management is a critical component for many organizations, but offers also many challenges, as it is not a fully automated process. Automation of Case Management is necessary in streamlining activities, eliminating human error, diminishing costs of education and retention of knowledge regarding processes (which are often to be found at the temporary personnel of the organization). The case-oriented BPM is considered to be the best solution of automation of Case Management [12].

3. AN APPROACH ON THE MIX AMONG KNOWLEDGE, PROCESSES AND BUSINESS INTELLIGENCE

Development of a BI system is an activity that involves many challenges, being under the constraint of authenticity of information. Developers must understand the business needs, the format and the deficiencies of data sources, the existing systems, the various needs of the users, etc. The goal of the development of the BI system is that of understanding the factors that affect performance metrics, providing for the managers expressive representations on the information that is modelling the business.

Starting from the basic dimensions [6] in the designing, implementation and use of BI systems, from the basic process for BI development [13] and from the need of combining BI with different technological methods, techniques and instruments, we propose the following approach concerning offering an agile solution for business management within collaborative environment (figure 5):

- business dimension – involves a series of methods and techniques of management which include knowledge used at the moment of the BI system development;
- functional dimension – involves determining the functionality of a BI system within an organization;
- technological dimension – involves a series of instruments, methods and solutions for the BI system development;

- organizational dimension – is based on determining the methodology of implementing the BI system in an organization.

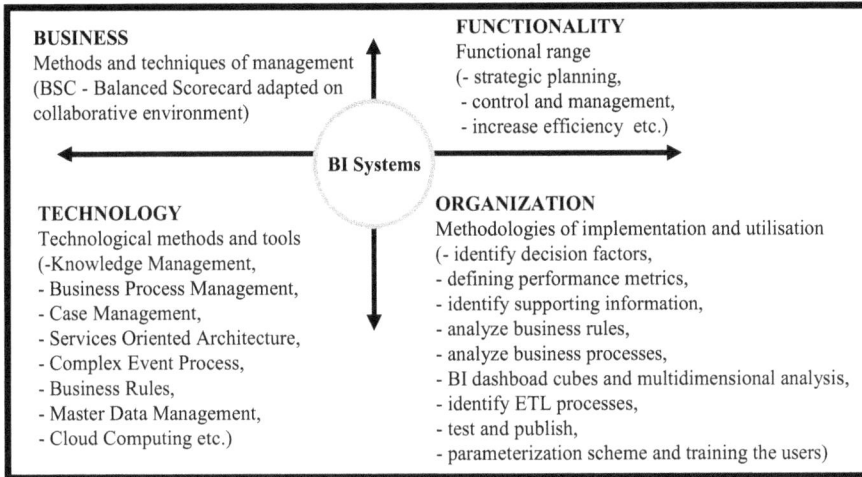

BUSINESS
Methods and techniques of management
(BSC - Balanced Scorecard adapted on
collaborative environment)

FUNCTIONALITY
Functional range
(- strategic planning,
 - control and management,
 - increase efficiency etc.)

BI Systems

TECHNOLOGY
Technological methods and tools
(-Knowledge Management,
- Business Process Management,
- Case Management,
- Services Oriented Architecture,
- Complex Event Process,
- Business Rules,
- Master Data Management,
- Cloud Computing etc.)

ORGANIZATION
Methodologies of implementation and utilisation
(- identify decision factors,
- defining performance metrics,
- identify supporting information,
- analyze business rules,
- analyze business processes,
- BI dashboad cubes and multidimensional analysis,
- identify ETL processes,
- test and publish,
- parameterization scheme and training the users)

Figure 5: Basic dimensions of BI systems

a) Business dimension of BI systems. BI systems have to allow integrated analysis and evaluation of the organization, which entails a complex approach that imposes the need for the creation of an environment of evaluation and control. Starting from the model most used in the implementation and control of an organization's strategy (BSC—Balanced Scorecard developed by Kaplan and Norton) adapted to the collaborative environment (figure 6) and taking into account the research in the field of measurement and control of performance, an integrated environment for expressing, measuring and controlling performance may be built [14].

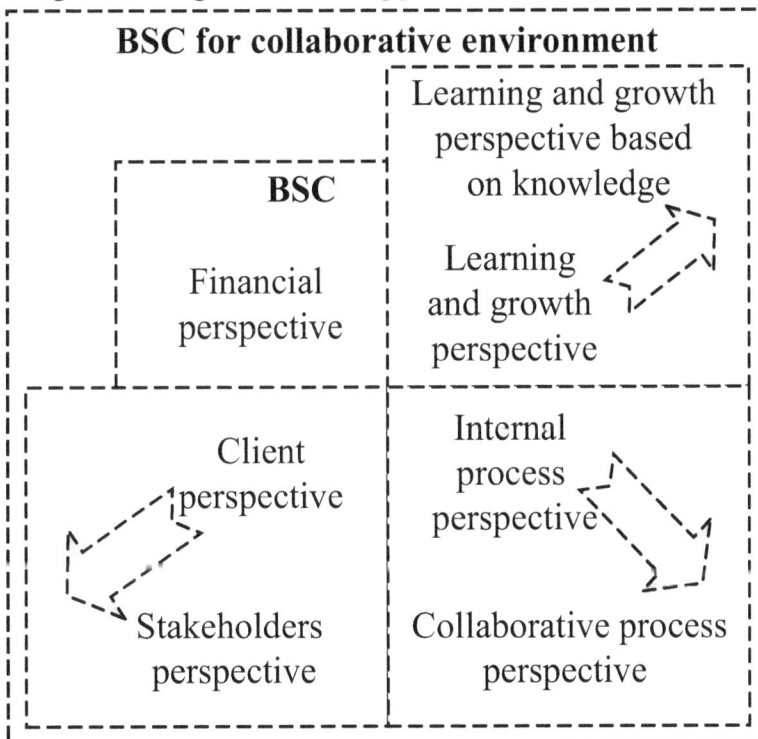

BSC for collaborative environment

BSC

Financial
perspective

Learning and growth
perspective based
on knowledge

Learning
and growth
perspective

Client
perspective

Stakeholders
perspective

Internal
process
perspective

Collaborative process
perspective

Figure 6: BSC Model adapted to the collaborative environment

In creating the model there must be set the business objectives and the metrics depending on the four perspectives of the adapted BPM model. The model will be used and improved with the help of the control systems situated on each level (figure 7). Within the model financial and non-financial indicators should be used that measure the performance of internal and external, tangible and intangible factors and monitor the drafting, implementation and optimization of business strategy.

Also, there is the need for optimization or redefinition of the strategy because it regards the long-term (two-three years), and the environment is in a continual change. The system of performance measurement must be made by the managers from the upper level of the organization and built in such a way that would ensure a balance between the systems' perspectives. Because BPM is based on a managerial approach, it helps to create the environment for measuring the business performance (used as BSC, the six sigma strategy, etc.) and offers a global image of the business.

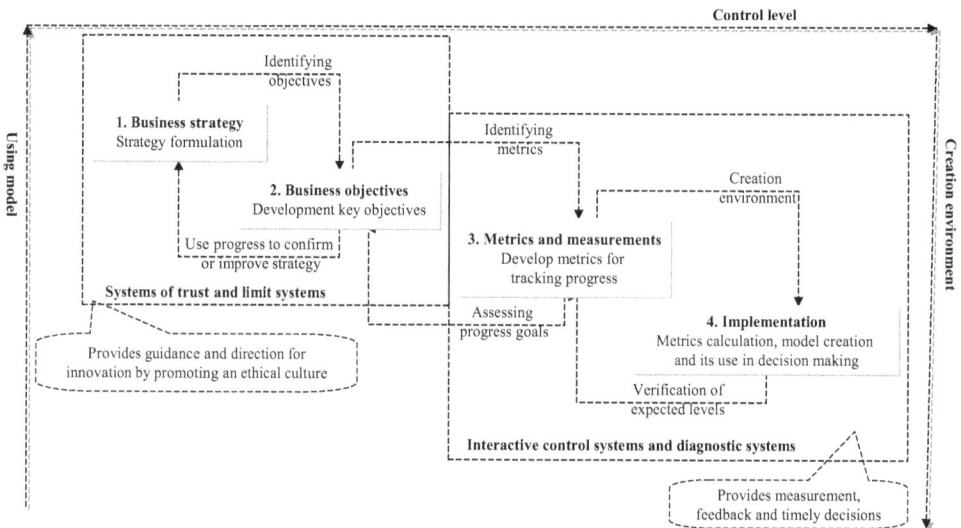

Figure 7: The business evaluation environment

b) *Functional dimension of BI systems.* BI systems have to be analyzed considering the benefits they may provide by their implementation in the organization. Based on research in this field, BI is mainly used for strategic planning, control and management, increasing efficiency, profitability assessment of products/services and improvement of quality of services provided to the main stake-holders.

c) *Technological dimension of BI systems.* The technological dimension involves mainly methods and techniques for knowledge creation and management (KM) and information technology instruments. Among the most important instruments are BPM, Case Management, SOA, MDM (Master Date Management), CEP and BR (Business Rules), which, in combination with BI allow the organizations to be connected in real time, on each level, in the process of daily activity and the making of strategic decisions.

Creation of a BI system involves the building of an analytical data deposit for managers. In most institutions, the most important metrics of decision are calculated based on information obtained through various systems. Therefore, BMP and Case Management represents an important technique of gathering this information and, along with the database, constitutes a method of integrating different sources of information. Analysis of business processes and rules (BR) represents a support for the analyses necessary for the creation of the solution of BI, BR helping the definition of dimensions and metrics. One of the key factors for the success of development is the use of BPM and BPM/BR analyses to improve the data scheme of the database.

A service-oriented architecture may bring many benefits, such as: promoting reuse, ability to combine services for the creation of new composite applications, use of decoupled services through standard interface, offering at the same time a technological behavior for the development of Business Intelligence solutions. Implementation of MDM in SOA strategy ensures data consistency, adjustment of information resources of the organization, correct dissemination of information in the interior/exterior of the organization, as well as delivery of all potential benefits by SOA initiatives.

CEP is a rule-based technology that groups in real time information from systems, databases and distributed applications in order to provide benefits for the BI solution. Each organization acts according to a set of rules, business rules, which may be external rules, (regulations in force that may be observed in all organizations operating in a specific field) and internal rules (which define the business policies of the organization and have the purpose of ensuring competition advantage on the market).

d) Organizational dimension of BI systems. The first step in the process of developing a BI system is identifying the system of indicators in the organization. This involves three stages: ❶ identifying general objectives; ❷ identifying key processes needed in reaching the objectives, and ❸ identifying the necessary organizational resources (figure 8). The identified objects will provide a general image on the existing environment and the future demand for knowledge. Analysis and design of key processes will lead to converting intelligence into action and will underline the flow of knowledge. Identification of organizational resources will allow setting of responsibilities, hierarchies and premises for the proper setting of processes.

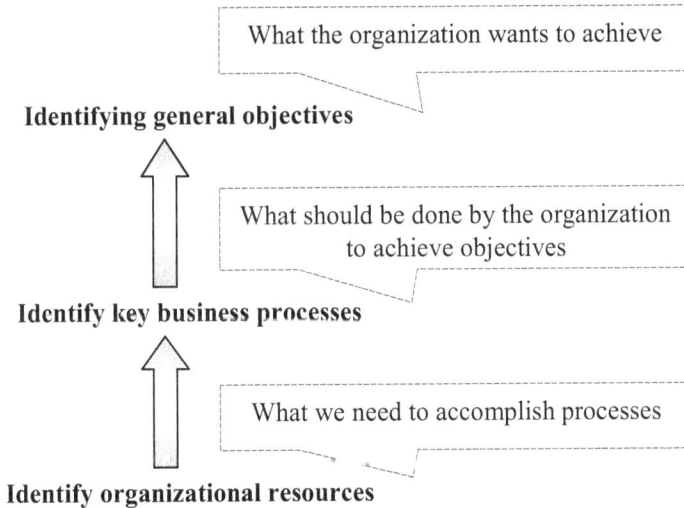

Figure 8: Stages in creating the indicators system

Then follow, in the development process, the definition of performance metrics, identification of the necessary information, analysis of business rules, analysis of business processes, drafting of dashboards and multidimensional analyses, identification of ETL processes (Extract, Transform, Load), testing and publication.

The last step is represented by the parametrisation of the BI system by use of proper knowledge and training of users.

An assessment of the implementation of the BI solution within the organization must be made in terms of costs as well as in terms of value to return, both at the start and during utilization. The audit of Business Intelligence solutions proves its importance and utility in relation with ensuring the quality of economic activities and processes within organizations [15]. Through the audit processes we can relatively quickly discover the weaker spots and the parameterization problems of BI solutions in relation with the specific activity that represents the object of implementation and with the ways of execution and improvement of the solution.

4. UTILIZATION OF AN AGILE BI SOLUTION IN THE EDUCATIONAL FIELD. CASE STUDY ACADEMY OF ECONOMIC STUDIES (ASE – WWW.ASE.RO) BUCHAREST

In the modern, knowledge-based economy, universities have to behave like any other business, for the purpose of becoming intelligent universities. The increasing competition between universities, the possibility of distance learning, high mobility of students, the efficient use of resources and application of the Bologna accord make necessary the use of agile BI systems in the educational environment. Also, increased pressure in the educational environment involves the drafting of reports, documents and watching of educational, demographic and financial information from the moment of students' registration (coming for admission or through the ministry) to the end of the educational cycle. The educational component connects the results obtained by students with the learning activities [16], providing to the leading board of the university a real image of the educational environment (figure 9)

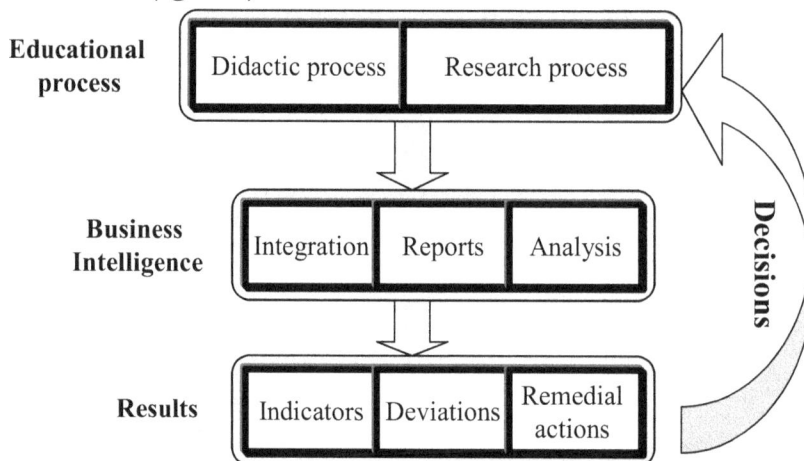

Figure 9: BI in the educational process of ASE Bucharest

One of the activities of university management is evaluation of the processes in the university, for which purpose many of the BI indicators of the economic-social environment have to be adapted to the university environment. Success of the use of a BI system within the university environment will depend mainly on assessment and measurement of the educational process (figure 10).

Assessment of the educational process

Indicators

Didactic process

Students and resources:
- number of students involved in research;
- using multimedia support;
- online education, resources and testing;
- planning and communication tool.

Research process

Results obtained

Projects:
- national research projects;
- international research projects;
- projects with business environment;
- structural funds projects.

Publications:
- studies in volumes of national and international conferences;
- articles in journals with or without impact;
- scientific books;
- monographs;
- textbook.

The number and degree of teachers involvement in:
- projects;
- publications.

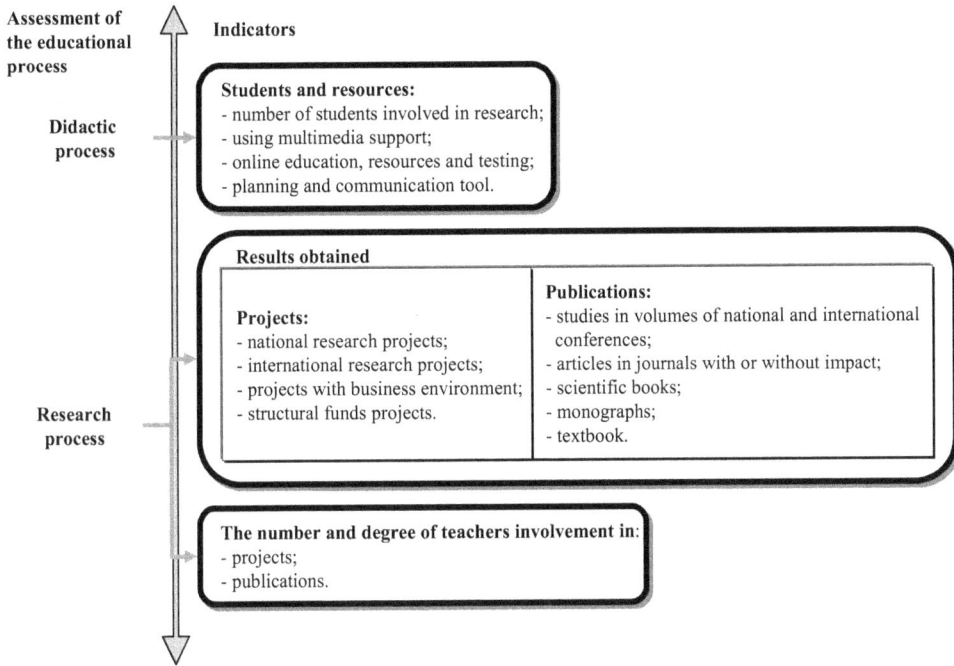

Figure 10: Assessment of the educational process

The Academy of Economic Studies of Bucharest (ASE), coordinator of an international consortium of five universities (ASE, Babeş Bolyai University of Cluj-Napoca, Polytechnic University of Timişoara, Naval University of Constanţa, George Baritiu University of Braşov) and two software development companies (Kion Italia and Crystal System) have started development and implementation of an Integrated Information System for University Management (SIIMU). The solution will concern the management of the education process (teaching and research) and the support activities, (finance, acquisitions, human resources, etc.) leading to operational efficiency, agility, and improvement of services provided to the main stakeholders (students, employees, the Ministry of Education, Research, Youth and Sport).

The need for the implementation of SIIMU appeared from the fact that ASE Bucharest, as well as other universities, is confronted with problems/difficulties in adapting rapidly to the demands of the market and to the present economic context. Among the main problems/deficiencies are:

- lack of IT application in certain activities and/or integration of existing applications;
- lack of BI components in the evaluation of processes;
- faulty operation of certain existing modules;
- the need to access in real time all data in the information system of the university;
- lack of modern interoperability with other external systems, etc.

Concerning the SIIMU objectives, it aims at solving the existing problems of the university through reaching certain primary objectives, such as:

- informatization of all activities within the university and implementation of an audit system for stored data (example: informatization of tasks met by a teacher - figure 11);

Figure 11: Example of informatization of a teacher's activity

- ensuring interoperability with systems of ASE and of the exterior (example: the Unified Register of UEFISCSU – the Executive Unit for Financing Higher Education and University Scientific Research);
- simplification and streamlining of flows (example: workflow implemented for teacher's documents - figure 12);

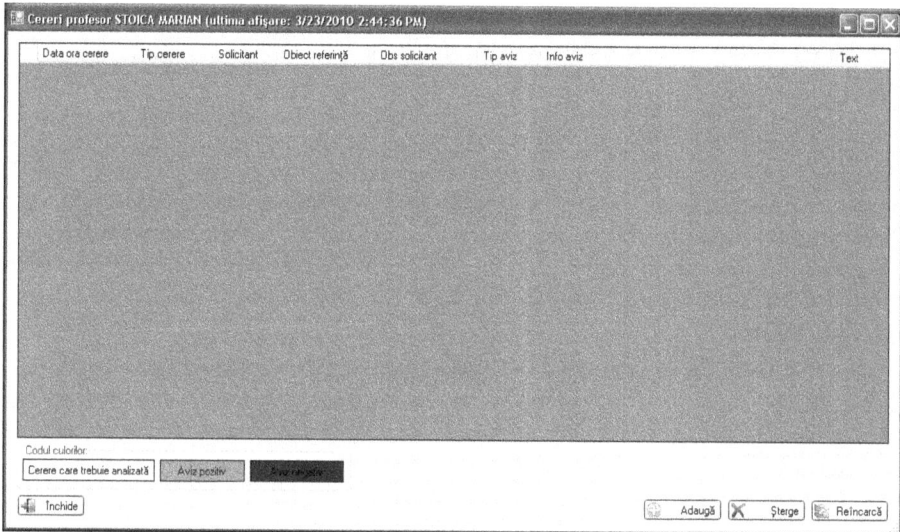

Figure 12: Workflow Example

- implementation of the concept of electronic register and of a configurable marking system (example: the evaluation commissions, composed of teachers from a certain chair, enter the marks of the students in electronic registers, based on clear rules - figure 13);

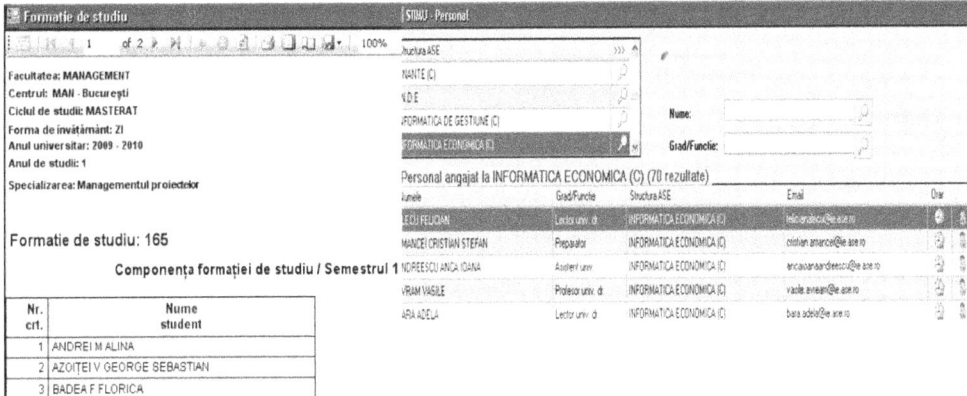

Figure 13: Example of study group and chair members

- providing a component dedicated to students (educational Case Management – display and update of information, interface for online payment of taxes, student-orientation etc.);
- implementation of BI components for the decision factors for the purpose of real time supervision of basic processes and support actions of the university (example: indicators on results on a certain discipline - figure 14).

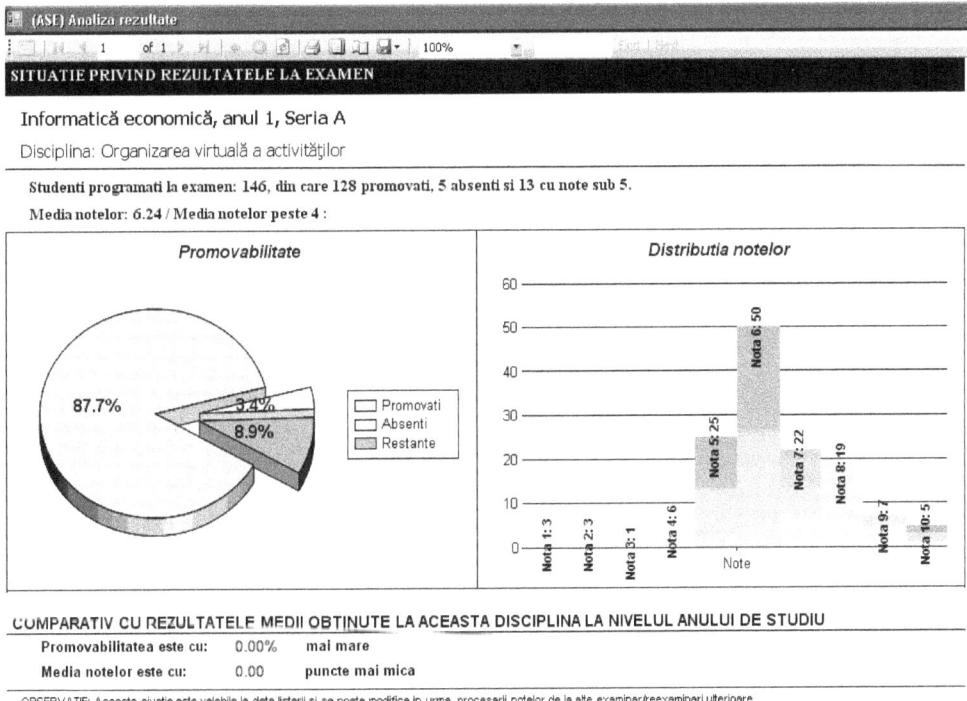

Figure 14: Example of analysis of results on a specific discipline

Regarding the value to be added by the combination of knowledge, processes, intelligence within a higher education institution of Romania, the main following benefits are obtained by the means of SIIMU:

Well grounded decisions. Creation of reports and analyses of trends will lead to well grounded decisions on the teaching disciplines, specializations within the institution, opening/closing of master courses based on the identified needs.

Strategic planning and quality assessment in education. Integration of SIIMU system with certain systems will entail assessment of success on the workforce market and underline the quality of education compared to other universities.

Reducing costs. The solution is built on SOA architecture and supports all front-office and back-office processes, thus providing rapid organized workflows and efficient management processes. By the introduction of the electronic register 40 pecent of the time allocated for entering data has been saved.

Reducing errors. SIIMU leads to reduction of errors from data duplication or delay. At the present have been eliminated the errors related to duplication and to the gap between tax payment or expelling a student and the possibility of taking part to an exam.

Unifies people, information and processes. The solution provides mobility, portal, collaboration, knowledge management, BI, MDM, BPM and SOA in a single solution.

Compliance with the government's demands. Provides reports, transparency, dashboards, security, identity management (connection to the solution IDM – Identity Management), workflows, business process management, according to the provisions of Bologna declaration.

Customer orientation. ASE Bucharest makes the effort of differentiating itself by offering easy, real-time, personalized, 24/7 access to information. Also, it will ensure a students' lifecycle management (admission, promotion, academic counselling, orientation, course management, management of academic program).

Ensuring quality and quality management. SIIMU is built in such a way that it complies with the legislation in force on ensuring quality and quality management, as well as with the ASE policy on quality improvement. Some of the regulations in force are:

- Standards and Guidelines for Quality Assurance in the European Higher Education Area, Bergen 2005;
- Emergency ordinance No. 75/12.07.2005 on ensuring quality of education and the Law No. 87 of 10.04.2006 approving it;
- Order MEdC 3928/2005 on ensuring quality of education service in higher education institutions;
- Methodology of external evaluation, standards, benchmarks and the list of performance indicators of ARACIS, 2006;
- ARACIS Guides on the evaluation: institutional, license programs and ID, master studies, requests for authorization and periodical certification, 2006;
- SR EN ISO 9001:2008 – Quality Management Systems. Conditions;
- IWA 2: 2009 – Quality Management Systems – Guidelines for application of ISO 9001:2000 in education (adopted as Romanian standard in 2006);
- ISO 9004:2009 – Leading an organization to steady success. An approach on Quality Management;
- Criteria of national quality awards: Education Criteria for Performance Excellence, Baldrige National Quality Program.

5. CONCLUSIONS

In the end we may notice that unidisciplinary approach is replaced by pluri- or multi-disciplinary approach, that mono-qualification is replaced by poli-qualification, that the philosophy of a single focus is replaced by that of dispersed focus, and this approach may continue. Therefore, within a hostile environment concerning economic, sociable, politic, ecologic, and other dimensions, characterized by globalization and externalization, organizations and business in general have limited solutions for development.

One of these solutions has its advantages and drawbacks presented in this paper: combination by interfunctionality of technologies in order to achieve development. This entails the use of knowledge, processes, business intelligence, Case Management, SOA architectures for the purpose of ensuring organization's agility in a collaborative context.

Furthermore, the present study brings the theoretical aspects into material application by the presentation of an agile BI solution in the field of higher education (ASE Bucharest). In conclusion, we may say again that this study is a solution, but not the only one. The spectacular development of technology corroborated with the general human evolution seen from the perspective of clusters of economic, social, cultural aspirations will certainly generate new opportunities for research, analysis and implementation of new solutions in response to the challenges of the market.

Acknowledgment:
This work was supported by ANCS-CNMP, project number PNII – 91-049/2007.

6. REFERENCES

[1] Jandi, T. (2008), "Process Oriented Business Intelligence", *Interfacing Technologies Corporation;*

[2] Ventana Research (2006), "Business Intelligence Meets Business Process Management", Powerful technologies can work in tandem to drive successful operation;

[3] Savvion Inc., "Making Intelligence Actionable: Business Process Management and Business Intelligence";

[4] Cunningham, M. (2010), "Cloud Computing Enables Self-serve BI", http://www.dashboardinsight.com/articles/business-performance-management/cloud-computing-enables-self-serve-bi.aspx

[5] Barlow, G. (2009), "Business Process management and Cloud Computing", *Cound Harbor,* http://www.bpminstitute.org/articles/article/article/business-process-management-and-cloud-computing/news-browse/1.html

[6] Olszac, C. and Ziemba, E. (2003), "Business Intelligence as a key to Management of an Enterprise Informing Science", http://www.informingscience.org/proceedings/IS2003Proceedings/docs/109Olsza.pdf

[7] Swenson, K. (2010), "The Nature of Knowledge work", *Workflow Management Coalition,*http://www.wfmc.org/webinar-on-case-management-for-knowledge-work.html

[8] Northrop Grumman, "Knowledge & Case Management", http://www.is.northropgrumman.com/by_solution/homeland_security/solutions/km/index.html

[9] Hogg, L. (2009), "Case Management Strategies and Best Practices: Taking Traditional BPM way beyond conventional workflow, routing and collaboration", *BPM Institute,* http://www.bpminstitute.org/uploads/media/Pallas_Athena_082609.pdf

[10] Ryan, M. (2007), "Case Management: Why Doesn't Every Law Firm Use It? Criteria for Use, Success and Failure", *Legal Files Software,*

http://www.legalfiles.com/docs/white_papers/Why%20doesnt%20every%20firm%20use%20CMS.pdf

[11] Shepherd, T., "Top Case Management Misconceptions", *Global 360*;

[12] Singularity (2009), "Case Management: Combining Knowledge With Process", *BPTrends*;

[13] Debevoise, T. (2007), "Business Process Management with a Business Rules Approach. Implementing the Service-Oriented Architecture", ISBN: 978-1-4196-7368-9

[14] Ghilic – Micu, B. And Mircea, M. (2007), "The E-business Strategy Management", *Economy Informatics*, v1, no. 4;

[15] Ghilic – Micu, B., Stoica, M., Mircea, M., Sinioros, P. (2010), "Cost – Performance Evaluation Environment for the Adoption of a Case Management Solution", *Journal of Economic Computation And Economic Cybernetics Studies*, v. 44, no. 1, pg. 63-80, ISSN 0424-267X

[16] Cech, P. and Bures, V. (2006), "Utilisation of Business Intelligence in an Education Environment", *Formatex*, http://www.formatex.org/micte2006/pdf/210-214.pdf

Using BPM to Drive Clinical Intelligence and Process Oversight in the Acute Healthcare Setting

Ray Hess, The Chester County Hospital, USA

INTRODUCTION:

The environment of the acute hospital setting is a complex compilation of intricate processes. The healthcare worker is challenged to manage and coordinate many diverse aspects of their patients' care effectively. There is an ever-increasing burden of care options and requirements that need to be considered. The use of business process management to help automate and control patient care has been shown to be effective in improving this care burden. However, the healthcare sector has been very slow to adopt BPM. There are many reasons for this phenomenon. Clinical care processes are very complex and often do not have easily defined beginning and ending points. They tend to overlap and disrupt other workflows based on the details of the individual process. A complex matrix of conditions can change the logic for dealing with event-based data elements and the way a system should react to those events. The clinical users tend to be very mobile and are not electronically connected for extended periods of their day. These are just a few of the challenges facing healthcare process automation.

One of the most daunting hurdles for creating effective BPM solutions in the acute healthcare setting is the ability to understand and map the process flow. The variables involved are very complex and intertwined. Multiple end-users all interact with patients in varied and changing ways based on the specific disease conditions and external variables that are present in the care environment. The challenges are extensive but the need is great. The payoff is significant if automated processes can be developed, deployed, and managed successfully. Ineffective management of processes is a problem that exists extensively in the healthcare arena even when accurate BPM flows are running. This primarily revolves around the ignoring of alerts and action reminders by the clinician. Unlike many industries, healthcare workers cannot always stick to defined work lists and a structured order for the actions they need to take. Situations arise regularly which force a deviation from the planned events. The responsibility for the care is regularly delegated, triaged, and handed-off. The priority of what care to deliver in what order is often in a state of flux. The patient or any patient can cause disruption or delay in following a planned schedule. Finally, the caregivers themselves can represent the problem if they do not act on their electronic directions in a prompt and consistent manner. Many well developed processes are thwarted by the staff not being consistent and timely in addressing their BPM related alerts and directions.

This chapter will focus on the use of BPM to support Clinical Intelligence Management. BPM driven oversight tools have proven to be a vital cog in the wheel of overall BPM success and improved outcomes in the hospital healthcare setting. Without it many of the processes do not achieve the desired effects. This chapter will review how the BPM system can be used to aggregate data in an effective manner for centralized oversight and management in addition to the normal expected patient level directives. The use of BPM has allowed The Chester County Hospital in West Chester, Pennsylvania to have a significantly enhanced patient care oversight and control capability. The result of having this capability has been more efficient and effective patient care outcomes.

Healthcare Systems Overview: Systems used within healthcare are designed to provide for patient care and to support clinical tasks. These systems contain functions such as ordering (tests or medications), documentation, and displaying results. The clinical care systems used in today's hospital almost universally have hierarchical database structures and are optimized for transactional activity. This means that they respond very quickly to individual events and actions regarding an individual patient. Examples of this may include: new test results, entering orders, pulling up charted documentation, or entering a clinical note. The systems and their databases are designed and granulated in such a way that the database indexes optimize on a single patient or event data. The goal is very rapid responses for the clinician at a patient level.

While this transactional structure works very well for managing an individual patient's care, it creates significant problems for anyone trying to aggregate data to obtain a more global view of the current status of groups of patients or disease conditions. Attempting to query a transactional database to get this type of data can result in very long query run times, table scans, and possibly system performance degradation while the query is running. Healthcare systems are not designed for relational querying. They usually have functions to export this data periodically to a separate reporting database that is relationally optimized. This is where analysis is expected to occur. Unfortunately, the use of an external dataset does not provide the real-time information needed to oversee and manage care. The data to accomplish proper oversight must be current and therefore must come from the production database.

Most clinical information systems have some level of rules-based clinical decision support capabilities which results in alerts to the clinician concerning proper actions and care options. The most advanced systems are now starting to include BPM in the product allowing for more extensive process management and automation. In all cases these systems are designed to analyze and react to transactions or discrete events related to each patient as they occur. This is very effective for overseeing and directing the care for single patients via the caregivers that are involved in the case. These BPM systems often give basic information about what processes are running, what steps are currently being executed, and what alerts/tasks are currently open. In short, they give adequate BPM oversight related to the BPM system operation and BPM activity monitoring.

The harvested information described in the previous paragraph represents clinical intelligence for an individual patient. This is defined as the knowledge of the aggregate disease conditions, current care status, and what actions should be considered or taken next for a specific patient. However, this type of information does not support the needs of the supervisor or a care specialist who needs to see the aggregate information for a population of patients. Hospitals often have "specialists" who deal with certain disease conditions or types of care such as congestive heart failure, diabetes, IV therapy, wound care, or managing stroke patients. Furthermore, departments such as Quality Management or other operational units need to see global status conditions for compliance with regulatory requirements or quality initiatives. Supervisors need to see if their staff is responding appropriately to their assigned work items. None of this is accomplished easily in a traditional BPM process.

The data described above is often collected via tedious manual processes or is gathered from the reporting systems which do not represent current information. This results in information that is often inadequate and/or erroneous. Sometimes the departments settle for the stale data or else they go through time consuming chart reviews and aggregate data in spreadsheets. This results in lost productivity, reduced management capabilities, and sub-optimal patient care. The clinical care specialists and supervisors need timely and accurate information to properly oversee care.

Using BPM to Manage Clinical Information: Historically BPM's use in healthcare has been focused on patient-specific workflows. This is very appropriate but has not always been effective. The BPM processes listen for individual events and react according to the pre-defined logic. The data for the individual patient event is readily available because it is often included within the event. Alternatively, it is easy for the BPM system to query the transactional database for more complete event data since the database is designed for just such a query. The data is reviewed by the BPM system and appropriate actions are taken. At that point the system is normally finished with the data and waits for the next event or action to occur. However, there is an opportunity to alter the BPM process design at this point to harvest this valuable data for increased clinical intelligence.

The first step is to determine what data elements are needed for real-time monitoring of the key processes. These are the elements that exist with each patient but are stored in such a way that aggregation is difficult. It is also important to understand what the data represents and the range thresholds that indicate a problem or item that needs attention. The end-users on the supervisory or specialty level must be engaged in determining these elements. They are the key stakeholders and their input is imperative because they will be using this clinical intelligence to assure that the overall outcomes are positive.

Once the necessary data elements are cataloged a relational database table structure needs to be developed to hold this data. Ideally one table should be created for all the elements needed for any specific process that is to be monitored. However, the most appropriate design will need to be determined on a case by case basis. Next logical indexing strategies need to be developed based on the way the data will be queried. It is very important to understand the differences between hierarchical and relational database structures. Usually this work is handled by a database administrator (DBA). This fact cannot be overemphasized. The person working on this aspect of the project needs to have a solid skill set regarding databases.

After the table structure is created conceptually it needs to be created in the system's database itself. This step should also be performed by a DBA. It is strongly recommended that you create a separate database for the relational table structure you are creating. This keeps these tables isolated from the production database and protects the work from interfering with the existing database or from being overwritten during a system upgrade. If possible try to keep the new database on the same server instance as the system database. By doing this the BPM engine should have no problem interacting fluidly between these databases.

Once this pre-work is done the next step is to alter the BPM processes that manage the workflows these new tables refer too. When an event trigger is fired the BPM process should collect all the data associated with the event being handled.

This data, because it is coming from a transactional system, will be very easy to grab in a manner that does not have any significant time or system impact. As the BPM engine completes its actions based on the existing logic a new sub-procedure is added to the BPM flow. This new procedure takes the data and either adds it to the relational table(s) or updates the current data for that patient in the tables. If the function being monitored is ending or the patient is discharged the BPM process removes the table entry in its shutdown sequence. This clinical intelligence manager sub-procedure is designed to manage only active cases or issues. Historical data will be pulled out of the already existing reporting database in the clinical system.

The result of the alterations to the BPM flow mentioned above is substantial. The system now has small relationally optimized tables that have the current conditions for the entire population of patients, diseases, or devices. These tables represent a compilation of many data elements from the transactional database which is often too granulated and/or non-indexed for real-time reporting. The BPM engine is used to manage the new reporting database for the end-users. It also places information about the status of work items or patient care related processes to the data in these tables as well. The system creates customized BPM managed Business Activity Monitoring for real time oversight.

The final piece of the equation is to create reporting views of these tables for the end-user to query. We chose to use Microsoft's Reporting Services because it gave us the ability to add logic to cells in the report that pulls the viewer to key data elements and because it had no additional licensing fees. Any of the major reporting packages should work and almost all environments have a package in use. Whenever the user clicks on the report a real-time picture of the status of the environment is created for that person. It allows them to see the institution from a global perspective instead of just from a single patient's needs. The data represents the current state when the user runs the query that pulls up the report.

PINU	331601	IV1	0 R Antecubital	Peripheral IV	Apr 05, 2010	No pain, no erythema		0
PINU	331701	IV1	0 L Outer Forearm	Peripheral IV	Apr 05, 2010	No pain, no erythema		0
PINU	331901	IV1	0 R Inner Forearm	Peripheral IV	Apr 06, 2010	No pain, no erythema		0
PINU	332101	IV1	0 L Inner Forearm	Peripheral IV	Apr 06, 2010	No pain, no erythema		0
PINU	332201	IV1	0 L Outer Forearm	Peripheral IV	Apr 04, 2010	Drainage		0
PINU	332201	IV2	0 R Wrist	Peripheral IV	Apr 06, 2010	No pain, no erythema		0
PINU	332301	IV3	0 R Wrist	Peripheral IV	Apr 07, 2010	None		0
PINU	332401	IV1	1 R Upper Arm	Power PICC	Mar 30, 2010	No pain, no erythema		0
PINU	332501	IV1	0 L Antecubital	Peripheral IV	Apr 06, 2010	No pain, no erythema		0
SCU	W00101	IV1	0 L Dorsal Hand	Peripheral IV	Apr 06, 2010	No pain, no erythema		0
SCU	W00201	IV1	1 R Upper Arm	Power PICC	Apr 04, 2010	No pain, no		0

Figure 1: A portion of a BPM-managed report showing IV detail

Figure 1 shows a good example of how this concept is used in real life at the Chester County Hospital. This is a screenshot of the report that shows every IV on every patient currently in the hospital. The user, in this case the IV team, is charged with overseeing the care of patient IVs. These nurses are able to get up to the second IV information for all patients anytime they click the report. Because this report is coming from the relational tables it returns in at most one to two seconds. The real report is in color. The lighter gray on the black and white image in this chapter is actually yellow on the report. The darker gray is red. Yellow represents current work or issues. On this report there is an IV that needs changed today and one that is missing documentation, both are cells that are in yellow. The red cell is for an IV with an issue that needs attention by the IV team. By adding filters (not seen) the user can instantly hone in on the specifics they need to see. If we had tried to create this report off of the transactional tables it could easily take up to 60–90 seconds to run on the same server.

The implications of this type of information availability are incredible for the hospital. Before this methodology was created the BPM process could monitor individual patients and alert the responsible nurse concerning the IV, specifically when it needed changed or evaluated. It could also send alerts to the IV team when a nurse noted in the documentation that there was a problem with an IV. The BPM workflow was good at the individual patient or nurse work level but not for the global team's oversight. By adapting the BPM process to take the data it was already evaluating to maintain a table of all IVs with their current status global management capabilities were greatly enhanced. The IV team now pulls up this list, uses various filters they have requested, and quickly and seamlessly gets a picture of the IV status for the entire facility. This allows them to prepare their work plan based on pressing needs and real-time clinical intelligence.

The original BPM process was developed to alert the IV team for specific issues that required their attention. However, by using the formatting logic to highlight and color specific cells in our report the IV team has found that these alerts were often not needed. The report became their worklist and they use it effectively. As the IV teams gleaned information from this global report they were able to see trends and changes that were needed in how the floor nurse documents IV statuses. They requested these changes and education has been conducted with the staff. This oversight has resulted in a steady clean up the accuracy of the source data documentation. This positive outcome was only possible because of the capabilities provided by the improved oversight via this enhanced BPM process. Retrospective analysis from the traditional reporting system, while important, did not give this type of insight and control.

The methodology described above has been used for multiple processes within the hospital. It has been used for devices such as IVs and Foley catheters. BPM managed reports exist for conditions or diseases such as pressure wounds, diabetes, congestive heart failure, and stroke. This methodology has also been used to provide the supervisor staff with exact knowledge of the current work status in their area of responsibility. The BPM engine is being used to manage the management of processes as well as the processes themselves.

Healthcare has had ongoing problems with alert items being ignored by the clinical staff. This has been well documented in the healthcare literature. At the Chester County Hospital there are alerts on hundreds of patients on a dozen floors. The nursing alerts need to be addressed by many different nurses on different shifts. There are hands-offs constantly occurring. Trying to get over 700 nurses consistently all to do the right things 24/7 has proved to be as difficult for this hospital as it has been throughout the industry. Consequently the BPM automated workflows had been compromised in their effectiveness. The BPM-managed clinical intelligence methodology has provided hospital management with the tools needed to oversee and therefore improve the effectiveness of the BPM processes.

The new approach described in this chapter has proven to be a key in addressing multiple problems. The BPM engine is used to roll disparate alerts from many diverse processes into summary compilations by floor and areas of responsibility. On any given shift there is a supervisor responsible for each of the dozen patient care floors. Each of these supervisors is tasked with reviewing the status of their floor's alerts by the middle of their eight hour shift and having them addressed (whenever possible) by the end of the shift. This management mandate has reduced the oversight burden from hundreds of nurses to 12 supervisors. The nursing manager over these supervisors assures that they accomplish their task. Because the supervisors are on top of the staff and the staff knows they will be challenged for not handling their alerts, the alerts get handled whenever possible. The bottom line has been better and more consistent patient care.

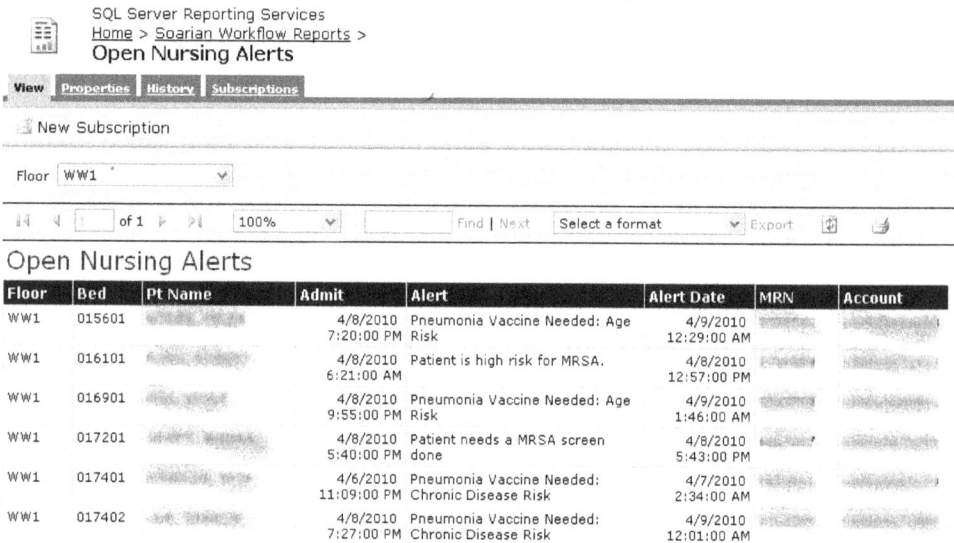

SQL Server Reporting Services
Home > Soarian Workflow Reports >
Open Nursing Alerts

View | Properties | History | Subscriptions

New Subscription

Floor | WW1

| | of 1 | | 100% | | Find | Next | Select a format | Export |

Open Nursing Alerts

Floor	Bed	Pt Name	Admit	Alert	Alert Date	MRN	Account
WW1	015601		4/8/2010 7:20:00 PM	Pneumonia Vaccine Needed: Age Risk	4/9/2010 12:29:00 AM		
WW1	016101		4/8/2010 6:21:00 AM	Patient is high risk for MRSA.	4/8/2010 12:57:00 PM		
WW1	016901		4/8/2010 9:55:00 PM	Pneumonia Vaccine Needed: Age Risk	4/9/2010 1:46:00 AM		
WW1	017201		4/8/2010 5:40:00 PM	Patient needs a MRSA screen done	4/8/2010 5:43:00 PM		
WW1	017401		4/6/2010 11:09:00 PM	Pneumonia Vaccine Needed: Chronic Disease Risk	4/7/2010 2:34:00 AM		
WW1	017402		4/8/2010 7:27:00 PM	Pneumonia Vaccine Needed: Chronic Disease Risk	4/9/2010 12:01:00 AM		

Figure 2: Open work items for nurses on floor West Wing One

The management technique of a hierarchical chain of command and responsibility is not new. It is a key to making sure that operations are accomplished properly. In the acute healthcare setting there have been many challenges to effectively automating processes. The use of the BPM engine itself to manage the relational reporting capabilities for effective control has been the key to unlocking the power of the BPM processes at The Chester County Hospital. Figure 2 shows a simple view of multiple alerts that need to be addressed for one floor (patient identifiers have been removed to maintain their privacy). Note that the alerts are from different processes. These alerts are the responsibility of multiple nurses but all fall under one supervisor who will make sure they are addressed in an appropriate manner. It was actually hard to find a good example of this report since there were few unaddressed alerts available for any given floor. The example shown has no alerts older than the threshold established that would have changed the color on the report.

BPM Process with Enhanced Relational Database

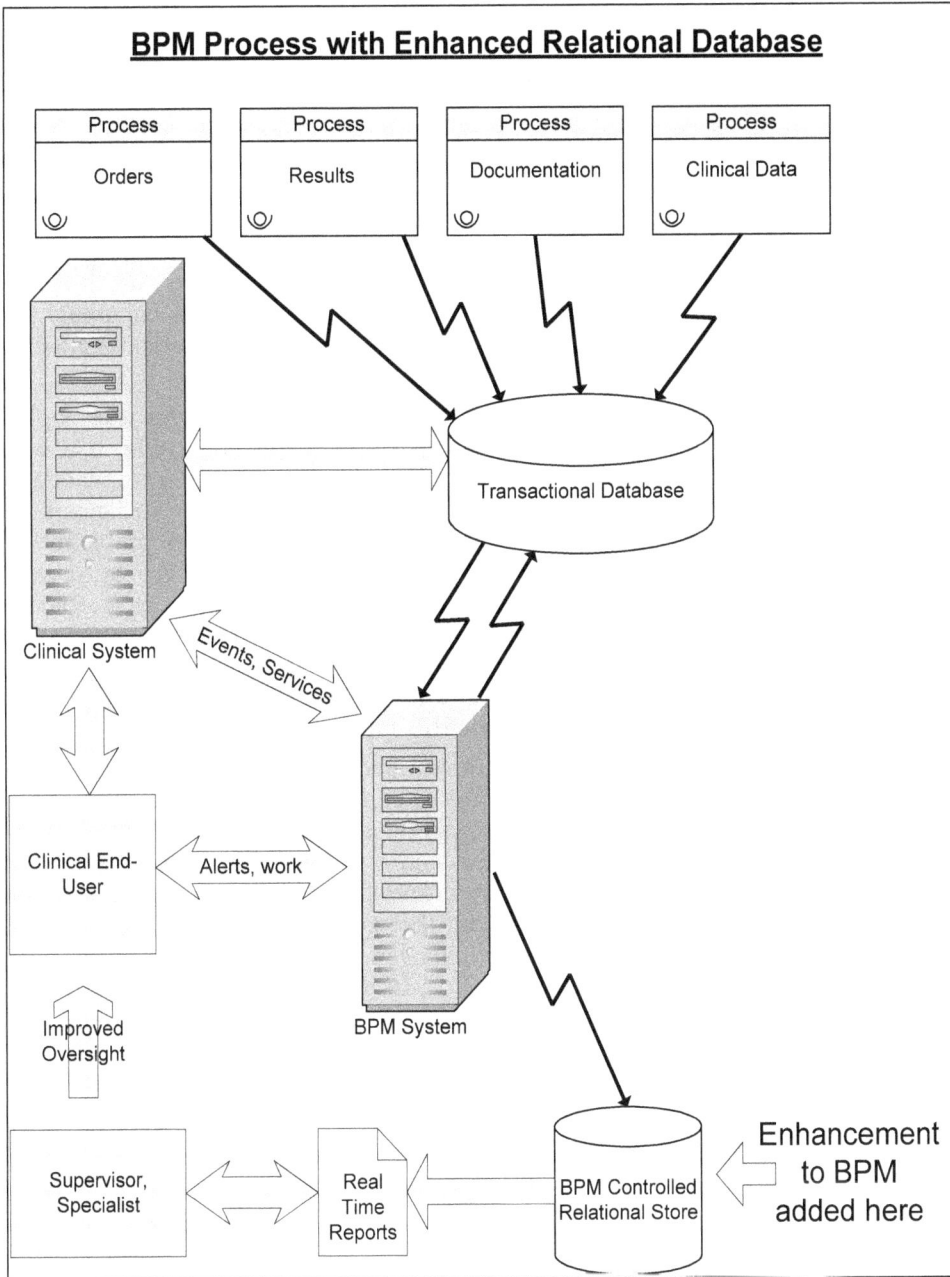

Figure 3: The BPM Process with the added Relational Component

Figure 3 shows a visual representation of the basic BPM schematic. The boxes across the top of the diagram are examples of internal and external data events that occur in the clinical information systems. These processes may be end-user initiated, system initiated, or come from external sources. The clinical system processes the data, stores it in the transactional database and sends out events and updates. The BPM system subscribes to the events and calls services to retrieve data from the transactional database. Using the data obtained, the BPM system creates alerts and work for the end user who is interacting with either the clinical system or the BPM system. These actions are all patient centric. The enhancement is graphically represented at the bottom of the picture. The BPM system manages a relational database which is used to create on-demand real time reports showing the current state of affairs. These reports are used to provide better control or oversight for better outcomes.

The use of the BPM engine to manage a relational reporting database in a hierarchical environment has created many diverse opportunities for the hospital. The key advantage it has provided is that it has given a method to aggregate disparate data elements into focused clinical intelligence. In the healthcare environment the term "clinical intelligence" is correlated to "business intelligence" in other sectors. These data elements are extremely valuable for individual patient care but now they are leveraged in new and exciting ways. As stated earlier, this capability has dramatically improved the ability to oversee and manage the care delivery within the institution.

Non-Healthcare Application: The process described in this chapter was applied in a healthcare setting. However, the concepts should be applicable in a wide range of industries and scenarios. If the industry is functioning in a transactional world and is having problems obtaining and controlling business intelligence the BPM engine should be considered as a possible way to address the problem. It is a powerful tool that is already handling the data as it manages automated workflows. Most high-end BPM systems have very robust database interaction capabilities. There is almost always an existing reporting package that the company is using and it can be formatted to present the data. The industry details may change but the core functionalities are usually very similar. Therefore it should be fairly straightforward to replicate this type of methodology.

There are four key knowledge-sets that are required to create this type of solution. The first is a DBA (database administrator) or someone who can work effectively within the database associated with the system. The second is the BPM process engineer who has the knowledge set necessary to alter the process flow for this task. The third skill set is that of a report writer. This person needs to know how to create effective and focused reports from the created tables. The final requirement is the most important and can often be overlooked or minimized. This is the key management or knowledge experts who can define the precise items needed for effective Business Activity Monitoring. Without their input the other resources will not know what is needed to assure success.

Achieving this type of solution is easiest if it is planned for during the initial BPM process definition. In the hospital's case the need became apparent because of the inconsistent way the staff handled their alerts and work items. Key existing automations were reworked based on priority. Once the initial wave of modifications were made and tested, the power and importance of this new approach was clearly demonstrated. From that point forward this new methodology was incorporated into most of the process automation projects that were already in development and is a standard part of all new work that is being started.

In conclusion, the Chester County Hospital has been able to effectively use the BPM engine to manage relational reporting structures in a hierarchical database environment. By using this approach the hospital has been able to obtain aggregated information that has significantly improved its ability to oversee and manage key processes. As stated earlier, the BPM engine is being used to manage the management of processes as well as the processes themselves. This methodology should be applicable to other industries if the industry is having difficulty in obtaining key business management information and/or views on a real time basis.

Using BPM and Business Intelligence to Improve Healthcare

Jonathan Emanuele and Cynthia Mascara, Siemens, USA

INTRODUCTION

The healthcare industry has seen an expanding focus on clinical outcomes as they are increasingly tied to reimbursement and meeting regulatory requirements. Hospitals must be able to improve and report on more clinical outcomes than ever before. These demands on the health care organizations require leveraging technologies such as business process management (BPM) and business intelligence (BI) to help tackle these challenges.

WHY MEASURING CLINICAL OUTCOMES IS ESSENTIAL

Recent examples of regulatory requirements related to reporting of clinical outcomes include the American Recovery and Reinvestment Act (ARRA) of 2009 and Joint Commission/Centers for Medicare & Medicaid Services (CMS) core measures specifications. The ARRA legislation authorizes reimbursement incentives for eligible professionals and hospitals who successfully demonstrate that they are "meaningful users" of certified electronic health record (EHR) technology. [1] The ARRA requirements include the submission of reports to CMS, and both Medicare and Medicaid will provide financial incentives for meeting the meaningful use definitions.[2]

Hospitals have been required to report clinical outcomes even before ARRA. For example the reporting of core measures is an effort by both the Joint Commission and CMS to provide a uniform set of quality standards for patient care. These guidelines outline evidence-based standards for the care of patients with a particular diagnosis such as acute myocardial infarction (AMI) or heart failure (HF). In addition to meeting reimbursement requirements, following the core measures guidelines should benefit the patient and hospital in terms of decreased mortality, improved patient health status and decreased length of hospital stay. The first version of the *Specifications Manual for National Hospital Inpatient Quality Measures* was published in 2005 for reporting of patient outcomes collected in that year. The most recent version of the specifications manual is 3.2, and will be used for reporting outcomes data collected for patients discharged between October 1,

---

[1] *Meaningful Use.* (2010, March 10). Retrieved April 12, 2010 from Health Information Technology website:
http://healthit.hhs.gov/portal/server.pt?open=512&objID=1325&parentname=CommunityPage&parentid=1&mode=2

[2] *Overview of ARRA Funding, EHR Certification, and Meaningful Use.* (2010, March 15). Retrieved April 12, 2010 from HIS Office of Information Technology website:
http://www.ihs.gov/recovery/documents/Overview%20of%20ARRA%20EHR%20Cert%20Criteria%20and%20MU.pdf

2010 and March 3, 2011. These manuals provide explicit details regarding the data elements to be collected for a patient's episode of care.[3]

The ultimate goal of collecting and reporting metrics is to learn from the data and improve patient care and outcomes. Reporting requirements developed by regulatory and reimbursement agencies are designed with the goal of guiding hospitals and care providers in interventions and practices that will result in improvements in the quality of care and better clinical outcomes. The adoption of evidence-based standards of care has potential for a positive impact on the quality of patient care, which may then reflected in reporting as improved clinical outcomes.

THE TECHNOLOGY

Business process management, or workflow technology, can be used in health care to coordinate communication, send reminders, and automate tasks for staff in various roles and across a period of time. These processes can result in improved patient care, more complete documentation, and better adherence to hospital protocols.

Many healthcare information systems (HIS) send or receive messages to communicate information between systems. Traditional integration and interfaces, such as HL7 V3 Messaging Standard, have been successfully deployed for years.[4] These standards are the basis for communicating and exchanging data between health care systems and networks. For example when a patient is admitted, hospital admission/discharge/transfer (ADT) systems will send a HL7 ADT message with the A01 code outbound to other systems that may need to know about the new patient.

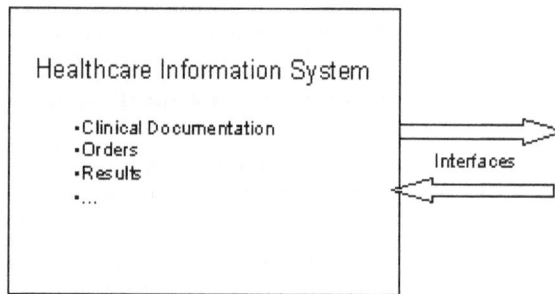

Figure 1: Traditional HIS

The need developed within healthcare systems to provide more robust coordination, orchestration, and even automation of some processes. Taking a page from other industries, the next evolution in healthcare IT was to create a healthcare information system built on a service-oriented architecture through which a workflow engine could be coupled. In this way the healthcare IT landscape exposes core functionality through events/services which workflow technology can use to drive clinical processes. Following the HL7 A01 example, the workflow concept

---

[3] *Specification Manual for National Hospital Quality Measures.* Retrieved April 12, 2010 from QualityNet website:
http://www.qualitynet.org/dcs/ContentServer?c=Page&pagename=QnetPublic%2FPage%2F QnetTier2&cid=1141662756099

[4] *V3 Messages.* Retrieved April 12, 2010 from Health Level Seven International website:
http://www.hl7.org/implement/standards/v3messages.cfm

allows information systems to go beyond communicating information about the new patient by helping to make certain that the patient's care is coordinated within and between all the systems and people involved in patient care. The combined workflow/healthcare system should be able to follow up to ensure that the admitted patient had a completed admission assessment documented in the clinical information system and has been evaluated and started on the appropriate care plans for patient problems such as skin breakdown and fall risk.

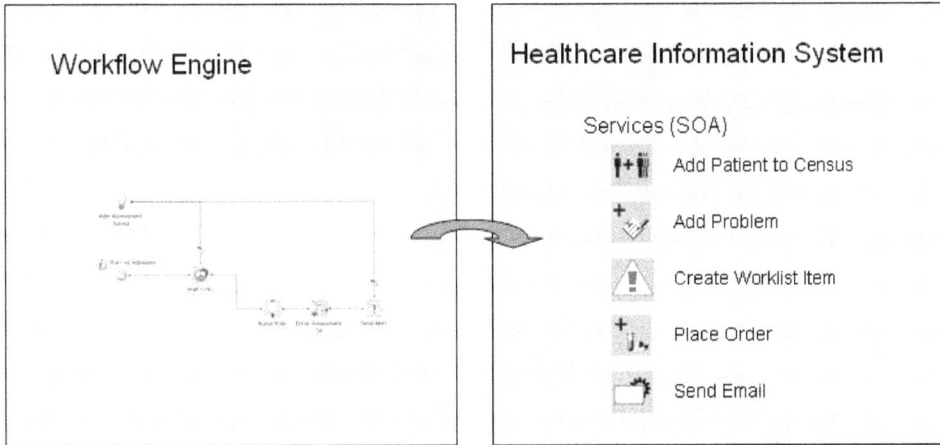

Figure 2: Workflow-Enabled HIS

Implementing a workflow-enabled healthcare system is only one aspect of an automated solution. Equally as important is the ability to evaluate both clinical and process data in a meaningful way which will enable the hospital to derive knowledge and insight into the effectiveness of their processes and where improvements may be needed.

Historically, clinical data warehouses have been a valuable medical research tool. If you wanted to look for effective medications for a certain diagnosis in a certain population, having a well-populated warehouse is invaluable. Manually performing chart reviews for any more than a handful of patients is simply too labor intensive for large-scale research.

These clinical data warehouses are typically limited to just the clinical data entered for the patient into their medical records. There is a huge amount of process data that is often not captured or not integrated into the clinical data within the warehouse. For example, the clinical data often doesn't show how many phone calls were needed, how many escalations were sent, or how much time passed. By combining the process data from the workflow engine and the clinical data from the healthcare information system, a more complete picture of the patient care practices can be developed.

The integration of healthcare information system data, workflow engine process data and reporting analytics is known as Healthcare Process Management (HPM) by Siemens Healthcare. This is the technology platform that supports an organization through process management coupled with advanced analytics. The goal of this technology solution is to support a culture of continual process improvement within health care.

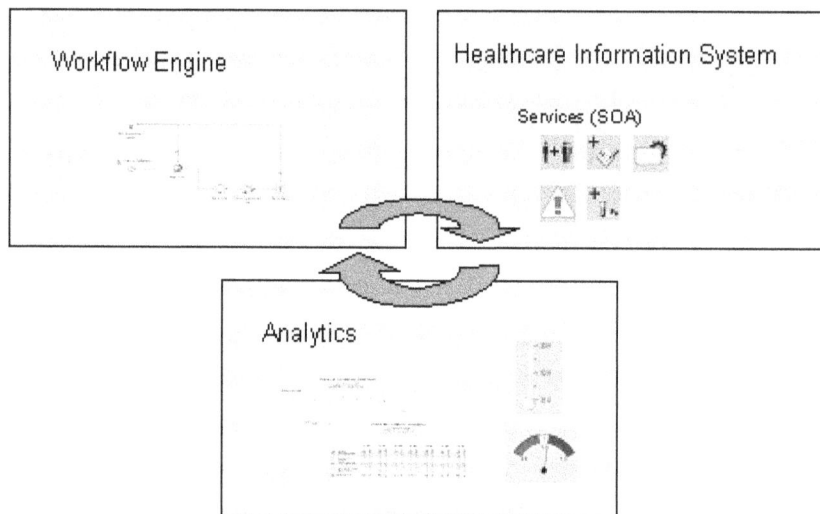

Figure 3: HPM-Enabled HIS

AN APPROACH TO MEASURING CLINICAL OUTCOMES

The Metrics that Matter program, developed by Siemens Healthcare, uses integrated workflow and analytics designed with the goal of helping providers improve clinical outcomes and report complex information for use by hospital administration and clinical leaders. This program addresses key clinical processes related to falls, pressure ulcers, acute myocardial infarction, heart failure, pneumonia and venous thromboembolism. Each process includes a workflow, an electronic clinical documentation form in the HIS and an analytics report.

The workflow template provides a standard workflow design that can be implemented by a hospital. The workflow can provide notifications such as the availability of critical results. In addition the workflow can automate portions of the care process based on hospital policy, such as the placing of consult orders. The workflow supports nursing in achieving more complete and on-time clinical documentation in a format that can be used directly by the reporting system.

The HIS clinical documentation form used along with the workflow may be a standard pre-existing form of documentation, such as a fall risk or skin assessment. The workflow can pull already charted information from these existing forms and populate a new form that is used specifically for recording information that will be reported by analytics. Examples include the specific documentation forms designed for the capture of data related to diagnoses such as acute myocardial infarction and heart failure forms.

An analytics report mines and evaluates retrospective data that is documented in one or more HIS forms. This report is used to trend clinical outcomes related to a specific metric, and can be used to compare performance to hospital benchmarks as well as national benchmarks. Reports can be scheduled for generation at predefined times or can be generated on demand by clinical and administrative personnel. The report specifications include details defining the patient population inclusion and exclusion criteria, including such factors such as the time period, age, diagnosis and other defined criteria specific to the metric being reported.

One example of the Metrics that Matter program is related to heart failure core measures. A workflow is implemented that identifies potential heart failure patients based on data entered such as admitting diagnosis and starts monitoring for new data such as test results and clinical care orders related to this diagnosis. The workflow queries the HIS database at twenty-four hours after admission to retrieve certain information then automatically pre-populates the heart failure documentation form with this information, precluding a clinician from having to look the information up and value the appropriate fields on the form. One example is that the workflow checks to see if the patient is a smoker, and if so, has smoking cessation education been documented. The corresponding fields on the heart failure form are then populated by the workflow. All information populated on the form by the workflow is presented to clinicians for validation.

Some data that must be included in core measures reporting is not available in the database as discrete data. An example is the HF-2 measure, which includes an evaluation of the left ventricular systolic (LVS) function. The information that must be reported for this measure is whether a heart failure patient has documentation in the hospital record that the LVS function was evaluated before arrival, during hospitalization, or is planned for after discharge. Since this documentation is often done by physicians on a paper progress note in the patient chart it most likely will not be available in the electronic patient record as a discrete data element. In these cases a clinician such as a nurse or case manager, or possibly a chart abstractor, will document the information in the electronic heart failure clinical documentation form. The combination of automated data retrieval by the workflow and manual documentation provides a complete and efficient manner for collecting the data elements in the EHR for use by business intelligence for reporting metrics data.

A workflow is also used to promote quality care and possibly improve outcomes. After the initial population of the heart failure form, the workflow sends notification alerts to the nurse, case manager and abstracter informing them that the patient is identified as having heart failure. This notification is an alert in the healthcare information system that includes a link to launch the heart failure documentation form that has already been started by the workflow. The workflow sends other alerts also designed to improve outcomes, including reminders to provide smoking cessation education or discharge instructions if not documented.

Finally an analytics report is used to retrieve data on discharged patients with a diagnosis of heart failure. The report collects and analyzes data from the heart failure documentation form as well as other patient data in the electronic patient record and other information systems.

It is expected that an integrated design process for workflow, documentation and reporting can lead to both improved clinical outcomes as well as more efficient and effective reporting. Initial feedback related to this implementation approach is positive, and actual results are expected to be available in late 2010.

Section 2

The Business Value of BPM and Workflow

BPM-on-Demand: Fantasy or Fast Track to Agility?

Jon Pyke, WfMC Chair, United Kingdom

The automation of processes is a key enabler of the Cloud phenomena—without *process*, the Cloud remains a passive environment that undoubtedly saves you money and removes some of the operational headaches, but does little else. The Cloud without process cannot deliver on the promise of Business Technology or the Service-Oriented Enterprise. All of the thoughts and ideas around assembling applications quickly to support a business imperative simply won't happen without process technology.

However we need to be very clear; process management in the Cloud is not just about BPM Suites-on-Demand. Indeed, the term BPM-on-Demand is beginning to take on a new meaning when used in conjunction with cloud computing.

The traditional use of BPM-on-Demand is often used to describe Software as a Service that delivers a BPM Suite as a Service (BPMSaaS) much like customer relationship management (CRM) applications are delivered as a service (e.g., Salesforce.com). Both use a pay-per-usage or subscription pricing model. BPMSaaS provides a full suite of BPM lifecycle capabilities, from modeling to deployment, and on to analysis and optimization. It's a third party, Cloud-hosted alternative to bringing in a BPM Suite in-house. This approach is, without doubt, a key enabler for Cloud deployment.

But there is much more to BPM-on-Demand than would at first appear to be the case. If we take the stance that the Cloud can deliver an infinite number of business software Services to all who need them, then we need a mechanism that makes that easy to orchestrate those Services and delivers the maximum flexibility. This is where "Process-on-Demand" comes in.

Process-on-Demand means having the capability to call up business Services when needed to change or augment a process that is *already being executed.*

This capability is in intrinsic part of the Service-Oriented Enterprise. The Services we are talking about are not the usual, fine-grained ones normally associated with the SOA world. These services are far more sophisticated than simple "get data/put data" activities. What we have are Services that contain:

- User Interface
- Business Rules
- Key Performance Indicators
- Meta data

In short, we have everything that makes a self-contained application all wrapped up as a Service that can be incorporated into an end-to-end business process.

Why do I need this type of capability? In a word—*simplicity*.

The concept of Process on Demand enables you to build dynamic processes that can be changed "on demand" to meet changing business needs. This dynamic process selection provides a substantial improvement in flexibility and agility plus reduction in design complexity. But we have to see if those advantages are sufficient enough to achieve the gains in agility, scalability, and robustness to meet the ever changing needs of today's business environment.

When developing business processes it is quite often very difficult to determine what will ultimately be needed in terms of documentation, sub-processes, timing and dependencies of tasks to accomplish some given requirement. For example, in designing a process to handle an insurance claim for a traffic accident, the analyst may know that the customer will need to get his car assessed for repair and that a payment may or may not be forthcoming, but may not know the types of documentation (e.g., the mechanics costing, police witness reports, and hospital bills) that will potentially be required to process the claim, nor will he or she know the dynamics that determine which one or ones of possibly many documents to use.

These interrelated paths through the claim process may already have been defined by different people, in different parts of the organization as self-contained business Services or sub-processes, and may be changed frequently as the procedures and rules change. In such cases, it is not possible for the main claim process to determine, even dynamically, what particular Services to use. All the developer knows is that a particular goal is to be achieved, but exactly which Service can be used to achieve it cannot be easily determined. Nor, in fact, does the developer really care—he or she simply wants the goal accomplished in an appropriate way.

To solve this problem, we need a repository where we can keep the Services for use by the company. What differentiates these Services from sub-processes or data integration tools is that our Cloud applications know what each Service does, the circumstances in which it can be used; the goals and outcomes that are required.

In addition, each Service is tagged with the circumstances in which it can be used, defined as an "entry condition" for the process. The entry condition is a conditional statement defined over the case data and any sub-process parameters. For example, the Service "Assess mechanical condition of vehical" may be tagged with the entry condition "CarAge > 10" where CarAge is a field of the case data. Other services would be similarly tagged.

This enables us to define which required Services are available "on demand." By this means, the calling process simply needs to access a Service in the process flow, leaving it to the system to determine which business Service best achieves the goal in a given circumstance. During the execution of the process all those Services that satisfy the goal are known so that on evaluation of a value or the detection of an event, the Service that is required can be incorporated and executed one second before the transaction occurs—making each iteration of the process totally different from and previous or subsequent processes depending on the dynamics in play at the time.

Modern BPM capabilities allow us to use different Services for different goals and desired outcomes—all with no coding required.

The important point is that the condition that defines the "applicability" of the Service is attached to the Service, not the calling process. The calling process need not know or specify the selection criteria. This greatly simplifies the construction of the overall end-to-end process. The developer of the overall process need not know how many Services are available to achieve the desired outcome, their names, or the criteria that determines their use—all that needs to be known is that at least one such service exists.

This approach improves significantly the development, agility, and scalability of business processes. The main process is simple, the "happy path," and is therefore easily understood. New services can be added or removed without any change whatsoever to the calling process or processes. For example when an airplane lands at, say, London's Heathrow Airport, a sequence of events (a process) is triggered to quickly and safely prepare the plane for its next flight. The top-line process—*prepare plane*—is always the same, but the companies and individuals performing the parts of the overall process will change according to time of day, availability of components (e.g., jet fuel), next destination and myriad other reasons. The important thing is that the plane has everything done to it that needs doing—regardless of the Services used. The needed Services are changed dynamically depending on need.

So Process-on-Demand provides a simple and effective way of defining processes that completely encapsulate their definition in self-contained, semantically complete business Services, significantly increasing agility and scalability as a side effect. However, how do we handle the exceptions, and less formal tasks of the case worker? What do we do when things don't go to plan or they can't be defined ahead of time?

We all work in complex, unpredictable business environments. So to understand how process-on-demand can help we need to understand what people do. Knowledge workers have well-defined objectives and goals but how they meet them depends on many factors; availability of documentation, response from others etc. Therefore they have to keep track of their goals and their current situation, and then choosing the sequence of tasks and processes that, given the situation they are in, can accomplish their needs. In short, at each moment in time they select a process that gets them from where they are to where they want to be. And they continue to do this, even as processes fail and unexpected events occur.

It should come as no surprise to learn that the same mechanism for handling exceptions and failures and the unexpected comes into play. For example, suppose a business service has been selected to achieve a given goal. If a service fails or causes an error condition during execution, the calling process detects the event and swaps in a service designed to handle errors. If a document arrives unsigned or filled in incorrectly this can be noted and a different set of actions are initiated to complete the task in hand. As a result, applications are far more robust to exceptions, failure, and incomplete process specification than conventional BPM systems.

WEB SERVICES

Needless to say, external applications and Web Services from the cloud can also be invoked using the same mechanisms as described above. To achieve this, the cloud-based application or Web Service is considered also to be a service, differing only from others in that it is to be achieved by one or more external service providers rather than by some internal process, effectively handing off the goal to a well known trusted service partner.

Because there may be many services and methods for achieving a given goal, so there may be many providers that can deliver or make available a given service; which means that as an internal service can be selected on the basis of its applicability to the given objective so can external services be pressed into play. Process delivered on-demand makes the loose coupling of Web Services far more important to the main processes since it makes them easier to maintain, more robust and more elastic, reflecting the key benefits obtained from cloud computing as a whole.

However, the notion of process-on-demand as described here adds greatly to the robustness of Web Services applications. Conventional Web Service deployments tend to ignore the impact of possible failure of a service provider. What we have outlined here is a well-grounded method for handling such situations. If a particular service provider cannot meet its service level agreements the on-demand nature of this approach ensures that another provider will be contacted and brought into service. So if Company A cannot respond within the requisite and agreed timescales the process will turn its attention to company B and fulfil its needs from them without user intervention or even knowledge.

THE REAL BENEFITS FROM PROCESS-ON-DEMAND

What we have defined here constitutes an entirely different approach to the way we think about application development. Providing services on demand removes almost all of the complexity of handling multiple options, exceptions, change, and uncertainty—all of that is transferred from the process developer to the system. The consequences of which are dramatic. More complex applications can be built, far easier and faster simply because it is no longer necessary to encode all the special cases for dealing with a complex, unpredictable world.

In summary, the benefits of this approach are:
- Applications that can be developed far quicker
- Faster ROI and time to value
- Applications are easy to change and maintain
- Software becomes more extensible and easily reused
- Software is more robust and reliable
- Reduced complexity:
  - simple, modular components,
  - easily validated and inspected,
  - self contained,
  - accessible to both business analysts and IT developers
- Develop in bite-sized chunks.

A Generic Framework for Business Process Management

Philippe Declercq and Vincent Fauliot, CNAMTS, France

ABSTRACT

This article introduces a generic framework for business process management. It is largely inspired from BPM and other new IT standards. Functional architecture is used as a link between process definition and implementation of IT new standards, such as BPM, BI, BAM or BRMS technologies.

This framework demonstrates how BPM solutions can bring added value to business users, and allows IT professionals to quickly deliver applications corresponding to business and users needs.

This article is illustrated with real case studies, issued from our experience in the French National Healthcare Insurance. This efficient way for designing business processes and implementing them is now successfully used in some of our main projects.

BUSINESS AND INFORMATION SYSTEM OF THE FRENCH NATIONAL HEALTH INSURANCE FUND

The national health insurance fund: An actor of the social security

Created in 1945, Health Insurance General Scheme presently covers about 55 million salaried people from industry, trade and services. It notably includes Health Insurance, a term which means protection against risks of health and consequences (illness, maternity, disability and life) together with occupational accidents and illnesses. Created in 1967, the National Health Insurance Fund for Salaried People (CNAMTS) is an administrative national public establishment that manages the information system and the course of actions of the different regional and local health structures. Health Insurance was initially founded to reimburse patients for healthcare providing a reliable, quick and secured process. Following this early mission, the main production system of CNAMTS was designed to pay social security benefits while controling supporting documents afterwards.

A context undergoing majors changes: Curing better by spending better

During the last twenty years, Health Insurance experienced a deep transformation of its sector. This was due to changes that occur in social economy (demography, economic crisis...) that still threatens funding, in technology and culture through public expectation in terms of services and involvement.

These changes revolve around CNAMTS and several reforms occured between 1996 and 2004 to progressively involve CNAMTS in balancing the healthcare system by medical control of expenses. Therefore, the surpassing of its historical mission led to pursue a risk management policy for both insurance and operation.

A	B	C	D	E
Contribute to planning and management of healthcare system	Define, evaluate and promote the range of prestations	Manage contracts between interested parties	Deliver products and services of Health Insurance	Manage customer relationship

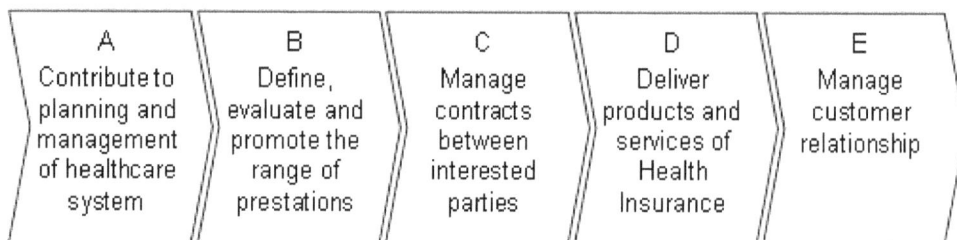

The value chain of Health Insurance: Risk management to affirm and justify the active role of CNAMTS in steering and controlling the healthcare system.

From an insurance industry point of view, Health Insurance has to enter into a contract with each actor of the health system (insured people, healthcare professionals and structures) in order to manage risk in advance, develop prevention, closely follow patients that suffer from chronic pathology, recommend the best medical practices and use of the more effective and less expensive pharmaceutical products.

From an operational point of view, this policy leads to achieve global quality of business processes all along their life cycle by means of monitoring and optimisation. This approach comes down to "an automated and exended production system". Its implementation is expected to have significant effects on the information system.

An Information system undergoing major changes: business process as the cornerstone of the information system.

The early aim of production focussed on the technical levels of the information system. Changes in social laws and health regulation, excessive business and territorial compartmentalization of information system together led to the design of applications with many successive layers (sedimentation), traditional point-to-point data links and large redundancy in data and business rules.

Such a production system, built upon the most variable foundations which are also highly responsive to changes in organisation, outsourcing or connection with new partners, was no longer able to respond to the service level of Health Insurance activities and missions. This remains true even by running new projects in certain sectors or focusing on partial recoding of applications.

Consequently it was mandatory to modernize the information system in its whole to meet the requirement of the new strategy of the establishment. That is to say extended, kept under control, fully integrated and in position to communicate with all the healthcare partners of Health Insurance.

The turning point of the modernisation occurred in the mid-2000s. It consists of strategically aligning the information system by considering it as a means to provide the operational and optimised processes that business units implement to achieve their missions and reach their goals.

It follows a strong need to represent and model business processes from business activities to application services, in order to implement them accurately using local components or COTS (Components Off-The-Shelf). Jointly, industrial processes must be set up to design, validate, bring into operation and deploy information technology products.

From this viewpoint, business processes and their functionnal representation acquire a clear and independant existence with regards to applications and infrastructure. All levels of representation take place into a new modular architecture which exposes four levels. This configuration allows us to easily and rapidly adapt to requested evolutions, taking advantage of improvements of communication and information technologies.

The upshoot of all this is that management, control and steering of business processes is the cornerstone of the information system.

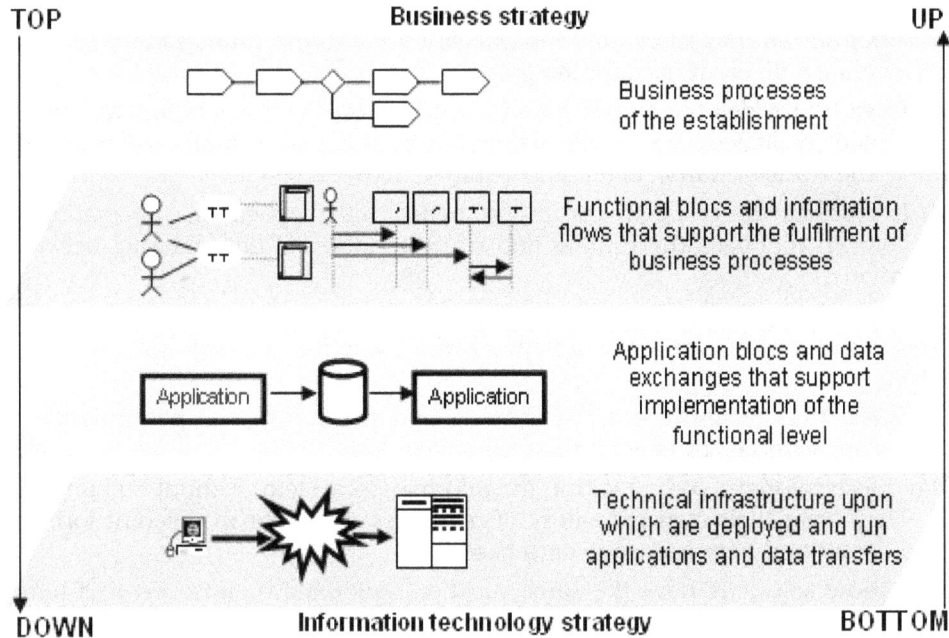

The four architecture levels of the modernized information system

These reviews which we won't discuss at any greater length as they are not specific to Health Insurance. They appear in many structures due to the ageing process of the information system facing business and technology changes.

Nevertheless, it is necessary to understand that these changes deeply impact organisation, techniques and concepts.

STEERING, MANAGEMENT AND INTEGRATION OF BUSINESS PROCESES IN THE INFORMATION SYSTEM

I have a dream!

- How quickly could we make changes if we were able to draw our business processes, display and link them graphically to make up an extended production process?
- How easy could it be to merge new business processes or modify existing ones if their display was sufficient to run and steer them?
- How agile would an enterprise become if it could simply modify its business processes to improve them without weakening them change after change?

It is this capability of directly using the modelled processes, as if drawing them directly enabled their implementation that is the key to mastering processes within the information system.

A strategic vision of business process integration

The concept of integration is one of the major challenges of the future information system of Health Insurance because it is at the heart of the coordination of its activities. Indeed, the user runs per task, company by the process, information system applications by data transactions.

For several years, different technologies have attempted to answer this need for integration. The automation of certain tasks involves using an application integration solution in place of a workflow. When activities are outsourced EAI or Workflow solutions need to work with B2B solutions (eg health insurance with the state). This implies implementations of these solutions on the other. However, experience shows that there are four categories of process management solution each meeting a different need for integration.

Workflow: It provides the orchestration of interactions with actors to manage the flow of activity affected to people within an organisation. It also provides the routing and transformation of data transmitted between people.

EAI: It provides the orchestration of interaction with applications for managing data flows. It manages the routing and transformation of data passing between applications.

B2B: It provides the orchestration of message stream between enterprises. It manages the transaction protocol between electronic information systems of two entities.

Scheduler: It is responsible for organizing and monitoring the performance of different applications, thus ensuring their scheduling.

Today these solutions coexist within the information system, without real integration. They have their own repository of processes and data in different formats and, different and heterogeneous data bases.

Yet all these solutions have the same vocation, enforcing the steering and management of business processes. This is precisely what is meant by the notion of "Business Process Management.

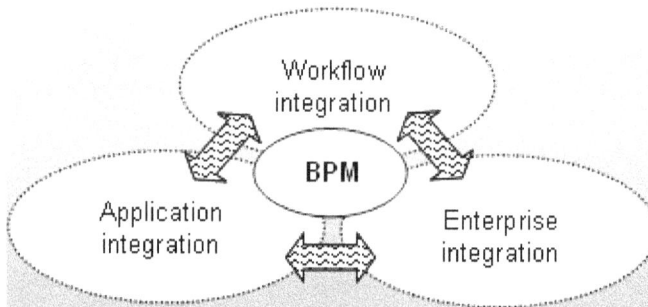

Location of the notion of Business Process Management

Thus the concept of Business Process Management includes the following ideas:
- A total management processes that cover both exchanges between applications, between companies and between people.
- The achievement of reliable and unique simple transactions such as long and complex sequences.
- A structure for the development of applications that allows the company to be more agile and faster deployment of new organizational models, new partnerships, new ways of working and new strategies.
- Deployment aware of the exact model of the process that will lead the integration and automation of activities while ensuring the changes in the processes that will be taken into account by the system software information.

The BPM appears as the golden key of strategic alignment of information system.

The functional model of business process management

There is a common functional model of management and process control, resulting from the convergence of studies and proposed standards by the standardization groups (type OSI and BPM) and functional views proposed by the editors of the relevant solutions (workflow, EAI or e-business solutions / B2B and scheduler). The business process management covers four broad sets of services that are organization, control, automation and integration of business processes.

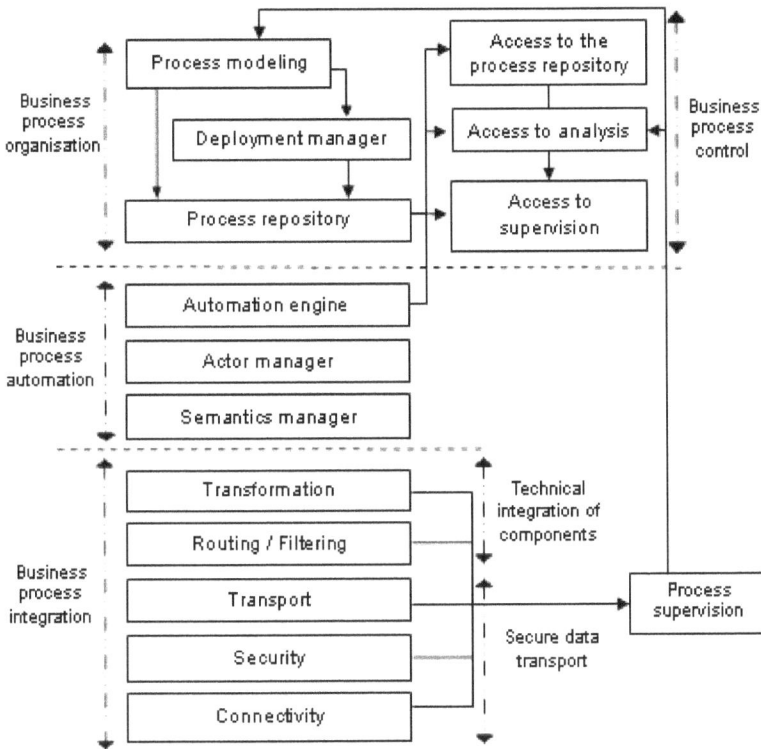

The functional model of business process management

RECONCILIATION WITH THE FUNCTIONS OF THE FUNCTIONAL ARCHITECTURE TARGET

The functional architecture target of the Health Insurance

As we know, the functional architecture is a vital link between the automated processing of information, the value chain and the organization of the institution. As such, it takes into account its requirements for modernization and adaptation to its environment. Thus, the service of business processes management is positioned within the targeted functional architecture as a component in phase with strong structuring qualities of the future strategic information system, namely:

- Decompartmentalized: information used / generated by a subset of the system for a field of activity is accessible to other areas.
- Trans-structure: non-dependent organizations in its architecture and in its general operation.
- Stable and therefore urbanised: Based on major invariant areas of activity.

- Interoperable: Allowing exchanges with other schemes, partners and actors of the social security sector.

The functional architecture that embodies this vision is notably composed from:

"Generic" functions, to a large extent independent of the missions of the Health Insurance and purposes of its activities. They are transverse and common to the whole system and contribute to its opening-up.

"Business" functions which are grouped according to a uniform pattern within extended production sets representing the main domains of the business activity model of Health Insurance.

One class of these functions is dedicated to steering and management of processes.

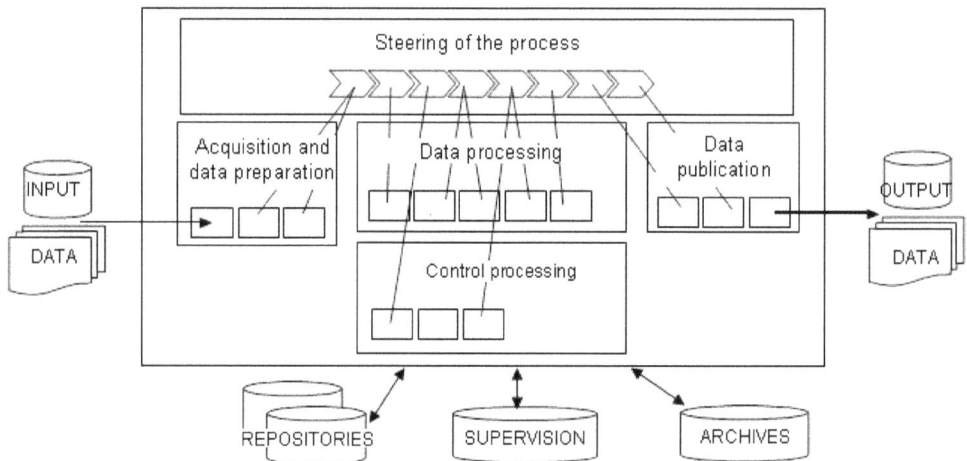

Categories of functions and dynamics of information flows within a set of extended production

The functions of steering and management of processes within a set of extended production

These functions will resume the functional model of BPM as described above in a manner appropriate to the needs of the Health Insurance. The detailed description is as follows:

E1—Organize the process: A set of functions for modeling, editing and storage of business processes, workflows and related components.

E2—Control the process: Features required for control, the detection of statement and the establishment of indicators on the process. Allows monitoring, analysis and optimization of business processes.

E3—Automate the process: Contains all the functions to initialize, to execute, stop, suspend a business process.

E4—Managing actors: In conjunction with E3 and E5 can build conversations between actors, while managing the information characterizing those involved in the process.

E5—Managing semantics: Allows management rules of translation between different formats that will be transmitted to the transformation engine. Includes the possible links between semantics, types of flows and groups of actors.

E6—Transform Data: Provide data transformation to translate messages based structures and data formats for transmitters and receivers. Based on the semantics of E5.

E7—Routing / Filtering data: Guide information inside or outside to the process by applying the selection criteria involving only the message header.

E8—Transport data securely: Manages the technical connection with the components related to the process. Ensures delivery of messages by managing all modes of communication.

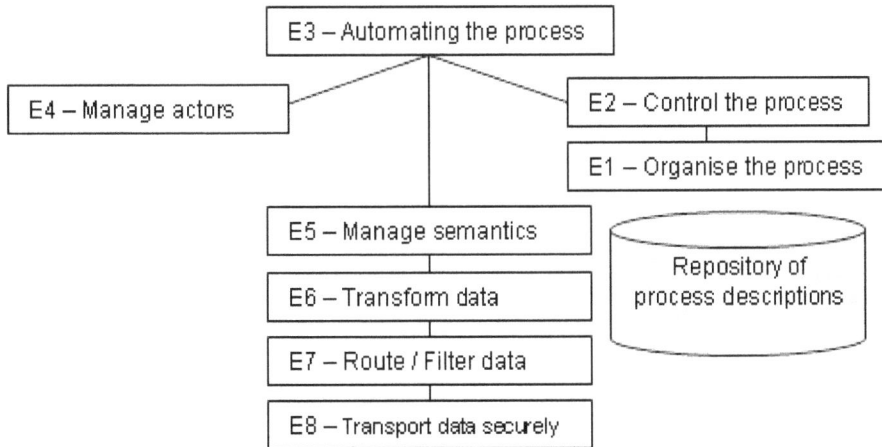

Detailed structure of the steering functions within a set of extended production

These functions are positioned in the new functional architecture within the six business blocks (set of extended production) namely Payment of benefits, Management of contract with actors, Accounting, Statistics, Customer relationship management and Health care provision. These business functions are supported by generic functions from interface and communication, rights management, data and information system administration.

Interface and communication	
A-Acquire data	B-Edit and transmit

Rights management	
C-Identify and authenticate	D-Manage habilitations

Extended production

E-manage and integrate

E1 Organise processes	E3 Automate processes	E5 Manage semantics	E7 Route / Filter data
E2 Control processes	E4 Manage actors	E6 Transform data	E8 Transport data securely

F-Prepare data for processing	G-Processing	H-Format the data processed

K-Process controls

Administration

L-Manage repositories	M-Manage and supervise IS	N-Archive

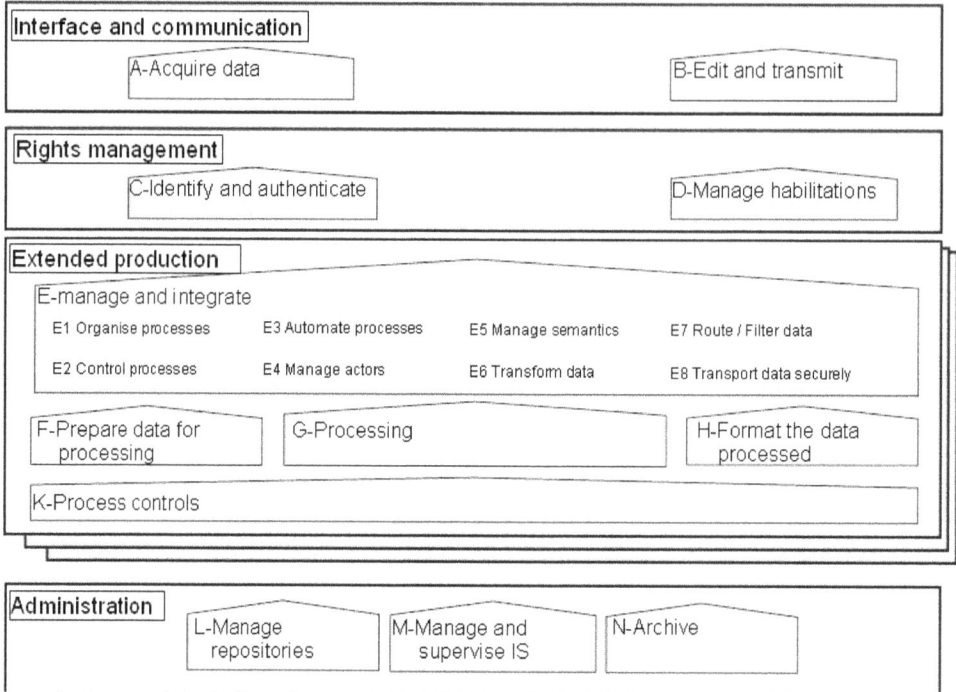

Functional architecture and Business Process Management

IMPLEMENTATION OF THE FUNCTIONAL ARCHITECTURE FOR PROCESS MANAGEMENT

Coverage of process management by families of market solutions

It is a fact that the solution that covers one aspect of BPM is sold as a solution for managing business processes. When managing and driving complex processes in production environments which combine collaboration between actors, treatments overseas and mass treatment, no solution covers all the functionality required. However, pairs of well-chosen tools like those listed above which would be added tools for analysis and monitoring (BAM / BI), data interoperability and repository management (MDM), modeling and mapping, semantic management (BRM, ETL), can cover the spectrum needed.

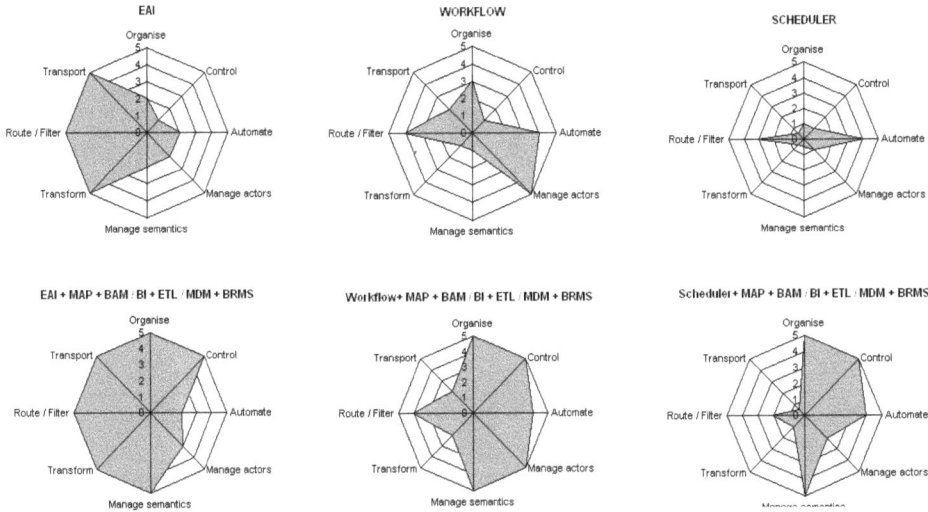

Qualitative coverage of process management and steering functions through integration of families of solution

Outlook for the information system of Health Insurance

The historical information system of Health Insurance was designed to handle large volume of data and consequently fell within the scheduler solution for managing and steering the work. While respecting legacy, the modernization of information system has therefore resulted in light of the functions identified in the functional architecture of the target by:

- The implementation of the EAI. Firstly, for the transport functionality then transforming functionality.
- The implementation of workflow for processes that require cooperation between local actors.
- The integration of the main system of production with EAI and workflow to make extended production.
- The operational preparation of a tool for modeling, simulation and mapping process nationally.
- Studies of implementing a BRMS solution in support of principal solutions.
- Exploratory projects of BAM and MDM solution.

These achievements and these approaches are carried out jointly with actions of:

- Standardization of message templates for data exchange.
- Standardization of business data.
- Streamlining and simplification of business rules.

Moreover, these initiatives are conducted in line with the functional standards and technological standards (BPMN, Web Services ...) that support the BPM vision. This ensures the sustainability of our functional architecture and gets benefits from the growing maturity and integration capacity of solutions.

CASE STUDY: THE MEDICO-ADMINISTRATIVE PROCESS FOR BENEFIT DELIVERY

French National Healthcare Insurance delivers several kinds of benefits, such as:

- Reimbursement of a medical visit,
- Coverage of transport costs due to a medical exam or a surgery,

- Compensation in case of sick leaves.

To harmonise the benefits delivery process description, a generic framework has been designed. Here is a macroscopic representation:

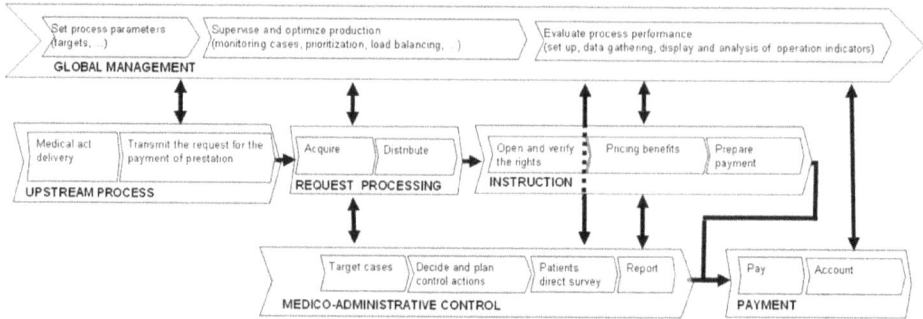

This generic process framework presents six sub-process:

- **Upstream process**: delivery of medical acts (care...) and transmission of supporting documents to Healthcare Insurance. This process is performed by an external actor (hospital, doctor...).
- **Supporting documents processing**: incoming documents processed at Healthcare Insurance including acquisition, acquittal and delivery.
- **Instruction**: executive process for supporting documents: rights checking, computation and generation of payment order.
- **Medico-administrative control**: control of the supporting documents before payment, to ensure that the corresponding act is medically as well as administratively justified. Controls are not systematic but targeted according to the national and local risk management policies. The system performs multi criteria analysis to set the control pattern.
- **Payment**: payment management process which consists of sending to bank and accountancy.
- **Global management**: this process allows actors to manage the whole medico-administrative process for benefits delivery.

We will explain how automated activities of these processes are implemented in the Information System.

We will focus on the instruction and medico-administrative processes to show how they can be functionally described following the generic model described in the previous paragraphs.

The automation level is different in the two sub-processes: instruction process is built with automatable rules while control activities are largely in the scope of human expertise.

Functional architecture of the instruction process

In the instruction process, treatments are performed by several technically heterogeneous systems (Cobol, Java Web services, NSDK...). These systems are invoked by the process steering functions in charge of the performing of the process. The following figure illustrates the sequence of function calls:

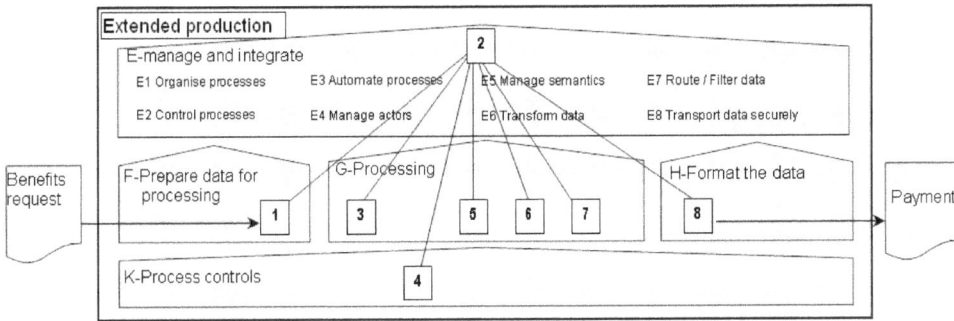

Description of performed functions:

1 – Benefits request receipt

2 – Request analysis, search for the process and performing

3 – Search the applicable contract

4 – Contract obligations checking

5 - Calculation of the reimbursement paid by the Health Insurance

6 - Calculation of fixed contributions at the policyholder's expenses

7 - Creation of a payment order

8 - Transmission of the payment order to the bank and accounting systems

All functions implemented here are automated. The manual functions of the process are the functions of recycling treatment, not shown in the figure above.

Implementation:

The receive flow (1) and transmission (8) are implemented by an EAI.

The business functions of treatment and control (3 to 7) are implemented by the existing system. We have a work in progress for redesigning this part of our system with a rules engine.

The steering functions (2) are implemented either by scheduler (for mass treatment of large volumes), sometimes by the EAI (for unit treatment). The functions used here concern transformation and transport flows from a computer system to another.

Functionnal architecture of the medico-administrive control

With the same representation of instruction process, the functions performed in the medico-administrative control process are presented in the following figure:

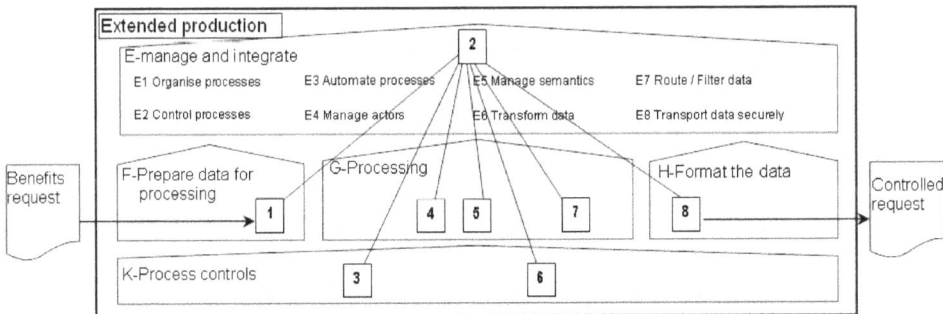

Description of performed functions:

1 – Benefits request receipt

2 – Data analysis, search for the process and performing

3 – Multi criteria analysis: Is this benefits request to be controlled?

4 – Request study and decision whether or not a control action must occur.

5 – Control action planning

6 – Control action realisation

7 – Report and conclusion of the control

8 – Transmission of the conclusion results to payment and accounting systems.

The functions 4 to 6 are mainly manual. Human expertise is required (anti-fraud unit, control provided by doctors...) to determine whether a request will be supported or not. However, the steering functions must ensure the flow of human activities associated, thanks to a workflow system.

Implementation:

The main differences with the instruction process are on the functions 3 to 7:

The function 3 is implemented by a rules engine, in charge of executing business rules for selecting requests, according to request's information and others business data of information system, in order to determine whether the request should be checked or not.

The steering functions (2) are implemented by a workflow system. There is no transformation flow to achieve, but a search of the right actor for the treatment to be performed.

This is represented by the following figure:

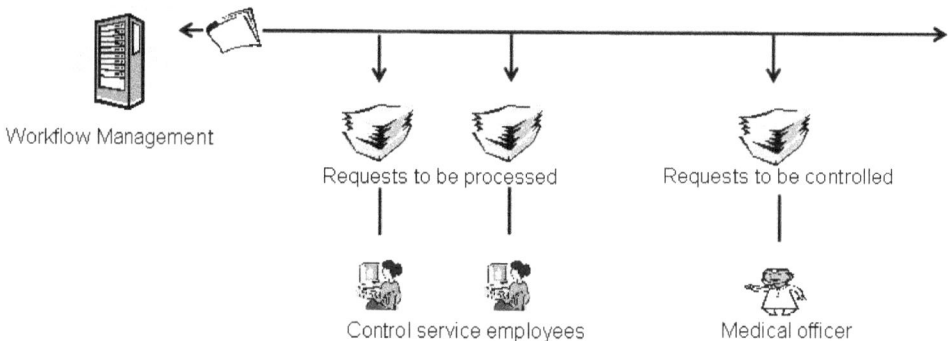

Workflow Management

Requests to be processed   Requests to be controlled

Control service employees   Medical officer

Conclusion

These works represent an important step in modernizing the information system of health insurance, by providing:

- A common description framework for all benefits requests business processes,
- A structural pattern to the organize the implemented functions, isolating the steering functions and the processing and control functions,
- Recommendations to increase the use of COTS, particularly for the implementation of steering functions.

The information system becomes more coherent and more modular, and therefore its quality and its ability to evolve are increasing.

Enterprise Process Automation– Providing the Gift of Time

Roy Altman, Peopleserv Inc., USA

PREMISE

I recently embarked on a project to improve Human Resources processes for a client. My methodology was to interview stakeholders from various points of view, from line-level managers through executives, globally. Following the interviews, I presented my observations, findings, and recommended actions. Toward the conclusion of the discovery phase, I was interviewing a senior executive from the London office; one of the highest ranking women in the financial services industry.

My parting question: "What would bring you the most value?"

She replied: "Well, more hours in the day!"

My initial inclination was to put her on a supersonic jet flying westerly, so she could be constantly gaining time each day. But after considering her statement, it occurred to me that if we could eliminate the work that can be effectively automated, it would have the effect of creating more time, and the added benefit of being able to use that time for tasks more enjoyable for the worker, and more of a value-add for the company. I called the resulting action plan: *"Enterprise Process Automation."*

OBSERVATIONS & CONCLUSIONS

My observations about this client, and many clients that I serve, was that work is disorganized. Too much time is spent doing administrative tasks. There were too many manual touch points of information. The company had many software applications in house, but they weren't integrated well. Often, Excel spreadsheets are used to bridge the gaps between point solutions. Thus the information was changed outside of controlled processes, and then uploaded into the next point solution. The solutions, therefore, worked in silos rather than as a well-integrated whole. Yet the end-to-end business processes involved touch points in several systems, so they were screaming for better integration. Procedures weren't well defined. Often managers didn't know what system to use to get the information they needed, or how to use that system if they did. Each system, in addition to having a URL starting point, required a userid/password to access. These were often forgotten or misplaced. In desperation, managers would ask their HR generalist to access the information they needed, which meant that HR was bogged down with administrative work and couldn't concentrate on being a partner to the business.

Employees are also experiencing media overload. Emails are used as the primary means of disseminating information or requesting that an action be performed. Most of the point solutions in the enterprise had an automated workflow component, and each of these prompted for an approval by sending an email. As a result, most managers received hundreds of emails a day. Sending an email to a busy manager is akin to casting a twig into a fast-moving stream from a bridge. The twig is swept away before it can be considered. Thus emails containing important information, or requesting approvals in an automated process, were buried before they could be acted upon.

Compounding this problem is instant messaging, text messages, and constant phone calls which effectively act as an interruption scheme when a prioritization scheme is needed.

The net result is everybody is working longer hours, less work is getting done, the quality of work suffered as deadlines are in danger of missed, and workers are constantly stressed, which leads to mistakes and low morale.

RECOMMENDATIONS

The recommendation was to implement a process portal. The portal focused on the end-to-end business processes, not the systems that are involved with automating parts of those processes. Thus the portal was to contain links such as: "Compensate my team" or "Promote an employee" rather than naming the compensation system or Human Resources Information System (HRIS) that actually processed those transactions. Single sign-on was to be implemented, which was integral in making the process-orientation seamless. The portal was to include personalization, so that when a user logged in the system knew who they were and what functional privileges they were entitled to. Pagelets on the portal were reserved for important announcements, and targeted based on the person, so that those informative emails wouldn't get lost. Finally, the portal was to contain an integrated worklist, so that all actions and approvals required of the employee would appear in one place and could be prioritized. The portal, implementation methodology, and underlying technologies comprise Enterprise Process Automation.

ENTERPRISE PROCESS AUTOMATION

Enterprise Process Automation (EPA) is a plan of action whereby existing assets in the company are harnessed to make work easier, allow work to be done faster, and with more accuracy, and more accountability. This is accomplished by using these assets in a more logical way, and focusing on the end-to-end business processes rather than the systems required to accomplish each part of a task. The design imperatives inherent in EPA are:

- *Flow-through processing:* Information is only entered once. Reentry of information is not permitted. Once information has been entered and validated, it will flow through to each asset requiring that information automatically.

- *Minimize mouse clicks:* Each task is accomplished using a minimum number of steps. No extraneous mouse clicks are permitted.

- *Information remains in controlled processes:* All steps in each process occur in controlled processes: information does not leave a form where it is part of a centralized system. For instance there are no downloads to Excel spreadsheets for processing; only reporting.

- *Interfaces are automatic:* Intervention by IT is not required to initiate interfaces between systems. Whether an interface is real-time, near real-time, or scheduled is a design decision. However interfaces occur when they need to occur in order to accomplish the end-to-end business process.

- **Complete audit trail:** All transformations of information, including but not limited to transaction initiations and all approvals, are stored in a system which can be reported on when needed.

- **Emails are used only for notifications:** Approvals are not accomplished by emails, but by controlled workflow processes. This provides the persistence necessary to ensure that the approval is acted upon.

- **Existing assets are leveraged to the greatest extent possible:** EPA is a methodology, not a software product. A company should use software assets that currently exist in the enterprise where possible. The objective is to use existing software better, not create extensive new software initiatives. However, there are instances where a necessary software tool is missing and must be obtained.

- **Manage worker relationships:** An organization is like an organism in that it is constantly changing. Workflow recipients and business rules require a comprehensive and up-to-date understanding of all of the worker relationships in an organization. The section on People Relationship Management will discuss this in more detail.

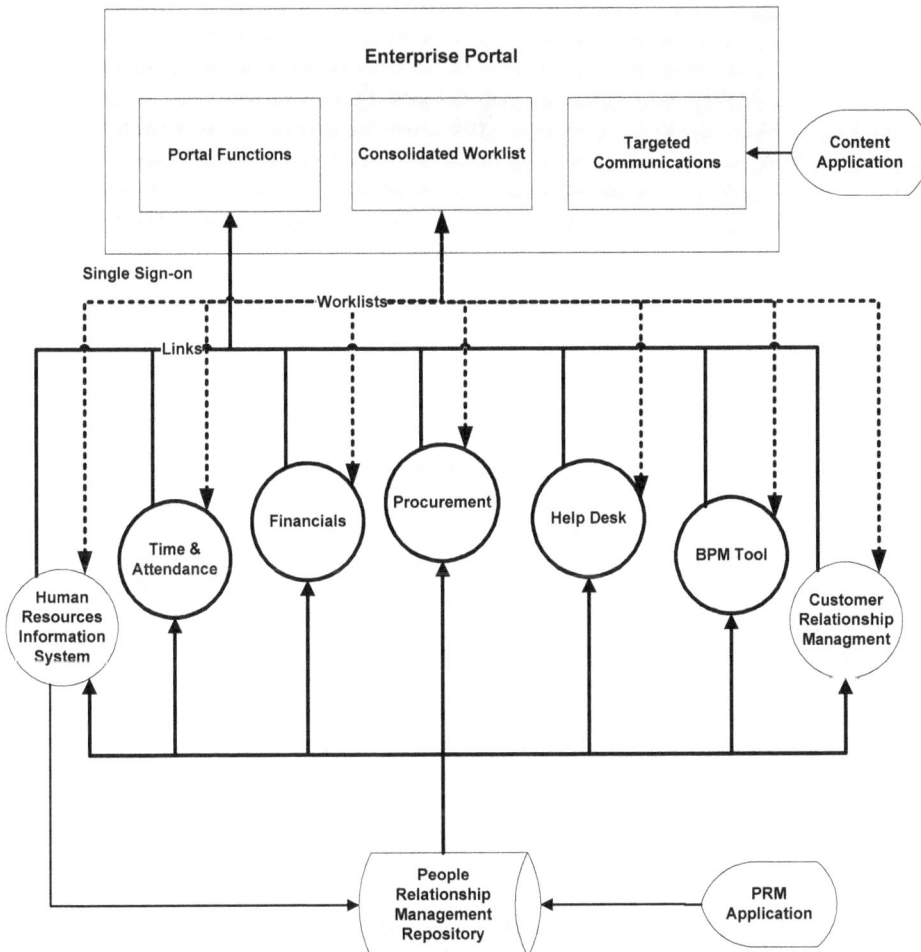

Fig. 1: Enterprise Process Automation architecture

BENEFITS

Since EPA promised the "Gift of Time," it is appropriate to enumerate the time-saving opportunities and other advantages:

- Tasks using workflow complete faster
- Work is managed better on a consolidated worklist
- Time saved locating the place to get the needed information and hunting for passwords
- Time saved searching for the email that you need to complete a task
- Consolidated and complete audit trail of all decisions
- Enhanced data quality due to flow-through processing

COMPONENTS OF ENTERPRISE PROCESS AUTOMATION

The necessary components of Enterprise Process Automation are as follows:

The Portal

A portal is a Web page that contains a link to each "business process" that a user performs. The portal should be "process-oriented" so that the user needn't be aware of the software behind the link that's processing the request.

Single Sign-On

Single sign-on is technology whereby the login credentials are passed to each software application, so that the user needn't remember the logon id and password of each software product. Not only does this allow seamless access to system functions, but it actually *enhances* security because the passwords for multiple systems are not scrawled on scraps of paper and left around the office.

Point solution application software

This is all of the application software used in the enterprise. This includes, but is not limited to: Enterprise Resource Planning, Human Capital, Payroll, Financials, Workforce Management, Talent Management, Help Desk, Customer Relationship Management, etc. There are many best-of-breed solutions on the market for any conceivable application, and each usually contains its own workflow engine, whereby transactions are routed to appropriate parties throughout the organization. Many have their own portals. Thus, each point solution views itself as the "Center of the Universe" in that it should be the controlling point for all activities in the organization. This ethnocentric approach rarely serves the best interests of the corporation. The problem is that business processes span across the "gaps" between what the point solutions provide. The gaps are bridged by knitting together the services involved in a process with workflow.

It is clear, therefore, that the "universe" has no center (just like the time-space universe). Enterprise Process Integration can be viewed as the unifying element in the corporate "universe."

Automated workflow

As stated earlier, each application point solution has its own workflow engine. Some are more robust than others, but each serves the needs of its own business problem. Typically, workflow is used for approvals of a transaction, although it can be used for collaboration on a process. Workflow is often initiated by an email. The problem with emails is that we receive too many of them to be effective. Emails are not prioritized, so we don't know which are important and which are part of the "noise" that engulfs us during the work day. Therefore, there is no way to control a process initiated by an email. The other way workflow items are organized is on a worklist. In a worklist, items can be prioritized based on due dates. Aging algorithms can ensure that the workflow item is acted on in a timely manner. Thus the process can be controlled in ways that it couldn't when initiated by emails alone. The problem with the worklist is that it exists in each point solution, so the user needs to know to access that application to check his worklist. When a user accesses several systems each day, this adds to the burden incumbent on the user to get their work done. Often, emails are used in conjunction with worklists to cover both bases. Emails are useful, however, as notifications, but not to be relied upon to control events.

"Umbrella" workflow

Although each silo has its own workflow engine, sometimes it's important to have an "umbrella workflow" engine – so that the touch points that fall in the gaps between the silos are covered. In order to do this, one must choose the most robust workflow engine available. Most point solutions have workflow engines that are specifically geared toward the process served by the application. ERP software tends to have fairly robust workflow engines. BPM tools generally have the most flexibility.

Consolidated worklist

A portal presents the user with a process-oriented view of his work. In this view, the user needn't be concerned with the system behind the link servicing parts of the business process. In like fashion, the portal should have a consolidated worklist, which contains items from all of the applications that have a workflow component. Thus the consolidated worklist acts as an electronic "to do" list, containing all items requiring the user's attention. This can then be prioritized to maximize use of a busy executive's time.

Service Oriented Architecture interfaces

A service-oriented architecture is a general term for the use of integration technologies based on widely-accepted standards. Thus, architectures can be designed so that functions within system are accessed as "services" rather than as an entire system. This very much lends itself to the portal approach espoused in this paper. Each business process presented on the portal can access services from within the point solutions that provide a set of functions involved in the business process.

People Relationship Management

People Relationship Management (PRM) is a class of software that maintains the relationships between assets in an organization (I say "assets" rather than "people" because they don't have to be human assets), and stores them in a central repository. Think of it as "Swiss Army Knife" software, a tool that can be applied to a myriad of problems. Since workflow connects people in automated processes, it's critical to identify the right people. Enterprise software (EPR, HR, etc.) only stores one company hierarchy which must be used in all business contexts. This is clearly not aligned with the business processes. For instance, the person who would approve a promotion may not be the same person who would approve a purchase or sign off on an audit. Thus, when automating these diverse applications, implementers often modify the corporate structure to fit their application. So the "master" copy is stored within the point solution, and not in a system-of-record repository, which is sensitive to changes in the workforce. Even if the workforce changes are manageable, the solution wouldn't scale to the enterprise level. Processes that are automated on a limited scale often identify the individual actors in a process, rather than abstract out to their role. For instance, new hires are routed to Cheryl, the recruitment manager, for final approval. If the company subsequently acquires a company overseas, who has a recruitment office in each country, the system needs to know who the recruitment manager is in each country. Using PRM, the automated solution could be applied to all offices immediately, thereby assisting in streamlining the merger process.

Without PRM, the possibility of broken business processes exists, if the correct recipient of a workflow item cannot be identified due to movement within the organization. Without the ability to assign business rules to groups of employees, an application needs to be implemented to handle each individual case. For example, a company can have different sales commission plans based on location, and different equity grants based on salary grade. In order to automate this, one would need to segregate groups of employees based on salary grade for the equity grants, and location for the salespeople. PRM would handle both situations without any custom code.

THE PORTAL

Evolution of portals

In the early days of the Web, portals were merely a collection of disassociated websites. As portals evolved, they took on a consistent look and feel, added personalization and search capability, and implemented single sign-on to many of the applications behind them. Thus, the portal knew the user logged in, their access rights, and their preferences. For instance, if a user signed on to the portal, it may display the Employee Self-Service transactions available to her, relevant stock quotes, and the weather in her home town. Still, the portal remained folder-dominated, meaning that she needs to know what she wants to work on, and how to navigate to the appropriate link. Current portals are more process-oriented, in that they are able to integrate the back-end applications to automate the end-to-end processes.

As they continue to evolve into more intelligent assistants, future portals will have the ability to anticipate the actions of the user by learning her work habits.

Personalization

A portal should have a degree of personalization. This means that when a user logs into the portal, the portal knows who she is, what her interests are, and what she's authorized to do. The portal should display links to all functions authorized. It may contain a prioritization scheme, whereby more commonly used functions float to the top of the list. Regardless, the links should have a *process* orientation rather than a *function* orientation, which means that the user shouldn't have to search among layers of menus to find the next function in the process. For example, a process can be: "I'm having a baby," which may comprise the following functions:

- Apply for FMLA
- Apply for State Disability
- Check company maternity and baby bonding leave policy
- Update my employment status
- Change my medical insurance coverage

- Change my dependents and beneficiaries
- Reassign my tasks to others
- Have my correspondence forwarded

A person who is in the late stages of pregnancy cannot be expected to know all of the options and steps involved in the process. The portal should guide them through all of the steps, posting worklist items for the steps that can't be concluded in the initial transaction.

Many portal products separate personalization from security, which means that the portal can display a link, but when the user takes that link he is informed that he doesn't have the proper authorization to perform the function. This is a suboptimal practice, which can be mitigated by using People Relationship Management to synchronize security with personalization.

Using single sign-on and deep links, the user is secluded from the system fulfilling the step in the business process. This can be useful as the company migrates from legacy systems, in that the link to the user remains the same even though the underlying system is changing as needed.

One of the challenges is that point solution software sometimes does not provide the deep links into the target sub-process, just a link to the solution's home page. Vendors should be apprised of the EPA strategy and encouraged to provide deep links, or ways to expose services through SOA-based methods. If not available, organizations should provide a link to the home page of the application.

Targeted communication

In today's global companies, enhancing communication is one of the greatest challenges and opportunities to convey a sense of common purpose to associates separated by great distances.

Remember how emails are swept away like a twig in a fast moving stream? Well, many of those emails contain important announcements that should not be ignored. A portal should have the ability to display targeted information to the user. Think of it as "emails with stickiness." For instance, if an employee is in the United States and benefits open enrollment is from November 1–15, there can be an announcement to that affect on the portal. However, a UK employee needn't see that announcement because it doesn't apply to him. Similarly, information pertinent to a specific business unit, job function, or even project team can be displayed as appropriate. This requires that a person administer the content for each interest area. It is important to identify the person with ownership of the portal content for the interest area, and secure his cooperation.

Consolidated worklist

The ideal state is to have a consolidated worklist because it becomes an electronic to-do list for all tasks required of a worker. This eliminates the interruption factor: when you are working on one thing and are interrupted in order to address a higher-priority item. This renders for naught any attempt at organizing the work efficiently. In the perfect world, all business process would be automated through workflow, and all workflow items would be able to be integrated so that they can be controlled on a consolidated worklist. Then, business rules can be applied to the worklist so it can be prioritized to maximize the worker's attention.

However, we know that the world is not perfect. Vendors are less likely to expose workflow items as Web services as they are more common interface items. Therefore integration of workflow items into a consolidated worklist may be difficult. Integration can occur at the data level, rather than the process-level, but that requires an intimate knowledge of the data model. In the worst-case scenario, a process can monitor the company's email server, and compare "from" address to a table that can identify the item as one that should appear on the worker's consolidated worklist.

Integration with the consolidated worklist is even more complicated than that. The first problem is inclusion of all of the necessary items. The second problem is their removal. There are basically three options as far as this is concerned:

- **Remove the worklist item as soon as the link is taken.** This ensures that the item is removed, but does not ensure that the item is "worked." You can include a link on the approval function to re-add the item to the worklist if the work on it isn't concluded.

- **Deep integration with the point solution.** This would involve a two-way Web services integration with the point solution, whereby the software would send a message to the portal to remove a worklist item once it is worked.

- **Allow the user to remove items when "worked."** This involves providing a way for the user to explicitly indicate when an item is worked.

Portal Architecture

There are many options for a portal. The major ERP software suites include a portal product. Middleware vendors provide portal products which are usually based on the emerging BPML standard. If you were to opt for this platform, BPML might be a choice for the "umbrella-workflow."

However, something as simple as a Web page with some code behind it can serve the purpose quickly and easily. An important consideration, however, is that regardless of the approach, the PRM is essential to categorize workers and to provide dynamic personalization and security.

CULTURAL CONSIDERATIONS

As with any change, the cultural challenges are often greater than the technical ones. Moving toward an automated enterprise means embracing the self-service methodology, where managers are empowered with ownership of their information. However, not all managers see it that way. Sometimes, managers are used to having administrators or their HR reps process transactions for them. They don't necessarily see automation as helpful to them, because it requires more action than was previously required. It is necessary to get buy-in from all stakeholders if the new methods are to be adopted. This is best accomplished by inclusion of the stakeholders at all stages of the discovery and implementation process.

EXECUTIVE SPONSORSHIP

The most important aspect in easing the cultural adoption curve is to obtain executive sponsorship up front. Enterprise Process Automation is the realization of a strategy through the tactics espoused in this paper. It should be a C-level executive who decides to enact such a strategy. Having a clear mandate from the CEO's office will do wonders to mitigate resistance to adoption.

MEASURING SUCCESS

It is important to measure and document the results of the project, in order to validate, make adjustments, and create a business case for progressing further down the road. Collect and publish the metrics identified in earlier phases. For those benefits that are not quantifiable, distribute post-implementation surveys to the stakeholders. This will serve to reinforce buy-in and gain important insights as to how to serve the business even better in subsequent phases.

MATURING WITH THE PROCESS

As more business processes are added to the portal, and workflow items added to the consolidated worklist, the convergence of work processes and information will reach a tipping point, and the portal will rapidly gain in importance and evolve into a hub of information and activity. The result will be an ecosystem of services available through integration technologies, and linked by workflow to humans, who make the nuanced judgments. Lifting the administrative burdens from the process will enable workers to focus on optimizing their decision-making. Thus, workers become more "human" because there is an increasing focus on the tasks for which humans are required. This will result in maximal use of resources for the company and maximal job satisfaction because the barriers to productivity are removed.

Once the pain points are mitigated, we can concentrate on ways to optimize talent by applying advanced analysis. An example is organizing tasks to maximize attention levels.

Companies typically evaluate software products based on the cost savings and risk mitigation that can result from them. However, the use of EPA with PRM offers an opportunity to change the way we manage. *An organization is a group of people who work together to produce value.* Business Process Management software has focused on the processes, but the process cannot be separated from the participants. Better understanding of the way people interrelate in an organization can drive a radical shift in the way relationship-based assets are managed; and provide illumination into the way humans interact.

CONCLUSION

The techniques espoused here are by no means a "magic wand" which will cause all problems in the enterprise to disappear. Try as you might, magic just won't work. Despite notable controversy, reengineering business processes is still more art than science. And like an artist, one should try to perceive the negative space in a business process—the aspects that should be there but aren't, and the aspects that are there but shouldn't be; and seek to make that perception a reality.

Transforming Security through Enterprise Architecture and BPM

Christine Robinson, Christine Robinson & Associates and Daniel Turissini, Operational Research Consultants, USA

ABSTRACT

This unified Enterprise Architecture (EA), Business Process Management (BPM), and security approach offers the potential to radically transform security on all levels, providing leadership and practitioners alike the tools to benefit from a strategic to a granular level. Security often suffers from cultural barriers, inadequate funding, insufficient attention, bolting it on the back end, lack of understanding, lack of uniformity, and many more ills. This approach enables organizations to plan and implement security throughout an enterprise and beyond through harnessing EA frameworks and integrated business process management (BPM) software to enable the EA.

An EA/BPM approach provides business-rule driven process automation that offers visibility, access across stovepipes, accountability, and transparency into security operations according to a need to know. EA/BPM offers leadership and security specialists alike the potential to cut across stovepipes to see the true security posture. This applies to governance, planning, design, and operations. Improved security could potentially help facilitate telework and cloud computing adoption. Cyber security, physical security, biometrics, business continuity and disaster recovery, and more can benefit from rule-driven process automation that provides the ability to automatically anticipate, defend against, and create new processes in real time. EA/BPM can address some of the unique characteristics of the Next Generation U.S. Airspace, energy, and health care, which are some of the U.S. and world's largest information-sharing environments and integral parts of the country's critical infrastructure.

INTRODUCTION

Security, and particularly cyber security, represents some of the most critical challenges to our personal security, our homeland security, and national defense. Although much attention and detail focuses upon various elements of problem definition and resultant solutions, we have failed to develop effective solutions that our present day business practices and technologies can provide. The skills and the technologies exist today so it is a matter of how we put them all together. How powerful would it be to capture institutional knowledge in software, manage regulatory and legislative compliance activities, pre-define human and system responses that can anticipate and defend against a security threat, and offer the ability in real time to modify or create new processes to address a different and perhaps more insidious threat? By applying enterprise architecture frameworks using rigorous Business Process Management (BPM) and BPM software, security solutions can become far more powerful, focused, precise, flexible, and more effective. The precedent lies in the powerful capabilities and BPM's proven history of success. This approach can offer transparency, access, and visibility into operations for leadership and practitioners alike.

SECURITY DEFINED

Security covers a broad spectrum of disciplines. Each segment of security has legions of "specialists" with associated technology solutions often little understood by people in other disciplines. For example, the Transportation Security Agency, responsible for safeguarding U.S. transportation systems, must manage myriad security systems, has a presence at 457 U.S. airports, screens two million people per day, and employs nearly 50,000 security officers. Security requirements cross myriad disciplines, involve many complex processes, and necessitate multiple technology solutions.

Security by definition is "something which guarantees or safeguards." Information Systems Security is defined as "The protection of information systems against unauthorized access to or modification of information, whether in storage, processing, or transit, and against the denial of service to authorized users, including those measures necessary to detect, document, and counter such threats." That which is to be guaranteed or safeguarded is primarily the information asset residing within an enclave, enterprise, database, desktop, laptop, etc. Thus, Information Security applies to anyone using a computer, PDA, cell phone, and so on. In other words, it applies to most everyone in American society today.

There are numerous facets that wage a continual tug-of-war, such as protection, privacy, availability, and so on. Today we find the convergence of Cyber, Information and Physical security is necessary to protect against the plethora of unethical individuals using malicious code to wreak havoc daily. The news bombards us with reports of viruses and worms spreading to businesses, grids, networks and households alike. The vulnerabilities are both physical and logical access points, each with protections that can be defined by business processes.

The target we should be striving to attain is the highest level of security, without sacrificing availability to authorized parties, and without encroaching upon the civil liberties under which our country was founded and has operated for over two hundred years. Moreover, it is critical that we understand that we cannot allow technology to be the driving force behind the policies governing their use. Instead, it must be common sense, sound policies, prudent laws, all translated as business rules and managed by business processes that dictate how technology can complement and augment the safeguards and protections. Too often, a new technology is devised and we make the mistake of compromising our processes and procedures so that the new technology can be used. This is analogous to building a brand new automobile in order to properly accommodate a newly-invented radio. If a technology or device requires the comprehensive reconfiguration and reconstruction of the existing resources, policies and business processes, it is not a proper fit.

Security in our society is complicated by people skeptical of universal identification credentials containing vital personal information. Or fears of personal data residing in a database somewhere that can potentially be hacked, causing data to be compromised. Unfortunately, in the haste of the Internet boom, vast amounts of personal data were willingly and/or unwittingly made available by individuals themselves, marketing groups, businesses, even some government agencies along with a host of others. Now, we are left with trying to lock-down as much as possible while simultaneously reeling back in that which has escaped. Society's collective sense of feeling jaded by the Internet is quite well founded. However, cyberspace was never intended to afford privacy. On the contrary, the Internet was devised for the open sharing of information to anyone and everyone with a connection. Nonetheless, this is the state we are currently in, and some measure of privacy is still attainable.

EA AND BPM DEFINED

Enterprise Architecture (EA), simply defined, means all of the business processes and supporting technologies that enable an organization to perform its mission. The Federal Enterprise Architecture (FEA), Department of Defense Architecture Framework (DODAF), federal segment architecture (FSAM), The Open Group Architecture Forum (TOGAF), and other frameworks provide powerful sets of tools with which to assimilate information, draw relationships between various elements, and create roadmaps for improvement. EA can provide the structure within which an organization can build views of its current state business and technology architectures upon which to design future states that enable an organization to achieve its mission and strategic objectives. These frameworks allow an organization to optimize existing structures, incrementally retire those that are no longer suitable or as efficient as they need to be, and build new ones that better enable the organization to succeed and thrive.

BPM rule-driven process automation can be a powerful enabling mechanism to carry out the organization's priorities as established through the EA. BPM can operate independently of and integrate with different professional disciplines and systems across the enterprise. Incorporating BPM can also help identify and fill the gaps between stovepipes whose boundaries so often seem impossible to cross.

In the following discussion, we apply EA with BPM (business rules and business process automation) to security, which has tremendous potential to become an emerging and common practice.

POTENTIAL BENEFITS OF AN EA AND BPM APPROACH

BPM has proven to be of great value in industry and government. According to the Gartner Group, BPM is becoming more and more often a component of most major IT implementations. An EA/BPM approach can transform security and EA from necessary evils and compliance exercises into strategic resources.

A BPM approach can help establish "defense-in-depth" crossing organizational boundaries by cutting across stovepipes throughout an enterprise and beyond to supply chains, customers, governments, and others. This approach offers a means to manage highly detailed security processes rolled up to provide leadership with a current picture of the EA. This will enable leadership to manage more effectively and in a more timely fashion, based on strict audit trails for every action.

Building security up-front into all the processes and technologies using BPM within an EA framework drives out human inefficiency, avoids differences of opinion during critical operations, and reduces or eliminates lag time caused by waiting for instructions to act. BPM can automatically initiate predefined responses to anticipated and unanticipated threats that lock down network infrastructure access, direct human resources and other assets, and provide auditable access to systems based on business rule-driven processes.

An EA/BPM approach offers the benefits of capturing and defining best security practices that may vary widely between organizations, optimizing them, standardizing across communities of interest, and sharing proven practices versus reinventing the wheel at each event. This is particularly true for some of the largest information sharing environments such as the Next Generation U.S. Airspace, health care, and energy.

BPM offers the potential to collect activities and information across multiple security disciplines where information collected solely through stove-piped security systems cannot effectively indicate a threat.

STEPS FORWARD IN U.S. FEDERAL GOVERNMENT

The U.S. federal government has taken great strides forward in revising how it requires agencies to address security. The National Institutes of Standards and Technology (NIST) and Department of Defense (DOD) have worked together to develop a common catalog of security controls that establish interagency trust partnerships. Establishing common standards and guidelines facilitates auditable transparency.

EA provides a common understanding for the enterprise and sets the stage for identifying and mitigating duplication and waste. NIST Special Publication (SP) 800-37, Guide for Applying the Risk Management Framework to Federal Information Systems, revised in February 2010, describe how to integrate security throughout the system development life cycle (SDLC) with an integrated life-cycle approach. The Federal Chief Information Officer's Council and the Federal Enterprise Architecture also created the Federal Identity, Credential, and Access Management (FICAM) Roadmap and Implementation Guidance.

Federal (DoD and NIST) guidelines also required certification and accreditation (C&A) before placing a new system or subsystem onto a network or into service; that includes quarterly security reporting and full audit refresh every three years after Authorization to Operate (ATO) is granted. Some systems require more frequent audits and subsequent controls and audits in the case of upgrades. While the intention is to ensure that security is addressed up-front into all of the business processes and technologies, unfortunately, in practice, it has placed security on the back-end that are noted as outstanding findings to be addressed during Interim ATO operations.

The revised Security and Privacy Profile that links security to the FEA could dramatically change how the federal government integrates security and privacy throughout an agency's architecture. However, it does not yet appear that anyone in the federal space has successfully connected EA and BPM to manage security governance and operations.

CHALLENGES TO PROVIDING IMPROVED SECURITY

We face immense challenges to properly safeguard our personal, corporate, and government identities and assets, some of the most troubling include:

- Less than effective leadership access, visibility, and transparency into operations,
- Stovepipes composed of highly focused and highly skilled product experts who have little or no understanding of how all the components should work together across the enterprise,
- Targeting by individuals and nation-states who increasingly intrude and steal personal, corporate, and government assets,
- Unnecessary complexity causing many people to avoid security practices or don't even know where to begin,
- Hesitance to publicize or alert authorities about security threats for fear of the consequences of adverse publicity,
- Immunity to the constant news about adverse events,
- Underfunding and understaffing or wrongly applied funding and wrong staffing,
- EA which struggles to prove it is more than a very costly compliance requirement but adds real value to the organization,
- Organizations are overwhelmed by the amount of data to assimilate and process,
- Existing culture of damage control; buy more and add it on, and,
- Overall reluctance to share data and knowledge about operations for a variety of reasons.

OPPORTUNITY TO TRANSFORM SECURITY OPERATIONS THROUGH EA AND BPM

Governance

An EA/BPM approach can help manage conformance to government mandated security requirements such as the Federal Information Security Management Act (FISMA) for the U.S. federal government, Sarbanes Oxley for the financial industry, and Health Information Portability and Accountability Act (HIPAA) of 1996 for health care. For example, one of the leading BPM software packages is used to automate Sarbanes Oxley internal governance processes for testing and security. Agencies could use BPM to capture and automate many of the massive number of processes associated with conforming to FISMA requirements for both security and business continuity and disaster recovery. This could include everything from automatic notification to interfacing disparate systems and running test scenarios.

Security operations

An EA/BPM approach building security up-front into all the business processes and technologies can enhance both normal operations as well as automatically set in motion contingency operations using rule-driven predefined processes. Using BPM within an EA framework to help run enterprise security operations can help provide transparency and visibility across different stove-piped disciplines as different as cyber security to biometrics and identity management. This approach can facilitate vast opportunities for optimizing, sharing across domains, standardizing, and many other possibilities.

EA/BPM can facilitate information-sharing environments with multiple instances of BPM in different organizations under a "federated environment." Federated solutions would be especially useful in large information-sharing environments such as the Next Generation U.S. Airspace, energy, and health care where security issues compound exponentially.

Cyber security

We are constantly at risk from cyber threats that do incredible damage to our personal information, economy, intellectual property, government systems, and potentially anything else that is connected to the internet or accessible through listening devices.

For example, on April 30, 2009, a hacker broke into a Commonwealth of Virginia system containing nearly 36 million patient prescription records, eight million patient records and demanded $10M in ransom with a note reading "ATTENTION VIRGINIA I have your sh**! In *my* possession, right now, are 8,257,378 patient records and a total of 35,548,087 prescriptions. Also, I made an encrypted backup and deleted the original. Unfortunately for Virginia, their backups seem to have gone missing, too. Uhuh."[1]

Cyber security has its own unique sets of complications. Who is in charge of cyberspace? Cyber threats can develop quickly and instantly propagate around the world. The barriers to entry are low as people around the world have access to computers and handheld devices capable of cyber crime. Legions of highly-skilled people around the world focus solely on using their knowledge and expertise for illicit or malicious purposes. Some cyber criminals lease out networks of computers that they have taken over around the world, known as Botnets, to other cyber criminals. Malware, viruses, trojans, and other problems may appear undetectable and only become apparent when they are activated. Preventing those needing to access websites from obtaining access by performing Denial-of-Service attacks cause untold economic damage and other hardship.

An EA/BPM approach can provide predetermined rules and processes that can anticipate and instantaneously respond to cyber and other threats. Linking up-to-the-minute information coming from the SANS Institute and other resources about new cyber threats could allow BPM to automatically notify personnel and other resources that a new threat exists and that the organization will need to develop the steps to mitigate the situation. An EA/BPM approach could automatically initiate processes by which individuals and organizations could take series of steps to troubleshoot and correct problems without having to figure out what to do and who to involve each time a new threat occurs.

Another powerful application for which an EA/BPM solution might be appropriate is the public/private partnership framework on cyber security that Riley Repko, senior advisor to the Air Force for cyber security, is actively advocating across government, industry, and academia. Our current practices inhibit our ability to quickly respond to threats that may instantly propagate around the world, while the U.S. may take months or even years to develop a

---

[1] Thomas Claburn, "Virginia Health Data Potentially Held Hostage," Information_Week, (May 4, 2009).

new solution operating through the current military-industrial complex. Riley Repko said, "We need an agile method to engage the adversary both on the operational and strategic levels to know how he thinks and how he acts and, because we are often reactive, we need to have access to all capabilities to enable us to come up with a solution in a real-time environment. We need access to knowledge, resources, tools, and innovative thinkers to build mission assurance solutions that are in synch with the adversary with which we are dealing. We have to have awareness, access and the ability to influence this domain. These need to be dynamic and change as our adversaries change."

John Toomer, Chief, Cyberspace Operations Division, Deputy Chief of Staff for Plans and Operations for the Air Force said, "There is no CEO for this domain. This domain demands global collaboration between government, industry, and academia. We must have process in order to perform it."[2]

To meet this need, BPM offers the potential for helping create a new culture of collaboration for this domain to quickly seek out prime intellectual capital from private industry, academia, government, private individuals, or major corporations who can quickly create solutions. BPM has the potential for managing the end-to-end business rules and processes for the public/private partnership Riley envisions.

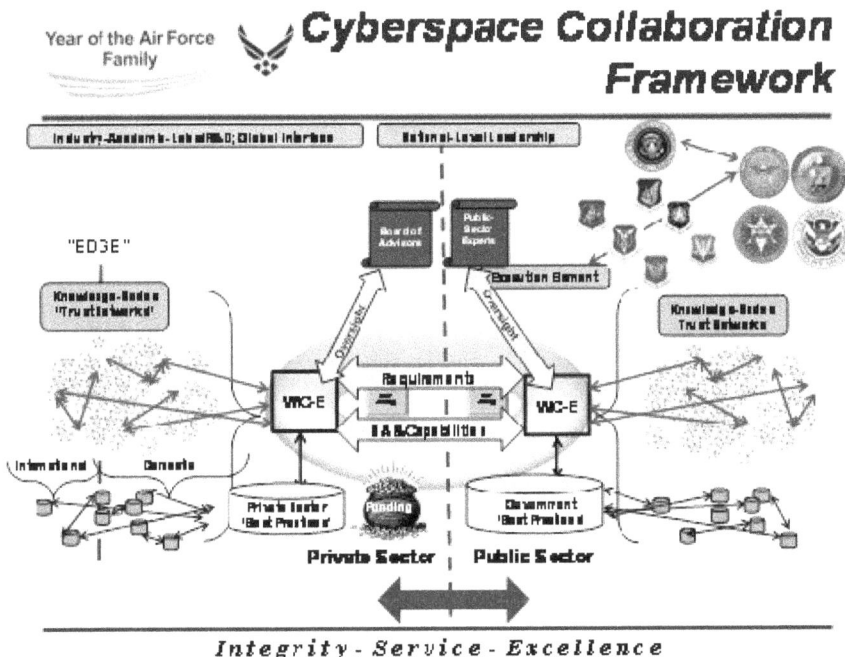

Figure 1: Riley Repko's concept for public/private partnership

---

[2] Riley Repko, John Toomer, Personal interview, 23 April 2010.

Identity Management and credentialing

Strong Identity Management and credentialing entities involved in transactions over the Internet provide the foundation for "trust." These entities include, but are not limited to, individuals, devices, application servers and software code. The governance structure under which to manage entity identity and assign trusted credentials requires a rigorous BPM definition and BPM automation. This can help ensure a highly-scalable, secure, auditable solution set, whereby participating parties can authenticate and validate the credentials issued to entities from various organizations and individuals with whom they desire to do electronic business. BPM rule-driven process automation can help develop a federated model trust defined by agreements, standards and technologies that make identity credentials portable across many organizations.

Leveraging rigorous BPM can enable participating organizations to achieve strong, and interoperable, identity verification and authentication based on trust credentials that authorized organizations provide. Because identity management and credentialing is specifically separate from access rules (discussed later in this paper), federated identity, based on BPM, can transcend verticals and stovepipes. That is to say, multiple communities of interest (e.g., Health, Energy, First Response, and many others) can reap substantial benefits from a well-designed federated identity system(s). In a federated system, each participating organization maintains or controls its own data store of enrolled entity data sponsored by that organization. Privacy and security are maintained because minimal identity information is held centrally or maintained in the infrastructure except in the employee's host organization domain server and each organization is compelled by the governance agreements to maintain the appropriate levels of assurance and controls on their participating systems[3].

At the present time, the U.S. Federal Government has defined four recognized levels of trust, where each level is defined by two distinct processes; one that defines the vetting process that is accomplished prior to issuing a credential; and the second defines the standards for the data, its cryptographic protection, and the standards and specifications for the credential itself. The current Government sanctioned nomenclature for "Levels" is numerical (i.e. 4, 3, 2, 1)[4]. Applying rigorous BPM to these definitions can enable government agencies, first responders, and industry partners to reliably authenticate the identity of individuals who seek access to both physical and logical assets in each other's environment. In all cases, however, the privilege or authority actually granted is a decision of the cognizant system owner/manager.

Based on each application owner's Business Processes, this would support access to applications handling sensitive value information based on the ap-

---

[3] The Federation for Identity and Cross-Credentialing Systems (FiXs) foundational document suite.

[4] NIST SP 800-63, Electronic Authentication Guideline, <
http://csrc.nist.gov/publications/PubsSPs.html>

plication owner's assessment. For example, applications may accept level 3 credentials for:

- Non-repudiation for small and medium value financial transactions other than transactions involving issuance or acceptance of contracts and contract modifications
- Authorization of payment for small and medium value financial transactions
- Authorization of payment for small and medium value travel claims
- Authorization of payment for small and medium value payroll
- Acceptance of payment for small and medium value financial transactions

However, in the case of a higher level credential, aligned with Homeland Security Presidential Directive 12 (HSPD 12)[5], may be appropriate for access which requires a higher degree of assurance and technical non-repudiation:

- All applications indicated above, plus
- Mobile code signing
- Applications performing contracting and contract modifications

By trusting federated credentials at multiple levels, application owners and those concerned with physical security can make sound access decisions based on established Business Processes and dynamic threat environments. A recent DoD pilot "to determine the policies and operating rules governing the use of 'certified' identity credentials issued by a non-DOD, Industry-based organization could be used in a federated manner, and accepted within the DoD, for identity authentication purposes. Upon affirmative authentication of the individual's identity, the credentials could then be utilized to make decisions, within the existing DoD infrastructure, for granting access privileges (authorization) for both physical and logical applications, consistent with the 'rules' of the facility or application owner."

The pilot "proved that the technology and processes are in place to utilize a 'federated model' for certified identity credentials issued by non-DoD issuers to contractors and to electronically verify the identity of those credential holders who were seeking access to designated government assets; as well as, access the SPOT application for enrollment purposes. Setting up the interoperable infrastructure, issuing the credentials, and using the credentials as prescribed by the requirements of the pilot posed no problem and proved very successful. However, the issues with policy, and existing DoD operating rules were major stumbling blocks towards achieving the goals set forth for the pilot. The major outcome of the pilot was a reaffirmation that DoD has a scalable enterprise solution capable of identifying and tracking contractor

---

[5] HSPD 12, dated August 27, 2004, entitled "Policy for a Common Identification Standard for Federal Employees and Contractors" which directed promulgation of a federal standard for secure and reliable forms of identification for federal employees and contractors. In March 2006, the National Institutes of Standards and Technology (NIST) issued Federal Information Processing Standards 201 (FIPS 201) for Personal Identity Verification (PIV) of federal employees and contractors. The PIV standard consists of two parts – PIV-I and PIV-II. PIV-I satisfies control objectives, including enrollment requirements, of HSPD 12.

assets authoritatively and in near-real-time, if the DoD can resolve the internal discrepancies by the major DoD stakeholders over policy and operating rules issues."[6]

Federated BPM encourages maximum participation among industry at-large to adopt this common set of standards to create a consistent, seamless, and secure operational framework and avoid the disruption and risks of implementing differing internal practices and platforms. The overall objective is to establish a secure and interoperable "Chain of Trust" for all members (including contractors, delivery and repair personnel, transport workers, law enforcement, first responders and others, needing access to facilities). The BPM documentation must provide the specific requirements for the vetting of sponsored individuals requesting credentials within specific market/ functional venues.

Access privileges

Identification and Authentication (I&A), and resulting non-repudiation, can occur in several ways. They vary in cost, sophistication and resistance to spoofing. The need to achieve a reasonable level of authentication and non-repudiation is raised by public expectations, the Government Paper Elimination Act, the Privacy Act and local policies and regulations.

Among high assurance communities, Public Key Infrastructure (PKI) has been implemented and policy exists to meet information and assurance requirements (I&A). The credentials used (e.g., ACES[7] FiXs[8], DoD PKI[9], and ECA[10]) can be issued to citizens, government employees, vendors, contractors and members of the Armed Forces. Other means of credentialing exist within the same communities, but there is no interoperability among them, within or outside public-private key technology. Those who cannot afford the up-front cost of PKI, are intimidated by the questions they cannot answer, or do not seek to be Information Technology "pioneers", await introduction of a government-wide solution.

It is the purpose of this paper to introduce the beginnings of an I&A solution, by defining a solid BPM framework and then steadily improving upon it such that it continually provides more functionality with time and experience. This is accomplished by implementing various authentication schemes that represent a spectrum of confidence and elaborateness, providing "users" a one-time access as a registered subscriber. While there can be several specific authentication mechanisms in place, authentication itself does not assure

---

[6] Consolidated Final Report, Synchronized Pre-deployment Operational Tracker (SPOT) Interoperability Engineering, Integration, and Operations Support, CONTRACT NUMBER: HC1028-08-D-2006, Task Order: E200025.00, dated 31 October 2009

[7] Access Certificates for Electronic Services (ACES) Program <http://www.gsa.gov/Portal/gsa/ep/contentView.do?contentType=GSA_DOCUMENT& contentId=21578>

[8] The Federation for Identity and Cross-Credentialing Systems (FiXs) < http://www.fixs.org/about>

[9] Department of Defense Public Key Infrastructure (DoD PKI) <http://iase.disa.mil/pki/>

[10] External Certificate Authority (ECA) PKI Program <http://iase.disa.mil/pki/eca/>

access unless the party at the receiving end recognizes and trusts that manner of authentication.

Processes that leverage existing methods of authentication can be used to allow organizations already connected by the Internet and should be considered before exercising unique and costly I&A policies and mechanisms. Once we begin using BPM for security, subscribers can develop increasingly mature policies to ensure that those entitled gain access to their enterprise resources while facilitating trusted communications with their partners and customers. Adoption would also expedite development of an increased number of standard authentication methods with confidence that can only increase with use.

Technology is available today with a design that is guided by standards, such as the Liberty Alliance (Kantara)[11]. "The Liberty Alliance's vision is one of a networked world in which individuals and businesses can more easily interact with one another while respecting the privacy and security of shared identity information" [12].

By leveraging commercially available modules that address initial specific I&A needs and optimizing response time to application servers relying on Internet accessibility, organizations can rely on multiple federated credentials to service and attract many communities of interest. The can be deployed as an evolutionary approach consisting of a repository to store user information, an on-line subscription module (providing level 1, 2, 3 and 4 credentials), a credential validation module, and a relying party interface module. As depicted in Figure 1, the components pull and cache information from the Internet so that relying applications can draw on this information with confidence.

---

[11] http://kantarainitiative.org/

[12] From the Liberty Alliance web page www.projectliberty.org. The Liberty Alliance is a consortium of over 160 corporations, which are producing, published specifications. Their goal is a true federated network identity management. Federated identity management makes it possible for an authenticated identity to be recognized and take part in personalized services across multiple domains. The characteristics of that identity do not reside in one place but are federated among many locations. The individual decides just how much information is to be known among the sites.

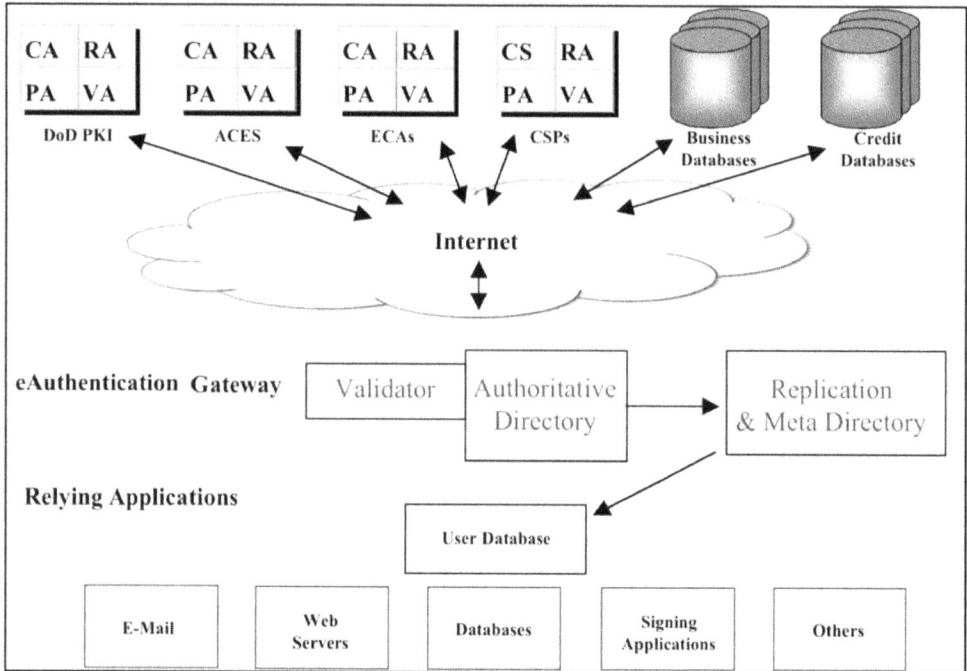

Figure 2: On-line subscription model for level 1, 2, 3, and 4 credentials

Each relying party's business processes can interface via BPM with all five services of an enabling infrastructure whose interface specification can be defined in three phases:

- Phase 0--Current operational capability, applies an Identity Management and Authoritative Directory service. Account information vetted by external credential providers and created in a local Authoritative repository transferred to the Relying Parties by accepted, secure industry-proven directory replication and meta-directory techniques and products.
- Phase 1--Upgraded operational capability can add standards-compliant products to achieve Security Services and Access Management functionality to those Relying Party applications that require that capability.
- Phase 2--Future capability can add the Provisioning and BPM Workflow Services portion of the infrastructure to achieve complete federated identity management.

A relying party interface module enables primary authentication and validation of individuals, linked to a given identity. If a user accesses an application directly, the application has the option of validating the user's credential using its own authentication processing or using a centrally-managed capability. Each relying application will manage the information to effect proper access control rules. Phase 0/1 primary authentication can include userid/passwords, tokens and trusted PKI certificates (levels 1 - 4). Phase 0/1 primary validation could include Lightweight Directory Access Protocol over Secure Sockets Layer (LDAPS) for validation of credentials or On-line Certificate Status Protocol (OCSP) validation of trusted PKI certificates. Phase 2 is developmental and may include standards-compliant authentication/ validation mechanisms and various "authenticator token" options.

Relying applications can independently maintain their access controls for each server supported by a user database. By employing their user databases in LDAP, Active Directory, X.500 directory or other SQL user database repositories, the data or process owner can support controlled user access. Addition of a CSP provides vetted users to an Authoritative Directory, which replicates or transfers those user accounts in the above type of directories via meta-directory technology, begins to lower administrative overhead. The relying party now only needs to concentrate on access control. The help desk calls for user administration are now going to the external credential providers for user administrator issues such as password reset and personal information maintenance.

The relying applications can execute an LDAPS bind to Authoritative Directory(s) for user validation or can choose to replicate certain information to enhance local reliability and performance. At each local directory level user group/ role administrators at any location can manage accounts. Both user and group/ role management are accomplished using the Hyper Text Transfer Protocol over Secure Sockets Layer (HTTPS). Once user and group/ role information is available in the authoritative directory, the application can communicate with the directory using LDAPS to determine access privileges for a user that has already been authenticated via various level credentials represented by a separate directory branches.

The next phase, Figure 2, adds Security Services and Access Management to the infrastructure. The relying party interface module will manage the access policies and rules and authentication enforcement; and will produce an authenticator token, which allows agency applications to recognize that primary authentication, and validation has been performed. For example:

- Mobile digital certificate – when a subscriber requests a userid/password in accordance with Appendix A. The created user account will include a digital certificate that defines the user in accordance with the level 1 or level 2 credential requirements. When the user authenticates to a relying application, the user is authenticated and validated (via userid/ password). The associated digital certificate is then presented to the relying application where it is trusted as a level 1 or 2 authenticator token, as defined in the token.

- SAML artifact - When the user authenticates the user is authenticated and validated (via userid/ password). A non-persistent cookie can be set in the users browser indicating that the user has successfully logged into the gateway and a SAML artifact in the Uniform Resource Locator (URL) query string. The relying application checks the SAML artifact where it can be evaluated to be trusted as a level 1 or level 2 authenticator token, as defined in the token.

Leveraging standard mature Commercial Off-The-Shelf (COTS) components and BPM software that have been proven in the technology market places the efficiency of a common solution for multiple applications on the same network or applied to multiple or distributed applications at multiple locations across an enterprise. Local trust policy is inherent in such a system, even as it is scaled. Technology refresh in the face of improved technologies is easily accommodated. If desired, BPM tools to manage policy can be employed for access control rules without human intervention.

This sample BPM/EA approach, defined above, affords the following advantages:

- Provides applications with multiple I&A/ validation interfaces rapidly;
- Allows applications to have enterprise or local access to account data;
- Centralizes the configuration management requirement of managing information from multiple authentication methods;
- Allows local policy to determine trusted authentications by each application (i.e., application does not inherit trust);
- Implements components designed to manage specific tasks so that applications do not have to support all authentication functions natively; and
- Provides an easy migration path from less elegant authentication schemes through higher assurance, including full PKI implementations and Federated Identities.

This EA/BPM approach results in open and improved interoperability between multiple standards-based-authentication mechanisms, enhance performance, and provide cost savings. This can be best realized by applying EA approaches that require the least modification of existing application systems and business processes. The largest area of expected return on investment is that specific programming does not have to be done application by application to enable all of an enterprise's authentication functions defined by their business processes.

Cryptographic Tokens and Biometrics

Where biometrics are concerned, the most important benefit provided is the third factor of authentication; something you *are*. The primary objective of cryptographic tokens[13] (such as smartcards) and biometrics is to ensure to the greatest degree possible that the individual presenting himself or herself is, in fact, who or what they claim to be. With tokens *and* biometrics combined it is possible to achieve 'three factor identification.'

- One-factor authentication is generally something one knows, such as a pin or a password.
- Two-factor authentication involves something one knows, coupled with either something one has (smart card) or something one is (biometric).
- Three-factor authentication involves presentation of something one knows, something one *has*, **and** something one *is*.

As the number of factors of authentication increase, so does the probability that the individual is who he claims to be. Conversely, the probability that the individual is being 'spoofed' or mimicked by an intruder or interloper decreases.

It is with good reason that most people in the today's society are skeptical of a universal identification card that contains vital personal information. Or they fear their personal data resides in a database somewhere that can potentially be 'hacked' into, causing their data to be compromised. Unfortunately, in the haste of the Internet boom, vast amounts of personal data were

---

[13] Cryptographic tokens compliant with the Federal Information Processing Standards (FIPS) FIPS Publication 140-2 level 2 or higher.

willingly and/or unwittingly made available by individuals themselves, marketing groups, businesses, even some Government agencies, and a whole host of others. Now, we are left with trying to lock-down as much as possible while simultaneously reeling back in that which has escaped. Society's collective sense of being jaded by the Internet is quite well founded. However, the Internet was never intended to afford privacy to anyone. Quite to the contrary, the Internet was devised for the **open** sharing of information to anyone and everyone with a connection. Nonetheless, this is the state we are currently in, and some measure of privacy is still attainable.

Smart card technology and biometrics can provide the additional security needed to afford all parties a high level of confidence that individuals attempting access to resources are who they claim to be. We can achieve this without compromising or infringing upon the privacy of the individual. It is simply a matter of adhering to established standards, policies and procedures to enforce the proper use and integration of the technologies, and laws that penalize transgressors.

Forensics

Forensics represents another critical aspect of security that is a prime candidate for an EA and BPM approach. Crime labs perform their functions in a variety of ways and many of them are tremendously backlogged. West Virginia University is presently exploring business transformation for crime labs and BPM could become a key component. One expert says, "Crime labs are screaming for business transformation." Well-backed lobbying and special interest groups such as Project innocence have lobbied extensively for congressional legislation to reduce the credibility of forensic evidence. The Supreme Court saddled a tremendous burden upon the criminal justice system by requiring that the already understaffed and underfunded professionals who process forensic evidence testify in court in order for forensic evidence to be included in a criminal trial. Crime labs everywhere could potentially benefit from an integrated EA and BPM approach to help facilitate their internal and external processes, without having to reinvent the wheel for every different crime lab. EA and BPM offer the potential to help save money, improve efficiency, replicate across local, state, and federal levels, and above all, facilitate providing the testing and availability of reliable forensic evidence. We have a personal and societal stake in prosecuting criminals and protecting the innocent.

AREAS WHERE ENHANCED SECURITY CAN PROMOTE ADOPTION

Telework

Adopting an EA and BPM security approach could help facilitate telework adoption by defining and automating the security rules and processes necessary for workers to perform their particular work at remote locations. The adoption of telework in industry, government, and other areas holds vast implications for our environment, quality of work life, productivity, morale, safety by keeping people off the roads, economy and maximization of resources, efficiency, and other potential offshoots.

Telework requires strict security policies to prevent the loss or theft of critical information, as employees are able to work at a variety of remote locations. At the April 8 Telework Exchange conference in Washington, D.C., Kareem Dale, the White House Disability advisor to President Obama, told the audience that, "any agency should be able to provide sufficient security" if the White House could provide him the security to work at home during the 2010 blizzard and its aftermath.

The theft of a VA laptop in 2006 made headlines and caused fears of mass identity theft. Fortunately, authorities recovered the laptop and its external hard drive stolen in 2006 from a Veteran's Administration analyst's home in Maryland containing the names, birth dates and Social Security numbers of 26.5 million current and former service members.[14] Authorities determined that thieves had not accessed the data. This computer theft drew Congress' attention and led to wide publicity about the VA's loose policies for controlling computer security. Had strict processes been in place for reporting such a loss immediately, the agency could have assured that administrator quickly learned of the computer's loss rather than 13 days later. The VA quickly instituted tighter controls. It was far better prepared when thieves in Austin stole a laptop with an encrypted hard drive and authorities knew quickly exactly what equipment was missing. BPM-enabled processes could make responses even more efficient.

According to Darren Ash, Chief Information Officer of the Nuclear Regulatory Commission (NRC), NRC has standardized on strict security policies for its teleworkers as much of its data may be sensitive.[15] NRC employees are only allowed to use wireless air cards provided by the phone company and does not allow access to public wireless, which can be insecure.

The U.S. Patent and Trademark Office (PTO) offers a prime example of successful telework policies. PTO officials recently shared the following latest figures on telework: 6707 of Positions at USPTO are Eligible for Telework (71% of total population) and 5518 Eligible Positions are teleworking between 1 and 4 Days per Week (82.27% of eligible positions are teleworking).

2512 Positions are Teleworking	4 Days per Week
61 are Teleworking	3 Days per Week
172 are Teleworking	2 Days per Week
2661 are Teleworking	1 Day per Week
Approximately 73 are Teleworking	on a non-regular/recurring basis

Figure 3: U.S. PTO statistics provided by PTO on April 19, 2010

Cloud computing

A concerted EA and BPM approach can also be a potential means by which to more effectively manage security solutions for cloud computing services as well as other concerns. Many people think that cloud computing is a new and different technology and is all the rage. To others, cloud computing is simply a new buzzword because we have been designing secure solutions in the cloud for decades, so cloud computing is not really something new. What is new are the ways in which services are provided and the means to acquire them.

[14] Christopher Lee and Zachary A. Goldfarb, Stolen VA Laptop and Hard Drive Recovered, *Washington Post*, June 30, 2006

[15] Darren Ash, Telework Exchange conference, 8 April 2010

Security in cloud computing environments is often one of the top concerns. Organizations will need to carefully think through the sensitivity of their information before determining which type of cloud computing solution is right for them or whether it is a potential solution at all. Sensitive defense and law enforcement information has vastly different security requirements than sales lead information.

The U.S. federal government is working with commercial providers of cloud computing services to certify a cloud computing capability once so that each agency procuring similar services doesn't have to perform the costly security certification and accreditation (C&A) process time and time again. Assuming that General Services Administration, the Department of Interior, and other potential providers of cloud computing services to the federal government are able to provide sufficient security measures, this will save the government untold sums of money in just C&A expenses alone. BPM business rule and process-driven security could provide significant advantages for cloud computing as well.

ENHANCING SECURITY FOR CRITICAL INFRASTRUCTURE

Information Sharing Environments

We have increasing needs to integrate outside of our own systems in larger and larger information-sharing environments. The Suspicious Activity Reporting System established after 9/11 created through a cooperative effort among local, state, federal and international parties provides information based on a need-to-know to aid the law enforcement community. These efforts led to establishing the National Information Exchange Model using a common vocabulary for the exchange of information. Security complexity for these large environments expands exponentially. Three of the largest ones with great impact on the U.S. are the Next Generation (NextGen) U.S. Airspace, energy, and health care.

NextGen

What better opportunity to prove the potential for EA/BPM-driven security than the world's largest and one of the most complex information-sharing environments? NextGen entails an IT implementation of unprecedented magnitude with a mandate to place all U.S. airspace operations over net-centric operations by 2025. Of extreme importance to the U.S., NextGen is key to U.S. economic prosperity and continued dominance in international aviation.

Recognizing that the U.S. airspace is larger than the Federal Aviation Administration (FAA) or any other single U.S. agency, Congress established the Joint Program Development Office (JPDO) to develop the guidelines and oversee its development. Representatives from multiple agencies officially come together at the JPDO to oversee the development of everything from the commercial airspace, air homeland defense, air military defense, other commercial interests, and more, all with varying levels of criticality and needs for security.

"NextGen has some unique security requirements that are much more complex than other types of environments," according to Patty Craighill, who is in charge of overseeing the guidelines for developing all of NextGen net-centric operations. "Our stakeholder community extends from public to private sector, across security domains, and warrants special protections for data types such as law enforcement, intelligence, and privacy data."[16]

Security requirements cover a wide spectrum. Defense and commercial airline requirements demand absolutely strict security to prevent tampering with mission critical data and information. Law enforcement information demands strict security controls to allow access but control who can obtain information. Flight information and air traffic control systems have immense security requirements. Commercial systems such as those that might notify passengers of special restaurant specials or sales on merchandise at passenger destinations would require vastly lesser security than air traffic control systems.

Many of the systems necessary to run and support the airspace, a great number of which are decades old, today operate in closed environments. The evolution to net-centricity requires placing closed systems with life and death consequences on net-centric operations and that they be accessible around the world.

Rather than having each work group approach security with a different twist, working groups and specialists in given areas could create a common framework that builds security into all of the processes and systems up-front using EA and BPM that participating organizations could potentially customize to meet their own specific requirements. BPM can also capture the processes through which each of these groups performs their security work for weather, surveillance, and other areas. This would enable the JPDO to not only capture security processes, but optimize, replicate, and adapt them across the different working groups and communities of interest involved in developing NextGen.

Dennis Wisnosky, the Chief Technology Officer and Chief Architect for the Department of Defense, has championed a methodology using "primitives (basic components) and patterns (of behavior)" for development that could also, when used with an EA/BPM approach, hold vast potential for helping develop NextGen security initiatives across the board.

Health Care

Health care represents another of the U.S. largest information-sharing environments with stringent security requirements at all levels. We must assure that health care information doesn't fall into the wrong hands, yet make it available to those who need access to the information. Electronic health care records could help prevent dangerous or even fatal drug interactions, share information about pre-existing conditions, provide a composite history of health care information available to individuals throughout their lifetimes, and provide the health care community a vast knowledge base about national health care for research and other purposes.

Security is fundamental to our health care, beginning with safeguarding personally identifiable information contained in patient records, to protecting our society from disease, pandemic, the aftermath of a natural disaster, from radiological and biological terrorist threats, and other consequences. How do

---

[16] Patricia Craighill, Personal interview, 7 April 2010.

we protect our own personal health information as well as that of the largest health care systems?

"Establishing guiding principles to protect privacy and security of health information, developing procedures for patient identification, and ensuring minimum necessary data are released are key functions that the health information management (HIM) professional can lead. HIM professionals need to accept a leadership role in the privacy and security of a Health Information Environment," according to Joyce Hunter, CEO of Vulcan Enterprises.

HIPAA, FISMA and other legislative and regulatory mandates incur strict requirements to provide security on a variety of levels, making health care even more complicated because of the added burden of complying with these requirements.

An EA/BPM approach to health care could accelerate the gains in health care modernization and provide many more individual and collective benefits. BPM can help direct and manage the workflow for all of the security requirements to include managing individual patient data, satisfying legal and regulatory requirements, and helping manage health care systems on a larger basis for hospitals, local and other jurisdictions, health care networks, government, and many others. For enterprising organizations that develop them, EA/BPM models of varying purposes and sizes could be replicated, shared, packaged, and sold across the country to help us realize advantages from an individual to a national or even international basis.

Energy

Energy represents yet another one of the most critical and most vulnerable aspects of our critical infrastructure. In addition to monumental physical security required to secure nuclear and other utility systems, our energy infrastructure depends upon computer systems and the Internet. This includes utilities, the Department of Energy (DOE) environmental cleanup efforts, protecting nuclear facilities and nuclear materials around the world, scientific advancement, developing wind and solar power, and vastly more.

Some people believe that hackers caused the Northeast blackout and, whether it is true or not, the potential exists to cause immense damage by attacking our energy critical infrastructure. Cyber criminals who hack into our energy systems could wreak havoc, causing loss of life and economic chaos as has occurred during major outages.

Because the utilities are run by private industry whose primary motivation is profit, not security, we lack sufficient focus on fixing the cyber vulnerabilities in this critical sector. The Aurora Project conducted by Idaho National Labs tested the theory that if one could hack into a generator's control system, hackers could cause a power system to destroy itself. Members of Congress were incensed at the energy industry for not having sufficient security controls in place.

The National Labs, with their vast computing powers and support for DOE activities, the energy industry, and DOE would benefit dramatically from an EA/BPM centered approach to security. Enterprising organizations could create standardized EA/BPM security solutions of varying purposes and magnitudes that the energy industry and government could replicate across the nation. Specific solutions could address different segments of industry such as nuclear versus coal power. In the end, we reap huge benefits by employing an EA/BPM approach to create rule-driven process automation to improve DOE's efficiency and that of private industry and, most importantly, improve our personal and national security.

An EA/BPM Approach for Security Holds Vast Potential

Our personal security, our homeland security, and national defense are at undue risk unless we adopt new and better ways of approaching security such as described in this EA/BPM approach. EA/BPM offer the framework and the means through existing practices and technologies to develop far more effective and repeatable solutions for providing security on all levels. Because of BPM's proven history in business and government we know that we can apply this to security. We can capture institutional knowledge in software, manage governance activities, predefine rule-driven responses that can anticipate and defend against a security threat, and provide real-time responses to new and different threats.

This approach can provide leadership and practitioners alike with the powerful means to achieve transparency, access, and visibility into operations to vastly improve our security capabilities. We can use BPM to integrate across stovepiped security disciplines with particular benefit to three of the largest information-sharing environments with critical impact on the nation: Next-Gen, health care, and energy. This holds true for physical security, cyber security, and any other type of security.

Customer Experience Transformation—A Framework to Achieve Measurable Results

Vinaykumar S Mummigatti, Virtusa, USA

INTRODUCTION

The era of extreme competition is creating immense importance for customer experience and how companies manage their customers' expectations. The ability to successfully manage the customer value chain across the life cycle of a customer is the key to the survival of any company today. Most companies realize this but are struggling to measure and influence the customer experience. This paper is an attempt to look at various facets of customer experience and how to transform customer experience to achieve measurable business goals. **Business Process Management** and the **convergence** of technologies *(such as Portals, web 2.0, BI, Content Management)* are two key elements of this transformation and hence we will focus on how the convergence of various technologies led by BPM will help achieve the business goals around **Customer Experience Transformation (CET)**.

Customer experience can be defined as the sum total of customer perception about a company and its offerings, based on multiple touch points that a customer faces such as branding, marketing, buying process, education, presales and post sales support, merchandising, website visits and the exposure through social media. It is measured by how customers translate this experience through buying behavior, purchase patterns, maintaining their relationship or how they voice their perceptions in larger forums.

Customer experience should be a seemingly easy topic to manage. Most large enterprises have built sophisticated CRM systems over the years, implemented ERP systems to achieve high transaction efficiencies, developed Portals that are loaded with information, and established global call centers that are supposed to handle customer service 24x7 as per SLAs (Service level agreements). Significant investments have been made in Data Warehouses and Business Intelligence systems. Large content repositories using the best of content management systems for web content and documents have been established.

However, all these investments have failed to deliver the desired outcomes in managing customer experience. There is a still a big disconnect between these investments as they are built in silos. There is no cohesive strategy binding these investments to the CEM goals.

Gartner research states "Increasingly, companies are turning to customer experience initiatives to boost the bottom line, but it's an effort that requires cooperation across the organization and extends beyond just CRM. In fact, targeting, attracting and retaining new customers remains a top priority for CIOs, a Gartner survey of 1,500 CIOs worldwide found. Yet CIOs have little involvement in customer experience initiatives," according to Ed Thompson, research vice president with Gartner.

The focus of this article is to present the different tenets of Customer Experience Management (CEM) which help in (1) acquiring customers (2) managing the sum total of experience at various touch points (3) measuring the customer experience KPIs in real time, and (4) taking initiatives based on outcomes to ensure we achieve the business goals. Let us look at how we move beyond CRM into CEM and what kind of solutions we need to develop to convert customer experience into measurable business goals through a combination of technologies related to data, content and process management.

BUSINESS AND TECHNICAL CHALLENGES IN CUSTOMER EXPERIENCE MANAGEMENT

Most large enterprises have redundant systems created by diverse departments or lines of business. Due to these silos, the structure does not permit a cohesive strategy to offer unified customer experience. As we set strategic goals and vision around delivering ultimate customer experience, we fail to execute the strategies as we have still not been able to pull together a well defined approach and framework defining roles, metrics and processes with an ability to track customer experience KPIs (Key Performance Indicators).

Sam Walton clearly articulated the importance of the customer, "There is only one boss. The customer. And he can fire everybody in the company from the chairman on down, simply by spending his money somewhere else." This simple but powerful statement states the single most important constituent in our company's performance is our customer.

According to Bernd Schmitt, CEM is the process of strategically managing a customer's entire relationship with a product or company. It moves beyond the outcome-based concepts of customer satisfaction and loyalty and focuses on the *process* a company engages to develop customer knowledge, align the organization, design the customer experience, and continuously *innovate*. CEM provides the key principles and frameworks for orchestrating the total customer experience.

In one of my previous engagements with a Fortune 500 Consumer Electronics company, the CIO posed us a challenge. In the CIO's own words *"We are rated either number one or two in product-quality research in most of the product segments in which we're present. Whereas we are rated number eleven in customer satisfaction research compared to our peers. While we stand out in product quality as the best, we are unable to leverage our engineering excellence in delivering customer value and satisfaction. We have seen declining revenues and profitability while our competition is eating into our market share. What can we do to achieve the desired improvement in customer satisfaction as it is hurting our entire business performance and we have recorded one of the lowest revenues during current year?"* From televisions and cameras to laptops and audio devices, this company has more than 50 product lines and has been rated as an innovator and known for its high-end quality. This situation brings out a common problem seen across most enterprises—why does our product or service excellence in itself does not ensure high level of customer experience?

It would be very relevant to present some of the findings from the study we conducted on the business- and technology-related challenges. Some of the business challenges that were identified in this scenario were:

- **Quality:** Inability to track defects and product failures beyond call centers all the way to product service and engineering groups.
- **Service Operations:** Turnaround time for the average customer request was much higher than industry benchmark. The processes for customer returns

and warranty claims management were in chaos. Repeat requests for parts and service were a direct reflection of existing inefficiencies.

- **Call Center Management:** Percentage of "first-call resolution" was very low with a high rate of abandoned calls. "Call waiting" and "average call" durations were much above the industry average.
- **Parts Management:** Huge back-order on parts requests. The inventory management was not aligned to the service center.

From a technology perspective the challenges identified were:

- **Redundant Data:** Diverse systems of records created silos of customer data and services data. Majority of the customer requests needed the Call center operator to access a minimum of 4 back end systems. The call center operator's ability to interpret the information and generate solutions for a customer's query or problem was very limited.
- **Disparate Systems:** Lack of integration between systems handling parts and model details, inventory status, customer details and product registration details., Sales data and service data were completely isolated. Reports were often inaccurate mostly due to legacy data integration issues.
- **Lack of Collaboration:** Multiple surveys were conducted by different teams and systems. For example, phone surveys, chat surveys, repair surveys and support surveys were not synthesized to create one single version of the truth for executive decision-makers.
- **Poor Knowledge Management:** Lack of a single Knowledge management system caused delay in accessing the right support information from manuals, bulletins or specifications.
- **No Process Management Capabilities:** Lack of event processing, workflow automation, alerts, notifications, work allocation, dynamic correspondence, BAM (Business Activity Monitoring), and tracking of KPIs. the process for tracking technician availability to schedule appointments for Fields Service was not in place. There was no system in place to measure efficiency and productivity of service teams.
- **No Portals/User Friendly Web Interface**: Corporate websites provided only the basic information about company and products but lacked any self-service capabilities for end-users around service or purchases.

This scenario might present an extreme case of inefficiency when measured against the standards of some of the companies who are on the leading edge of customer experience management. But this case presents a comprehensive set of parameters which influence the customer experience. Although this scenario is from a manufacturing segment, it is no different from a wealth management firm or a retail bank or a life insurance and annuities carrier. We can map these situations to any industry with multiple customer touch points.

James Richardson, CMO at Cisco Systems, summarizes the level of seriousness every company needs to have around CEM, "Orchestrating the total customer experience is a very realistic and worthy goal, and one we strive to achieve at Cisco. For example, we work closely with our customers through all stages of a network implementation—plan, design, implement, and operate. And customers buy our products and services both directly from us, as well as though many other routes to market. We couldn't provide the level of customer satisfaction that our customers expect if we did not orchestrate our marketing around the *total experience.*"

BUSINESS CASE FOR CUSTOMER EXPERIENCE TRANSFORMATION (CET)

Most enterprises have made significant investments in their customer service departments and activities. Hence it is very difficult to initiate a transformation as it calls for a fundamental change in the organization, processes and systems. The biggest hurdle to CET is the resistance to change. CET is about making a fundamental change to the portfolio of customer experience activities and investments in alignment with the corporate strategy.

According to 2009 Customer Experience Management Benchmark Study by the Strativity Group, 48 percent of the surveyed companies increased investments in customer experience over the past three years by 10 percent driving a 60 percent average improvement in satisfaction scores. Such statistics are easy to reference after the fact.

How do we create a business case and what areas do we need to address while calculating the ROI from a CET program? The below diagram is a high level representation of parameters which help drive customer experience programs.

Figure 1: Business Drivers for a CET Initiative

Let us start with some fundamental questions that will determine why we should make investments in CET:

- Are we able to measure KPIs such as customer retention rate, ability to up-sell/cross-sell, customer loyalty, customer satisfaction across all product lines and service lines, and new customer acquisition rate?
- Are we able to capture and convert customer feedback and responses into meaningful actions?
- What is the competition doing in terms of branding, customer acquisition, and benchmarks around key customer services? Are our competitors growing faster than us? Are we losing customers to competition?
- How efficient are our call centers in terms of various call metrics and operational efficiencies? Are they inundated with customer and product data and information? How much time is spent in accessing content and data?
- Are we using the latest Web 2.0 technologies to enhance customer experience and to collaborate internally and externally? Are we able to influence customer experience directly and indirectly?
- Do we have any metrics on customer experience across each channel and are we able to track the same kind of metrics across all channels?

- Today's customers want 24x7 access to services irrespective of time zone or geography. What levels of self service are we providing vis-à-vis our competition?
- Have we segmented our customer base and defined a strategy addressing the service levels and positioning targeted for each segment? Is this built into our systems and do we collect data which can help us drill down into each micro segment to present customers with targeted services and products? Are we able to make our customers feel that they are being treated as individuals with tailored data, content and information offered at their finger tips?
- Do we have clearly-defined processes driving all aspects of customer interaction and fulfillment? Are the processes aligned to overall strategy and are able to deliver measurable outcomes.

BUSINESS FRAMEWORK FOR CUSTOMER EXPERIENCE TRANSFORMATION

According to Forrester's "Customer Service Innovation and Assessment Report" almost 50 percent of respondents said that an obstacle to improving customer experience was the lack of defined customer experience management processes. The overall Customer Experience Transformation (CET) framework is based on our ability to tie business strategy to customer service goals, measuring outcomes and continuously optimizing to bridge the gaps. This is described in the framework below.

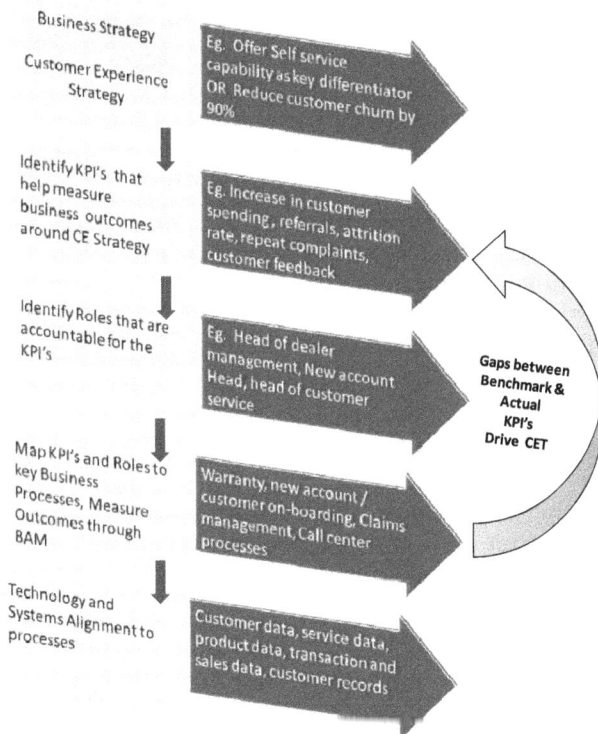

Figure 2: Business Blueprint for CET

CET stands out compared to CRM or other customer service activities in its strategic importance and long-term if not permanent impact. It is also a more holistic approach spanning different organizational elements therefore requiring a fundamental change. The key elements of such an initiative are elaborated below:

- **Define the Customer Experience Strategy:** Any CET initiative begins with the definition of the overall strategy and business goals around customer experience management. A clear articulation of the CE strategy sets the overall direction.

- **Define KPIs:** The next step is to identify the key metrics that help us track customer experience, i.e., data points related to transactions, operations and processes that are critical from a customer experience standpoint as well as their larger impact on product and service quality, branding and positioning, channel productivity, revenues, and profitability.

- **Define Roles:** We need to map roles to KPIs at points of customer interaction and larger levels of aggregation. Key roles in product development/management, distribution, pricing and promotions need to be identified and assigned KPIs. Only then we can reap the benefits from a sophisticated CEM system.

- **Define Processes:** We need to define the key processes at every level of customer touch points that will help trigger follow-on activities based on customer behavior and synthesize people and systems in a seamless flow. These processes must enable automation across all customer service activities and ensure measurement of relative performance through BAM (business activity monitoring) dashboards. Process automation also drives uniform communication across stakeholders and the integration of systems to eliminate redundant data access and entry by operators.

- **Align Technology Investments:** Investments in technology systems need to be aligned to the above parameters. One of the biggest hindrances to customer experience improvement is the rigidity of legacy systems. Also how we leverage leading edge technologies such as Web 2.0 and collaboration tools, portals, content management systems and search engines, determines our ability to deliver best-in-class customer experience.

Forrester analyst Natalie L. Petouhoff states, "Customer service drives brand perception, customer loyalty, and repurchase probability, and it's a core element in an enterprise's competitive strategy. Customer service is the last differentiating competitive factor with price and product no longer driving customer preferences." This message conveys the importance of *total customer experience* in all stages of the customer life cycle.

As we have seen in the example provided in the previous section, a company's fortunes are driven by its customers. As market dynamics change and competition evolves there is a constant threat of customer churn. Every company needs to measure customer experience, align business goals to these metrics, define roles and processes that help in optimizing the customer experience, and build systems that support the overall framework.

CET is about driving fundamental change in the way we manage customers across multiple touch points through all phases of the customer life cycle. As we continue to measure the customer experience and benchmark those metrics, we need to align the processes bringing together people, data, systems and content. Business processes are the underlying linkages between people, systems, and external entities like suppliers and customers. The best CET programs integrate strategy, organizational structure, people, processes, and technology in a holistic approach.

A conceptual representation of such a solution (applicable to multiple industries) is shown below:

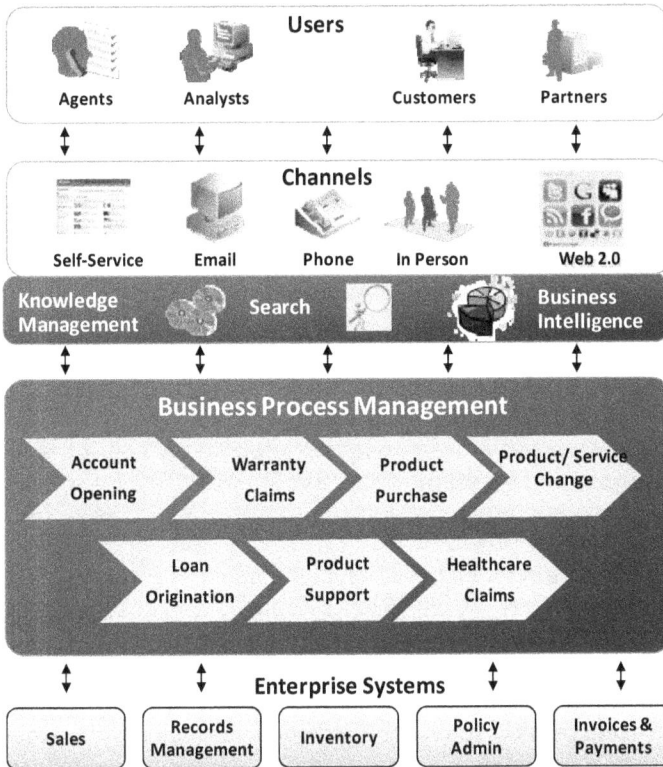

Figure 3: Conceptual Framework for a CEM solution

This diagram depicts the need for a cohesive approach where customer experience is delivered through multiple channels but the underlying data, processes and information layers are seamless and unified. Enabling unified delivery channels with a set of collaboration, knowledge management and search tools helps users with information delivered per specific context thus enabling self-service capabilities. The BPM layer orchestrates the overall dynamics between data, process, KPIs, roles and systems. Lastly we need to wrap the back-end systems with unified data entry and access layers so as to eliminate redundant data entry and insulate the users from being forced to access multiple legacy systems for each transaction.

TECHNOLOGY CONVERGENCE & ROLE OF BPM

One of the biggest challenges facing CET is that no single technology or product vendor can help achieve all customer experience functions. By its very definition, CET programs are meant to bring diverse systems, people and processes together toward the achievement of customer-related goals. Hence, we need to conceive a solution spanning multiple technology products bringing together the best of breed capabilities offered by each stack.

Let us explore the key components in an integrated CEM solution which would address the various topics we have discussed thus far:

- **Integrated Portals** for Customers and Agents/Call Center Operators: The role of a Portal is to aggregate information from multiple sources. Portals must offer an ability to personalize and bring in context sensitive information in order to make customers feel a sense of relationship with the portal. The portal must also act as a work management interface where the customer/operator will carry out all kinds of requests be it for online purchases or information request or complaints and claims. Embedding the collaboration features such as Chat and IM on portals and agent desktops can help in productivity improvements and real time resolutions of cases increasing overall "call resolution" rates. It is also important for the Portal to provide intelligent search on data and content scattered across multiple sources to improve work-completion times and achieve customer delight. Customer empowerment is the crux of satisfaction; the more we empower customers to manage their own service requests, the better perception we are creating in terms of our brand, products and services.

- **Business Process Management:** As we automate various processes around customer management and call center operations the role of the BPM layer becomes critical. Most of the user experience we create through portals and self-enablement will be based on workflow and process automation sourced in the back-end. The BPM layer provides Process and Rules automation to integrate diverse legacy systems, measuring work and allocating work dynamically thus improving overall productivity. The BPM layer also provides the ability to keep customers in the loop as the work progresses through dynamic correspondence thus providing audit trails. Customers can view the real time status of their work requests thus feeling a sense of intimacy and transparency from the provider. The BPM layer can also trigger departmental and customer facing processes addressing product quality, logistics issues, supply chain updates, campaigns, market research and surveys based on events generated during customer interactions.
- **Business Intelligence:** Business Intelligence (BI) is a key component of any CEM solution, invaluable in terms of gaining customer insight, triggering customer interactions and continuously optimizing marketing investments.

From a customer insight standpoint, BI tools provide quality customer data, predict customer behavior and profile/segment customers as outlined below:

- *Data integration* Pulls data from any source and ensures customer information is organized as a single source of truth and provides 360 degree view of customer.
- *Web behavior tracking* helps get the most out of e-business channels and improves the effectiveness of marketing campaigns.
- *Forecasting* helps in trend analysis and decision making.
- *Analytics* provides descriptive and predictive insights through response models, churn analysis, customer value and profitability analysis.
- In terms of helping manage customer interactions and optimizing investments to generate the highest ROI, BI tools help in:
- *Campaign management* helps send the right offers to the right customers across the right channels.
- *E-mail/mobile marketing* provides large-scale multimedia messaging capabilities, including e-mail and SMS within single-channel or multi-channel marketing campaigns.
- *Event trigger alerts* inform most opportune time to reach out to customers.

Here, it is relevant to mention a quote from Forrester analyst Connie Moore published in internetnews.com, "I think the BI vendors are missing the boat on process. They don't really understand process because they focus on analysis of data. Operational data, tactical data, strategic data; the data needs to be put into action. The BI vendors don't understand the whole process world. BPM vendors are increasingly realizing they need to improve their business processes, rules and event management with greater intelligence or analytics capabilities. As BPM goes beyond process, some BPM vendors are cleverly adding integration with collaboration, portals and BI."

This quote sums up the foundation of convergence solutions proposed in this section.

- **Web 2.0:** Web 2.0 is a broad set of technologies and concepts including wikis, blogs, mash-ups, and social networking sites that are dramatically changing the way we are using the Internet. Web 2.0 technologies have led to a sharp increase in community-based collaboration and a proliferation of social media activities. At an individual company level, we are no longer able to direct the customer opinion as there are much larger influences at play through social media. How companies leverage communities and blogs, participate and influence the flow of discussions, and trigger back-end processes based on information captured through social media are key to a sustained customer experience strategy. The customer-facing portals need to have Web 2.0 features in order to achieve stickiness with the viewers inducing them to buy products/services and contribute to surveys.

- **ECM, Collaboration, Search:** As we collect and store volumes of customer content and records, our ability to organize this content and make it accessible across multiple channels is very important. We also need to incorporate search engines across the channels to have seamless access to these records and content. Collaboration tools such as IM and Chat can be crucial in keeping customers engaged with contact centers.

We see five key components to any CEM solution. How well we bring these components together through a seamless business architecture and design is the key to CET. The next generation CEM solution must have all five components and provide a seamless ability to manage the customer across all channels with a single set of KPIs. A high-level solution is represented below.

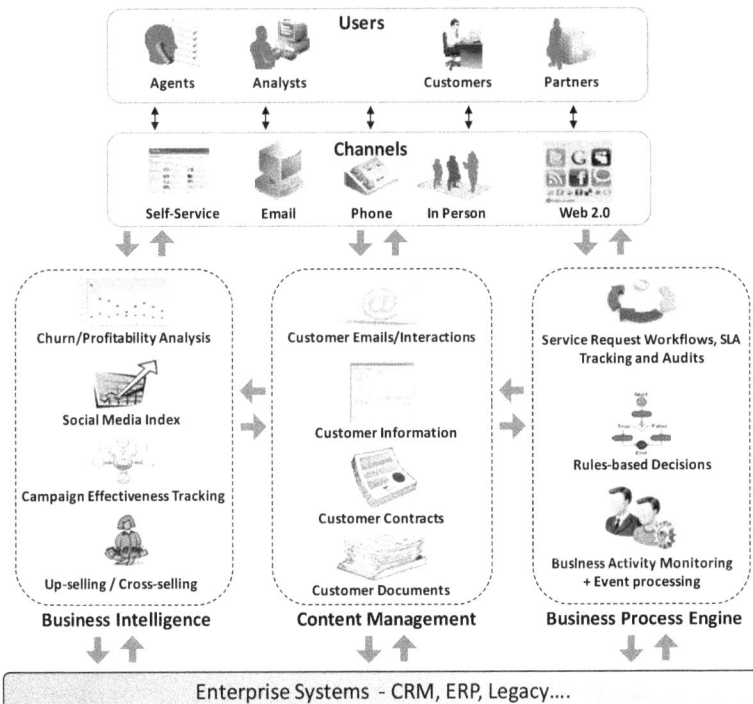

Figure 4: Technology blueprint for a CEM solution

An underlying assumption behind this solution is that we are not replacing any of the core transactional systems which have been built over the years.

SUMMARY AND KEY TAKEAWAYS

Having discussed various aspects of a typical CET initiative in detail, here is a summary of key takeaways:

- Start your CET initiative with the definition of your overarching customer strategy.
- Define and weight your metrics according to outcomes desired. Remember, if you can't measure it you can't manage it.
- Make sure that all roles and KPIs are identified and communicated to key stakeholders.
- There is no single technology that meets all CEM requirements. Assess the technology landscape and plan a solution as described in Figure 4.
- View CET as not a one-time project but an ongoing initiative. Constant measurement and alignment to goals and changing business conditions are key to sustained success.

CET is a widely applicable topic across all industries. The changing business dynamics has created so many uncertainties. Our customers are the last thing we can afford to lose sight of. Inability to manage our customers, forecast customer trends and influence broader perceptions can mean a debacle for every enterprise. Let us realize this fact and put concentrated effort to manage our most important assets; OUR CUSTOMERS!

REFERENCES

Forrester's "Customer Service Innovation Framework and Self-Assessment" by Natalie L. Petouhoff, Ph.D.

Gartner webinar on "Customer Experience Management : Raising Customer Satisfaction, Loyalty and Advocacy" By Ed Thompson & Jim Davies http://www.sas.com : Product white papers

Business Intelligence and BPM: Merging? Article by Clint Boulton

"Customer Experience Optimization" article by David Jacques

"Customer Experience—The Marriage of Marketing and Business Process" article by Victor Howard.

Section 3

Standards and Technology

How to Optimize Capability-Centered Enterprise Integration

Nathaniel Palmer and Jason Adolf, SRA International, Inc., USA

OVERVIEW

During the last decade, the lines between enterprise application integration (EAI) technology and workflow blurred, morphing into what is now widely recognized as the "Integration-centric BPM" market sector. Ten years later, much progress has been made in meeting the challenge of integrating legacy applications and their more modern counterparts, allowing enterprise IT organizations to expose the necessary functionality from each system.

Increasingly, COTS BPM and SOA platforms are leveraged as the bones of architecture and approach, allowing for the maximum amount of flexibility while reducing the need for tenuous custom coding. Yet the 'Integration-centric' approach most commonly followed obviates the inherent benefits offered by BPM, notably the ability to deliver business capabilities, rather application functionality.

Taking a capability-centered approach to extracting and exposing existing application functionality, while mapping these to new processes and interaction models, allows organizations to realize optimal value from current generation COTS BPM and SOA platforms. This approach begins with modeling business concepts as addressable capabilities, and then extending these into specific deployment models which leverage BPM and SOA for capability-centered business integration.

STARTING WITH THE PROCESS

Developing process models provides a critical early or often first step in validating how a system or service should perform, as well as defining the roles, rules, and other attributes. Without an easily understood definition of how services are delivered, organizations struggle to provide a consistent experience to customers, citizens and other stakeholders. The advantage of a well-defined process is to provide consistent results as well as the ability to continuously improve over time.

From delivering a more consistent and predictable citizen experience, to providing better visibility into the status of work and lower risk change. Process modeling is a core capability that cannot be bypassed if the organization is intent on improving its results. It is also a critical step in the development of any system or service. Modeling processes *before* developing code allows for validating expectations for how the system or service will behave. Models are far easier to change than code. Thus the better the model, the more accurately it is validated by stakeholders, the less rework will be required during the development process.

MODELING WITH UML

The Unified Modeling Language or "the UML" (although for casual references, the "the" is usually silent) is a visual modeling language created to allow the visualization of application logic prior to developing actual code. It is not, however, intended to be a visual programming language, in the sense of having all the necessary visual and semantic support to replace programming languages. This is core concept and should be understood, it is *not* a programming language, it is language-, tool- and process-agnostic.

It should be understood that UML is a *notation*—it presents basic symbols (while allowing for some variation among modeling environments) and guidelines for how these should be used (referred to as abstract syntax.) It is not a programming language, nor a rigid standard, but rather is intentionally ambiguous to allow for accommodation of local "dialects" or domain-specific practices. For this reason, the level of detail used is intended to provide a working understanding of the UML.

Specifically, it is an explicit set of parameters defining how to visualize, specify, construct or otherwise document the *artifacts* of software-based system or service. Because it is not a programming language and defines execution semantics, each and every UML-defined model must be transformed into executable code. For this reason, the accuracy of each model is critical to the success of the development initiative.

In other words, models themselves represent the common link, arguably the *language*, between the business stakeholder and the system builder. If the models are not well-understood, the development effort invariably requires substantial rework to "get it right."

Defining Classes and Hierarchy

The UML is inherently object-oriented, as it is based foremost on the identification of objects. An object is a noun (person, place, or thing) and can be users, offices, servers, reports, events or other "things" related to the system or services. Objects "know things" (i.e., they have attributes) and they "do things" (i.e., they have methods and performance parameters.)

Objects exist within a class, which is essentially the "blueprint" or template defining the construction of that object:

"Cup of Coffee" exists in the Object Class of "Beverages"
    Sub Class = "Hot Beverages"
        Sub Sub Class = "Caffeinated Hot Beverages"

As previously described, the UML is not a programming language but a modeling language. It is represented by a various symbols and diagrams. Each diagram type shows a unique facet of the system or service being modeled. As a result, by having multiple views of a system or service, there is much greater opportunity to enable more accurate validation by stakeholders and others involved in determining requirements.

Although the UML 2.x consists of over a dozen diagram views, for the purposes of capabilities modeling, the focus here is on the five most frequently used and most relevant to business process illustration: *Use Case Diagram, Activity Diagram, Class Diagram, Sequence Diagram,* and *Component Diagram.*

To ensure that each view is correlated, however, requires specific management of the relationships between each view—that a given Use Case Diagram relates to an Activity Diagram relates to a Class Diagram, and so forth. This is done by the use of a common, declarative meta-model and is managed by the specific modeling environment used. The meta-model defines the basic rules for how each diagram relates to one another, and the broader UML specification informally describes the meaning of the various meta-model elements. Within these parameters, the five primary diagrams fit on four fundamental areas of depiction (i.e., what is intended to be shown): Documenting Required Capabilities and Resources

The most common mistake made in a process modeling initiative is beginning with pictures: visual diagrams, lines and boxes. Although a seemingly logical starting point, this inevitably results in models that cannot be adequately understood by stakeholders and which create ambiguity and uncertainty in their interpretation, and likely unusable by anyone other than its author.

Nuanced definitions of words and terms will lead to a series of subtle disconnects that collectively result in assumptions that are mistrusted or simply wrong. Building a picture based on ambiguous definitions and faulty assumptions results in little more than a process-oriented Rorschach test. For this reason, the first step in process modeling is to develop or validate a written narrative of the process.

To achieve this, some basic questions should be answered: What outcomes is the system or service expected to deliver? What data and/or resources will be consumed or produced? What specific activities will provide the desired capabilities? What roles (who) will be involved?

The answers to these questions can be group into specific categories, for example:

What outcomes? (Capabilities)	Objectives, Features, Services
What data and/or resource?	Objects (Nouns)
What specific activities?	Actions (Verbs)
What roles (who)?	Roles, Actors (Performers)

This approach mirrors work recently done at the U.S. Department of Defense Business Transformation Agency, principally led by Dr. Michael zur Muehlen. The goal of this work is to provide a standard approach for defining business capabilities using a common vocabulary model. It is currently part of the DoD's DODAF enterprise architecture framework. The interplay between vocabulary components, as described above, is also depicted in the diagram on the page which follows.

Source: Dr. Michael zur Muehlen, U.S. Dept of Defense

Another objective during the first stage of documenting the process is to identify common terms, homonyms and synonyms—different ways that different people use to describe the same thing. The goal is ultimately to create a standardized and disambiguated vocabulary to define the process. For smaller, simplistic processes, this can be done simply be flagging common or redundant terms and phrases. For anything larger than a very simple process, however, it is important to define a taxonomy showing the linkage between terms and meanings.

Questions should be asked through interviews with the stakeholders and intended end-users, as well as review existing documentation such as "Con-Ops" (Concept of Operations) and other requirements documentation. Start focusing on the "What" questions, rather than "Why" perspectives. For example, ask a stakeholder *"What* do you do?" not *"How* do you do your job?" or *"Why* do you do that?" Or look for the answers to these questions from the stakeholder's perspective, reading existing requirements documentation.

What do you...?   When do you...?

How often do you...?   How much do you...?

The answers resulting from the preceding questions should start illustrate a clearer picture of the intended performance characteristics. These answers should also start to outline the required set of *capabilities*; both what will be required for the system or service to perform a required function, and what's the expected outcome.

The next area of examination is the "why" and "how" of the system from the standpoint of stakeholders and system interactions. Questions here include:

• Why do you...?   • How well do you...?

• What happens after you...? • What happens before you...?

Answers to these questions can be organized either formally (i.e., as artifacts) or informally (as memos and unstructured documents) depending on the scope of the system. The result should be a set of clearly identified parameters (objectives, features, capabilities, resources and participants) and the ability to construct these into a narrative. To illustrate, here is an example: *Hiring a New Employee*

Objective: Hire a new employee

Questions:	Answers:
How do they apply?	By submitting an application.
Who receives the application?	A recruiter.
Who makes the hiring decision?	The hiring manager.
How do they make the decision?	By reviewing the applications.
Then what do you do?	Notify the applicant that they got the job.

With these questions we've identified the required resources of application, recruiter and hiring manager, and activities of submitting and application, reviewing the application, and notifying the applicant.

> *To make a hiring decision, the organization must receive a submitted application, a recruiter must assign that application to a hiring manager who reviews it and makes a decision. Once a decision is made, the applicant is notified.*

Form this narrative, the next step is to identify specific use case and beginning the steps of visualizing the process.

IDENTIFYING USE CASES

Once the core capabilities and resources have been captured in a document, the first phase of visual modeling is to design Use Case Diagrams (UCDs.) The UCD is used to describe the level functionality of the system or service in terms of interaction and associations between "Actors" (users and resources) as Verb:Noun combinations (i.e., "Print Document") which comprise Uses Cases. UCDs are used to depict functionality in what is called a "horizontal" manner, or specifically all available functionality at one time. It should not be confused with a flow chart or other UML diagrams (e.g., Activity or Sequence) as they do not depict the actual sequence or number of iteration activities, nor do they depict exceptions or conditions.

Core Use Case Symbols

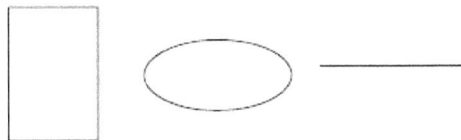

| Actor | System | Use Case | Association |

Although there is no definitive standard, there are four core elements or symbols that define the notation. These consist of a stick figure representing "Actors," rectangles which define the boundaries of the "System" in question, horizontal ovals which present the individual "Use Cases" and solid line which define associations. Because UCDs offer only a very high-level depiction of a system, UCDs should include a written user narrative (developed previously.)

For example, a user narrative describing the process for making a hiring decision reads like this:

To make a hiring decision, the organization must receive a submitted application, a recruiter must assign that application to a hiring manager who reviews it and makes a decision. Once a decision is made, the applicant is notified.

A representative UCD would look like this:

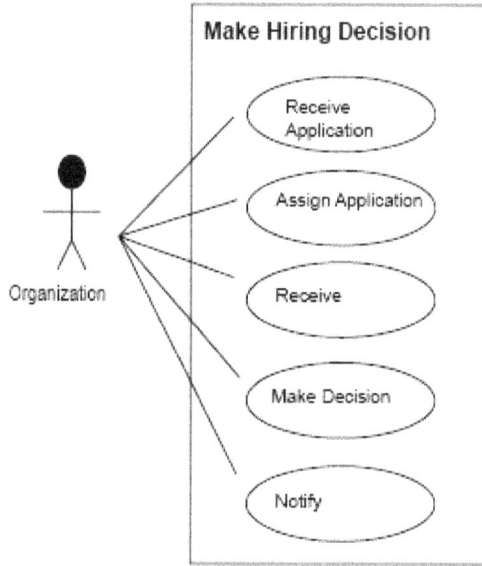

Define Activities and Responsibilities

The next step is to diagram activities and responsibilities using an *Activity Diagram*. The basic building block of a process description in UML is the *Activity*. From a system or service perspective, an activity consists of either separate or sequenced steps (sometimes referred to as "atomic" and "composite" steps) that perform a particular function to deliver a predefined capability, or otherwise transform resources to achieve a specific objective or outcome.

The symbol set for UML Activity Diagrams is similar to that of other common notations, such as BPMN, however, it is limited to the ten basic symbol elements show below (with their respective BPMN counterparts):

	●	◉	⊗	→	▭	◇	[text]	⊢	⊣	—
UML	Start/ Initial Node	Activity Final Node	Flow Final	Flow	Activity	Decision	Condition	Fork or Split	Join	Partition or Swimlane
BPMN	Start	End Terminate	End Cancel	Flow	Transaction, Subprocess, Task	Gateway	Annotation	XOR-Split, AND-Split	XOR-join, AND-join	Pool or Lane

As described previously, an Activity Diagram visualizes the "flow" of actions to be performed including control flow and data flow. This diagram type follows the traditional flowchart format, and is a close approximation of a Data Flow Diagram (DFD) from the structured design method. The Activity Diagram includes considerably more context than UCDs and introduces the notion of transitions or conditional logic, as well as the separation of responsibilities depicted by "swimlanes."

This should also be understood as distinct from a BPMN diagram,, which although sharing a common look to the UML Activity Diagram, depicts actual execution syntax of intended enactment environment. In other words, the BPMN model is intended to have enough information to be executable, and in order to accomplish this consists of over 100 unique elements (rather than only 10) and presents concepts not depicted in an Activity Diagram, such as message flow and specific syntax around workflow control patterns.

Activity Diagrams show the basic flow of a process, but in much finer grain detail than an UCD. This allows for easier validation for missing steps; for example, realizing that the candidate data should be entered into the recruiting system in order to track the applicant over time, we also uncover several steps for the recruiter that were previously unidentified. Using the same user narrative and use case as defined in the previous steps, an Activity Diagram would look like this:

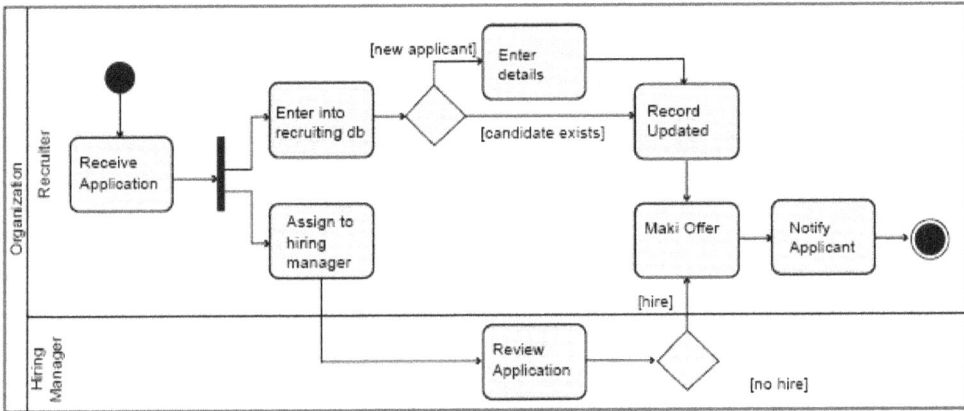

Another advantage of the Activity Diagram is that it helps to identify changes in the process. Although it is not commonly used or necessarily appropriate for large-scale business process reengineering initiatives, by visualizing the

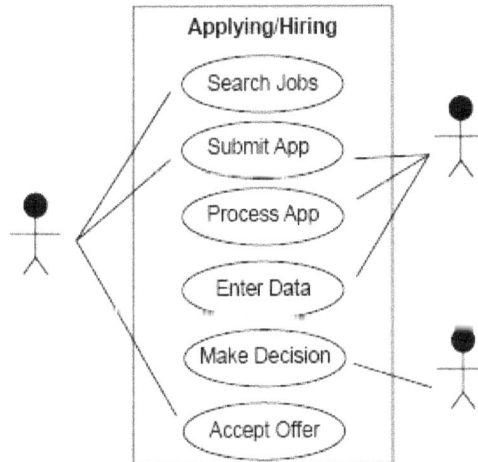

process in the more "business friendly" notation that an Activity Diagram provides, it does allow for identification of basic process improvements.

In fact, in many cases these process improvements may result in the identification of a system capability which should be extracted and encapsulated as an externalized service (i.e., external to the core system or otherwise a web service.)

For example, after visualizing the initial hiring process, it was identified that there should be a separate use case for a more holistic and complete view of the process. As such a new UCD should be developed which identifies the new actors of an "Applicant," "Recruiter," and "Hiring Manager" who each have different associations to a new set of use cases, now involving entities external to the organization.

The Activity Diagram would also change (or a new one would be created) to reflect the new use case, with new roles and responsibilities. In this simple example we depict all the activities that comprise the process of hiring a new employee, as well as the control flow from the point the application arrives until the offer is accepted.

It would be just as appropriate, however, to show the Activity Diagram simply from the perspective of the end user, in this case the Applicant, and abstracting how the hiring decision is made from the recruitment process. This is how web services can be incorporated into the process depicted in an Activity Diagram. The main process manages primary activities and interfaces to nested subprocesses or external services. This can be depicted as shown above, or simply as an activity with a subprocess, interface points, data and message flow, as well as classifications that define relationships and properties of objects exchanged between activities and services, such as the structure of messages and data flows. These classifications are modeled using UML Class Diagrams.

Validate Classes

Class diagrams show the static structure of the object, their internal structure, and their relationships. Classes are depicted as boxes with three sections, top contains the class name, in the middle are attributes, and the bottom methods relating to the attributes.

Class Name
Attribute 1
Attribute 1
Method 1
Method 2

Classes can represent tangible or physical objects (people, products, documents, real estate) as well as information sets and logical concepts (product types, departments.) Class can be *abstract*, representing a superset of other classes but not instantiated in the system and represented in the UML 2.0 notation by an italicized name, or *concrete* indicated by a name with normal text. Concrete classes define a set of common properties or attributes where each instance of the class assigns specific values to class type. "Applicant" has property of "Application" and each Application had one or more codes or "AppCode" relating to different hiring criteria. This model shows that each application is assigned a specific value based on the defined method, in this case "GetAppCode" which consists of the codes define in the *Hiring Codes* class.

An *association relationship* is depicted as a solid line between classes and is used to define a link between two objects. Associations need to be defined in terms of multiples; one-to-one, one-to-many, many-to-one, many-to-many (albeit should be normalized to avoid many-to-many wherever possible.) A small solid arrowhead next to the association name indicates the direction for purpose of reading association names.

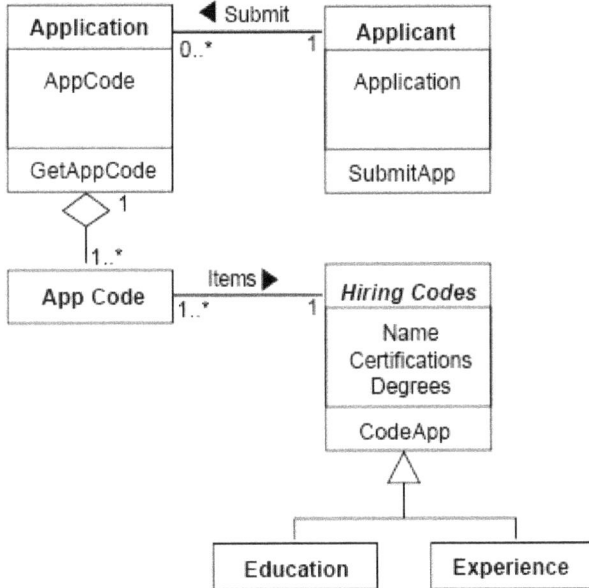

An *aggregation relationship* is depicted by a diamond symbol next to the container class and is used to indicate used to model object types which have other objects as parts, for example *App Code* is made up of *Hiring Codes* which is a superclass of *Education* and *Experience*. Class diagrams depict properties and relationships between objects, but not interaction or message flow between activities. These are depicted using a *Sequence Diagram*.

Define Sequencing and Interaction

The *Sequence Diagram* is used primarily to show the interactions between objects in the sequential order that those interactions occur.

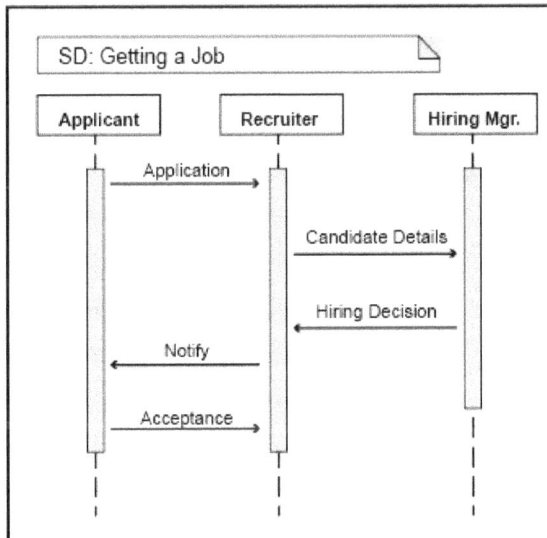

At a high level, these are effective for visualizing stakeholder input and answers to questions asked during Step 1 concerning "What happens after you..." and "What happens before/after you..." in order to capture how various business objects interact. The three primary notions depicted in a sequence diagram are *services*, *methods* and *usage scenarios*.

Services—an invokable service called by an activity or other function. Commonly a web service or otherwise a system-specific transactional procedure, and visually depicted as a high-level method.

Methods—a more granular depiction of the logic of an operation, function, or procedure.

Usage Scenarios—the description of how a system or service is used, typically one complete iteration per use case (as shown below.)

Ultimately sequence diagrams are used to document how an intended system or service should behave. Typically this is done individually for each unique permutation of a use case. In other words, where both the UCD and Activity Diagram present a horizontal view, where all possible pathways and outcomes are shown in one picture, the sequence diagram depicts a one-way trip or complete iteration of one pathway. Where there are significant variations in potential paths and outcomes, unique sequence diagrams should be created.

The basic depiction of the sequence diagram is shown below, with the object in a box at the top, the "activation" of the object in a vertical box and message flow depicted by arrows, with sequence flowing top-down. Iteration can be depicted with a looped arrow from/to the activation box.

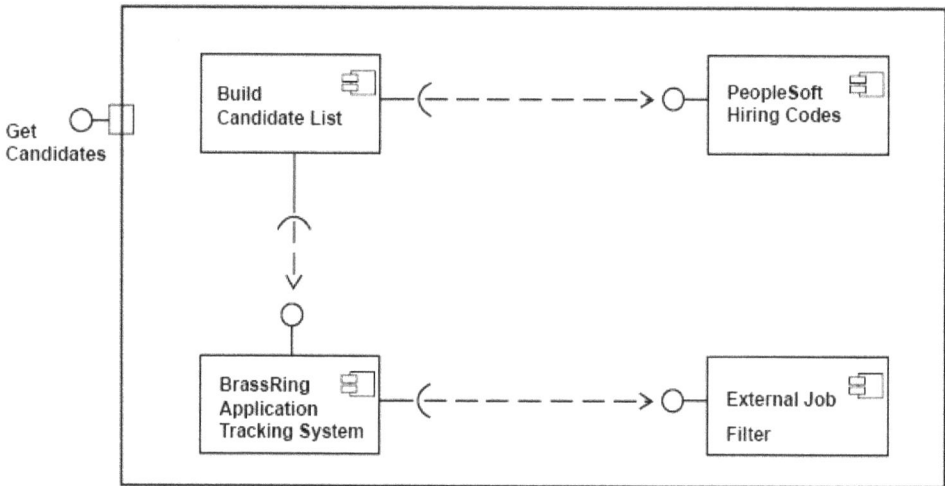

Sequence diagrams are also used to document how objects already existing legacy system currently interact. This will typically include the identification of the message flow and interaction with legacy systems and a new system or service. The specific role and interface points to legacy systems, however, are depicted by a Component Diagram.

Refine Components and Dependencies

The last diagram and in this sequence the final step is the Component Diagram. Unlike the UCD and Activity Diagram, which depict objects (nouns) that are not necessarily tied to any specific software-based system, the Component Diagram specifically depicts system components. Components are by definition logical, design-time constructs representing autonomous, encapsulated units within a system or subsystem that provide one or more interfaces. Component diagrams are used to validate the initial architectural landscape of the system or service, and represent the logical building blocks of component-based development (CBD).

For this reason, Component Diagrams are essentially orthogonal to traditional business process modeling (as more closely approximated in an Activity Diagram) yet are a critical component to services modeling. They provide an essential tool to communicate to non-implementers (stakeholders and end users) how a service will work, as well as to provide a generalized understanding of the system being built.

Components are connected via an *assembly connector* from one component's *provided interface* to another component's *required interface*. The provided interface represents the service contract defining what services the component as service publisher provides to service consumers. The required interface defines dependencies of services provided by other components. A component may have either provided or required interfaces or both, however, it not a functional requirement to have both.

The notation for components in the current version of UML is in part a holdover from previous versions, with the image of the previous component symbol (a box with two small rectangles straddling the right-side edge) now inside the box, as well as the provided interface is a depicted as a ball on a line, and the required interface is shown as a "socket" or half-circle on a line.

A Component Diagram may depict logically assembled components as an entire system, or as the decomposition of a subsystem. For example, on the previous page is a Component Diagram depicting the UML notation for the activity defined earlier for obtaining applications.

The role of the Component Diagram is to illustrate the building blocks which compose "coarse grain" capabilities without having to define the specific execution within the individual pieces. They offer a view of the high-level software and/or service components between them. For this reason they are often referred in more casual terms as "wiring diagrams" as they illustrate components that are wired together. Component Diagrams provide a perspective which is not easily gleaned from a BPMN diagram or other UML models, as they are not intended to depict actual execution syntax but rather the interplay between components and capabilities.

SUMMARY

As more and more organizations face the challenge of how to successfully integrate legacy and modern applications to expose the necessary functionality from each system, BPM and SOA are likewise increasingly viewed as the answer. The assumed benefit is most often the anticipated flexibility and reduced need for tenuous custom coding. Yet these deployment environments generally lack a means for modeling capabilities which reside out of the direct control of the BPMS or otherwise that will be built within the SOA deployment environment. Following this basic five-step process, which in most cases, should be performed iteratively permit us to refine the models through repeated validation. These steps allow taking a "development first" approach which may start with a complete process model, but which typically lacks validated definition of capabilities with a controlled vocabulary, obviates the inherent BPM benefit being able to build complete systems based on stakeholders' understanding of operations. It will instead result in a repeat of the traditional IT-centric model that will be difficult to adapt to changes in the business environment.

In contrast, by starting with a common vocabulary and business-centered understanding of required capabilities, then building out the constructs of the system based on these controlled terms, permits us to develop a system which maps to true business architecture and allows for a more agile and more manageable environment that optimally leverages the best qualities of a BPMS environment.

XPDL 2.2: Incorporating BPMN 2.0 Process Modeling Extensions

Robert M. Shapiro, Global 360, USA

INTRODUCTION

In June 2009 the OMG[1] voted to adopt the BPMN 2.0 specification which then entered the Finalization Task Force (FTF) phase. At that time the WfMC[2] initiated work revising XPDL2.1. The new version, XPDL2.2, is described in this paper.

As of March 1, 2010 the FTF was still hard at work. Many issues in BPMN2.0 remain unresolved. If the FTF completes its task in June, the original objective, it will do so only by deferring a large number of issues. The principle reason for this is that many new ideas were introduced that extend or change what was in the previous version, BPMN1.2.

XPDL2.2 is intended as a preliminary release which supports the graphical extensions to process modeling contained in BPMN2.0. In fact, the BPMN specification addresses four different areas of modeling, referred to as:

- Process Modeling
- Process Execution
- BPEL Process Execution
- Choreography Modeling

We focus only on Process Modeling. Within that we define several subclasses to support process interchange between tools. This is discussed in a later section of this paper.

For a review of XPDL we refer the reader to a prior paper which describes the historical development of XPDL and a review of the major elements in XPDL2.1[3] . Here we discuss significant additions in XPDL2.2.

Another part of the process interchange story is the serialization of a process diagram, which is used to persist a process model and to transport it to other tools. XPDL has been used for this purpose and XPDL2.1 is the only standardized way of serializing earlier versions of BPMN[4]. The OMG is committed to providing a serialization of BPMN2.0, but the draft specification contains a serialization only for the semantic portion of the specification; the graphical aspects of diagram interchange are being worked on by the Diagram Interchange subgroup of the FTF. We return to this topic in a later section of this paper.

OVERVIEW OF ADDITIONS AND CHANGES

In the next sections we discuss changes in the following areas:

---

[1] Object Management Group

[2] Workflow Management Coalition

[3] XPDL 2.1 - Integrating Process Interchange & BPMN

  http://www.wfmc.org/Specifications-Working-Documents/XPDL/

[4] 1.0,1.1,1.2

- Pools and Lanes
- Call Activity/Re-usable Sub-Process
- Event Sub-Process
- Event Types
- Data Objects, Data Flow and Input/Output Specifications

For a complete description of BPMN2.0 refer to the OMG specification[5]. For a complete description of XPDL2.2 refer to the WfMC specification[6].

POOLS AND LANES

In prior versions of BPMN all the process modeling elements pertaining to flow, i.e. Activities, Gateways, Events and SequenceFlow, were always contained in a Pool. All the flow elements in a Pool were part of the same process. Multiple processes were depicted using multiple pools. Message communication between processes was depicted by message flow between Pools. The Pool boundary was optional for a single Pool in the diagram. Lanes were a way of subdividing Pools.

In BPMN2.0 a distinction is made between Collaboration diagrams and Process diagrams. A Collaboration diagram involves two or more Pools with Message flow between them. A Process diagram has no Pool. To support the Lane construct, a new element, LaneSet, was introduced. The Lane structure is contained in LaneSet. Both Pool and Process may have LaneSets.

Eliminating Pool from a process diagram creates an inconsistency between prior versions of BPMN and BPMN2.0 with little apparent benefit. Consequently in XPDL2.2 we retain the idea of a background Pool for a single process with no pool border displayed. Lanes remain a way of subdividing Pools.

CALL ACTIVITY/RE-USABLE SUB-PROCESS

BPMN2.0 introduces a graphical distinction between embedded Sub-Process and Re-Usable Sub-Process which is incorporated in XPDL2.2. However, the manner in which input and output parameters are passed between the caller process and the called process remains complicated and confusing. XPDL retains the mechanisms provided for accomplishing this: providing conventional parameter lists (actual and formal parameters) as well as straightforward data mapping between data fields in the two processes upon entry and exit.

EVENT SUB-PROCESS

An Event Sub-Process is similar to an Embedded Sub-Process. It shares the data environment of the Process or Sub-Process in which it is defined. The instantiation is different. Instead of being instantiated by a SequenceFlow, it is triggered by an Event. In XPDL both Event and Embedded Sub-Process are defined by Activity Sets within a Process. An Embedded Sub-Process is instantiated by execution of a Block Activity in the Sequence flow of the containing Process, whereas the Event Sub-Process is triggered by an Event.

---

[5] OMG, BPMN (version 2.0 – June, 2009)

[6] WfMC, XPDL 2.2 WFMC-TC-1025 (Version 1.0 April 2009)

An attribute of Activity Set 'TriggeredByEvent' distinguishes between Event and Embedded.

EVENT TYPES

Event Types in BPMN2.0 are more complex for three reasons:

- Support for both interrupting and non-interrupting Events.
- Introduction of the Event Sub-Process.
- Introduction of a new Event type: EscalateEvent.

Changes in XPDL to support this are minimal:

- A new attribute 'Interrupting' with a default value 'true' for the appropriate Start and Intermediate Events.
- Addition of Escalation Event for:
  - Interrupting or non-interrupting Start Event in Event Sub-Process.
  - Interrupting or non-interrupting Boundary Intermediate Event.
  - Intermediate or End Throw Event

The following chart (from the specification) portrays all the Event types and the contexts in which they may occur.

Types	Start			Intermediate				End
	Top-Level	Event Sub-Process Interrupting	Event Sub-Process Non-Interrupting	Catching	Boundary Interrupting	Boundary Non-Interrupting	Throwing	
None	●			●				●
Message	●	●	●	●	●	●	●	●
Timer	●	●	●	●	●	●		
Error		●			●			●
Escalation		●	●		●	●	●	●
Cancel					●			●
Compensation		●			●		●	●
Conditional	●	●	●	●	●	●		
Link				●			●	
Signal	●	●	●	●	●	●	●	●
Terminate								●
Multiple	●	●	●	●	●	●	●	●
Parallel Multiple	●	●	●	●	●	●		

DATA OBJECTS, DATA FLOW AND INPUT/OUTPUT SPECIFICATIONS[7]

Data and data flow, as represented in the diagram by the *data object* shape and *association*, were classified in BPMN 1.x as *artifacts*, meaning essentially annotations of the diagram with no defined semantics.

That has all changed in BPMN 2.0. Data has been elevated to a first-class semantic element. A data object, together with a handful of other types of *data-aware elements*, now signifies a *process variable*, defined with a specific schema. It is no longer connected to flow elements by a regular association, which still just applies to artifacts, but with a new type of connector, a *data association*. The details of the data association actually define the mapping of data from one flow element to the next.

The *data object* is the primary construct for modeling data within a process. Each data object is contained within a specific process or subprocess element, and its lifetime and visibility are constrained within that element. In other words, a data object could represent a *global variable* for the process or a *local variable* for a particular activity. The lifetime of a data object is limited to the lifetime of the process or activity instance.

Data Object   Collection
                 Data Object   Data Store

A data object representing a *collection* of variables is depicted in the diagram with the multi-instance marker. A *data store* represents a data structure that the process can read or write but which persists beyond the lifetime of the process.

Processes, tasks, and global tasks specify their input and output parameters, or data requirements, as *data inputs* and *data outputs*. A data input represents information needed to start an activity, and each data input can be defined as required or optional; it cannot have incoming data associations. If a required data input is unavailable when a process or task is invoked, start is delayed until that data input becomes available. A data output represents information that may be output from an activity; it cannot have outgoing data associations.

Data input (left) and data output (right)

The collection of data inputs and data outputs required by a particular activity is called an *inputSet* and *outputSet,* respectively, and together these comprise the *ioSpecification* for the activity or process. It is possible to define multiple inputSets and outputSets, in which case the implementation determines which ones apply.

---

[7] This section is taken from BPMN Method and Style, Bruce Silver 2009

A *data association*, depicted in the diagram using the dotted line connector, represents a mapping between a data object, property, or data store (i.e., persisted data) on one end and a data input or data output (i.e., parameter) on the other end. A data association connected to an activity or event in the process diagram represents a visual shorthand for connection to the data input or output of that activity or event. Activities have two types of data association, *dataInputAssociation* and *dataOutputAssociation*, respectively. A catching or throwing event has only one, as appropriate.

A data association defines a *source* and a *target*, and optionally a *transformation*. When a data association is executed, data is copied from the source to the target, and possibly transformed in the process.

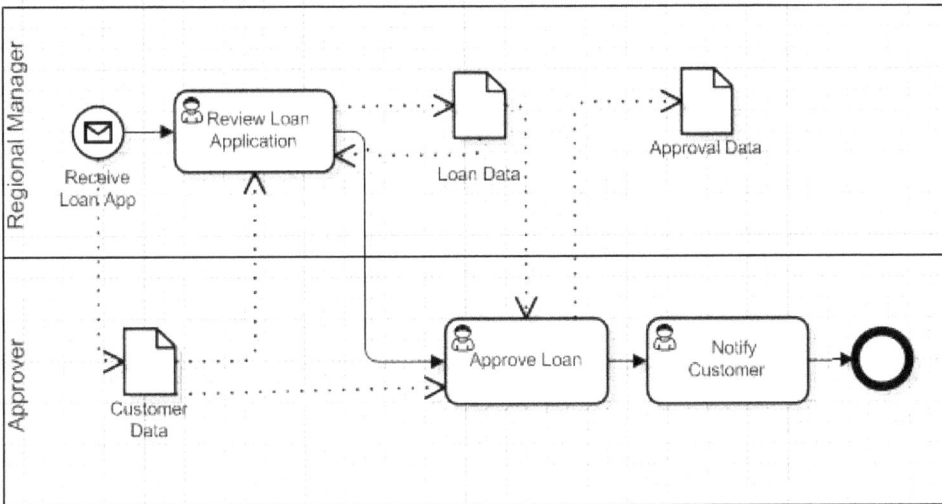

The example shown above illustrates the use of data objects and data associations in executable BPMN.

> For non-executable modeling,

- Data Input and Data Output are typically omitted from the model.
- Data Object is used in the same way as the Data Object artifact of XPDL2.1.
- DataStore is used to graphically emphasize **persistent data**.

PROCESS METAMODEL

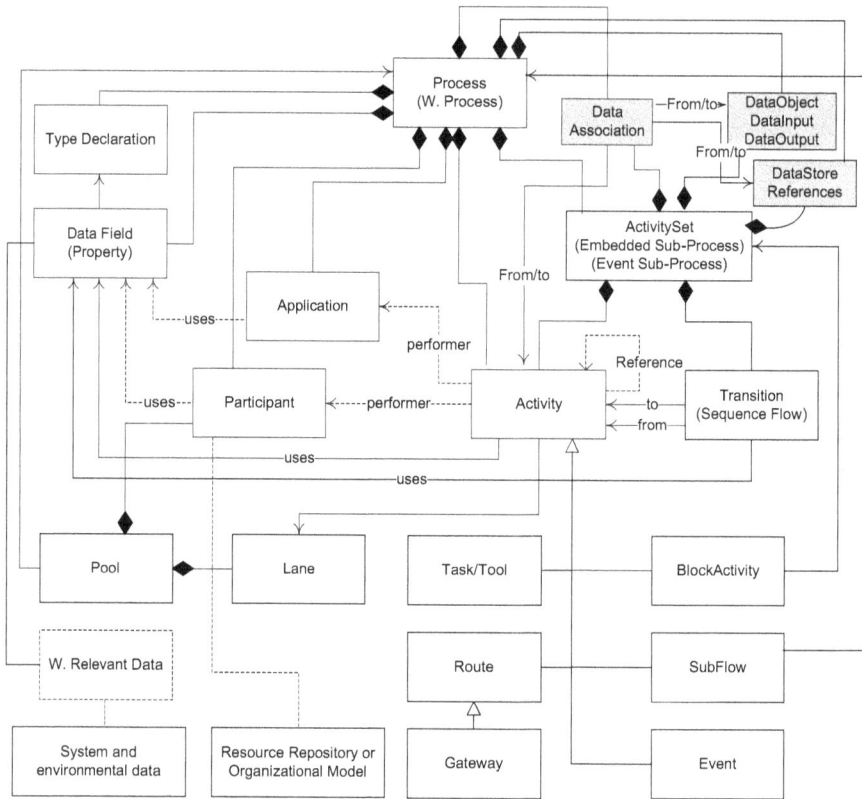

The meta-model depicts the relationships between all the elements in a Process. The shaded elements represent new graphical elements added to XPDL.

PACKAGE METAMODEL

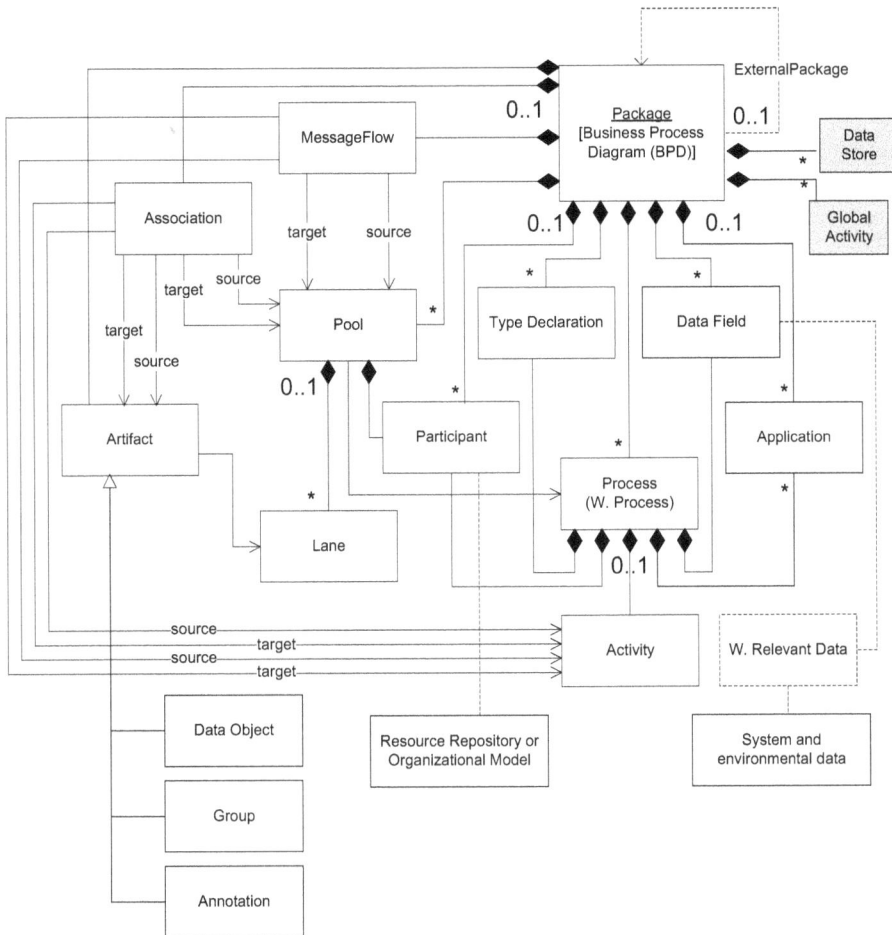

ExternalPackage

0..1

Package
[Business Process
Diagram (BPD)]

0..1

Data Store

Global Activity

MessageFlow

Association

target   source

target   source

target

source

0..1

0..1

0..1

Pool

Type Declaration

Data Field

Artifact

0..1

Participant

Process
(W. Process)

Application

Lane

0..1

source
source

target
target

Activity

W. Relevant Data

Data Object

Resource Repository or
Organizational Model

System and
environmental data

Group

Annotation

This meta-model describes the relationship between elements on the Package or Business Process Diagram level. The shaded elements represent new graphical elements added to XPDL.

PROCESS INTERCHANGE

Common meta-model allows tools to exchange models
Type of tools:

- Simulation tools
- Monitoring tools
- Execution tools
- Modeling tools
- Repository tools

The following diagram illustrates the use of process interchange in a BPM suite.

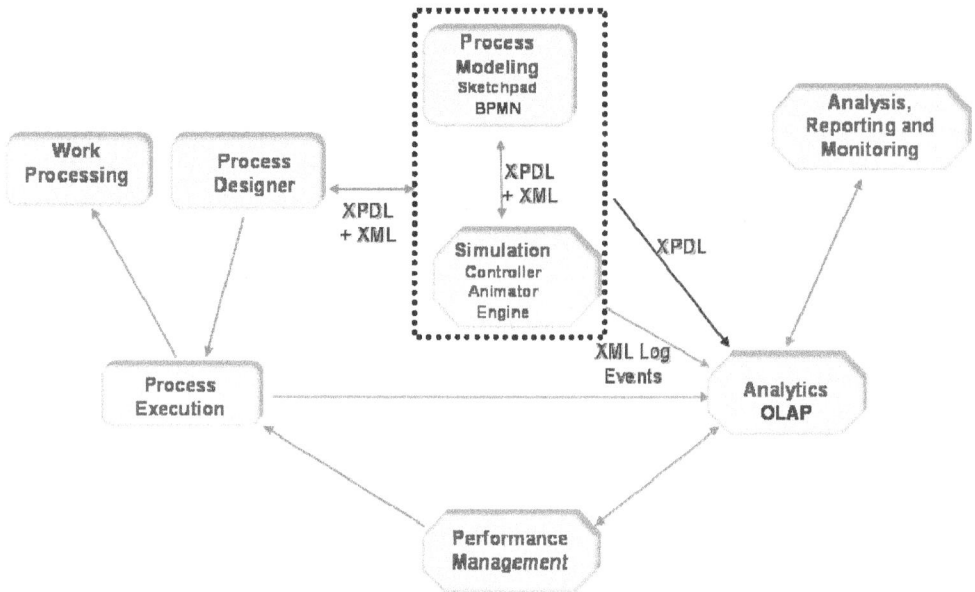

BPMN Model Portability Conformance

BPMN can be used for both "abstract" activity flow modeling and for complete executable design. Many tools, however, make use of BPMN for the abstract modeling but add executable detail in tool-specific activity properties. One goal of XPDL 2.2 is to promote portability of abstract activity flow models between tools. This requires separating the elements and attributes of BPMN related to activity flow modeling from those related to executable design. The BPMN2.0 spec does not define this separation, but a proposal being considered by the OMG BPMN2.0 Finalization Task Force would add Conformance sub-classes for this. XPDL2.1 did this, in the form of BPMN Model Portability conformance classes. XPDL2.2 modifies and extends the conformance classes.

In broad terms, the "abstract model" elements are those that represent BPMN constructs that are printable in the business process diagram, such as those defining the flow object type or subtype (e.g., looping User task, collapsed sub-process, exclusive gateway, timer event), including only attributes specifying the subtype, label (Name attribute), and unique identifiers for the object itself and pointers to other identifiers in the diagram. Elements and attributes representing data, messages, or other implementation detail are omitted from the abstract process model. In other words, the model describes the "what" and the "when" of process activity flow, but not the "how" of flow object implementation.

There are three conformance sub-classes defined:

- SIMPLE
- DESCRIPTIVE
- ANALYTIC

SIMPLE is contained in DESCRIPTIVE, which is, in turn, contained in ANA-LYTIC.

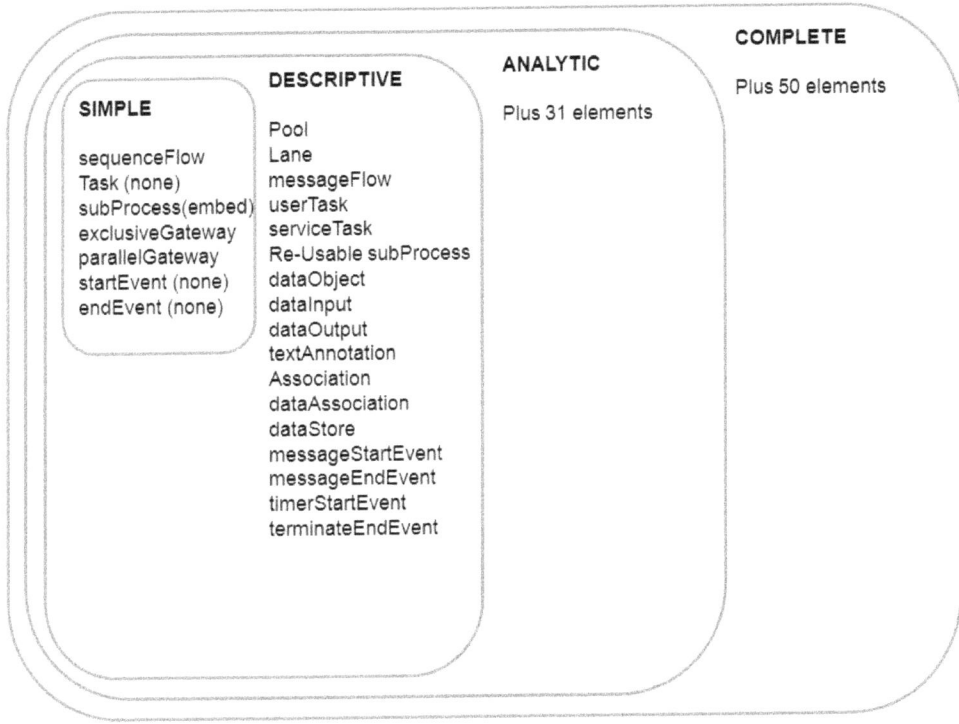

SIMPLE

ELEMENT	ATTRIBUTES
sequenceFlow (unconditional)	id, name, sourceRef, targetRef
task (None)	id, name
subProcess (expanded)	id, name, flowElement
subProcess (collapsed)	id, name, flowElement
exclusiveGateway	id, name
parallelGateway	id, name
startEvent (None)	id, name
endEvent (None)	id, name

DESCRIPTIVE

All the elements in SIMPLE plus:

ELEMENT	ATTRIBUTES
participant (pool)	id, name, processRef
laneSet	id, name, partitionElement, childLaneSet, flowElementRef
messageFlow	id, name, sourceRef, targetRef
userTask	id, name
serviceTask	id, name

callActivity	id, name, calledElement
dataObject	id, name
textAnnotation	id, text
association/dataAssociation	id, name, sourceRef, targetRef, associationDirection*
dataStoreReference	id, name, dataStoreRef
messageStartEvent	id, name, messageEventDefinition
messageEndEvent	id, name, messageEventDefinition
timerStartEvent	id, name, timerEventDefinition
terminateEndEvent	id, name terminate EventDefinition

* associationDirection not specified for dataAssociation

ANALYTIC

All the elements in DESCRIPTIVE plus:

ELEMENT	ATTRIBUTES
sequenceFlow (conditional)	id, name, sourceRef, targetRef, conditionExpression*
sequenceFlow (default)	id, name, sourceRef, targetRef, default**
sendTask	id, name
receiveTask	id, name
Looping Activity	standardLoopCharacteristics
MultiInstance Activity	multiInstanceLoopCharacteristics
exclusiveGateway	Add default attribute
inclusiveGateway	id, name, eventGatewayType
eventBasedGateway	id, name, eventGatewayType
signalStartEvent	id, name, signalEventDefinition
signalEndEvent	id, name, signalEventDefinition
Catching message IE***	id, name, messageEventDefinition
Throwing message IE	id, name, messageEventDefinition
Boundary message IE	id, name, attachedToRef, timerEventDefinition
Non-int Boundary message IE	id, name, attachedToRef, cancelActivity=false, messageEventDefinition
Catching time rIE	id, name, timerEventDefinition
Boundary timer IE	id, name, attachedToRef, timerEventDefinition
Non-int**** Boundary timer IE	id, name, attachedToRef, cancelActivity=false, timerEventDefinition
Boundary error IE	id, name, attachedToRef, errorEventDefinition

errorEndEvent	id, name, errorEventDefinition
Non-int Boundary escalation IE	id, name, attachedToRef, cancelActivity=false, escalationEventDefinition
Throwing escalation IE	id, name, escalationEventDefinition
escalationEndEvent	id, name, escalationEventDefinition
Catching signal IE	id, name, signalEventDefinition
Throwing signal IE	id, name, signalEventDefinition
Boundary signal IE	id, name, attachedToRef, signalEventDefinition
Non-int Boundary signal IE	id, name, attachedToRef, cancelActivity=false, signalEventDefinition
conditionalStartEvent	id, name, condtionalEventDefinition
Catching conditional IE	id, name, condtionalEventDefinition
Boundary conditional IE	id, name, condtionalEventDefinition
Non-int Boundary conditional IE	id, name, cancelActivity=false, condtionalEventDefinition
message	id, name

* conditionExpression allowed only for sequenceFlow out of gateways, may be null.

**default is an attribute of a sourceRef (exclusive or inclusive) DecisionGateway.

***IE= intermediateEvent

****Non-int=nonInterrupting

For a tool to claim support for a sub-class the following criteria must be satisfied:

- All the elements in the sub-class must be supported.
- For each element, all the listed attributes must be supported.

The tool must be able to read and write syntactically correct serializations that include any other elements and attributes. In particular, if a tool reads in such a serialization and edits it, when writing it out all elements and attributes not in the supported sub-class must also be written out.

SIMPLE PERSONA

A common situation for use of the SIMPLE class is *process capture*.

- A business analyst is sitting in a room with a group of process owners.
- The session is attempting to map out a currently deployed set of processes that have never been suitably documented.
- Technology for such a session may range from a low-tech whiteboard to a laptop and projector.
- A process map is drawn by the business analyst as the process owners describe their operations step by step.

SIMPLE Example:

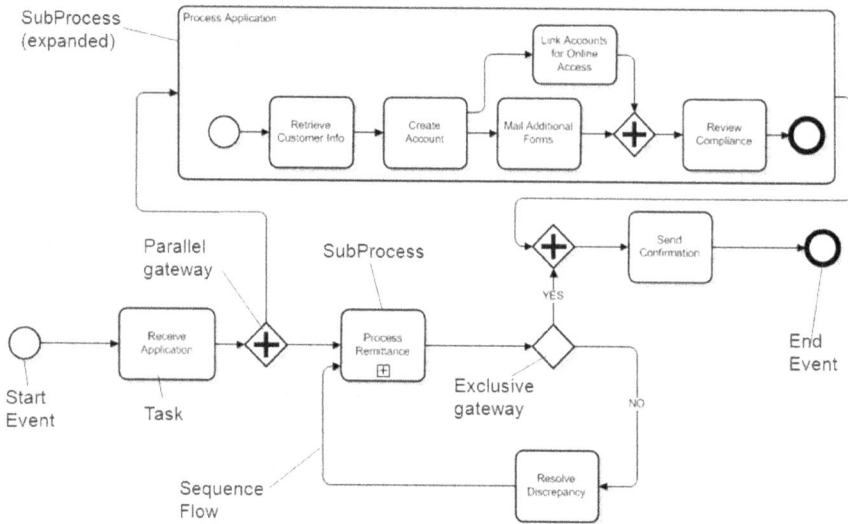

DESCRIPTIVE PERSONA

A common situation for use of the descriptive class is fleshing out the details omitted in a process capture session

Using elements familiar from traditional flowcharting, the business modeler

- extends the routing logic to include the more critical exceptions (such as time-outs) and special cases,
- adds information about resource or role requirements for performing activities,
- adds some basic information about data flow
- and provides an overview of communications between partici-pants/processes pertaining to the start and end of processes.

DESCRIPTIVE Example

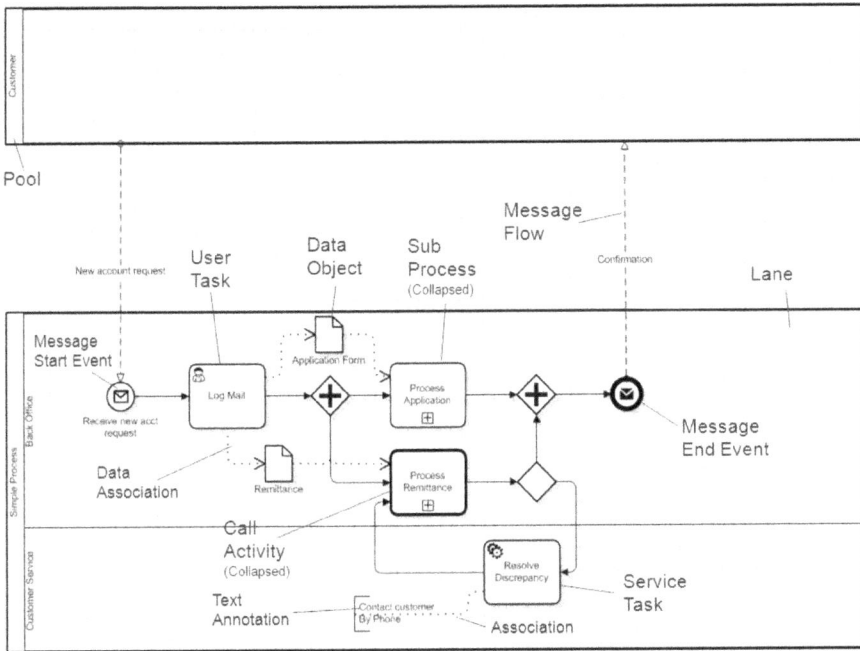

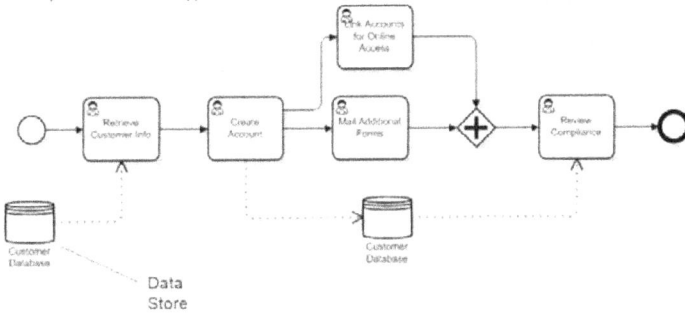

Expansion of Process Application

CONCLUSION

XPDL 2.2 provides a standard graphical approach to Business Process Definition based on BPMN graphics. XPDL 2.2 provides a standard file format for persisting BPMN diagrams and interchanging Process definitions. The file format is based on the WfMC meta-model which establishes a framework for defining, importing and exporting process definitions for numerous products including execution engines, simulators, BPA modeling tools, Business Activity Monitoring and reporting tools. The schema defining the format is extensible and provides vendor and user extension capabilities as well as a natural path for future versions of the standard. Mappings to specific execution languages (e.g. BPEL) and other XML-based specifications (e.g. ebXML) are possible. Finally, BPMN Model Portability conformance classes greatly increase the likelihood of true portability at the design level between a significant number of different vendor tools.

Workflow Control-path Intelligence and Its Implications

Haksung Kim, Dongnam Health University and Kwanghoon Kim, Kyonggi Univ., Rep. of Korea

In this paper, we describe the basic concept of workflow control-path intelligence and its implications on the arena of business process analysis, prediction and optimization. That is, we introduce a series of models, algorithms and frameworks for analyzing, predicting, optimizing and rediscovering the control-path intelligence from a workflow model. Conclusively, we strongly believe that the workflow control-path intelligence must be an essential factor for improving the quality of workflow model itself as well as a pioneering research issue in extracting other workflow-related knowledge and intelligence to rapidly and reliably deliver agile services to businesses and IT customers.

INTRODUCTION

According for workflow design and automation technologies to swiftly grow and be increasingly adopted by both traditional and newly-formed web-based enterprises, we need to deal with and attempt to analyze a new type of requirements and demands concerning about workflow intelligence and quality. Especially, in order to improve the quality of workflows with a high, consistent and predictable efficiency, emphasizing on the workflow intelligence from runtime executions is never enough at all; There might be several perspectives on the workflow intelligence; For instance, workflows should be correctly designed; control flow and data flow perspective and their executions should meet their workload requirements; behavioral perspective, and the process resources, actors, roles, and policies, should be assigned into the work items in a timely and skillfully reasonable fashion from an organizational perspective.

Out of those perspectives, the main focus of this paper is on the control-flow perspective, through which we are able to ratify the answers for both of the questions: "Is a workflow model correctly reflecting the control-flow aspect of the corresponding real-world business process?", and, "Is the enactment history and logs of a workflow model able to not only provide some valuable process-oriented business knowledge and intelligence, but also be embodied as business intelligence?" (Note that the control-flow perspective of a workflow model is especially called *workflow process*, and also each of the possible execution sequences of the workflow process is called *workflow control-path* in this paper.) In other words, we try to dig into the control-flow perspective embedded in a workflow model, which is dubbed especially workflow control-path intelligence, by systematically arranging a series of models, algorithms and frameworks for analyzing, rediscovering, predicting and optimizing the control-path intelligence. Based upon those fundamental theories, we try also to answer to the questions by showing how the analyzed and rediscovered workflow control-path intelligence is valuably used in monitoring and predicting the behaviors of workflow models (or business processes) as well as optimizing the structures of workflow models. Finally, the models and frameworks suggested in the paper ought to be a fundamental methodology that can be reused in digging into other perspectives of the process-oriented business knowledge and intelligence.

The remainder of this paper is organized as follows. In the next sections, we try to define the basic concept of workflow intelligence, and describe the details of analyzing, rediscovering and reconstructing approaches of the workflow control-path intelligence. Finally, we explain the implications and applications of the workflow control-path intelligence in terms of predicting the runtime behaviors as well as optimizing the structures of workflow models.

PRELIMINARIES

There are two of essential keywords; *workflow model* and *workflow intelligence* in this paper. I would say about the relationship of them, suchlike that workflow model embeds workflow intelligence, and reversely workflow intelligence affects structure and behavior of workflow model. Also, all of the models, algorithms and frameworks described in this paper require a concrete workflow model and a confined scope of workflow intelligence in order to algorithmically work out their detailed problems and goals. Therefore, in this section we would summarily describe the basic concept of information control net as a workflow modeling methodology, and define the basic concept of workflow intelligence and confine its scope.

Information Control Net for Workflow Model

All of the models, algorithms and frameworks of this paper are based on the Information Control Net (ICN) that is a typical workflow modeling methodology. The information control net was originally aiming to describe and analyze information flow by capturing several entities within office procedures, such as activities, roles, actors, precedence, applications, and repositories. It has been used within actual as well as hypothetical automated offices to yield a comprehensive description of activities, to test the underlying office description for certain flaws and inconsistencies, to quantify certain aspects of office information flow, and to suggest possible office restructuring permutations. In this section, especially, we focus on the activities and their related information flows by defining workflow process models through its graphical and formal representations.

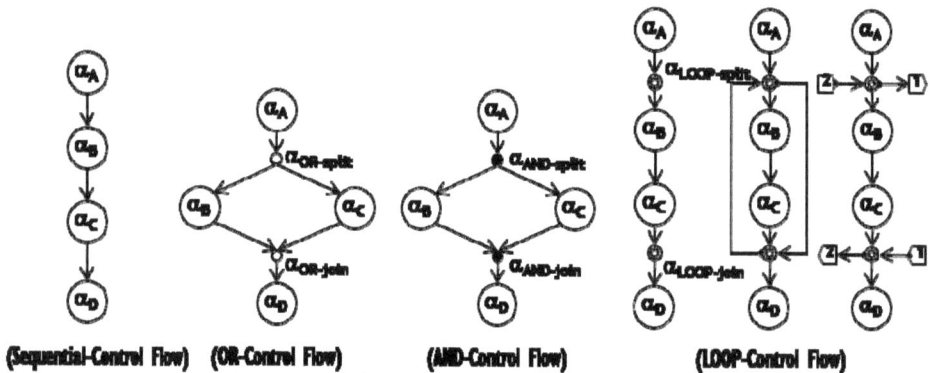

(Sequential-Control Flow) (OR-Control Flow) (AND-Control Flow) (LOOP-Control Flow)

Figure 1. The Graphical Primitives of ICN

A workflow process model consists of a set of activities connected by temporal orderings called activity transitions. In other word, it is a predefined set of work steps, called activities, and a partial ordering (or control flow) of these activities. As shown in Figure 1, activities can be related to each other by combining sequential transition types, disjunctive transition types (after activity a_A, do activity a_B or a_C, alternatively) with predicates attached, conjunctive transition types (after activity a_A, do activities a_B and a_C, concurrently) and loop transition types (after activity a_A, do activity a_B and next do a_C, repeatedly). An activity is either a compound activity containing another subprocess, or a basic unit of work called an elementary activity. An elementary activity can be executed in one of three modes: manual, automatic, or hybrid.

The workflow process model also needs to be represented by a formal notation that provides a means to eventually specify the model in textual language or in database, and both. The following [Definition 1] is the formal representation of the workflow process model:

Definition 1. **Information Control Net (ICN)** *of a workflow process model. A basic* **ICN** *is 4-tuple* $\Gamma = (\delta, \kappa, \mathbf{I}, \mathbf{O})$ *over a set of,* **A***, activities (including a set of group activities) and a set of,* **T***, transition conditions, where*

- *—* **I** *is a finite set of initial input repositories, assumed to be loaded with information by some external process before execution of the ICN;*
- *—* **O** *is a finite set of final output repositories, perhaps containing information used by some external process after execution of the ICN;*
- *—* $\delta = \delta_i \cup \delta_o$ *where,*
    $\delta_o : \mathbf{A} \longrightarrow \wp(\alpha \in \mathbf{A})$ *is a multi-valued mapping function of an activity to its set of (immediate) successors, and*
    $\delta_i : \mathbf{A} \longrightarrow \wp(\alpha \in \mathbf{A})$ *is a multi-valued mapping function of an activity to its set of (immediate) predecessors;*
- *—* $\kappa = \kappa_i \cup \kappa_o$ *where*
    $\kappa_i(\alpha)$ *: sets of control-transition conditions,* **T***, on each arc,* $(\delta_i(\alpha), \alpha), \alpha \in \mathbf{A}$*; and*
    $\kappa_o(\alpha)$ *: sets of control-transition conditions,* **T***, on each arc,* $(\alpha, \delta_o(\alpha)), \alpha \in \mathbf{A}$*;*
    where the set **T** $= \{default, or(conditions), and(conditions)\}$.

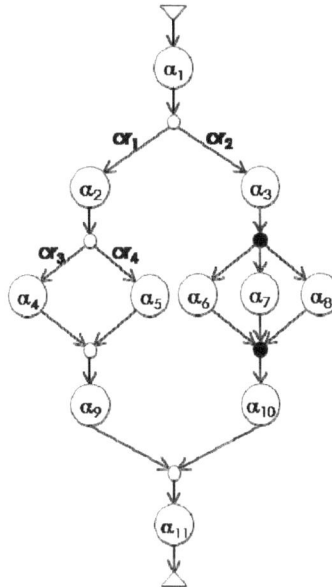

Figure 2. The Graphical Representation of an ICN-based Workflow Process Model

Figure 2 is to represent a simple example of ICN-based workflow process model with its graphical notations. In the graphical notation of ICN, circles represent activities, arcs, which may have transition conditions, such as or_1, or_2, or_3, or_4, represent the precedence partial orders, hollow dots represent or-split and or-join in a pair of nodes, filled dots represent and-split and and-join in a pair of nodes, and two small triangles represent start and end, respectively. Also, the following Table 1 is the formal representation for the example model.

Table 1. Formal Representation of the ICN-based Workflow Process Model

$\Gamma = (\delta, \kappa, I, O)$ over A, T /* The ICN-based Workflow Process Model

$A = \{\alpha_1, \alpha_2, \alpha_3, \alpha_4, \alpha_5, \alpha_6, \alpha_7, \alpha_8, \alpha_9, \alpha_{10}, \alpha_{11}, \alpha_I, \alpha_F\}$ /* Activities
$T = \{d(default), or_1, or_2, or_3, or_4\}$ /* Transition Conditions
$I = \{\emptyset\}$ /* Initial Input Repositories
$O = \{\emptyset\}$ /* Final Output Repositories

$\delta = \delta_i \cup \delta_o$

$\delta_i(\alpha_I) = \{\emptyset\}$;	$\delta_o(\alpha_I) = \{\alpha_1\}$;
$\delta_i(\alpha_1) = \{\alpha_I\}$;	$\delta_o(\alpha_1) = \{\{\alpha_2, \alpha_3\}\}$;
$\delta_i(\alpha_2) = \{\alpha_1\}$;	$\delta_o(\alpha_2) = \{\{\alpha_4, \alpha_5\}\}$;
$\delta_i(\alpha_3) = \{\alpha_1\}$;	$\delta_o(\alpha_3) = \{\{\alpha_6\}, \{\alpha_7\}, \{\alpha_8\}\}$;
$\delta_i(\alpha_4) = \{\alpha_2\}$;	$\delta_o(\alpha_4) = \{\alpha_9\}$;
$\delta_i(\alpha_5) = \{\alpha_2\}$;	$\delta_o(\alpha_5) = \{\alpha_9\}$;
$\delta_i(\alpha_6) = \{\alpha_3\}$;	$\delta_o(\alpha_6) = \{\alpha_{10}\}$;
$\delta_i(\alpha_7) = \{\alpha_4\}$;	$\delta_o(\alpha_7) = \{\alpha_{10}\}$;
$\delta_i(\alpha_8) = \{\alpha_3\}$;	$\delta_o(\alpha_8) = \{\alpha_{10}\}$;
$\delta_i(\alpha_9) = \{\{\alpha_4, \alpha_5\}\}$;	$\delta_o(\alpha_9) = \{\alpha_{11}\}$;
$\delta_i(\alpha_{10}) = \{\{\alpha_6\}, \{\alpha_7\}, \{\alpha_8\}\}$;	$\delta_o(\alpha_{10}) = \{\alpha_{11}\}$;
$\delta_i(\alpha_{11}) = \{\{\alpha_9, \alpha_{10}\}\}$;	$\delta_o(\alpha_{11}) = \{\alpha_F\}$;
$\delta_i(\alpha_F) = \{\alpha_{11}\}$;	$\delta_o(\alpha_F) = \{\emptyset\}$;

$\kappa = \kappa_i \cup \kappa_o$

$\kappa_i(\alpha_I) = \{\emptyset\}$;	$\kappa_o(\alpha_I) = \{d\}$;
$\kappa_i(\alpha_1) = \{d\}$;	$\kappa_o(\alpha_1) = \{or_1, or_2\}$;
$\kappa_i(\alpha_2) = \{or_1\}$;	$\kappa_o(\alpha_2) = \{or_3, or_4\}$;
$\kappa_i(\alpha_3) = \{or_2\}$;	$\kappa_o(\alpha_3) = \{d\}$;
$\kappa_i(\alpha_4) = \{or_3\}$;	$\kappa_o(\alpha_4) = \{d\}$;
$\kappa_i(\alpha_5) = \{or_4\}$;	$\kappa_o(\alpha_5) = \{d\}$;
$\kappa_i(\alpha_6) = \{d\}$;	$\kappa_o(\alpha_6) = \{d\}$;
$\kappa_i(\alpha_7) = \{d\}$;	$\kappa_o(\alpha_7) = \{d\}$;
$\kappa_i(\alpha_8) = \{d\}$;	$\kappa_o(\alpha_8) = \{d\}$;
$\kappa_i(\alpha_9) = \{d\}$;	$\kappa_o(\alpha_9) = \{d\}$;
$\kappa_i(\alpha_{10}) = \{d\}$;	$\kappa_o(\alpha_{10}) = \{d\}$;
$\kappa_i(\alpha_{11}) = \{d\}$;	$\kappa_o(\alpha_{11}) = \{d\}$;
$\kappa_i(\alpha_F) = \{d\}$;	$\kappa_o(\alpha_F) = \{\emptyset\}$;

Workflow Intelligence Perspectives

In describing an ICN-based workflow model, we would use the basic workflow terminology—workflow procedure, activity, job, workcase, role, actor/group, and invoked application including web services. These terms become the primitive entity types to be composed into the ICN-based workflow model, and also they have appropriate relationships with each other as shown in Figure 3. These primitive entity types and their relationships spawn and form some perspectives looking at knowledge and intelligence of workflows or business processes. By using the analyzed and rediscovered results from these perspectives of workflow knowledge and intelligence, it is systematically possible to provide high, consistent, and predictable quality of process-oriented services to reengineer and redesign the corresponding workflows and business processes, and consequently they become essential values to be able to achieve their business goals to attract and retain business customers. The followings are the basic primitives of the workflow intelligence that can be discovered from a series of workflow models deployed and enacted in an organization:

- **Intelligence from the workflow procedure perspective.** A workflow procedure is defined by a predefined or intended set of tasks or steps, called activities, and their temporal ordering of executions. As we introduced in the previous section, a workflow procedure can be described by a temporal order of the associated activities through the combinations of sequential logics, conjunctive logics, disjunctive logics, and loop logics. Multiple instances of a workflow procedure may be in various stages of execution. Thus, the workflow procedure can be considered as a class (in object oriented terminology), and each execution, called a *workcase*, can be considered an instance. A workcase is thus defined as the locus of control for a particular execution of a workflow procedure. A workflow management system helps to organize, control, and execute such defined workflow procedures with a high, consistent, and predictable quality. From a workflow procedure perspective, the system should be able to discover several levels of intelligence from the models themselves to their enactment histories: for example,

- Verifiability intelligence: how much the workflow procedures should be correctly designed.
- Validity intelligence: how much their execution should be met their workload requirements. And how much their execution should be satisfied with the expectation when they were originally designed and planed in the buildtime phase.
- Performance intelligence: how much the organizational resources should be able to perform their work items in a timely fashion.
- Reengineering intelligence: how to re-engineer (re-build, re-construct or re-design) the original workflow procedures after being elapsed a certain amount of period.
- Predictability intelligence: how to identify the possibility of exceptions or undesired behavior from the system level to the business level throughout the whole period of the system's enactment runtime.

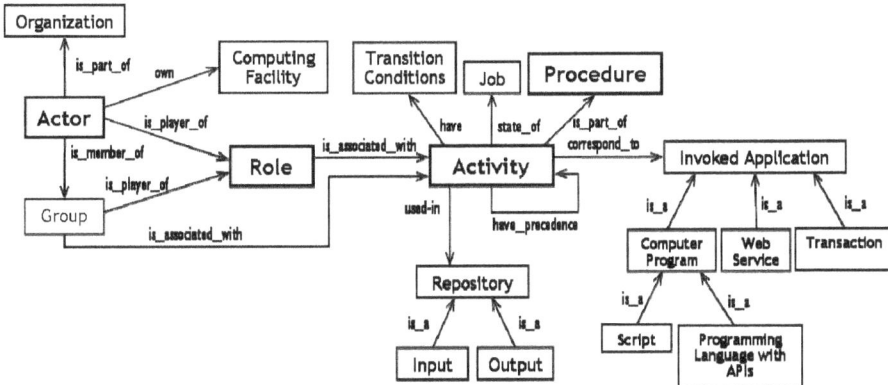

Figure 3. Perspective Elements for the Workflow Intelligence

- **Intelligence from the activity perspective.** An activity is a conceptual entity of the basic unit of work (task or step), and the activities in a workflow procedure have precedence relationships, each other, in terms of their execution sequences. Also, the activity can be precisely specified by one of the three entity types—compound activity, elementary activity and gateway activity. The compound activity represents an activity containing another workflow procedure, which is called subworkflow. The elementary activity is an activity that can be realized by a computer program, such as application program, transaction, script, or web service. And the gateway activity implies an activity that is used to controlling execution sequences of elementary/compound activities. The types of gateway activities consist of conjunctive gateway, disjunctive gateway and loop gateway, as explained in the previous section. Particularly, both the disjunctive gateway and the loop gateway need to be set some specific *transition conditions* in order to select one of the possible transition paths during the execution time. The transition condition itself can be defined by using the input/output relevant data on the *repository*. Additionally, each activity has to be associated with a real performer, such as organizational staff (role, participant) and system, who possesses all ownerships over that activity. From an activity perspective, the system should be able to discover the following types of knowledge and intelligence from analyzing models and their enactment histories and logs:

- Dependency intelligence: There exist four different types of dependencies—data dependency, activity dependency, role dependency and actor dependency—among activities in a workflow model, and they also could be rediscovered from the activities' enactment histories and logs. These discovered and rediscovered cases of the dependency intelligence focused on the activity perspective should be worthily used to ensure verifiability, maintainability and usability of the model.
- Predictability intelligence
- Structural pattern intelligence
- Performance intelligence
- Dynamic intelligence: The system should be able to support a various level of dynamic changes—organizational changes, structural changes and temporal changes—possibly happened on an activity during its runtime period. The various types of dynamic intelligence ought to be very valuable as business intelligence.

- **Intelligence from the organizational (roles and performers) perspective.** A logical unit of the organizational structure can be represented by role or actor/performer; A role is a named designator for one or more participants, which conveniently acts as the basis for participating works, skills, access controls, execution controls, authority, and responsibility over the associated activity. While on the other hand, an actor (performer) represents a person who can fulfill his/her roles to execute, to be responsible for, or to be associated in some way with activities and workflow procedures. The most essential intelligence to be discovered from the organizational perspective is about social networks or work-sharing networks among roles and/or actors involved in a workflow procedure or a group of workflow procedures of an organization. The social-related intelligence have something to do with not only discovering a work-sharing human network embedded on a workflow model, but also rediscovering a work-sharing human network from enactment and execution logs of the underlining workflow models. The discovered and rediscovered social-related intelligence can be analyzed for quantifying the degree of working-intimacy among humans through the essential notions of the centrality—degree centrality, betweenness centrality, stress centrality and closeness centrality—which have been well-defined in the social network analysis literature. Conclusively, the recent issues of social network intelligence discovery and rediscovery are about how to define a discovered or rediscovered human network, how to evaluate the degrees of working-intimacies in the discovered or rediscovered human network, and finally how to visualize the degrees of working-intimacies among humans associated with the corresponding workflow models.

- **Intelligence from the system (invoked applications and data) perspective.** An *invoked application* implies a physical realization of the corresponding activity, and it so may be implemented in a shape of script, transaction, computer program or web service. Furthermore, it needs a set of input and output *relevant data* (repository) in order to be invoked for its execution by the system. Consequently, the repository provides a communication channel between the workflow enactment engine and the invoked applications. From the system's perspective, the security and access control intelligence ought to be the most important knowledge for predicting the system level's unexpected behaviors. Also, both maintaining the concurrency control and keeping update history of relevant data might be the most valuable system-wide intelligence, because these two types of intelligence from the system perspective give opportunities to the workflow data mining issues.

Scope of the paper: Workflow Control-path Intelligence

In the previous section, we introduce the classes of workflow intelligence that can be discovered according to the perspectives. In this paper, we focus on a specific intelligence naturally discovered from the workflow procedure perspective, which is called workflow control-path intelligence that is possibly classified into the reengineering intelligence class. The basic concept of the workflow control-path intelligence was firstly introduced in the authors by proposing the control-path oriented workflow intelligence analysis algorithms. After introducing the basic concept, there have been several research results focused on this matter. The most essential issue in the control-path oriented workflow intelligence is to look for efficient workflow analysis and rediscovery algorithms, the results of which are eventually applied to redesigning and reengineering approaches for maintaining the higher degree of quality on workflow models. Based upon these research results that have been done by the authors' research group, we try to complete the summarization of workflow control-path intelligence concept, in terms of its analysis and rediscovery approaches and their applications to the business intelligence aspect. Particularly, the rediscovery issue should be a much more important contribution because not only the workflows and business processes are becoming massively large-scaled and much more complicated, but also, nevertheless, their life-cycle and recycling (reengineering) periods are becoming swiftly shorter. That is, the quality improvement and refinement works such as redesigning, reengineering, and restructuring of workflows should be done after analyzing their behavioral patterns on runtime, and so the workflow trace and rediscovery techniques ought to be the right approaches to explore them from the enactment audit and history information logged and collected from the runtime and diagnosis phases of the workflow models.

Conclusively, this paper summarizes a series of models, algorithms and frameworks coping with the workflow control-path intelligence issues by analyzing control-paths of a workflow model, by rediscovering the control-path oriented intelligence from the workflow logs gathered in the model's runtime execution history, and by reconstructing the original workflow model from the rediscovered control-path intelligence.

WORKFLOW CONTROL-PATH INTELLIGENCE

As a matter of fact, this paper describes a feasible framework to handle out the workflow quality issues through the workflow control-path intelligence. The framework consists of the analysis part and the rediscovery part for the control-path intelligence; The analysis part takes in charge of analyzing the control-path intelligence by generating a set of control-paths from an ICN-based workflow model; The rediscovery part is of rediscovering or mining the corresponding control-paths' instances (workcases) from the workflow warehouse built from workflow runtime execution logs. That is, this paper's goals are to define what the workflow control-path intelligence is, how the intelligence is generated from an ICN-based workflow model, and how to rediscover the intelligence from the enactment logs of the model. In this section, we give a series of formal descriptions to analyze the workflow control-path intelligence from an ICN-based workflow model, to rediscover the intelligence from the enactment histories and logs of the model, and finally to reconstruct an ICN-based workflow model from a set of the rediscovered workflow control-path intelligence.

Analysis of the Control-path Intelligence

As an analysis algorithm of the workflow control-path intelligence, we introduce a straightforward approach, because it analyzes and produces a set of control-paths, each of which implies a reachable execution sequence of activities from the start node to the termination node, by traversing the targeted workflow model. The following subsections devote to details and formalities of the approach.

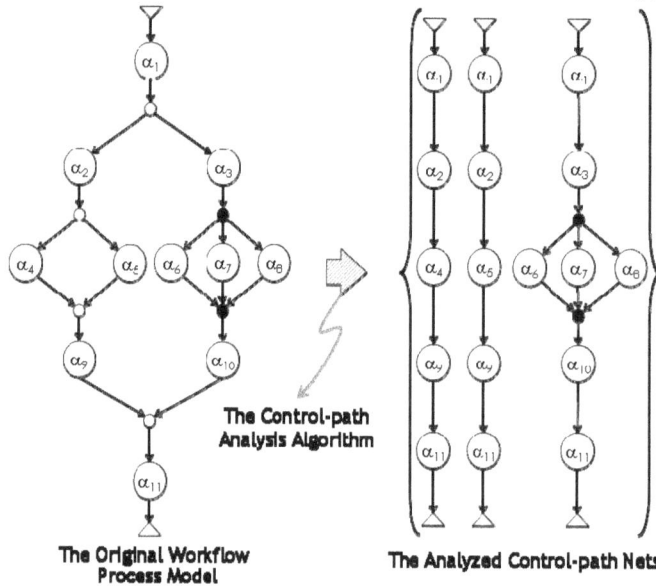

The Original Workflow Process Model

The Control-path Analysis Algorithm

The Analyzed Control-path Nets

Figure 4. The Basic Concept of Workflow Control-path Intelligence Analysis

Definition 2. Control-path Net of a workflow model (ICN). Let W be a CpN, a control-path net, that is formally defined as $CpN = (\varrho, \kappa, I, O)$ over a set of activities, $\mathbf{A}^{cp}$, and a set of transition-conditions, $\mathbf{T}^{cp}$, where

- $\varrho = \varrho_i \cup \varrho_o$
  where, $\varrho_o : \mathbf{A}^{cp} \longrightarrow \wp(\alpha \in \mathbf{A}^{cp})$ is a multi-valued mapping of an activity to its set of (immediate) successors, and $\varrho_i : \mathbf{A}^{cp} \longrightarrow \wp(\alpha \in \mathbf{A}^{cp})$ is a single-valued mapping of is a multi-valued mapping function of an activity to its set of (immediate) predecessors;
- $\beta = \beta_i \cup \beta_o$
  where, $\beta_i(\alpha)$: a set of control transition conditions, $\tau \in \mathbf{T}^{cp}$, on each arc, $(\beta_i(\alpha), \alpha)$; and $\beta_o(\alpha)$: a set of control transition conditions, $\tau \in \mathbf{T}^{cp}$, on each arc, $(\alpha, \beta_o(\alpha))$, where $\alpha \in \mathbf{A}^{cp}$;
- I is a finite set of initial input repositories of the corresponding ICN;
- O is a finite set of final output repositories of the corresponding ICN;

The Control-path Net and Its Analysis Algorithm. The workflow control-path intelligence is formally defined through the Control-path Net of [Definition 2], and its graphical representation is shown in the righthand side of Figure 4. Figure 4 shows the result automatically generated from the example workflow model of Figure 2. The detailed analysis algorithm, which is called the Generic Analysis Algorithm named **PROCEDURE TRAVERSE( )**, is pseudo-coded as the following:

```
The Generic Analysis Algorithm: PROCEDURE TRAVERSE():

Input An Information Control Net (ICN), Γ = (δ, γ, λ, ε, π, κ, I, O);
Output A Set of Control-path Nets (CpNs), ∀ W = (ρ, κ, I, O);
Initialize CpN ← {∅};       /* The empty net of CpN. */
PROCEDURE TRAVERSE(In s ← {αI}, CpN) /* Recursive Call. */
BEGIN
      v ← s; CpN.A^cp ← CpN.A^cp ∪ {v};
      WHILE ((u ← δo(s);) ≠ {αF})
         SWITCH (What type, u, is?) DO
               Case 'serial-type activity':
                     w ← u; CpN.A^cp ← CpN.A^cp ∪ {w};
                     CpN.ρo(v) ← w; CpN.ρi(w) ← v;
                     CpN.ϑo(v) ← κo(s); CpN.ϑi(v) ← κi(s);
                     break;
               Case 'conjunctive-type (AND-split) activity':
                     w ← u; CpN.A^cp ← CpN.A^cp ∪ {w};
                     CpN.ρo(v) ← w; CpN.ρi(w) ← v;
                     CpN.ϑo(v) ← κo(s); CpN.ϑi(v) ← κi(s);
                     FOR (eachof ∀a ∈ δo(u)) DO
                           x ← a; CpN.A^cp ← CpN.A^cp ∪ {x};
                           CpN.ρo(w) ← x; CpN.ρi(x) ← w;
                           CpN.ϑo(w) ← κo(u); CpN.ϑi(w) ← κi(u);
                     END FOR
                     FOR (eachof ∀a ∈ δo(u)) DO
                           Call PROCEDURE TRAVERSE(In s ← a, CpN);
                     END FOR
                     exit();
               Case 'disjunctive-type (OR-split) activity':
                     w ← u; CpN.A^cp ← CpN.A^cp ∪ {w};
                     CpN.ρo(v) ← w; CpN.ρi(w) ← v;
                     CpN.ϑo(v) ← κo(s); CpN.ϑi(v) ← κi(s);
                     FOR (eachof ∀a ∈ δo(u)) DO
                           Call PROCEDURE TRAVERSE(In s ← a, CpN);
                     END FOR
                     exit();
               Default: /* OR-join activity or AND-join activity */
                     w ← u; CpN.A^cp ← CpN.A^cp ∪ {w};
                     CpN.ρo(v) ← w; CpN.ρi(w) ← v;
                     CpN.ϑo(v) ← κo(s); CpN.ϑi(v) ← κi(s);
                     break;
         END SWITCH
            s ← u; v ← w;
      END WHILE
      w ← u; CpN.A^cp ← CpN.A^cp ∪ {w}; /* u is equal to αF. */
      CpN.ρo(v) ← w; CpN.ρi(w) ← v;
      CpN.ϑo(v) ← κo(s); CpN.ϑi(v) ← κi(s);
      PRINTOUT CpN
END PROCEDURE
```

The time complexity of the generic analysis algorithm is O(N), where N is the number of activities in an ICN-based workflow model, because the function, **PROCEDURE TRAVERSE()**, is recursively traversing each activity in only once. Therefore, the overall time complexity is O(N).

Rediscovery of the Control-path Intelligence

The rediscovery of the Control-path Intelligence starts from event logs stored in a standard format of BPAF (Business Process Audit Format). According to the logging format, the workflow event logging mechanism of a workflow enactment engine stores all of workflow enactment event histories triggered by the engine components. In general, the event logs might be produced by the following three types of workflow engine's components:

- Event triggering components: Requester and Worklist Handler
- Event formatting components}: Workcase Objects or Activity Objects
- Event logging components: Log Agent and Log File Storage

The *event triggering components* handle the workflow enactment services requested from workflow clients, and these services can be categorized into three levels of classification—Workcase level class, Running activity level class, and Workitem level class. The *event formatting components* try to compose event log messages according to the service classes after performing the requested services. Finally, the *event logging components*, especially the log agents, take in charge of the responsibility of the event logging mechanism. Once, a log agent receives the event logs and then transforms them into XML-based log messages, and stores the transformed messages onto the Log File Storage.

Based on the log file storage, we can build a workflow control-path intelligence warehouse that shapes into a cube with three dimensions, such as workflow models, temporal workcases, and activities. From the cube we extract a set of control-path intelligence by filtering the temporal workcases (traces) that is instantiated from a workflow model. Note that a temporal workcase is a temporal order of activity executions within an instance of the corresponding workflow model, and we would not describe the details of the temporal workcase model. Finally, the algorithm rediscovers a set of control-path intelligence groups by applying the filter, each layer of which is made out of a control-path net as shown in Figure 5.

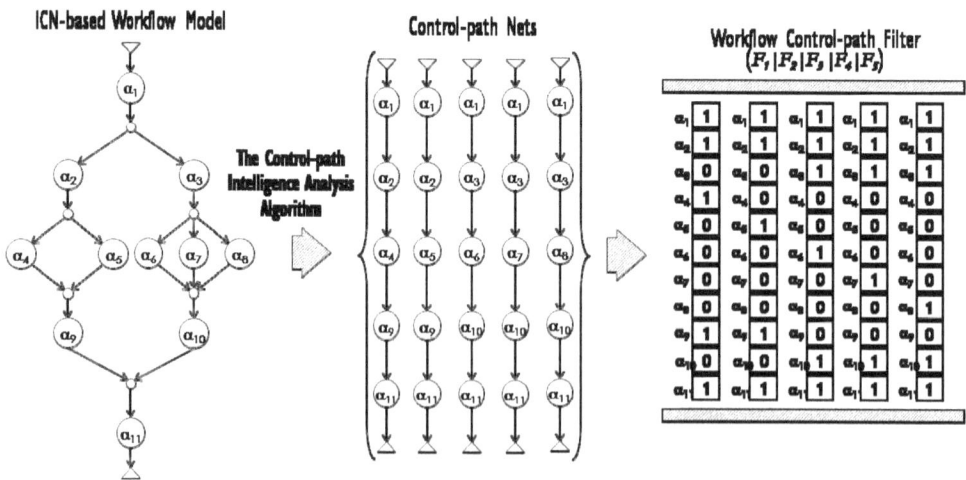

Figure 5. A Control-path Intelligence Filter

Reconstruction of a Workflow Model

As just conceptually described in the previous section, the control-path intelligence rediscovery algorithm eventually generates a set of control-path intelligence groups. Each of the intelligence groups is associated with one of the filter's layers. Finally, by amalgamating these intelligence groups, we are able to reconstruct an ICN-based workflow model. The basic idea of the amalgamation procedure is to incrementally amalgamate each layer of the filter, one-be-one. Note that each layer can be formally as well as graphically represented by the control-path net. Also, during the amalgamation procedure works, the most important thing is to observe and seek those three types of transitions.

Precisely, the basic amalgamating principles seeking each of the transition types are as follows: if a certain activity is positioned at the same temporal order in all control-path net models, then the activity is to be involved in a sequential transition; else if the activity is at the different temporal order in some control-path net models, then we can infer that the activity is to be involved in a conjunctive transition; otherwise if the activity is either presented in some control-path net models or not presented in the other control-path net models, then it has got to be involved in a disjunctive transition. As simple examples of the amalgamating principles, we algorithmically illustrate the amalgamation procedures reconstructing a conjunctive transition and a disjunctive transition through Figure 6 and Figure 7, respectively.

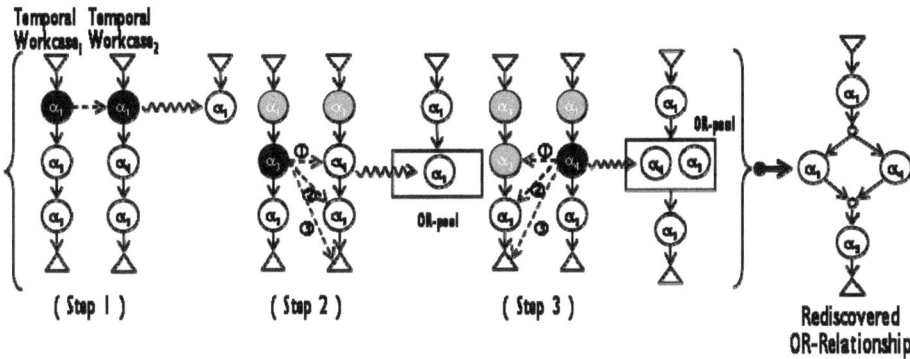

Figure 6. The Reconstruction Principle rediscovering OR-Transition

In Figure 6, suppose we examine the rediscovered layers of the filter of an ICN-based workflow model that has three activities, a_1, a_3 and a_4, and try to amalgamate two specific control-path net models; the temporal order of a_3 and a_4 in one control-path net model is reversed on the other control-path net model. Therefore, we can infer that the activities, a_3 and a_4, are involved in a conjunctive transition of the reconstructing workflow model.

In Figure 7, we also assume that we examine the rediscovered layers of the filter of an ICN-based workflow model that has four activities, a_1, a_3 and a_4 and a_5, and try to amalgamate two specific control-path net models; the temporal order of a_1 and a_5 in one control-path net model is same on the other control-path net model; also, the positions of a_3 and a_4 on the temporal order are same in these two control-path net models respectively, and, while on the other, the activities, a_3 and a_4, are not presented in these two control-path net models at the same time. Therefore, we can infer that the activities, a_3 and a_4, are involved in a disjunctive transition of the reconstructing workflow model.

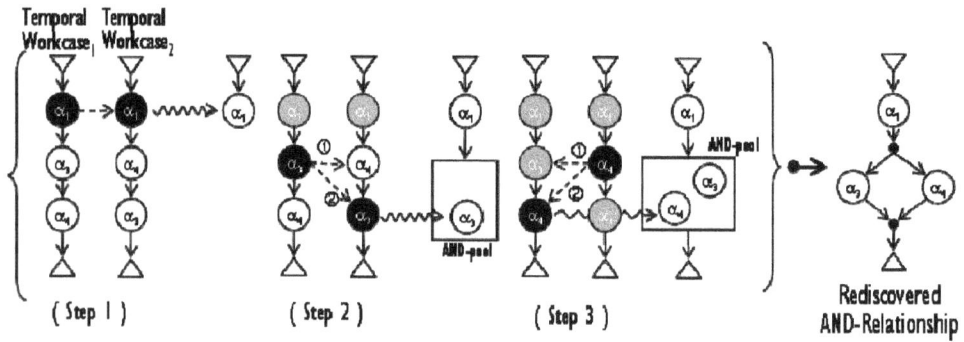

Figure 7. The Reconstruction Principle rediscovering OR-Transition

Based upon the basic amalgamating principles, we conceive a workflow reconstruction algorithm automatically generating an ICN-based workflow model by amalgamating a set of control-path net models, each of which represents a layer of the filter analyzed or rediscovered from the workflow model and its enactment histories or logs. Because of the page limitation we would not make a full description of the algorithm in here.

IMPLICATIONS OF THE WORKFLOW CONTROL-PATH INTELLIGENCE

In this paper, our emphasis is placed on the quality of workflow model by using the workflow control-path intelligence with the purpose of improving the optimization and predictability of the workflow model. In other words, what is the quality of a workflow model? And how can we evaluate the quality of a workflow model? Then, we try to answer for those questions through the concept of the workflow control-path intelligence.

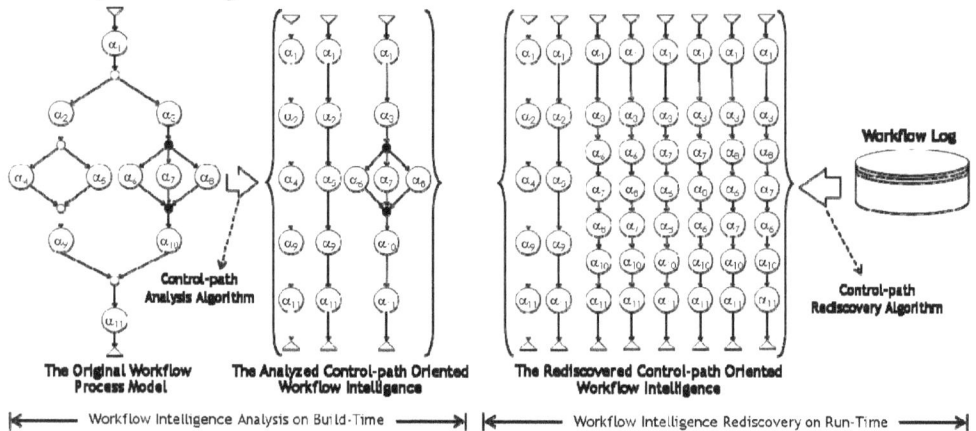

Figure 8. Predictions through the Control-path Intelligence

We would insist that the quality of a workflow model be defined by the degree of the discrepancy between the defined workflow model as it is built on modeling time and a set of activity firing sequences (classified by control-path intelligence groups), each of which is modeled by a control-path net model, as it is actually executed on running time. The discrepancy, as you can easily imagine, is caused by disjunctive and conjunctive control-paths presented on the model. The number of disjunctive control-paths on the model will effect on the number of *mutually exclusive activity firing sequences.* Also, the number of activities associated with a conjunctive path will effect on the number of *mutually inclusive activity firing sequences.* Based upon these theoretical terms, we would describe the implications of the workflow control-path intelligence in terms of enhancement of the predictability of the workflow model's runtime behaviors as well as increase the level of optimization with respect to reengineering the workflow model.

Figure 8 shows two faces of the workflow control-path intelligence of a workflow model. One face, like the left-hand side of the figure, shows the analyzed control-path oriented intelligence built on modeling time, and the other face, the right-hand side of the figure, represents the rediscovered control-path intelligence generated from running time traces and execution logs. That is, the workflow model in the figure has three mutually exclusive activity firing sequences, and the rightmost one of which possibly generates six mutually inclusive activity firing sequences.

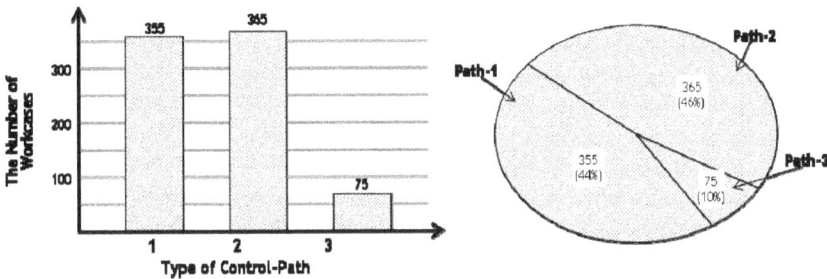

Figure 9. Filtering Measurements of the Control-path Intelligence

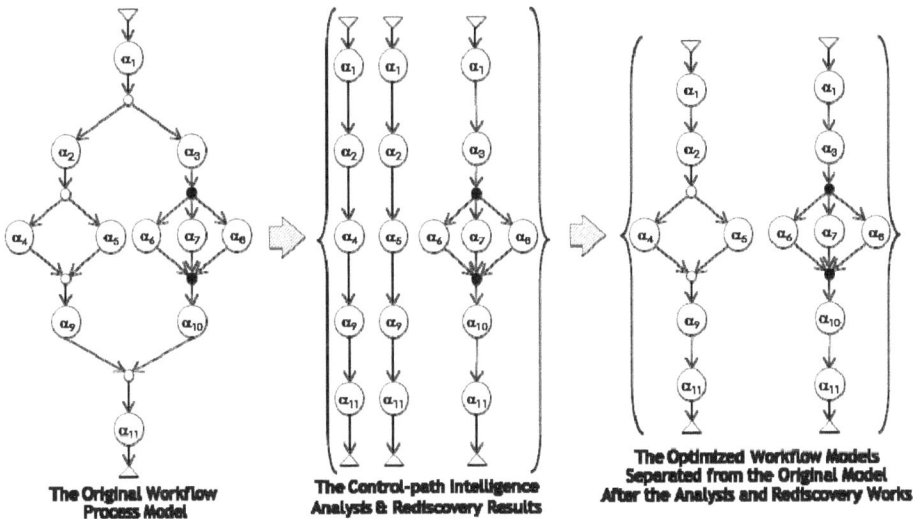

Figure 10. The Optimized Workflow Models

For example, after fetching a workflow instance from the logs, we need to know along which control-path (or firing sequence of activities) it has followed or enacted. This might be very useful knowledge for workflow administrators and designers to redesign and re-estimate the quality of the workflow model after being elapsed for a specific amount of period. Figure 9 shows a result of the filtering measurements based upon the concept of control-path intelligence, which may be possibly measured after being elapsed a certain amount of time. Based upon the filtering measurements, the workflow model can be reasonably optimized by eliminating the control-path having the smallest number of instances, as shown Figure 10. Conclusively speaking, the workflow control-path intelligence is able to give a sort of intrinsic knowledge for the quality improvement and refinement work of workflow models.

CONCLUSIONS

So far, this paper has introduced the concept of workflow control-path intelligence and it has also described the formal analysis approach, conceptual idea of the rediscovering intelligence, and the workflow reconstruction principles from a set of the rediscovered control-path intelligence. Particularly, in this paper we tried to classify the types of workflow intelligence possibly extracted from the different views of the workflow's perspectives. Also, we have described the implications of the workflow control-path intelligence that eventually gives us a much higher-level of efficiency in improving the quality of workflow models. In recent, the workflow literature needs various, advanced, and specialized workflow knowledge and intelligence techniques and architectures that are used for finally providing feed-backs of their analysis results to the redesign and reengineering phase of the existing workflow and business process models. We strongly believe that this work might be one of those impeccable attempts and pioneering contributions for improving and advancing the workflow intelligence technology.

ACKNOWLEDGEMENT

This work was supported by the GRRC program of Gyeonggi Province, Republic of Korea. We would like to extend our appreciation to our fellow researchers in the Collaboration Technology Research Lab (CTRL) at Kyonggi University. Also thanks to GRRC colleagues, especially to the officers of Gyeonggi Province, who have contributed greatly to establish our research center.

REFERENCES

[1]   Arthur J. Hedge III, "People Improve Processes, Not BPM Tools," e-Doc Magazine, AIIM (2005)

[2]   Clarence A. Ellis, "Formal and Informal Models of Office Activity," Proceedings of the Would Computer Congress, Paris, France (1983)

[3]   C.A. Ellis and J. Wainer, "Goal-based Models of Collaboration," Journal of Collaborative Computing, Vol. 1, No. 1 (1994)

[4]   Daniela Grigori, Fabio Casati, Malu Castellanos, Umeshwar Dayal, Mehmet Sayal and Ming-Chien Shan, "Business Process Intelligence," Journal of Computers in Industry, Vol. 53, Issue 3 (2004)

[5]   Dimitrios Georgakopoulos, Mark Hornick, "An Overview of Workflow Management: From Process Modeling to Workflow Automation Infrastructure", Distributed and Parallel Data-bases, 3, pp. 115-153 (1995)

[6]   Fabio Casati, et al, "Business Process Intelligence," Technical Report, HPL-2002-119, HP Laboratories Palo Alto (2002)

[7]   Kwanghoon Kim and Clarence A. Ellis, "Workflow Reduction for Reachable-path Rediscovery in Workflow Mining," Series of Studies in Computational Intelligence: the Foundations and Novel Approaches in Data Mining, Vol. 9, pp.289-310, Springer (2006)

[8]   Kwanghoon Kim and Su-Ki Paik, "Practical Experiences and Requirements on Workflow," Lecture Notes Asian '96 Post-Conference Workshop: Coordination Technology for Collaborative Applications, The 2nd Asian Computer Science Conference, Singapore (1996)

[9]   Kwanghoon Kim, "Control-path Oriented Workflow Intelligence Analysis on Enterprise Workflow Grids," Proceedings of the International Conference on Semantics, Knowledge, and Grid, Beijing, China (2005)

[10]   W. M. P. van der Aalst, B. F. van Dongena; J. Herbst, L. Marustera, G. Schimm and A. J. M. M. Weijters, "Workflow mining: A survey of issues and approaches," Journal of Data & Knowledge Engineering, Vol. 47, Issue 2, pp. 237-267 (2003)

[11]   W. M. P. van der Aalst and A. J. M. M. Weijters, "Process mining: a research agenda," Journal of Computers in Industry, Vol. 53, Issue 3 (2004)

[12]   Kwanghoon Kim and Clarence A. Ellis, "sigma-Algorithm: Structured Workflow Process Mining through Amalgamating Temporal Workcases," Proceedings of the 11th Pacific-Asia Conference on Knowledge and Data Discovery, LNAI, Vol. 4426, pp. 119-130 (2007)

[13]   C. Ellis, "Information Control Nets: A Mathematical Model of Information Flow," ACM Proc. Conf. on Simulation, Modeling and Measurement of Computer Systems, pp. 225-240 (1979)

[14]   C. Ellis, et al, "Workflow Mining: Definitions, Techniques, and Future Directions," Workflow Handbook 2006, pp. 213-228 (2006)

[15]   C. Ellis, et al, "Beyond Workflow Mining," Lecture Notes in Computer Science, Vol. 4102, pp. 49-64 (2006)

[16]   Kwanghoon Kim, "A Workflow Trace Classification Mining Tool," International Journal of Computer Science and Network Security, Vol.5, No. 11, pp. 19-25 (2005)

[17]   Kwanghoon Kim and Clarence A. Ellis, "Chapter VII. ICN-based Workflow Model and Its Advances," Handbook of Research on Business Process Modeling, pp. 142-171 (2009)

[18]   Kwanghoon Kim, "Mining Workflow Processes from XML-based Distributed Workflow Event Logs," Proceedings of IEEE International Workshop on Distributed XML Processing: Theory and Practice, Vienna, Austria, pp. 595-602 (2009)

[19]   M. Park and K. Kim, "Control-path Oriented Workflow Intelligence Analyses," Journal of Information Science and Engineering, Vol. 24, No. 2, pp. 343-359 (2008)

Workflow Design Patterns for Developing and Maintaining e-Business Workflow Systems

Farhi Marir and John Ndeta, Knowledge Management Research Centre, Faculty of Computing, London Metropolitan University, UK

ABSTRACT

Designing an e-business workflow system for your organisation using a traditional framework is not appropriate as it ignores the human dimension of organisational knowledge creation and the dynamic situations encountered in organisations collaborative work processes in the new e-business environment. As a result e-business workflows systems developed using this framework are less capable in dealing with the new e-business era which is characterised by an increasing pace of radical, discontinuous and unforeseen change in e-business processes.

This paper highlights the limitation of this traditional framework and presents an alternative framework for designing flexible and dynamic e-business workflow management systems that respond to the continual changes of e-business processes.

INTRODUCTION

Workflow management systems are designed to support business process modelling. Business process modelling is an effective tool for managing organisational change and is known to have brought benefits to many organisations. During the last decade workflow technology systems have become readily available. They are built using a traditional framework which is well understood for traditional intra-organisational workflow applications that span only structured and predictable business processes and business environment. Designing workflows using this traditional framework is limited to modelling four internal perspectives of the organisation as shown in Figure 1:

(i) Functional perspective for decomposing organisation process functionality into tasks to be allocated to workers or software agents of the organisation

(ii) Informational perspective for describing the organisation business data, documents and product specs which are consumed and produced within the organisation

(iii) Organisational perspective for specifying the roles and actors which are designated by the organisation management to be involved in the workflow execution and describes how the organisation configures its resources to perform business processes and

(iv) Behavioural perspective for specifying the way the information is channelled through the different steps of the process and the rules and constraints of the organisation business policies and practices.

Organisational Perspective

Actors

Roles

Routes &
Rules

**Behavioural
Perspective**

Processes & tasks

Data & Documents

Functional Perspective

Informational Perspective

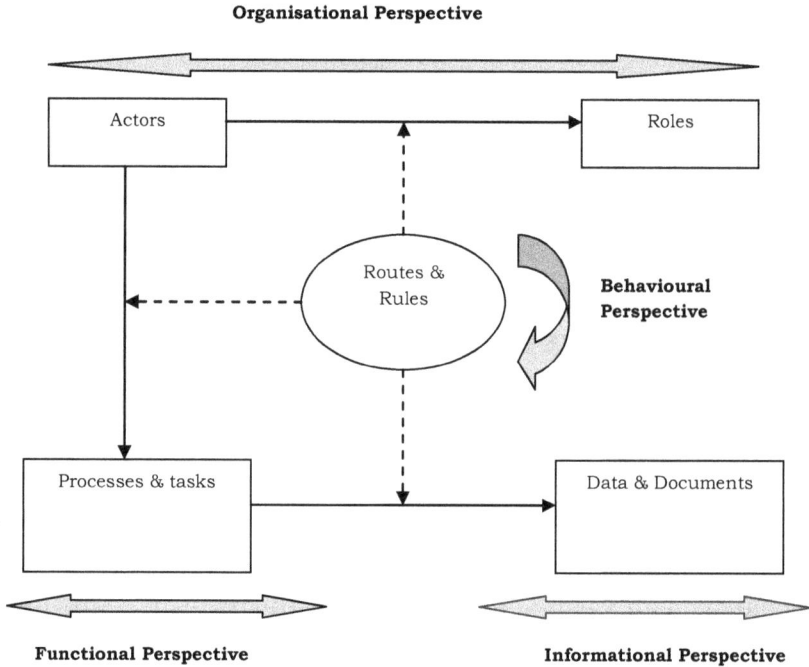

Figure 1: Traditional Framework for Workflow Development

It is clearly noticeable that all the above perspective focus on the organisation's internal business process and none of them deals with neither e-business processes shared between organisations nor the human dimension of organisational knowledge creation which is crucially important in the new era of global and knowledge economy. So developing an e-business workflow system using this traditional framework will end up with a rigid workflow system which can not cope with organisations and their e-business processes which undergo changes from time to time, and in some cases this changes are dynamic, discontinuous and complex [1].

The team presenting this paper has spent the last three years investigating with several organisations the limitation of the traditional framework. The team, in collaboration with Workflow Management Coalition, put online a questionnaire asking academics, managers and workflow developers their views on traditional framework for developing workflow systems. Around 30 percent of responses confirmed that they are not using a traditional framework to develop or maintain their workflow systems and amongst 70 percent who are still using a traditional framework confirmed that they are using different techniques to reflect the worker knowledge and to model business processes shared between organisations [2,3].

The results of this investigation confirms the need for an alternative framework for designing flexible e-business workflow systems which thus become a necessity due to the impact of e-business processes on organisation survival and growth in this global and knowledge economy.

This paper presents a framework and methods for developing e-business workflow systems that supports the dynamic and continual changes of e-business processes and a case study showing how this framework is used to reengineer a company e-business workflow system to cope with dynamic changes to its e-business processes.

THE KNOWLEDGE ENHANCED FRAMEWORK

To address the above limitations for developing e-workflow systems, we enhanced the traditional framework with a knowledge perspective as shown in Figure 2. This knowledge perspective is used to memorise explicit and tacit process-related knowledge generated within or outside the boundary of the organisation. The captured knowledge is used to trigger changes needed to both the organisation e-business processes and its four perspectives (functional, informational, organisational, behavioural) to reflect and satisfy new requirements of internal and external stakeholders of the organisation. Some examples of the role of this knowledge perspective could be extracting knowledge from data and information flowing between the four perspectives, memorising successful stories and best practices within or outside the boundary of the organisation, recording views of external stakeholders such as customers' views on the organisation e-business processes and learning from previous experiences in developing e-business processes.

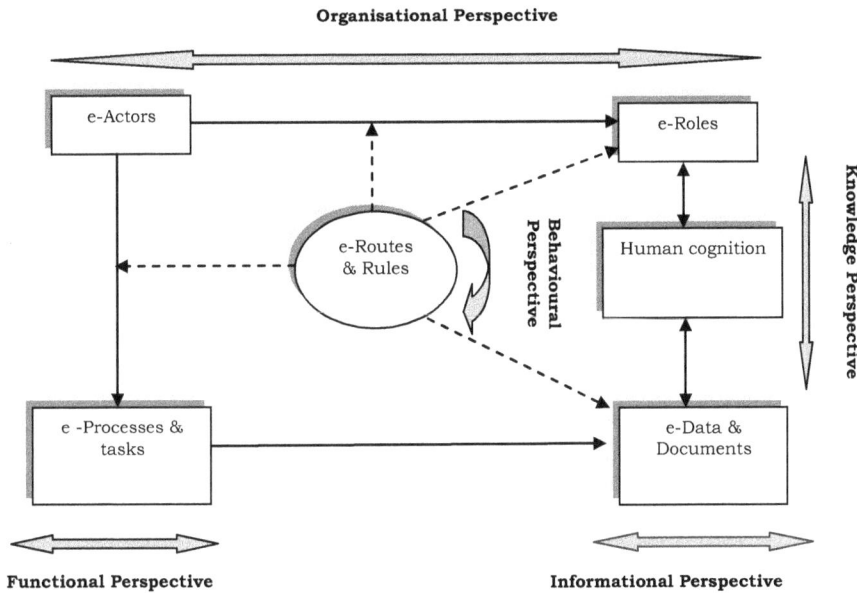

Figure 2: Knowledge Enhanced Framework for e-workflow Development

To achieve one of the roles of the knowledge perspective in memorising previous experiences we used two techniques and concepts: design patterns [4] and case-based reasoning [5]. We used the concepts of design patterns to create a process-related knowledge repository memorising reusable *e-business workflow design patterns* and we used case-based reasoning indexing, retrieval and adaptation techniques to *access, manage and reuse these workflow design patterns*. These e-business workflow design patterns can be either used to trigger changes to the organisation e-business processes to reflect new requirements of stakeholders and related external organisations or they can be reused to assist workflow developers in their design of flexible e-business workflow systems that reflect the new e-business environment.

KNOWLEDGE REPOSITORY OF E-BUSINESS WORKFLOW DESIGN PATTERNS

Each e-business workflow design pattern contained in the knowledge repository specifies a set of tasks, together with the ordering constraints and object flows between them. It represents one possible means of achieving a given type of task by breaking it down into sub-tasks. Each workflow design pattern specifies a single level of structural decomposition. However, the decomposition could be further partitioned into a set of tasks, each of which represents another workflow design patterns in the repository. These workflow design patterns may in turn be selected to specialise/instantiate the sub-tasks, and so a multi-level hierarchical process structure may be generated by composition of many design patterns.

As a result of this hierarchical structure, for any given task, there may be multiple possible workflow design patterns, expressing different ways of breaking the task down for different situations. A workflow process shown in Figure 3 depicts a simple workflow pattern for the e-business process of booking a travel service from a network-centric travel service provider.

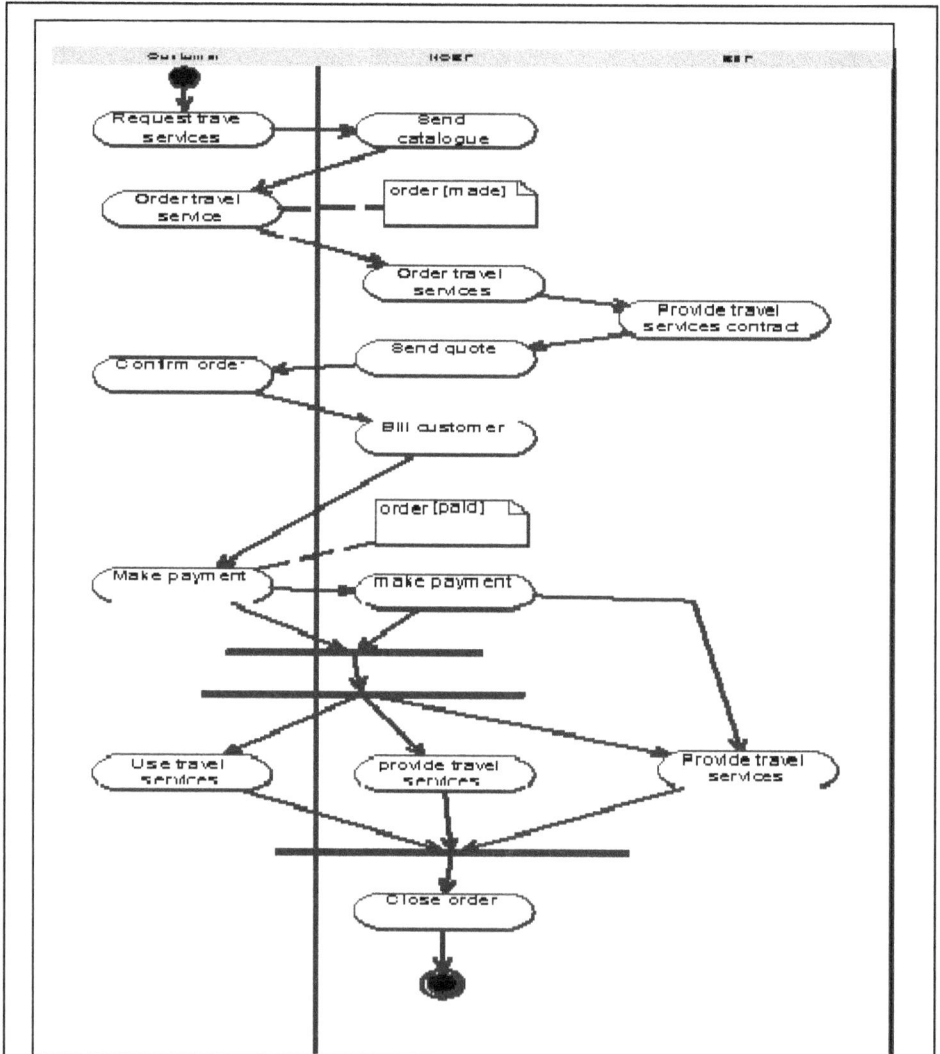

Figure 3: The travel booking service workflow definition

To be able to manage the above e-business workflow patterns contained in the knowledge repository, each one of them is associated to a template, which defines the pattern in an abstract and accessible format. An instance of the workflow design pattern template is structured as follows:

Name of the pattern: It is used for uniquely identifying the pattern in the workflow design pattern repository. As this name will become part of the design vocabulary, it must be chosen carefully.

Authors: each pattern has one principal author;

Problem: written in user-centred terms, i.e. what is the problem presented to the end user?

Intent: This section describes in few sentences the main goal of a pattern, i.e. towards which problem it offers a solution.

Classification: according to the categories and sub-categories of the workflow design pattern repository to allow users to browse by category;

Solution: This section describe possible solutions to the problem

Related to: establishing links among patterns to combine them in different structures;

Guidelines: provide suggestions to the user about possible usage and instantiation/personalisation of patterns

Keywords: which are a set of user-selected terms that can be used to refer (select, search, etc) to the available patterns in the repository; this field allows one to describe more precisely the topics of the pattern, especially to distinguish the different patterns of a given category in the classification;

Template: it contains the core specification of a pattern. The specification is given in terms of events, conditions, and actions. Unlike events and conditions, which are the main parts of the patterns, the action part provides only suggestions. This reflects the fact that exception patterns focus on how to capture exceptions, rather than on how to fix reactions, which are application dependent. The template contains parametric fields (also called generic terms in the following) to be filled in with specific values provided by the designer

Sample usage: since the user of the repository is anticipated to be an expert of the application under design but is not required to have detailed knowledge of the exception language syntax, the repository is provided with some user-oriented sample usage. This is a set of instantiations of patterns on specific examples. They show how patterns can be customised in different context and applications by illustrating how parameters of patterns can be supplied by the designer to produce a concrete workflow model. The sample usage description is a set of workflow-specific instantiations of patterns related to an application domain.

Pattern-based cycle for e-workflow design

Once each of the e-business workflow design pattern and its template are stored in the knowledge repository, the question that arises is how to manage and reuse these design patterns to benefit the organisation to maintain the dynamics and the continual changes of its e-business processes and to support workflow developers in designing flexible e-business workflow systems for their organisation. As mentioned earlier in the paper, we used a case-based reasoning paradigm to manage this knowledge repository. A case-based reasoning (CBR) paradigm is a problem solving method which solves new problems by adapting solutions that were used to solve old problems. Its process of solving problems can be represented by a schematic cycle of *Retrieve, Reuse, Revise and Retain* as represented. This CBR problem solving cycle is applied to manage our knowledge repository of e-business workflow design pattern as represented in Figure 4.

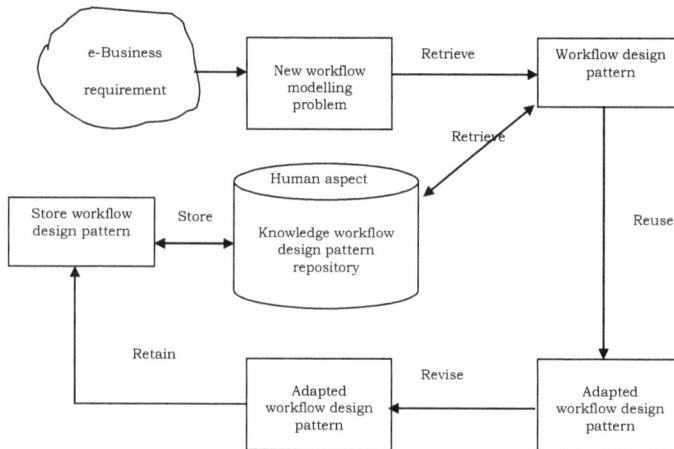

Figure 4: Pattern-based cycle for e-workflow design

So the process of reuse begins when new e-business requirements are identified. They will be used to initiate a search of the knowledge repository as depicted in Figure 4 above. Appropriate workflow templates and their associated e-business workflow design patterns are retrieved using CBR techniques such as nearest neighbour algorithms. Retrieved workflow design patterns are analysed (manually, possibly automated) to decide if any of the retrieved workflow design patterns are appropriate for further modification or a new solution needs to be generated from scratch.

In the reuse step, a retrieved workflow design pattern, possibly from multiple alternatives, may be modified. Appropriate domain knowledge may be added or deleted and constraints may be re-configured and reflected in the various workflow-modelling perspectives (functional, organisational, informational and behavioural). The adaptation and reuse of workflow design patterns are feasible because of the recurrence of similar business tasks, data and tasks dependencies in different business context, and recurrence of common types of business problems and constraints across a variety of business processes and domains. The adapted workflow design pattern is then subject to validation and verification based on domain dependent rules and formal approaches. Successful validation of the workflow model may trigger deployment and execution on the e-business workflow engine. This newly adapted e-business workflow solution is retained as a new e-business workflow design patterns in the knowledge repository and which can be reused in the future to solve new workflow problems in different e-business settings or contexts.

If we have identified the e-business workflow and its associated template as a case representation for CBR, what is needed now is how to index these cases i.e. e-business workflow template to be able to retrieve and adapt them.

The following section is devoted to indexing and retrieval of these e-business workflow design patterns.

WORKFLOW DESIGN PATTERN INDEXING AND RETRIEVAL

The importance of recognising the right e-business workflow design pattern templates from the knowledge repository will help to improve productivity as well as reduce the expert skill requirements of the workflow designers during the design and evolution of e-workflow applications in the new economy. In order for the mechanism of workflow design patterns retrieval to be applicable to retrieving context-sensitive workflow design patterns and sub workflow design patterns, the indexing scheme for patterns and sub-patterns must be at an appropriate level of generality of the global and local context and to reflect the hierarchical structure of the workflow design patterns. For this purpose, two main interconnected indexing schemes are provided in the workflow design pattern repository; workflow design pattern indexing scheme and the sub-workflow design pattern indexing schemes as shown on Figure 5. Each of the indexing schemes is composed of two types of indexes with different functionalities.

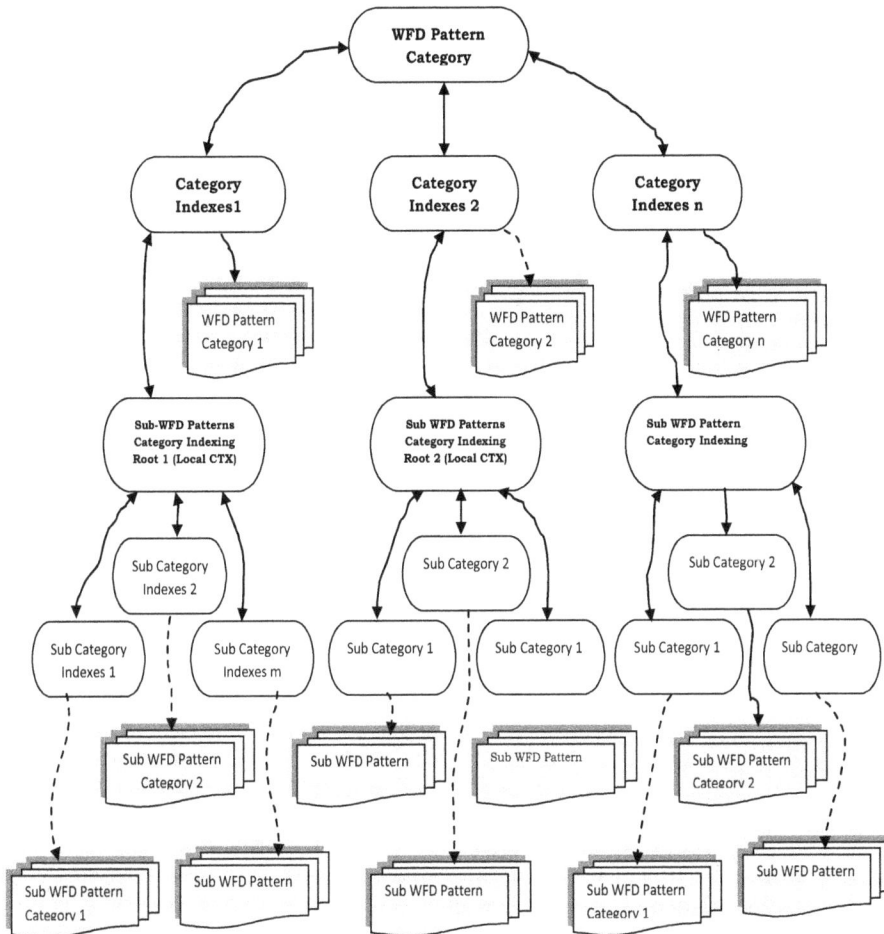

Figure 5: Workflow design pattern indexing scheme (Adapted from Marir & Watson, 1995)

Classification indexes represent the global and local context features of e-business workflow design patterns and their sub-workflow design patterns that represent the acquired knowledge and experience in the workflow domain. These indexes are considered as a difference-based indexing scheme by their main function of differentiating a workflow design pattern from another similar workflow design pattern. However, these indexes are mainly used to classify and direct the retrieval to context-sensitive workflow design patterns and sub-workflow design patterns. This reflects the importance given to the context information which expert domain retrieve and adapt patterns and also adds an advantage to the proposed e-workflow approach by reducing the scope of the retrieval search space of classes of similar workflow design patterns rather than the whole workflow design pattern repository.

CASE STUDY

To study the benefits of the proposed framework approach, we have chosen the illustrative example of e-business based on a web-based travel agency. The proposed framework approach was used to reverse engineer the e-travel agency's workflow model in order to identify problems and also to provide possible solutions. Conceptually this transaction can be demonstrated by the following example. The e-travel agency sells flight tickets, reserves hotel rooms and provides car rental services to its customers. In order to provide these services for its clients, the e-travel agency needs to establish business links with other organisations or business service providers (BSP), i.e. airlines, car rentals and hotels. The customer can select a service from the following services via the e-travel agency's web site (flight only, hotel only, car only, flight + car, flight + hotel, flight + hotel + car). In this context, a financial institution, i.e. a bank is required to facilitate the financial transaction.

This service is complex and may run into difficulties for instance in the following two scenarios:

(i) The e-business process may require change due to the need to capture some new business requirements or changes that happened to some of the business partners or

(ii) The customer two months later (after the initial booking) and two weeks before the departure date decides that they wish to change some aspects of the transaction, such as upgrades, extend, amend or cancel. This will trigger varying interactions between the service providers or business partners involved in the transaction. Beside the difficulties of actually changing details of the transaction, there are many difficulties concerning the service providers involved in the contract. Some will require compensation or have set procedures for going about amendment of their part of the contract. These exceptional situations present many difficulties and issues concerning the modelling and implementation of the e-travel agency's e-workflow virtual applications.

Step 1: Definition of the e-Workflow functional perspective

The workflow design process starts when new business needs or requirements are provided and used to initiate a search of the workflow design pattern repository. During the design of e-travel agency's workflow model, a knowledge workflow designer should be able to retrieve suitable patterns from the repository. A retrieved workflow design pattern chosen possibly from a number of alternatives may be reused or modified. Suitable domain knowledge may be employed to alter the e-travel agency's workflow process sequence; new tasks may be added or removed. After tasks sequencing, resource allocation may be taken into consideration in other to enable concurrent execution and infrastructural issues such as data location and agent's location to the e-travel agency's workflow model. Retrieved patterns are analysed manually to determine if any of the retrieved knowledge, particularly workflow design patterns, is suitable for further modification or a new solution to the e-travel agent's problem needs to be generated from scratch by using the framework for knowledge enhanced e-workflow modelling. The booking *flight only* e-business process workflow design pattern diagram below (see Figure 6) was developed from the first principle by reverse engineering the agency's workflow models from their website since there are no workflow design pattern templates in the knowledge repository that can be reused to develop the e-travel agency's workflow models.

Figure 6 represents the workflow design pattern while Figure 7 represents its associated template in knowledge repository which underlies the knowledge perspective.

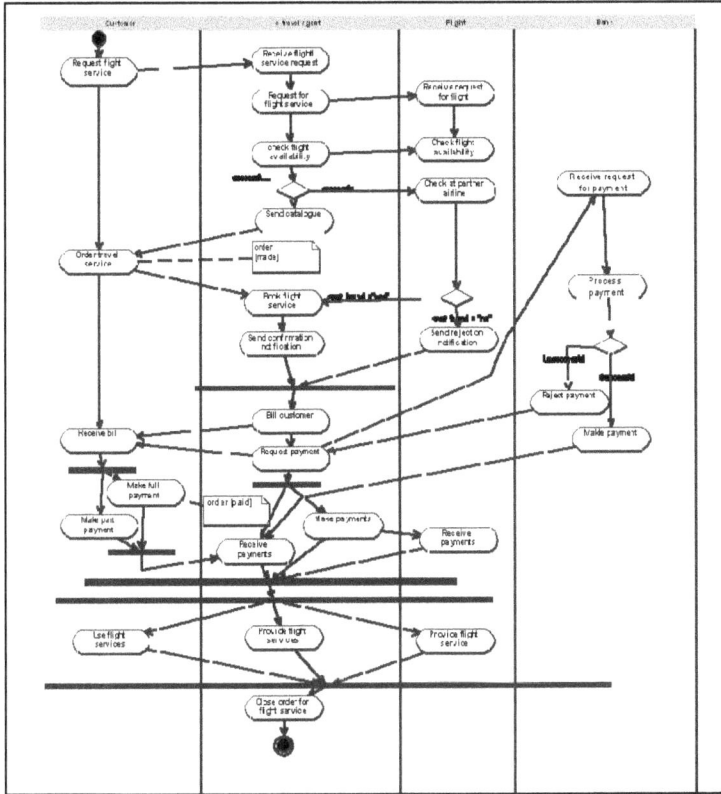

Figure 6: Booking Flight only business process workflow design pattern

Name: Book Flight only business process workflow design pattern template
Author: John Ndeta and Farhi Marir
Version: 1
Date: 12/05/2008
Intent: This pattern template allows the definition of a workflow process for achieving the flight only reservation business process
Classification: Sub workflow design pattern
Template:
Get request for travel
Get customer details
Check flight availability
IF flight available
    THEN Book flight seat
        Send confirmation letter
    ELSE
        Check flight availability at Partner airline
        IF seat available
            THEN Book flight seat

```
                    Send confirmation letter
                    Request payment
        ELSE
                    Send rejection letter
            ENDIF
ENDIF
```
Keywords: Book Flight only business process workflow design pattern

Related to:

Guideline: This workflow design pattern template may be used to compose workflow schemas for different workflow problems within different business context or setting.

Figure 7: Booking Flight only business process workflow design pattern template

In order to develop the *hotel only* business process workflow design pattern as shown below see Figure 8, the *flight only* business process workflow design pattern was reused by instantiating and specialising it with activities and resources in the context of *hotel only* business process workflow design patterns.

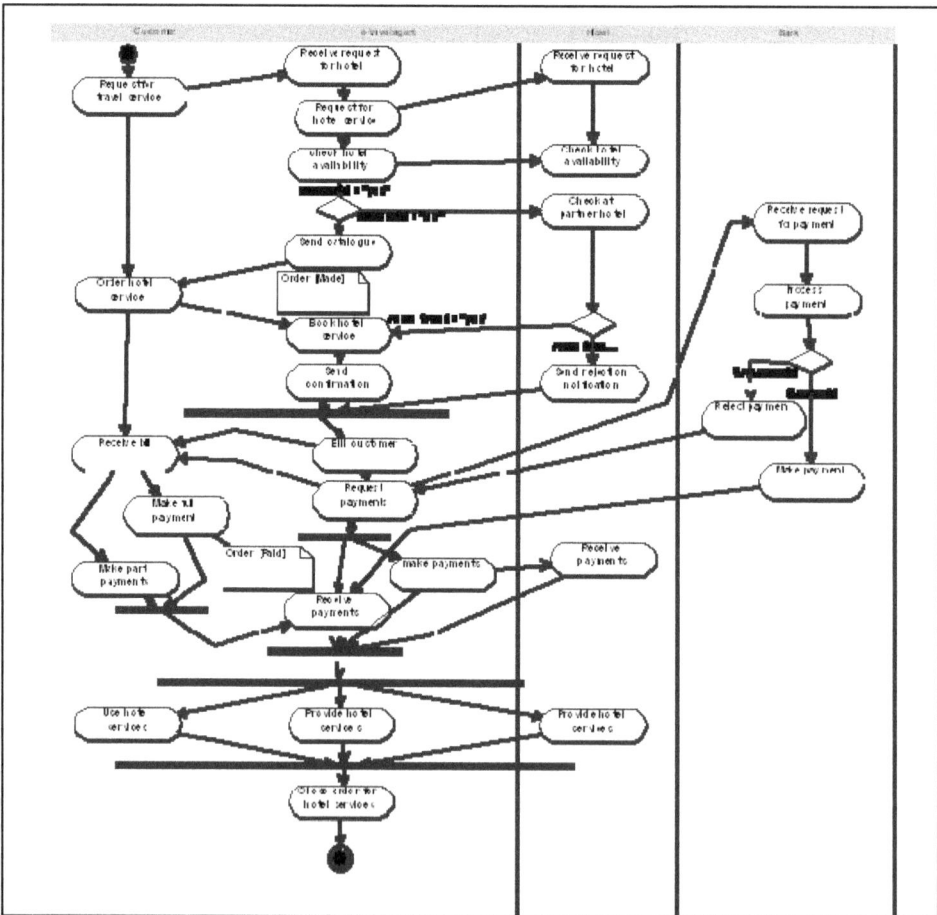

Figure 8: Booking Hotel only business process workflow design pattern

This was made possible by instantiating and specialising resources like *flight* with *hotel* and activities like *receive request for flight* with *receive request for hotel, check flight availability* with *check hotel availability*, etc. After tasks sequencing, resource allocations, pre-conditions and post-conditions was also taken in to consideration.

Step 2: Definition of the organisational perspective

In the e-workflow model, role view identifies the roles that will participate in the execution of workflow. Usually a role corresponds to a position that is filled by one or several stakeholders. Analysing roles allows the elimination of effort duplication and bottlenecks in the workflow process. Figure 9 below presents the workflow resource pattern of the organisational perspective. A role is associated with responsibility to fulfil a service, using different resources. In Figure 9, Service class depicts such responsibilities. Performing a role's service means implementing a service tasks to achieve a particular business process within the workflow. A service always represents a business process in which a number of different organisations and tasks are involved and these web services are always distributed across these various organisations. Actor class represents a physical entity that will play a role. Requirements class describes the features, which are required to fulfil a role e.g., expertise, years of experience, background etc. Finally, credential class stands for actors' or stakeholders' capabilities to meet role requirements. The organisational perspective can inherit properties of the workflow resource patterns from the algorithmic and textual representations of the business process workflow design patterns templates stored in the knowledge repository.

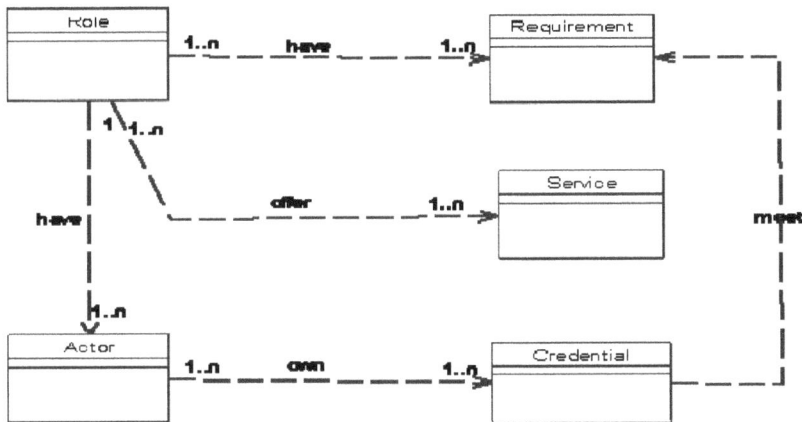

Figure 9: Workflow resource pattern

The workflow resource pattern may be reused as design knowledge from the knowledge repository during the design and evolution of complex e-business workflow applications for different workflow problems within different business domains. When a process-agent initiates a task, it identifies potential actors from the organisation's database (organisation perspective) that correspond to the roles specified in the task abstract description. The process-agent selects the appropriate actors via their respective role-agents such as actor's availability, actor's workload, task's deadline, and task's priority. The proposed framework provides appropriate mechanisms such as negotiation, and assessing the characteristics of the environment in which the business evolves. These mechanisms are used by the process-agents to assign tasks to appropriate actors.

STEP 3: DEFINITION OF THE BEHAVIOURAL PERSPECTIVE

The information required for the behavioural perspective has already been listed in the task list of the e-travel agency's workflow schemas. This perspective defines the routes and rules involved in the execution of the e-travel agency's workflow schemas. Routes define the way information is routed through the different steps of the process. It can either be routed serially, in parallel or conditionally based on the business rules and policy. Rules are the blend of policies and practices and can be triggered by the information on the process. This work uses ECA rules to control the routing of activities and the selection of e-workflow providers. When a workflow process is initiated, a fork node fires all output arrows in parallel, whereas a branch node fires the output arrows that satisfy the routing conditions. ECA rules can be used to describe the routing decisions. In e-workflow applications, the completion of preceding e-business processes is regarded as an event of routing rules. The behavioural perspective can also inherit the workflow control flow patterns from the algorithmic and textual representations of the business process workflow design patterns templates in the knowledge repository. The workflow control flow pattern may be reused as design knowledge from the knowledge repository during the design and evolution of complex e-workflow design problems for different workflow problems within different business settings. To help further understanding of the behaviour of the workflow model, animated models may provide better temporal representation than static visual diagrams and therefore are suitable as a communication tool for both the knowledge workflow designer and users. While tasks sequencing rules defined in the workflow schemas specify when a task needs to be done, organisational policies determine, in real time, which procedure is to be executed to accomplish the task, who to assign the responsibility and providing access to the required tools and information entities.

Step 4: Definition of the informational perspective

The workflow data pattern of the information perspective shown on Figure 10 below, describes the documentations involved in a workflow process definition and in its enactment. Such elements are information variables, available to all tasks in the workflow schemas within the functional perspective i.e., forms, documents, and folders. The proposed e-workflow uses these information variables about the e-service to establish the communication relationship between the various e-agent of that e-service. This could be a table or a class structure defining the business entities and the e-services or tasks that they provide. In the e-workflow model, information view describes the data that a workflow for Internet will manipulate and generate. Manipulation of data takes place during workflow execution while generation of data occurs at the end of execution. In the e-workflow model generation of data implies updating data. These processes are critical to the survival and growth of e-business organisations characterised by dynamic, global and knowledge economy.

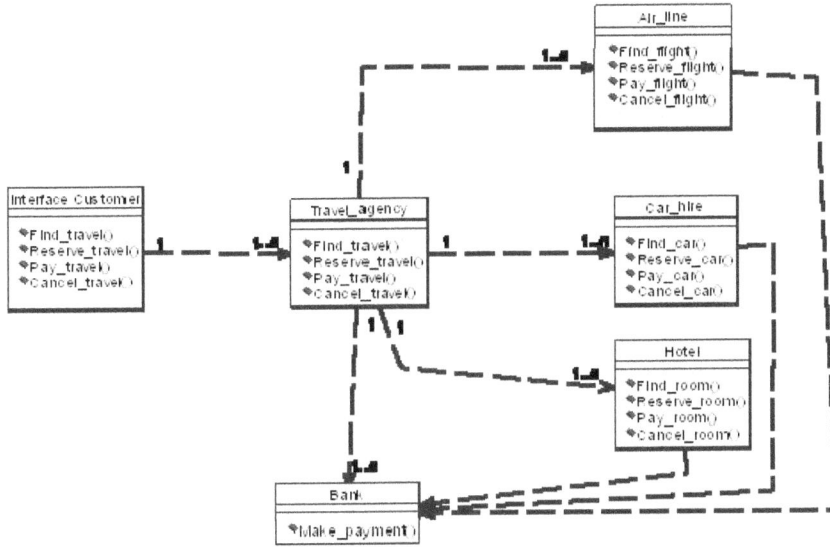

Figure 10: Workflow data pattern

Also, studying the workflow domain allows the structuring of data and permits a better appreciation of the context in which the workflow will take place. It may be possible that different tasks, from independent e-processes, are executed in parallel. Hence, these tasks could have to manipulate the same data simultaneously; however any deadlock in accessing this critical data is avoided by the concurrency control of the underlying database systems. In the e-workflow model, data coherence is ensured, through the information agents. The informational perspective can also inherit workflow data patterns from the algorithmic and textual representation of the business process workflow design patterns templates stored in the knowledge repository. Furthermore, the workflow data pattern may be reuse as design knowledge from the knowledge repository during the design and evolution of complex e-workflow applications for different workflow problems within different business domains. Thus the proposed framework approach aims at workflow applications scenarios requiring flexible and build time modifiable workflows, which may cross-organisational boundaries.

The knowledge repository within the proposed framework provides support for carrying out common tasks in any one of a standard ways. Knowledge creation, sharing, collaboration and reuse is enhanced by provision of e-business workflow design pattern templates at different levels of abstraction, so that each workflow designer can work with patterns expressed at the necessary level, without having to commit unnecessarily to lower-levels of details. Thus the refined workflow model is then reviewed or validated based on the e-travel agency's domain business rules, by simulation or formal approaches. If the review process is successful, the workflow model should be deployed for execution on the e-travel agency's workflow engine. And finally, all these business process workflow diagrams and templates may be used to compose workflow solutions for different workflow problems with different business context or settings

EVALUATION AND CONCLUSIONS

In this paper we have presented a new framework that takes into consideration the knowledge dimension for the development of e-workflow to support continual and unpredictable changes of current e-business processes. A significant contribution of our proposed framework is not only limited to adding a knowledge perspective to traditional framework but by setting new relationship and dynamics between this new perspective and its existing functional, organisational, behavioural and informational perspectives. In the proposed knowledge enhanced framework all perspectives are integrated and all of them harbour some knowledge through common access to a knowledge repository that memorise best practices, previous experiences and stakeholders experiences. Furthermore, the paper presents one realisation of the knowledge repository in the form of workflow design pattern repository. We have also provided templates for pattern creation, which would enable patterns content in the workflow design pattern repository to be structured and predictable. The paper also provides classification strategies for pattern indexing and retrieval in the e-business workflow design patterns repository of inter-related patterns and on providing strategies for specialising and instantiating workflow design patterns in the repository.

The proposed framework has been tried successfully by another travel agent to assess their e-business processes. One of the e-business processes assessed was Flight + Hotel booking web based service. In the initial flight + hotel booking service, the customer, while booking the flight, is not given the possibility to alter the number of days required to spend in the hotel. We changed the Flight + Hotel booking service by providing on the web a window for the user to put their comment why they did not proceed with the booking. When we analysed the comments of the customers we found that a large number of customers would like to book the flight with fewer days to spend in the hotel as they would like to spend some of the days with local friends or families. Once, we changed the Flight + Hotel e-business process changed allowing customers the flexibility to book Flight + Hotel with the possibility to alter the number of days to spend in the hotel, no customer has raised again that problem which might mean that more customers have booked for Flight + Hotel service.

REFERENCES

Van der Aalst, W.M.P., Reijers, H.A., Weijters, A.J.M.M., Van Dongen, B.F., Alves de Medeiros, A.K., Song, M. & Verbeek, H.M.W. (2007) "Business process mining: An industrial application", Information Systems, 32, pp. 713 – 732

Ndeta, J and Marir, F. (2005) Towards the Development of a Conceptual Framework fro Knowledge Enhanced e-Workflow Modelling, Proceedings of the 6th European Conference on Knowledge Management, University of Limerick, Ireland.

Ndeta, J. (2008) Knowledge Enhanced Framework for the Design and Development of e- workflow Systems, PhD Thesis, Knowledge Management Research Centre, Faculty of Computing, London Metropolitan University, UK.

Gamma, E., Helm, R., Johnson, R and Vlissidesn, J. (1995) "Design Patterns: Elements of Reusable Object-Oriented Software", Addison-Wesley Professional Computing Series. Addison-Wesley Publishing Company, New York.

Marir, F and Watson, I.D. (1995) Representing and Indexing Building Refurbishment Cases for Multiple Retrieval of Adaptable Pieces of Cases. First International Conference on CBR (ICCBR-95), Portugal.

Utilizing Process Definitions for Process Automation: A Comparative Study

Filiz Çelik Yeşildoruk and Onur Demirörs, Middle East Technical University, Informatics Institute, Turkey

ABSTRACT

Process modeling offers a very effective means for understanding and analyzing what needs to be improved. Process models are also used for many other purposes such as process automation, which increases the effectiveness of process improvement especially when organizations need to react quickly. Although there are numerous studies on various approaches to be separately applied to process modeling and process automation, the relationship and dynamics between the two still remains undiscovered. This paper presents the results of an exploratory study on the usability of process models developed for process improvement to be applied to the automation of processes with selected Business Process Management (BPM) tools.

The case study covers two processes in a software development unit of a large organization. The extended Event Driven Process Chain (eEPC) notation was utilized for process modeling and BizAgi, WebMethods and Intalio BPM suites for automation. A comparison was made concerning time spent to carry out the modeling and automation and the effectiveness of the BPM tools was analyzed.

INTRODUCTION

Business Process Management (BPM) has become a top business priority for systems interoperability and execution of end-to-end complex processes [2] [7] [8]. Aalst et al. describes BPM as "supporting business processes using methods, techniques and software to design, enact, control and analyze operational processes involving humans, organizations, applications, documents and other sources of information" [12]. This definition clearly identifies the wide range of issues to be considered in building better processes through BPMS.

The first and most important step in BPM lifecycle is process modeling [12] Business process modeling methodologies are useful for understanding, learning and teaching, monitoring, measuring, improving and executing the as-is processes of an organization. Process models represent the aspects in a process, which are considered important to the purpose of the modeling. When this purpose has a wide range, the notation to emphasize the important aspects of the model will require a wide spectrum of methods, ranging from informal i.e. natural language to formal i.e. computer programs.

In this study the focus is on process modeling from the perspective of improvement and execution. Process modeling and automation techniques are becoming more and more popular for improved quality and effectiveness of the processes [4]. In order to support process improvement, it is essential that various stakeholders, such as the process owners, business analysts, IT developers and enterprise architects, are able to understand and use business process models. Additionally, the notation must be formal and unambiguous if models are to be used as the input for process execution tools and the model should be able to fulfill the requirements of different perspectives.

Although there are numerous studies describing various approaches applied to process modeling and process automation, these are carried out separately and the relations between them has not been investigated thoroughly. Furthermore, these approaches are utilized by different sets of users. For example, business users may focus on high-level easy-to-understand modeling of business logic; however, these models lack execution parameters and details. On the other hand, processes modeled for execution purposes are not easily understood by business users because they are complex and require high level of technical knowledge. Therefore, the relationship and dynamics between process modeling and process automation need to be investigated in order that modeling tools and languages are able to hide irrelevant details for business users whilst providing an executable interface for those with technical knowledge.

In this study, the use of process models, in various process automation environments is investigated. As Terai et al, comments, the reuse of existing business models for automation purposes, makes it easy to adapt to business model changes [10]. We have modeled the processes looking from the business users' perspective, and then, we investigate the usability of these models for process automation efforts, rather than modeling the processes starting from scratch. The aim of this study is to investigate the ease of execution of processes modeled in eEPC notation with the selected BPM tools; BizAgi, WebMethods and Intalio.

RELATED RESEARCH

The automation of processes is becoming increasingly popular in organizations. Consequently, many vendors have introduced BPM suites. In 2008, four very large enterprise software suppliers—IBM, Microsoft, Oracle and SAP—made BPM a central element of their product portfolios and marketing efforts [13].

In order to benefit from advantages of business process management systems, the first step is process modeling which would enable organizations define and describe their processes in an understandable, unambiguous and reusable manner without losing any information. Process-modeling languages and representations need to present different perspectives, which underlie different aspects of information for analyzing and presenting processes [1]. Accordingly, there are many languages for business process modeling focusing on these different aspects [3]. Since these languages address different process abstraction levels they appeal to different user groups. Lippe et al. analyzed various business modeling approaches and identified that processes of an organization can be grouped in three levels each of which can be modeled with different languages and notations [2]:

- Business processes: EPC, IEM, Business Scenario Maps
- Technical processes: BPDM / BPMN, UML, ebXML, RosettaNet, BPML
- Executable processes: XPDL, WS-BPEL / WS-CDL, UML

Event Driven Process Chain (EPC) [9] is a modeling technique dedicated for business-oriented modeling, offering not only a notation but also a method for modeling. Non-IT people can easily understand it, mainly because of its simple notation which includes three basic elements; function, event, connector. The extended Event Driven Process Chain (eEPCs) notation used in this study describes processes with a sequence of functions and events including roles, organizational units, positions that perform the activities and information that are inputs/outputs to activities. We have used eEPC successfully in many projects for modeling and visualizing the processes making it possible to create a common understanding of the processes more easily.

BPMN [6][15], maintained by Object Management Group (OMG)[1], is a graphical notation to represent business processes and has become very popular. It includes diagrams to describe processes, as well as semantics by utilizing the attributes of the various elements. However, it does not have an official interchange format, and thus, sharing BPMN among different environments is a complex and ambiguous task. Moreover, converting BPMN models to executable forms is very overwhelming if not impossible. BPMN has a large range of concepts since it is intended to be implementation-oriented, which may cause it to be difficult for business users to learn.

XML Process Definition Language (XPDL) [14] and Business Process Execution Language for Web Services (BPEL)[5] are two popular specifications for enterprise system interoperability. Although they are separate specifications, they complement each other in executing BPMN models. XPDL is used as an interchange format for BPMN elements from a diagram portability perspective; however, BPEL only defines the executable aspects of a process. Since they are focused on execution of models, they are complex and therefore they do not appeal to business users.

Although there is no language supporting the needs of all levels, research has shown that models can be transformed among different levels [2][10][16]. For example, one-to-one mapping from EPC elements to BPMN elements or the transformation of each model to Petri nets and then making a comparison are possible transformation choices. However, since these methods are overwhelming and may cause loss of detail, bridging the gap between business processes and executable processes has not yet been achieved [11].

In this study, an exploration is undertaken of how these modeling notations interact with each other in real-world process automation suites.

REUSE OF PROCESS MODELS FOR PROCESS AUTOMATION

Three BPM suites; BizAGI, Intalio and WebMethods were selected. The focus in this study is not to compare these products, but using these products in order to explore the requirements to automate processes reusing business models.

BizAgi[2] offers a BPM solution that enables modeling and executing of business processes through a graphic environment and without the need for programming. The process wizard guides the users from modeling to automation in the following steps: modeling the process using the BizAgi Process Modeler, editing the data model to identify entities, attributes and relations, defining forms to interact with the users, defining business rules as specific conditions, defining performers in terms of people or resources, integrating with any other system in the organization and executing the process.

---

[1] Object Management Group, *www.omg.org*

[2] BizAgi, *www.**bizagi**.com*

Intalio|Works[3] is a modular BPM suite that consists of a BPMN modeler, forms editor, data mapper and a deployment manager that is built on an Eclipse platform. The suite has a built-in process modeler with BPMN support and can convert the process models modeled using BPMN to BPEL. BPEL is the main means for deploying process models on the Intalio|Server. Intalio has a forum for users to ask questions and get answers, which is very helpful for eliminating modeling problems for execution.

WebMethods[4] provides a web-based platform to design and automate processes, with simulation and monitoring features. The design of the business process management system features an Eclipse based environment in which process models can be developed by multiple researchers in collaboration.

In this study, we modeled the change management and moving to production processes in a software development unit of a large organization. In the change management process, users from various units (business units, help desk, software development team) report problems concerning software in production. These problems are analyzed by the development team and taking manager's opinions into consideration they decide whether to implement the changes and when. Moving to production process is related to the change management process in terms of the definition of how to reflect the implemented changes on the production environment. The processes chosen were related to each other to understand how interrelated processes are handled in automation environments.

After the selection of the processes, they were modeled with eEPC notation for an explicit definition. These models are referred to as software process improvement (SPI) models. In this phase, the roles, organization units and input/output relations are made clear. An example from the change management process modeled in eEPC notation, where the incident is entered in service center software, is presented in Figure 1.

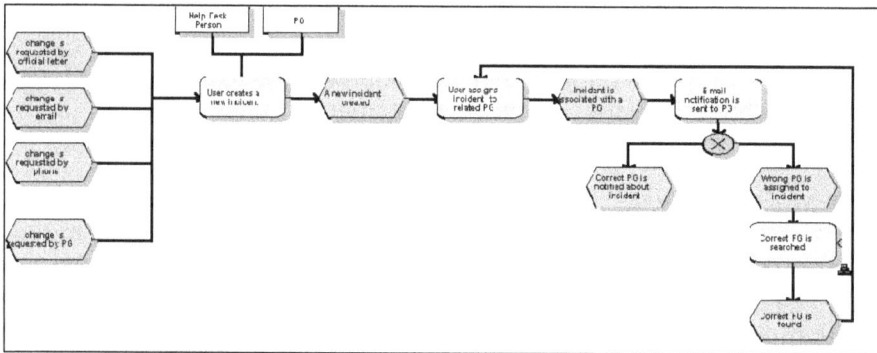

Figure 1 - Business models with eEPC notation

The next step in the study was to explore the reusability of the SPI model. The process models designed for BPM suites are referred as the business process automation (BPA) model. The possibilities of using SPI models as BPA models in BPM suites were identified in accordance with following aspects:

---

[3] Intalio, http://www.intalioworks.com/products/bpm/

[4] WebMethods, http://www.softwareag.com/corporate/products/wm/bpm/default.asp

Modeling Environment: the selected BPM suites offer either a stand-alone application or an Eclipse plug-in for process modeling. The Eclipse environment does not offer a user-friendly graphics interface and it is not easy to visualize the model, especially for end users who are not familiar with programming interfaces. Although stand-alone applications for business modeling are more user friendly, overall, the modeling environments which BPM suites offer are limited when compared to tools which are specifically designed for business process modeling, such as ARIS [9]. For example, the hierarchical organization of the processes is not permitted in BPM suites, in this case modelers have to deal with the whole process at once, which is not easy to handle.

Usability of SPI model: Processes modeled in eEPC cannot be reused in any of the BPM suites. There are implications that BPMN specifications can be imported into some suites but a one-to-one transformation cannot be achieved. In order to execute processes with BPM suites, modelers have to re-model the processes in BPMN notation using the modeling environment that the suites offer.

Interchange format: XPDL is used in some suites as an interchange standard but problems arise for some elements such as, connectors. Hence, exporting process models from BPM suites as well as importing is not free of problems.

Modeling: BPM suites support BPMN notation, however there are some problematic areas. Since the execution perspective is dominant throughout the modeling phase, there are some controls that make it very difficult to express the circular flows in the processes. Another issue is role definitions expressed as lanes in BPM suites. Defining role interactions may be quite difficult since each interaction requires the definition of execution parameters. In the SPI model, the focus is on understanding, therefore elements which are not immediately relevant to processes but enhance understanding are permitted. However, in BPA models the focus is on automation, therefore, these kinds of elements may be omitted and some knowledge may be lost, not all aspects of the SPI model can be reflected in the BPA model.

Model check: All suites provide a syntactic check for the notation they support.

Executability check: Intalio provides executability check during modeling, however, the support for resolving issues is very difficult and modelers need a high level of technical knowledge. For example, Intalio gives error messages for wrongly associated elements but it is necessary to have BPEL knowledge to understand what the error refers to. In other suites, modeling phase is separated from automation phase; therefore execution check is not immediately available.

Effect of changes in processes: Input/output relations maintain the interactions between processes. Therefore, one change in a process affects other processes only if there are any alterations in input/output definitions.

In Figure 1 below, Intalio Designer, the modeling perspective for Intalio suite is displayed. In this environment the errors are displayed as the model is designed, in a problems window, which is displayed in the lower part of the figure. BPMN elements are selected, from the palette displayed in the right hand side of the figure. However, the wide range of available elements makes it confusing for business users to model their processes. In Intalio, not only the business logic but also the automation details are modeled simultaneously which makes the modeling phase more difficult.

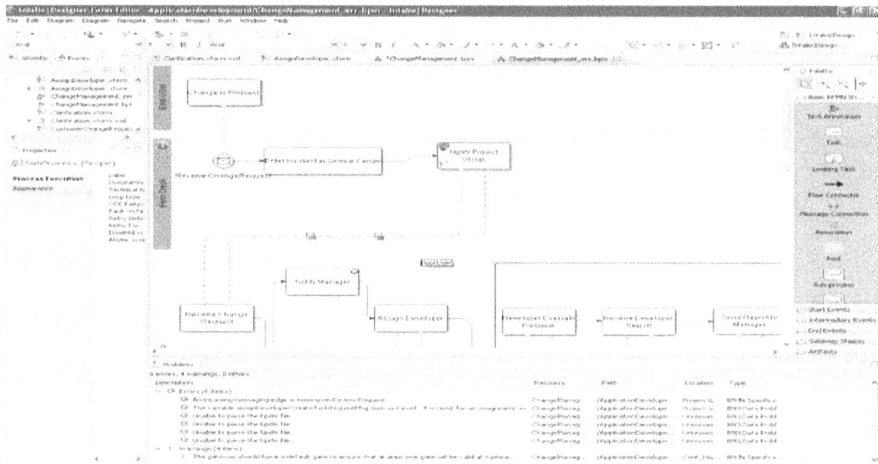

Figure 1 - Process Modeling in Intalio

In Figure 2, BizAgi Business Process Modeler interface is displayed. The interface is simpler and easy to use compared to Intalio, since the execution details are defined after modeling phase. However user's control over the screen is not very effective. For example, the size of lanes, describing roles, is not easily adjustable by the users, which causes the process to be less readable, as seen in the figure. Defining sub-processes is not permitted which increases the complexity, hence decreases the understandability of the model.

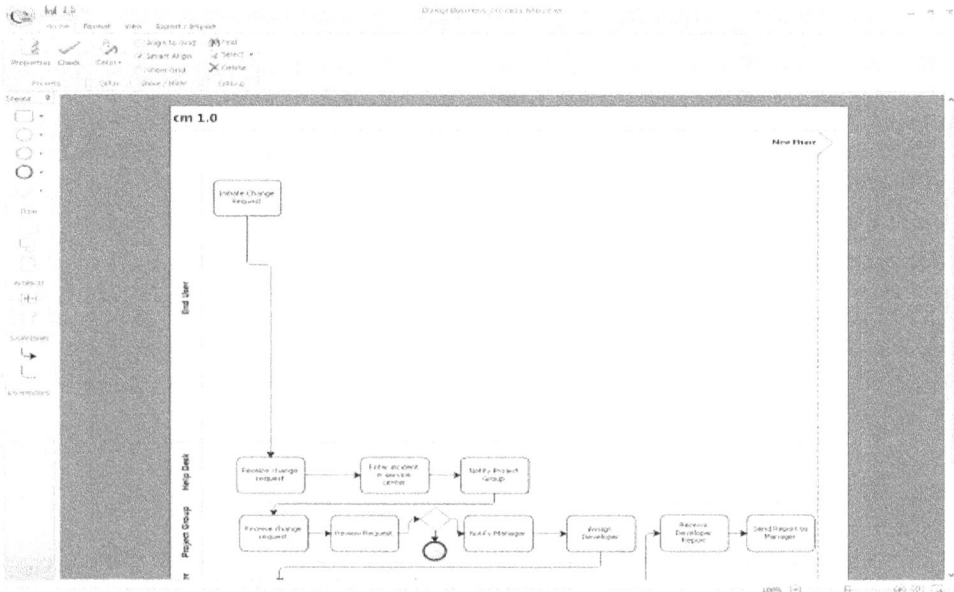

Figure 2 - Process Modeling in BizAgi

WebMethods process development interface is displayed in Figure 3. The modeling notation slightly differs from BPMN notation, unlike other suites. Webmethods permit using sub-processes, which make the whole process more understandable at first glance, however, modeling is not easy in this interface since the lane structure is not easy to manage.

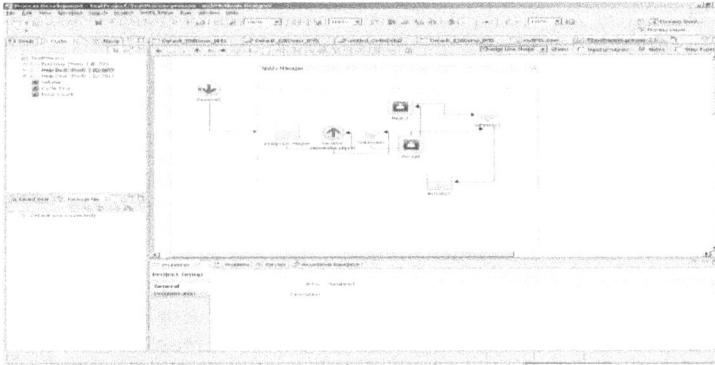

Figure 3-Process Modeling in WebMethods

The final step in the study was to execute the BPA models and it proved to be the most time consuming and difficult stage. This phase was undertaken in terms of the following aspects:

Execution Environment: All BPM suites use web technologies to execute the processes via Microsoft, Java or other proprietary solutions. Setting up the environment is time consuming and very difficult, since each suite has its specific requirements, for example, Intalio requires Java, Eclipse and J2EE knowledge to run the server. BizAGI requires familiarity with Microsoft technologies and Webmethods require high RAM and extensive knowledge of the suggested framework.

Automation parameters: Suites have different approaches for defining automation parameters. Some suites have separate definitions for each phase. Users model the process first, and then, later, add roles, inputs, outputs and relations with other organizational services. This approach is easier since it separates the modeling phase from execution, reducing the complexity of modeling. However, some tools require definition of forms, inputs, outputs while modeling, which requires both programming and BPEL knowledge. For example, there is more work to define conditions for expressing loops and exclusive gateways, and this cannot be done without technical knowledge and experience.

Figure 4 gives the time required to model the processes in BPM suites including setting-up BPM modeling environments and the learning phase as well as the time required to execute the processes in BPM suites including setting up BPM execution environments and learning phase.

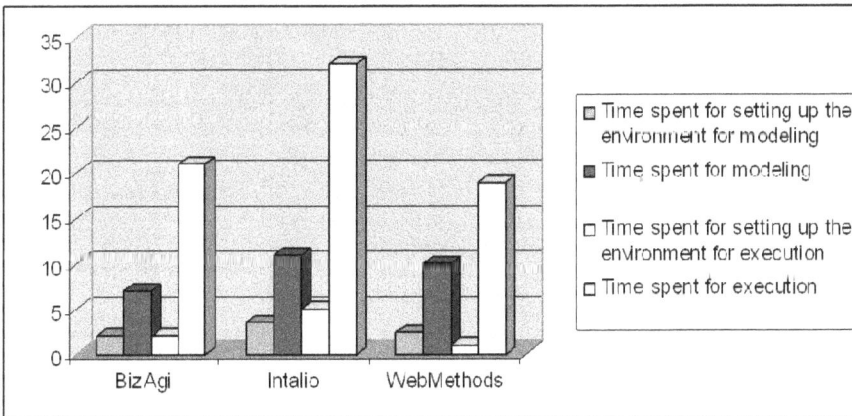

Figure 4 - Time spent for modeling and automation

CONCLUSION

Modeling business processes is a common task for process improvement and process automation and this study explored the extent of reusing process models rather than starting from scratch. It is revealed that the main users for BPM suites are those with technical knowledge since it is very difficult for business experts to understand the frameworks. However, the owners of the processes are business people; therefore, the BPM suites must be incorporated into a more business-logic perspective so that the owners can have more control over their processes.

The modeling phase of process automation requires a rework of the existing processes, for example, SPI models presented with eEPCs cannot be transformed into a BPA model in a way that business analysts are familiar with. To overcome this issue, BPM suites may benefit from the advantages that process modeling tools offer, rather than presenting their own modeling environments.

In a business model, all the elements in the process are described to enhance understanding even though they are not directly relevant, however in modeling for process automation, only related aspects are modeled, those which could cause SPI models to differ from BPA models are omitted. On the other hand, generally, information presented in the SPI model with eEPC is not adequate for a transformation to a complete, executable BPEL process that could be used as a base for BPA model, which is another reason why BPA models differ from SPI models.

From a business perspective, SPI models are well suited for high-level modeling and can include organizational issues such as its goals and structure. On the other hand, BPA models do not focus on the business context but rather only support the processes, the data definitions and the interactions between processes including more implementation level details. In order to transform an SPI model to a BPA model, the question "who will execute what, when, where, how?" must be answered.

Table 1- Questions to be answered for process automation

Who	Those taking part in activities defined in the processes are expressed with enhanced role definitions. However, activity flows between roles may be restricted in BPA models compared with SPI models. In order to increase the approximation between role definitions in SPI and BPA models, lane-structured role definitions may be utilized in SPI models to define roles for each activity together with controls for role completeness to assure interactions between roles will be not be problematic in BPA models.
What	Some activities in a process may require integration with other web services as defined by the organization. These types of interactions are difficult to identify during the modeling phase and may require an additional step. Moreover, in its current state, an SPI model lacks execution details since they are not intended for that purpose.
When	The timing of activity in the process life cycle depends on the synchronization managed by web server; when an activity is completed, the proceeding ones are activated. SPI models must be enriched with notations to enable the web server understand the orchestration. Moreover, the completion criteria for activities and the following action must be explicitly set.

Where	Web service is the dominant technology for executing processes. However, there are no standards for the implementation of web services; some suites use standards such as BPEL, others use proprietary solutions. Since web services are crucial to the execution, SPI models should be enriched with support for web service notations.
How	The way in which an activity is performed is defined by inputs, outputs and other web services. Forms are used to define input/outputs between activities; also other tools used by the organizations (email, messaging systems) can be integrated. To define input/output relations SPI models should incorporate systematic and formal means, which should also allow application and platform specific aspects to be considered.

This study shows that although the SPI and BPA models start at a similar point, then they take completely different roads and the users lose the effectiveness of strengths of each model. There is a need for an approach that would allow inclusion of execution parameters on the one hand, and hide the overwhelming details for business users on the other. Since the nature of the business and technical aspects of modeling differ, a modeling framework is required that will enable the collaboration and integration between technical and business aspects. Such a framework that could establish a common environment to facilitate interaction between technical and business people and allow a sharing of the context would be very beneficial in terms increasing the effectiveness of BPM suites.

Further work will be undertaken to elaborate on the questions listed in Table 1 for SPI models in order to directly bridge with BPM suites.

REFERENCES

Curtis, B., Kellner, M.I., Over, J.: Process Modelling. Communications of the ACM. Vol.35, no.9 (1992)

Lippe, S., Greiner, U., Barros, A.: A Survey on State of the Art to Facilitate Modelling of Cross-Organisational Business Processes. In: Proceedings of the 2nd GI-Workshop XML4BPM 2005, Karlsruhe, Germany. (2005)

Mendling, J., Nüttgens, M., Neumann, G.: A Comparison of XML Interchange Formats for Business Process Modelling. In: Proceedings of EMISA 2004 – Information Systems in E-Business and E-Government. LNI. (2004)

Nalepa, G.J., Mach, M.: Business Rules Design Method for Business Process Management. In Proceedings of the International Multiconference on Computer Science and Information Technology. Pp.165-170. (2009)

OASIS: Business Process Execution Language for Web Services Version 1.1 (BPEL4WS 1.1) Specification. (2006)

Object Management Group: Business Process Modeling Notation (BPMN) Specification 1.0 (2006)

Phifer, G., Hayward, S., Flint, D.: Technologies That Enable Business Process Fusion. Report by Gartner, October 2003.

Recker, J., Rosemann, M., Indulska, M., Green, P.: Business Process Modeling – A Comparative Analysis. Journal of the Association for Information Systems. Vol. 10. issue 4. article 1. (2009).

Scheer, A.W. ARIS – Business Process Modeling, 3rd Edition, Berlin, Germany (2000)

Terai, K., Izumi, N., Yamaguchi, T. : Coordinating Web Services based on business models. In ACM International Conference Proceeding Series: Proceedings of the 5th international conference on Electronic commerce, vol. 50, p. 473–478. (2003).

Tscheschner, W. Transformation from EPC to BPMN. Hasso-Plattner-Institute, Potsdam, Germany. http://bpt.hpi.uni-potsdam.de/pub/Public/OryxResearch/TransformEPC2BPMN.pdf. Last Accessed: 19.04.2010

van der Aalst, W.M.P., ter Hofstede, A.H.M, Weske. M.: Business Process Management: A survey. In Proc. Business Process Management: International Conference, BPM 2003, Eindhoven, the Netherlands (2003).

Ward-Dutton, N.: BPM Vendor capability comparison, 2H08. http://www.oracle.com/us/corporate/analystreports/infrastructure/059586.pdf. (2008). Last accessed: 19.04.2010

WfMC. Workflow Management Coalition Workflow Standard: Workflow Process Definition Interface – XML Process Definition Language (XPDL) (WFMC-TC-1025). Technical report, Workflow Management Coalition, Lighthouse Point, Florida, USA, 2002.

White, S. A. Business Process Modeling Notation - OMG Final Adopted Specification. On BPMN website, 2006. http://www.bpmn.org.

Ziemann, J., Mendling, J.: EPC-Based Modelling of BPEL Processes: a Pragmatic Transformation Approach. In Proceedings of the 7th International Conference "Modern Information Technology in the Innovation Processes of the Industrial Enterprises", Genova, Italy, September 2005.

Section 4

Appendices

Author Biographies

Our sincere thanks go to the authors who kindly gave their time, effort and expertise into contributing papers that cover methods, concepts, case studies and standards in business process management and workflow. These international industry experts and thought leaders present significant new ideas and concepts to help you plan a successful future for your organization. We also extend our thanks and appreciation to the members of WfMC Review Committee who volunteered many hours of their valuable time in the selection of the final submissions and who helped guide the content of the book.

JASON ADOLF

jason_adolf@sra.com

Director of BPM Services Business Process Management, SRA International, USA

Jason Adolf is Director of BPM Services Business Process Management expert with six years of design, development, and implementation experience with BPMS systems. Currently a member of SRA's Spectrum Solutions Group working a business development role to expand our Business Transformation Services practice. Responsible for talent aquisition, proposals, maintaining pipeline, vendor relationships and project execution. Previous experience at SRA includes Web 2.0 projects including standing up corporate Wiki and Instant Messenger system and pro-bono projects as well. Past jobs at SRA included a role as Business Operations Analyst managing project finances for over 30M in annual revenue.

ROY ALTMAN

roy@peopleserv.com

President, Peopleserv, Inc., USA

Roy Altman is the CEO and founder of Peopleserv, Inc. and inventor of its People Relationship Management product. He has been providing customers with resourceful solutions for several decades. He holds an M.B.A. from Pace University in New York, and has taught at institutions of higher learning. Altman is the architect of multiple commercial software products, has authored several published articles and papers, and is a frequent speaker for conferences and seminars. He serves as Chairman of the Electronic Music Foundation, an international not-for-profit music organization.

FRANCESCO BATTISTA

francesco.battista@respondo.it

Senior Consultant, Respondo, Italy.

Francesco BATTISTA is a Computer Science graduate. Since 1994 he worked for Procter & Gamble as Management System Project Manager in Italian and international projects, then moved to major it consultancy companies with account and project management responsibilities for process reorganizations involving SAP and web technologies. From 2004 to 2009 Francesco has been Marketing Director of an Italian BPM company (leading also corporate communications) and is now Organization and Processes Senior Consultant at Respondo. Published author, he is WfMC chairman for Italy and active speaker in BPM related events.

PATRICK BEAUCAMP

patrick.beaucamp@bpm-conseil.com

Founder and CEO, BPM-Conseil, France

Patrick Beaucamp is the founder and CEO of BPM-Conseil, a French company first dedicated to BI and BPM platforms integration. With almost 20 years of experience in the BI area, and a participation in early 90s to Cognos PowerPlay & Impromptu launch in West Europe, Patrick founded in 2007 the Vanilla Open Source BPI Project, rewarded by independent analysts as one of the Top 10 successful French Open Source Project (April 09), as major competitor of SAP Business Object, IBM Cognos and Microstrategy platform (November 09) and most recently nominated in the finalists of the RedHerring promising European companies (may 2010)

GIANPIERO BONGALLINO

gianpiero.bongallino@gmail.com

BPM Senior Researcher and Developer, Italy.

Gianpiero BONGALLINO is a Computer Science graduate, specialized in Intelligent System, AI and Software Engineering. Since 2005, he contributed to development of Web-based and Server-side tools for an Italian BPM company (openwork). Those activities included image recognition & processing, automation, digital sign, client/server integration and enterprise application developments, also involving him as BPM Consultant for processes related to document processing and digital sign, for technical and legal matters. He coordinated teams of last year undergraduates and acted as tutor for internship and thesis, collaborating with Universities in multi-company European projects.

Gianpiero is now BPM, SOA, Event Processing, BI Senior Analyst, Architect, Researcher & Developer and member of Workflow Standards, AI and Software Design teams.

PETER BOSTROM

Peter.Bostrom@oracle.com

Master Principal, Sales Consulting, Oracle Americas

Peter Bostrom has over two decades of technology industry experience in a wide variety of technical and executive management positions in innovative, venture backed start-ups and the largest enterprise software companies. Currently, Peter serves as a Master Principal on the pre-sales technical team of the North American Public Sector practice of Oracle Corporation. In this role, he works with Oracle customers throughout the U.S. Federal Government, as well as state, local and provincial government customers facing the dual challenges of budget constraints and increased demand for responsiveness from their IT assets. Previously, Peter served as the Federal CTO for BEA Systems, acquired by Oracle Corporation in June 2008. Prior to BEA Systems, Peter served in a similar capacity at TIBCO Software. Peter has served in leadership positions on numerous standards bodies, technical user groups, and as an advisor to investors and dozens of technology companies. He is a frequent speaker on technology topics around the country. A long time ago, Peter served in the 1st Battalion of the U.S. Army's 75th Ranger Regiment and the 11th Special Forces Group. He holds a BA in International Affairs from The American University in Washington, DC with a focus on U.S. Defense and Security Policy, as well as Middle East studies.

LINUS CHOW

linus.chow@oracle.com
Chair WfMC Public Sector Chapter
AIIM Ambassador
Principal Consultant, Oracle, USA
Linus Chow is the Chair of the WfMC Public Sector Chapter, AIIM Ambassador and a Principal Consultant for Oracle Corporation. He has over 16 years of leadership and management experience in information technology internationally with over 11 years in workflow, BPM, and SOA. He has played crucial roles in expanding the growth of BPM and SOA adoption first in the US and then internationally from Australia to Switzerland. Currently, Linus leads the adoption of BPM and SOA solutions for Public Sector customers. He has helped organizations win many industry awards for BPM/SOA/ECM implementations. He is a published author and an active speaker on the Best Practices of BPM and SOA. A decorated former US Army Officer, Linus has an MBA, a MS in Management Information Systems, and BS in Mathematics; and is a Certified BPM Professional.

He has spoken at the National Defense University (NDU), OMG, WfMC, BPMI, IQPC, AIIM, Brainstorm, IEEE, SSTC, JMETC, BPM Focus, ISSSP, BPM Strategies; Transformation and Innovation; Gartner, MITRE, University of Hong Kong, National University of Singapore, Computer Society venues; as well as several Government (US, Australia and ASEAN), events.

He has also been widely published: BPM and Workflow Best Practice Handbook 2003, 2004, 2005, 2006, 2007, and 2008 (6 times); 11 BPM/SOA Awards (2002 x 2, 2003, 2004, 2005, 2006, 2007 x 2, 2008 x 2, 2009, 2010 x 2), AIIM Awards 2010 x 2, CIO 100 Award; 2004 Business Management; Computer World Magazine (Australia); CIO Magazine (Australia); SDA Asia; BPM Strategies 2007 and 2008; Several Oracle publications 2007 and 2008; Systems Software and Technology Conference 2008; IEEE; MITRE Orchestration and Service Bus Study; and numerous other articles.

MARCELO CORDINI

mcordini@integradoc.com
Project Manager, INTEGRADOC, Uruguay
Marcelo Cordini is Project Manager at INTEGRADOC (www.integradoc.com), a Business Process Management and Workflow focused company. He was a Senior Developer, directly involved in the development and growing of the company's BPMS. He has worked in several international projects using several Workflow and BPM technologies. He has written several BPM related papers for international Congresses, and has been member of the translation team of the one of the most important BPMN Book to Spanish. His degree thesis focused on the application of Business Intelligence to Business Process Management Systems to monitor processes' key performance indicators.

MANOJ DAS

manoj.das@oracle.com
Director of Product Management, Oracle, USA
Manoj is Director of Product Management at Oracle, responsible for Oracle's BPM Suite of products. Manoj's BPM journey started at Siebel Systems, where he was responsible for the next generation process-centric and insight-driven application platform. He plays a leadership role setting BPM and SOA industry standards, especially in BPMN 2.0, BPEL, and Business Rules. He is widely rec-

ognized at industry conference and Information Technology publications. Manoj has a BS in Computer Science from IIT Kanpur and MBA from UC Berkeley. He has held senior Product Management, Development Management, and Product Development positions at Oracle, Siebel, Mentor Graphics, and others.

PHILIPPE DECLERCQ

Philippe.declercq@cnamts.fr

IT project manager, Caisse Nationale d'Assurance Maladie (CNAMTS), France, Associate Professor in Computer Science, IT Department at Evry University, France

Philippe Declercq is IT project manager. He manages projects for upgrading existing systems and building some reusable components based on service-oriented architecture. Previously he worked more than 10 years in the banking and financial services as a consultant and trainer, in the domain of architecture and design of information systems. He teaches modeling and design of information systems in IT Department at Evry University.

ONUR DEMIRORS

demirors@metu.edu.tr

Associate professor, chair Software Management Programme of Information Systems Department at Middle East Technical University, Ankara, Turkey

Onur Demirors is an associate professor and the chair of the Software Management Programme of Information Systems Department at Middle East Technical University. He holds a Ph.D. degree in Computer Science from Southern Methodist University. His research focuses on software process improvement, software project management, software measurement, software engineering education, software engineering standards, and organizational change management. He managed research projects on developing software process improvement and modeling techniques for SMEs and for establishing and implementing business process modeling approaches for large scale software intensive system specification/acquisition. He studies business process management for software organizations from measurement and modeling perspectives as well as process mining.

SHEILA DONOHUE

s.donohue@crif.com

Product Marketing Manager, CRIF Decision Solutions, Bologna, Italy

Sheila Donohue has twenty years of international experience in delivering risk management solutions to financial services institutions. She is an expert in automating decision-focused business processes, having implemented many risk assessment automation and workflow solutions for large, global companies, including D&B/AIG, IBM and Hewlett Packard, as well as for major financial institutions in Western/Eastern Europe and Russia with her endeavors at her current company, CRIF Decision Solutions. Presently, she is responsible for marketing and pre-sales activities for decision-centric process offerings used both to manage credit, fraud and operational risks as well as to improve competitiveness. Sheila obtained her Masters of Business Administration in Finance and International Business from New York University's Stern School of Business and holds a Bachelors degree in Computer Science and Mathematics from Manhattan College.

JONATHAN EMANUELE

jonathan.emanuele@siemens.com
Sr. Consulting Manager, Siemens Healthcare, PA, USA
Jonathan Emanuele is a Sr. Consulting Manager at Siemens Healthcare, responsible for clinical workflow and reporting implementations. Jonathan has a B.S. in Operations Research & Industrial Engineering and a M.Eng. in Computer Science from Cornell University. He is the co-author of the article "Workflow Opportunities and Challenges in Healthcare" in the 2007 BPM & Workflow Handbook.

VINCENT FAULIOT

Vincent.fauliot@cnamts.fr
IS Architect, Caisse Nationale d'Assurance Maladie, France
Dr Vincent Fauliot is an architect in functional management of information systems. He works in the field of operational urbanization of the information system of Health Insurance and more particularly to the design and implementation of generic functions in support to business activities. Ph.D. in applied physics, specialized in numerical modeling and signal processing, he worked as a researcher at the National Center of Scientific Research and spent more than 10 years in consulting and service information technology firms as a project manager and technical director.

LAYNA FISCHER

layna@FutStrat.com
Editor and Publisher, Future Strategies Inc.,
As the Official Editor and Publisher to WfMC and Director of the annual Global Awards for Excellence in BPM and Workflow, Layna Fischer was previously the Executive Director of WfMC and continues to work closely with the organization to promote industry awareness of BPM and Workflow. Ms Fischer was also the Executive Director of the Business Process Management Initiative (now merged with OMG) and is on the board of BPM Focus (previously WARIA, Workflow And Reengineering International Association), where she was CEO since 1994.

Future Strategies Inc., (www.futstrat.com) publishes unique books and papers on business process management and workflow specializes in dissemination of information about BPM and workflow technology, business process redesign and electronic commerce. As such, the company contracts and works closely with individual authors and corporations throughout the USA and the world.

Future Strategies Inc., is the also publisher of the business book series *New Tools for New Times*, as well as the annual *Excellence in Practice* volumes of award-winning case studies and the annual *Workflow Handbook*, published in collaboration with the WfMC. Ms. Fischer was also a senior editor of a leading international computer publication for four years and has been involved in international computer journalism and publishing for over 20 years. She was a founding director of the United States Computer Press Association in 1985.

BOGDAN GHILIC-MICU

ghilic@ase.ro, www.ghilic.ase.ro,
Head of Economy Informatics Department, Academy of Economic Studies Bucharest, Romania

Bogdan GHILIC-MICU received his degree on Informatics in Economy from the Academy of Economic Studies Bucharest in 1984 and his doctoral degree in economics in 1996. Between 1984 and 1990 he worked in Computer Technology Institute from Bucharest as a researcher. Since 1990 he teaches in Academy of Economic Studies from Bucharest, at Informatics in Economy Department. His research activity, started in 1984 includes many themes, like computers programming, software integration and hardware testing. The main domain of his last research activity is the new economy – digital economy in information and knowledge society. Since 1998 he managed over 25 research projects like System methodology of distance learning and permanent education, The change and modernize of the economy and society in Romania, E-Romania – an information society for all, Social and environmental impact of new forms of work and activities in information society.

Ray Hess
rhess@cchosp.com
Vice President, Information Management, The Chester County Hospital, West Chester, PA, USA
Ray Hess has a Masters Degree in Healthcare Administration and has spent the last seven years working on applying Business Process Management and process automation principles to the healthcare setting. He has published and spoken extensively on the subject. He has also won multiple awards for his work. These include the 2006 WARIA North America Gold Award, a 2009 CIO Top 100 Innovator and Plus One Award, and a 2010 Healthcare Informatics Innovator award.

Hansung Kim
amang@dongnam.ac.kr

Associate Professor, Dongnam Health College, and WfMC Member

Kwanghoon Kim
kwang@kgu.ac.kr
Director, Contents Convergence Software Research Center, Gyeonggi Province, Korea

Full Professor, Department of Computer Science, Kyonggi University, Korea and WfMC ERC Vice-Chair, Country Chair (Korea)
Dr. Kwanghoon Kim is a full professor of computer science department and director of the contents convergence software research center at Kyonggi University, South Korea. At Kyonggi, he is involved in research and teaching of workflow, business process management, groupware, coordination theory, computer networks, software architectures, and database systems. He had worked as a researcher and developer at Aztek Engineering, American Educational Products Inc., and IBM in USA, as well as at Electronics and Telecommunications Research Institute (ETRI) in South Korea. In present, he is a vice-chair of the BPM Korea Forum, a country-chair (Korea) and a ERC vice-chair of the Workflow Management Coalition. He has also been on the editorial board of the international journal, KSII Transactions on Internet and Information Systems, and the committee member of the several conferences and workshops. His research interests include workflow systems, adaptive case management, service-oriented business process management, workflow discovery/rediscovery, CSCW/ Groupware, collaboration theory, Grid/P2P/ Cloud distributed computing, workflow mining systems and RFID/USN middleware.

SETRAG KHOSHAFIAN

setrag@pega.com

VP of BPM Technology, Pegasystems Inc., USA.

Dr. Setrag Khoshafian is Vice President of BPM Technology for Pegasystems Inc. Dr. Khoshafian is a recognized BPM pioneer and thought leader who has done R&D, innovation, and productization in a number of domains including Business Process Management, Service Oriented Architectures, Business Intelligence, Collaborative Computing, Database and Content Management, and Object Orientation. Dr. Khoshafian's vision of enterprise software is captured in his recent book *Service Oriented Enterprises.* This vision combines a service-focused way of doing business with the latest BPM technology for a fresh approach in which each party or participant sees itself as a service provider as well as a service consumer integrated through BPM. Service Oriented Enterprises shows how Business agility could be achieved through BPM and focuses on the emerging architecture of service orientation. Dr. Khoshafian holds a PhD in Computer Science from the University of Wisconsin-Madison.

FARHI MARIR

f.marir@londonmet.ac.uk

Associate Professor, London Metropolitan University, UK

Farhi Marir is associate Professor and head of the knowledge Management Research Centre at the faculty of computing, London Metropolitan University. Dr. Marir has amassed fifteen years experience in teaching and research in the UK. He is teaching software engineering, advanced database, data mining and warehousing systems. His research covers knowledge management, workflow systems, information retrieval, semantic web and case-based reasoning. He led several UK and EU funded projects and published around eighty papers in the domain of knowledge and information management, database systems and content-based indexing and retrieval systems. He also led to completion ten PhD students in the domain of knowledge management, information retrieval, database systems and workflow systems. He is member of British Computer Society and also member of editing board for two international journals. He is also member of the program committees for four international conferences.

CYNTHIA MASCARA

cynthia.mascara@siemens.com

Principal Consultant at Siemens Healthcare, PA, USA

Cynthia Mascara RN, MSN, MBA is a Principal Consultant on the Clinical Outcomes team at Siemens Healthcare, with responsibilities for designing workflows and corresponding reports for measuring clinical outcomes, as well as outcomes and metrics consultation during hospital HIS implementations. Cynthia has a 29 year history in health care, having worked in various nursing clinical and informatics positions at the University of Pittsburgh Medical Center before coming to Siemens. She is co-author of the Handbook of Informatics *for Nurses and Healthcare Professionals,* first through third editions, and co-presenter of "IT Support for Clinical Workflow: Definitions, Requirements and an Example of a Healthcare Workflow Management System" at the AMIA 2007 Spring Congress.

CRISTIAN MASTRANTONO

cmastrantono@integradoc.com

Senior Developer, INTEGRADOC.

Cristian Mastrantono is part of INTEGRADOC development team (www.integradoc.com), a Business Process Management and Workflow focused company. He is a Senior Developer, directly involved in the development and growing of the company's BPMS. He has worked in several multinational software companies before. He has written several BPM related papers for international Congresses, and has been member of the translation team of the one of the most important BPMN Book to Spanish. His degree thesis focused on the relationship between Business Process Management and Business Intelligence, and how to extract useful knowledge to improve organization's performance.

Marinela MIRCEA
mmircea@ase.ro
Economy Informatics Department, Academy of Economic Studies Bucharest, Romania
Marinela MIRCEA received her degree on Informatics in Economy from the Academy of Economic Studies, Bucharest in 2003 and his doctoral degree in economics in 2009. Since 2003 she is teaching in Academy of Economic Studies from Bucharest, at Informatics in Economy Department. Her work focuses on the programming, information system, business management and Business Intelligence. She published over 35 articles in journals and magazines in computer science, informatics and business management fields, over 15 papers presented at national and international conferences, symposiums and workshops and she was member over 15 research projects. She is the author of one book and she is coauthor of three books. In February 2009, she finished the doctoral stage, and her PhD thesis has the title *Business management in digital economy.*

Juan J. Moreno
jmoreno@integradoc.com
Director, INTEGRADOC, Montevideo--Uruguay.
Juan J. Moreno is cofounder of INTEGRADOC (www.integradoc.com), a Business Process Management and Workflow focused company, holding the intellectual property of its INTEGRADOC BPM Suite. Having managed dozens of installations in different countries of South America, he has a deep understanding of the benefits organizations may obtain from BPM. He is also professor and researcher at the Engineering and Technologies Faculty of the "Universidad Católica del Uruguay". He holds a PhD in Computer Science, specialized in Software Engineering, from the "Universidad Pontificia de Salamanca", in Spain. He has dozens of technical and arbitrated publications, and has been recognized with the third prize of "Innovator of the Year 2003" in his country, Uruguay.

Vinaykumar S Mummigatti
vinaymummigatti@gmail.com
VP – Global Head of BPM Practice, Virtusa, USA
Vinaykumar is VP and global head of BPM practice at Virtusa, a global IT consulting firm. He is responsible for BPM strategy, alliances, consulting and delivery. He has contributed significantly to BPM Center of Excellence, Business Transformation, Convergence and BPM on Cloud initiatives. He has more than 18 years experience in the IT and Consumer Industries handling various leadership roles in Enterprise solutions, Business consulting, Global delivery, Strategic alliances and business operations. He has been involved closely with BPM, ECM, Portals and CRM initiatives across multiple Fortune 500 clients in defining roadmap for enterprise solutions and successfully implementing strategic

programs. He contributes regularly to his blog on www.BPM-experiences.com. He holds a Bachelors degree in Electronics Engineering and MBA in Finance and Marketing. He worked previously with Mahindra Satyam and IBM.

JOHN NDETA

Jon014@londonmet.ac.uk
Post-Doc Researcher, London Metropolitan University, UK
For the last five years he worked as a researcher/visiting lecturer in the Knowledge Management Research Centre (KMRC), Faculty of Computing, and London Metropolitan University, UK. His research interests include conceptual modelling and design of e-workflow application, adaptive and context-awareness in web applications, knowledge management, component-based web applications development, and business process management. John Ndeta holds a Ph.D. in Information Systems from London Metropolitan University, MSc in Information Engineering and BSC in Computing Studies from South Bank University, London, UK.

MARTIN PALATNIK

mpalatni@ucu.edu.uy
Independent Consultant, Uruguay
Martin Palatnik has worked in Software Development for many years both in South America and Europe, gaining a broad view of different technologies and disciplines. He has written several BPM related papers for international Congresses, and has been member of the translation team of the one of the most important BPMN Book to Spanish. His degree thesis focused on the application of several Knowledge Management tools, including Business Intelligence, to Business Process Management Systems to extract metrics, monitor indicators and predict user future workloads.

NATHANIEL PALMER

nathaniel_palmer@sra.com
Chief BPM Strategist of SRA International and
Executive Director, Workflow Management Coalition, USA.
Nathaniel Palmer is Chief BPM Strategist of SRA International and Executive Director of the Workflow Management Coalition (WfMC). In addition he was recently appointed Editor-in-Chief of BPM.com – the BPM market's most-trafficked destination site. He is also the founder and chairman of the successful Transformation and Innovation event series, widely regarded as the leading conference on business transformation. Previously he was Director, Business Consulting for Perot Systems Corp, where he worked for business process guru Jim Champy. He spent over a decade with Delphi Group as Vice President and Chief Analyst. The author of over several dozen research studies as well as co author of the critically-acclaimed management text "The X-Economy" (Texere, 2001) and the "BPM and Workflow Handbook" (FSI, 2007), Nathaniel has been featured in numerous media ranging from Fortune to The New York Times. He is on the advisory boards of many relevant industry publications, as well as the Board of Directors of Association of Information Management (AIIM) NE, and was nominated to represent the Governor of Massachusetts on the Commonwealth's IT Advisory Board.

Jon Pyke

CEO, Collaborate in Motion, UK

Jon Pyke has over 30 years experience in the field of software engineering and product development. During his career he has worked for a number of software and hardware companies as well as user organizations. Jon is one of the most influential figures in the Business Process Management (BPM) sector. As CTO of Staffware plc (now Tibco) for over 12 years, he can truly claim to be one of the founders of BPM as a means to implement a process improvement culture in business. He was personally responsible for defining many of the key software metaphors that enable BPM to work, and as Chair of the Workflow Management Coalition (WfMC), he has also overseen the development of standards. Jon was founder and CEO of the Process Factory and CSO for Cordys where he opened up the UK office, set their "total BPM" strategy, defined the Cloud proposition and headed Marketing. Most recently Jon has started a new venture – Collaborate In Motion due to launch onto the market in the fall of 2010.

As one of BPM's great thinkers, he has written and published a number of articles on the subject of Office Automation, BPM and Workflow Technology. Jon Co-Authored a book covering both technical and business aspects of BPM. The book is published by Cambridge University Press and is called – Mastering you Organization's Processes. More recently Jon co-wrote Enterprise Cloud Computing with Andy Mulholland and Peter Fingar.

Jon demonstrates an exceptional blend of Business/People Management skills; a Technician with a highly developed sense of where technologies fit and how they should be utilized. Jon is a world recognized industry figure; an exceptional public speaker and a seasoned company executive.

Christine Robinson

robinsoncf@yahoo.com
Principal-Enterprise Architect
Christine Robinson & Associates, LLC Arlington, USA

Christine Robinson, published author and award-winning technology professional, has received international recognition for her contributions to Enterprise Architecture, Business Process Management, and security. With a history of performing leadership roles at leading technology firms, Christine's business and technology solutions to protect and streamline U.S. government agencies and other organizations range from small initiatives to some of the world's largest. Her numerous published works include the recently published book she co-authored entitled "Future Cities, Designing Better, Smarter, More Sustainable and Secure Cities" which describes using her innovative security approach for designing future cities. Her thought leadership and creativity have led her to win awards for innovation and excellence, inspire government procurements, and even help pass congressional legislation and funding. Christine currently serves on the Arlington County IT Advisory Commission. Christine graduated with her BBA from the University of Texas at San Antonio and graduated with an MBA from George Washington University.

Robert Shapiro

robert.shapiro@global360.com
Senior Vice President, Global360, USA.

Robert Shapiro created the first open-architecture object-oriented graphical modeling toolkit for process modeling. It was the platform for Design IDEF in support of SADT (Structured Analysis and Design Technique) and used to build the first version of CPN (Colored Petri Net) modeling and simulation technology. Robert Shapiro is founder and manager of Process Analytica. He is Senior Vice President: Research, for Global 360. He founded Cape Visions (acquired in 2005) where he directed the development of Analytics and Simulation software used by FileNet/IBM, Fujitsu, PegaSystems and Global 360 Business Process Management products. Prior to founding Cape Visions, as founder and CEO of Meta Software Corporation, he directed the implementation of a unique suite of graphical modeling and optimization tools for enterprise-wide business process improvement Products based on these tools are used by Bank America, Wells Fargo, JPMChase and other major banks to optimize their check processing and Lock Box operations As a participant in the Workflow Management Coalition and chair of the working groups on conformance and process definition interchange, he plays a critical role in the development of international standards for workflow and business process management. He has been instrumental in the creation and evolution of XPDL and BPMN. In 2005 he was awarded the Marvin L Manheim Award for outstanding contributions in the field of workflow.

Marian STOICA

marians@ase.ro, www.marian.stoica.ase.ro
Marian STOICA received his degree on Informatics in Economy from the Academy of Economic Studies, Bucharest in 1997 and his doctoral degree in economics in 2002. Since 1998 he is teaching in Academy of Economic Studies from Bucharest, at Informatics in Economy Department. His research activity, started in 1996 and includes many themes, focused on management information systems, computer programming and information society. The main domains of research activity are Information Society, E-Activities, Tele-Working, and Computer Science. The finality of research activity still today is represented by over 50 articles published, 10 books and over 20 scientific papers presented at national and international conferences. Since 1998, he is member of the research teams in over 20 research contracts with Romanian National Education Ministry and project manager in 5 national research projects. IEEE member from 2010.

Keith Swenson

kswenson@wfmc.org
VP of Research & Development, Fujitsu America
Vice Chairman, Workflow Management Coalition
Keith Swenson is Vice President of Research and Development at Fujitsu Computer Systems Corporation for the Interstage family of products. He is known for having been a pioneer in web services, and has helped the development of standards such as WfMC Interface 2, OMG Workflow Interface, SWAP, Wf-XML, AWSP, WSCI, and is currently working on standards such as XPDL and ASAP. He has led efforts to develop software products to support work teams at MS2, Netscape, and Ashton Tate. He is currently the Chairman of the Technical Committee of the Workflow Management Coalition. In 2004 he was awarded the Marvin L. Manheim Award for outstanding contributions in the field of workflow. Mr. Swenson holds both a Master's degree in Computer Science and a Bachelor's degree in Physics from the University of California, San Diego. From 1995 to 1997 he served as Vice Chairman of the ACM Special Interest Group for Group Support Systems (SigGROUP). In 1996, he was elected a Fellow of the Workflow Management Coalition. In 2004 he was awarded the Marvin L. Manheim Award for outstanding contributions in the field of workflow.

JAMES TAYLOR
james@decisionmanagementsolutions.com
CEO and Principal Consultant, Decision Management Solutions, USA
One of the leading experts in decision management and decisioning technologies, James is passionate about using business rules and predictive analytics to improve decision making and develop smarter systems. He is an active consultant, speaker, blogger and author. He was lead author of "Smart (Enough) Systems," the book he wrote with Neil Raden, and has contributed chapters to books on business rules and BI. James appears frequently at events including keynoting BI 2010 and speaking at the IBM CIO Leadership Exchange, Predictive Analytics World and Business Rules Forums. James developed the concept of decision management and has been working on it for the past 8 years. The best known proponent of the approach, James helped create the emerging Decision Management market and has over 20 years developing software and solutions.

DANIEL TURISSINI
Operational Research Consultants, United States
Mr. Turissini is the CEO and founder of Operational Research Consultants, Inc. An innovator in systems engineering and integration he has focused ORC in the field of Information Assurance and Identity Management, providing integration & testing, operation & maintenance, and R&D for all aspects of Information Security. He has achieved Certificate Authority certifications across the Federal government, providing trusted eGoverment authentication capability and successful deployments of Federal Personal Identity Verification credentials for various Federal agencies. Mr. Turissini sits on the Board of Directors of the Federation for Identity and Cross-Credentialing Systems® (FiXs) where he chairs the FiXs Operations Committee, leading efforts in defining the requirements that need to be met for FiXs operations; and, concurrently, deploying a FiXs certified credential issuance solution - fully posturing FiXs to fulfill its mission to establish and maintain a worldwide, interoperable identity and cross-credentialing network built on security, privacy, trust, standard operating rules, policies and technical standards. He holds a Bachelor of Science degree in Marine Engineering and Nautical Science from the US Merchant Marine Academy and a Masters in Engineering Administration from The George Washington University.

FILIZ ÇELIK YESILDORUK
filiz.celik@tcmb.gov.tr
Researcher and Ph.D. student, Middle East Technical University, Ankara, Turkey
Filiz Çelik Yesildoruk is a researcher and a Ph.D. student in Information Systems at Informatics Institute, Middle East Technical University She holds an M.S. degree in Information Systems (METU) and B.S. degree in Computer Engineering and Information Science (Bilkent University). She has been working as a software engineer since 2000. Her research interests include; software process improvement, software process management and business process management.

WfMC Structure and Membership Information

WHAT IS THE WORKFLOW MANAGEMENT COALITION?

The Workflow Management Coalition, founded in August 1993, is a non-profit, international organization of workflow vendors, users, analysts and university/research groups. The Coalition's mission is to promote and develop the use of workflow through the establishment of standards for software terminology, interoperability and connectivity among BPM and workflow products. Comprising more than 250 members worldwide, the Coalition is the primary standards body for this software market.

WORKFLOW STANDARDS FRAMEWORK

The Coalition has developed a framework for the establishment of workflow standards. This framework includes five categories of interoperability and communication standards that will allow multiple workflow products to coexist and interoperate within a user's environment. Technical details are included in the white paper entitled, "The Work of the Coalition," available at www.wfmc.org.

ACHIEVEMENTS

The initial work of the Coalition focused on publishing the Reference Model and Glossary, defining a common architecture and terminology for the industry. A major milestone was achieved with the publication of the first versions of the Workflow API (WAPI) specification, covering the Workflow Client Application Interface, and the Workflow Interoperability specification.

In addition to a series of successful tutorials industry wide, the WfMC spent many hours over 2009 helping to drive awareness, understanding and adoption of XPDL, now the standard means for business process definition in over 80 BPM products. As a result, it has been cited as the most deployed BPM standard by a number of industry analysts, and continues to receive a growing amount of media attention.

WORKFLOW MANAGEMENT COALITION STRUCTURE

The Coalition is divided into three major committees, the Technical Committee, the External Relations Committee, and the Steering Committee. Small working groups exist within each committee for the purpose of defining workflow terminology, interoperability and connectivity standards, conformance requirements, and for assisting in the communication of this information to the workflow user community.

The Coalition's major committees meet three times per calendar year for three days at a time, with meetings usually alternating between a North American and a European location. The working group meetings are held during these three days, and as necessary throughout the year.

Coalition membership is open to all interested parties involved in the creation, analysis or deployment of workflow software systems. Membership is governed by a Document of Understanding, which outlines meeting regulations, voting rights etc. Membership material is available at www.wfmc.org.

COALITION WORKING GROUPS

The Coalition has established a number of Working Groups, each working on a particular area of specification. The working groups are loosely structured around the "Workflow Reference Model" which provides the framework for the

Coalition's standards program. The Reference Model identifies the common characteristics of workflow systems and defines five discrete functional interfaces through which a workflow management system interacts with its environment—users, computer tools and applications, other software services, etc. Working groups meet individually, and also under the umbrella of the Technical Committee, which is responsible for overall technical direction and co-ordination.

WORKFLOW REFERENCE MODEL DIAGRAM

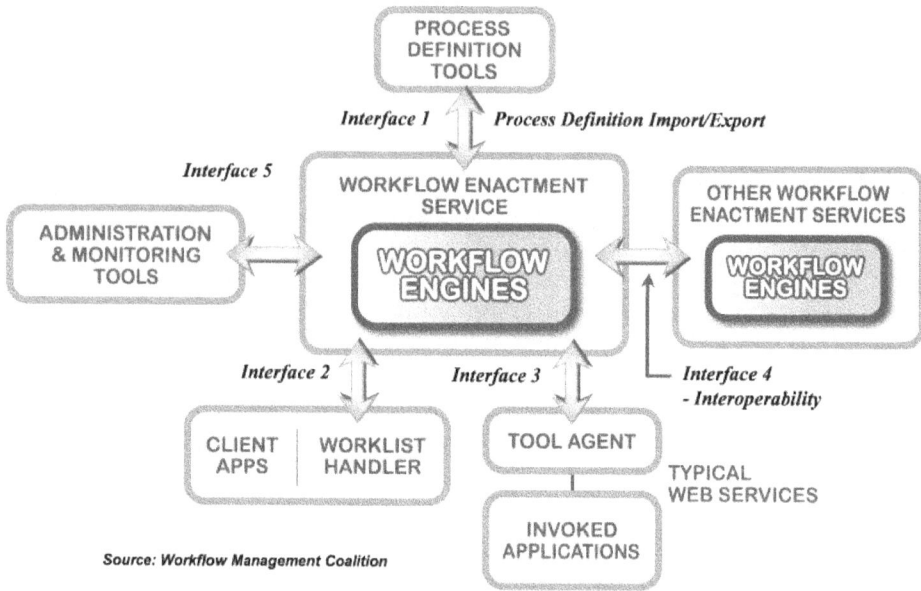

Source: Workflow Management Coalition

WHY YOU SHOULD JOIN

1. Gain Access to Members-Only Research and Q&A Forums
2. Participate in Members-Only "Brown Bag" Networking Sessions and Industry Speaker Series
3. Receive Free Admission to Business Process Focused Events and Programs (a Benefit Worth $1,000s Annually)
4. Access to Access to the Industry's Largest Research Library on Business Process Modeling, Workflow, BPMS
5. Assistance in Product Certification and Conformance, as well as Requirements Analysis and Procurement Strategy

Being a member of the Workflow Management Coalition gives you the unique opportunity to participate in the creation of standards for the workflow industry as they are developing. Your contributions to our community ensure that progress continues in the adoption of royalty-free workflow and process standards.

MEMBERSHIP CATEGORIES

	Full Member	Associate Member	Individual Member
Annual fee	$3500	$1500	$500
Hold office	Software Vendors, IT & Professional Services Firms, Government, Non-Profit & Commercial	Government or Non-Profit (incl academic); Any Commercial Firm Not Selling Software or IT Services	All open to all organizations; limited to observing roles, not eligible for officer or committee participation
Limitations	Eligible for All Offices & Committees	Eligible for All Offices & Committees	Observer Only
Events/ Research	Full Admission to WfMC Events (up to 3 individuals) and Full Access to the WfMC Research Library (up to 3 log-ons)	Full Access to the WfMC Research Library (single log-on) and Free Admission to All WfMC Events	Full Access to the WfMC Research Library (single log-on) and Free Admission to Select WfMC Events
Promotional Benefits	Logo on All WfMC Pages; Free Use of WfMC Banner Serving; Detailed Company Profile in WfMC Publications	Listed on WfMC Members List and Within Member Directory	N/A

ADDITIONAL BENEFITS OF MEMBERSHIP

This corporate category offers exclusive visibility in this sector at events and seminars across the world, enhancing your customers' perception of you as an industry authority, on our web site, in the Coalition Handbook and CDROM, by speaking opportunities, access to the Members Only area of our web site, attending the Coalition meetings and most importantly within the workgroups whereby through discussion and personal involvement, using your voting power, you can contribute actively to the development of standards and interfaces.

Full member benefits include:

- Financial incentives: 50 percent discount all "brochure-ware" (such as our annual CDROM Companion to the Workflow Handbook, advertising on our sister-site www.e-workflow.org), $500 credit toward next year's fee for at least 60 percent per year meeting attendance or if you serve as an officer of the WfMC.
- Web Visibility: your logo on all WfMC pages, inclusion in the WfMC web banner network, a detailed company profile in in online member directory as well as in all WfMC publications.
- User RFIs: (Requests for Information) is an exclusive privilege to all full members. We often have queries from user organizations looking for specific workflow solutions. These valuable leads can result in real business benefits for your organization.

- Publicity: full members may choose to have their company logos including collaterals displayed along with WfMC material at conferences / expos we attend. You may also list corporate events and press releases (relating to WfMC issues) on the relevant pages on the website, and have a company entry in the annual Coalition Workflow Handbook
- Speaking Opportunities: We frequently receive calls for speakers at industry events because many of our members are recognized experts in their fields. These opportunities are forwarded to Full Members for their direct response to the respective conference organizers.

ASSOCIATE MEMBERSHIP

Associate and Academic Membership is appropriate for those (such as IT user organizations) who need to keep abreast of workflow developments, but who are not workflow vendors. It allows voting on decision-making issues, including the publication of standards and interfaces but does not permit anything near the amount of visibility or incentives provided to a Full Member. You may include up to three active members from your organization on your application.

INDIVIDUAL MEMBERSHIP

Individual Membership is appropriate for self-employed persons or small user companies. Employees of workflow vendors, academic institutions or analyst organizations are not typically eligible for this category. Individual membership is held in one person's name only, is not a corporate membership, and is not transferable within the company. If three or more people within a company wish to participate in the WfMC, it would be cost-effective to upgrade to corporate Associate Membership whereby all employees worldwide are granted membership status.

HOW TO JOIN

Complete the form on the Coalition's website, or contact the Coalition Secretariat, at the address below. All members are required to sign the Coalition's "Document of Understanding" which sets out the contractual rights and obligations between members and the Coalition.

THE SECRETARIAT

Workflow Management Coalition (WfMC)
Nathaniel Palmer, Executive Director,
759 CJC Hwy, Suite #363,
Cohasset, MA 02025-2115 USA
+1-781-923-1411 (t), +1-781-735-0491 (f)
nathaniel@wfmc.org

WfMC Membership Directory

BIZMANN SYSTEM(S) PTE LTD

Associate Member

www.bizmann.com

BOC INFORMATION TECHNOLOGIES CONSULTING LTD.

Full Member

www.boc-group.com
The BOC Group is a software and consulting house specializing in IT-based Management Approaches. From its offices in six different countries and its Headquarters in Vienna, the BOC Group operates on a world-wide basis with Europe as its core market. Anticipating markets needs, the BOC Group offers expertise in Strategy Management by using the Balanced Scorecard concept, product ADOscore®, in Business Process Management based on the Business Process Management System Meta-Modelling concept, ADONIS®, in Supply Chain Management using the SCOR® concept, ADOlog® and in IT Architecture and IT Service Management by using, current concepts like ITIL®, ADOit®. The BOC Group performs projects and offers solutions in the banking, insurance, telecommunication, health care, public administration sectors as well as in the fields of E-Learning and Knowledge Management providing its customers with competence optimizing their processes, identifying their IT potentials, better utilizing their knowledge assets and deployment of their human and IT resources.

FLOWRING TECHNOLOGY CO. LTD.

Associate Member

www.flowring.com

FUJITSU COMPUTER SYSTEMS CORP

Full Member

www.fujitsu.com/interstage
Ranked as a leader in the Application Infrastructure Software market, the Fujitsu Interstage BPM Suite helps companies build SOA-enabled BPM applications by bringing business and IT professionals together to design, simulate, automate, analyze, and optimize business processes. Fujitsu's Process-Driven Approach to SOA using Interstage Business Process Manager, together with CentraSite, Fujitsu's SOA registry and repository, successfully brings business and IT professionals together. This top-down approach allows for collaboration on translating real business models into optimized, executable business processes while letting an organization reuse their existing Visio process maps, IT infrastructure and other SOA assets to reduce operational costs and maximize business agility and efficiencies. With ₵13 billion in annual revenues, Fujitsu is the third largest global IT Company. Its Interstage offerings are the enabling technologies of choice for companies building applications that can be shared across the enterprise to lower operating costs, accelerate business processes and react quickly to changing market requirements.

GLOBAL 360, INC

Full Member

www.global360.com

Insight 360 is Process Intelligence for BPM, providing bottom-line BPM benefits without the risk and cost of a BI project, and without relying on a competing application infrastructure that attempts to obviate existing investments. While most BPM Suites are not designed to address the management of processes that lie outside of their direct control, Insight 360 is unique because it offers an independent layer that can integrate with BPM Suites and other applications for providing end to end process visibility and alignment. Insight 360 benefits are focused in four distinct areas: Visibility, Alignment, Efficiency, and Agility.

HANDYSOFT GLOBAL CORPORATION

Full Member

www.handysoft.com

HandySoft Global Corporation is leading the way for companies worldwide to develop new strategies for conducting business through the improvement, automation, and optimization of their business processes. As a leading provider of Business Process Management (BPM) software and services, we deliver innovative solutions to both the public and private sectors. Proven to reduce costs while improving quality and productivity, our foundation software platform, BizFlow®, is an award-winning BPM suite of tools used to design, analyze, automate, monitor, and optimize business processes.

IVYTEAM-SORECOGROUP

Associate Member

www.ivyteam.ch

KOREA INSTITUTE FOR ELECTRONIC COMMERCE (KIEC)

Full Member

www.kiec.or.kr

Korea Institute for Electronic Commerce (KIEC) was established under the Korean Government pursuant to the Framework Act on Electronic Transaction legislated in August 1999. The state purpose is to promote Korea's e-Business in line with a rapidly global trend. KIEC has been positioning itself as the hub of Korea's e-Business industry to meet the needs of the times. The institute has created an e-Business-friendly environment nationwide by linking the public and private sectors and facilitating international cooperation.

LOMBARDI

Full Member

www.lombardisoftware.com

Lombardi believes that a Process-Driven approach is the best way to win. We deliver a suite of Business Process Management (BPM) software and services that enable organizations to quickly become Process-Driven. Lombardi is a recognized as a leader in BPM software for Global 2000 companies by both Gartner and Forrester Research.

MCL SYSTEMS

Full Member

www.mclsystems.com

The MCL Ganges product line offers Business Process Management solutions for building process driven solutions. The innovative approach of Ganges in seamlessly integrating BPM to any database application is fundamentally different from traditional solutions that provide a separate BPM solution. Ganges delivers process driven operations, workflow automation, collaboration, security, enforces best practices, and drastically improves quality, productivity and accountability.

METASTORM

Full Member

www.metastorm.com

With a focus on enterprise visibility, optimization, and agility, Metastorm offers market-leading solutions for Enterprise Architecture (EA), Business Process Analysis & Modeling (BPA) and Business Process Management (BPM). As an integrated product portfolio, Metastorm Enterprise™ allows organizations to maximize business results by unifying strategy, analysis and execution. Metastorm is the only solution provider to bring together these critical disciplines on a single software platform to enable an understanding of enterprise architecture and strategy, accurate impact and opportunity assessment, effective process execution, and accelerated value realization for organizations worldwide.

OPENWORK

Full Member

www.openworkBPM.com

openwork® is a pure Independent Software Vendor concentrating all efforts exclusively on its openwork Business Process Management suite. openwork features an original methodology that makes use of daily business, non-technical language and approach, introducing high-abstraction tools to map, share and maintain organizations shape and working rules. Those agile tools also allow to reflect organizations evolutions, keeping them always aligned with changing business needs. openwork is then able to act as an interpreter of graphic representation of organizations shape and working rules, enabling paper manual processes to become alive into finalized real-world web applications, integrated with other existing IT systems.

PEGASYSTEMS INC.

Full Member

www.pega.com

Pegasystems (NASDAQ: PEGA) provides software to drive revenue growth, productivity and agility for the world's most sophisticated organizations. Customers use our award-winning SmartBPM® suite to improve customer service, reach new markets and boost operational effectiveness. Our patented SmartBPM technology makes enterprise applications easy to build and change by directly capturing business objectives and eliminating manual programming. SmartBPM unifies business rules and processes into composite applications that leverage existing systems -- empowering businesspeople and IT staff to Build for Change®, deliver value quickly and outperform their competitors. Pegasystems' suite is complemented by best-practice frameworks designed for leaders in financial services, insurance, healthcare, government, life sciences, communications, manufacturing and other industries. Headquartered in Cambridge, MA, Pegasystems has offices in North America, Europe and Asia.

PROCESSMAKER

Full Member

www.processmaker.com
ProcessMaker is an open source business process software tool that allows private and public organizations to automate document intensive, approval-based processes across systems including finance, HR and operations. A web-based application, it allows users across multiple sites to create and share workflows, customize forms, manage processes, and enhance reporting. ProcessMaker includes tools to design forms, create documents, assign roles and users, create routing rules, interconnect with third-party systems including business intelligence (BI), document management (DMS), content management (CMS) and enterprise resource planning (ERP) systems through a service-orientated architecture (SOA). It is available free for download at
http://sourceforge.net/projects/processmaker/

QUALIWARE APS

Full Member

www.qualiware.com
Founded in 1991, QualiWare is a global consulting services and business modeling software provider. Our services and products help our customers succeed with their Quality Management, Business Process Management and Optimization initiatives, Business Excellence programs, Enterprise Architecture initiatives, and/or IT solution development needs, including the QualiWare Lifecycle Manager which supports XPDL 2.1 for process portability. QualiWare is a private company with offices in Denmark, Sweden, Norway, Ukraine and the United States. Our development team is headquartered in Copenhagen, Denmark and Kiev, Ukraine.

PROGRESS SAVVION

Full Member

www.savvion.com
Savvion is the leading provider of business process management (BPM) software that improves business performance and reduces costs. Savvion has a proven track record of turning process improvement ideas into real-world solutions quickly, often in as few as 30 days, and delivering a return on investment as high as 300%. More than 300 global business enterprises, public service agencies, and systems integration firms, including 20 of the Fortune 100, use Savvion systems to manage their business. Savvion is recognized by Intelligent Enterprise as one of the most influential companies in information technology today, and is cited as a leader by independent research firms.

SERENA SOFTWARE

Full Member

www.serena.com
For 30 years, Serena has been solving the tough problems facing organizations responsible for application development. Customers choose our industry-leading Application Lifecycle Management solutions whenever they need development

controls for mainframe, distributed or embedded development projects. From team-level management of source code to complex development projects that simply cannot fail, Serena delivers the governance needed to make software better. More recently, we have expanded the Serena solution portfolio to bring the same governance to other business processes. Our Business Process Management solutions quickly automate business processes to increase responsiveness while delivering built-in auditability.

SRA International, Inc.

Full Member

www.sra.com/bpm
SRA International, Inc. [NYSE: SRX] is the premiere provider of Business Process Management Services to the U.S. federal government. Named to FORTUNE Magazine's "100 Best Companies to Work For" list for ten consecutive years, SRA's staff of 7,000 across 50 offices worldwide represent some of the industry most recognized names in business process modeling, simulation, semantic web, enterprise architecture, and BPMS implementation. SRA has been an active Full Member of the WfMC since 2007 and regularly leads local BPM workshops for members and other interested parties inside of the Washington, D.C. area.

TIBCO Software, Inc.

Full Member

www.tibco.com/solutions/bpm/default.jsp
TIBCO digitized Wall Street in the '80s with its event-driven "Information Bus" software, which helped make real-time business a strategic differentiator in the '90s. Today, TIBCO's infrastructure software gives customers the ability to constantly innovate by connecting applications and data in a service-oriented architecture, streamlining activities through business process management, and giving people the information and intelligence tools they need to make faster and smarter decisions, what we call The Power of Now®. TIBCO serves more than 3,000 customers around the world with offices in 40 countries and an ecosystem of over 200 partners.

University of Nebraska

Academic Member

Email: emukusha@nebraska.edu

W4 (World Wide Web Workflow)

Full Member

www.w4global.com
W4, one of the leading European software vendors specialized in Business Process Management, supplies more than 270 customers, serving more than 1 million users. For more than 10 years W4 has been widely acclaimed for its expertise in Human Centric BPM. Whatever the particular need, there is a package available allowing customers to take full advantage of W4 technology. W4 BPM Suite is a complete package, from modeling to monitoring, dedicated to the enterprise process automation. This BPM package is managing the automation of complex work processes involving high volumes of users, connections to applications and integration to the IT. Process can be both support (finance, HR, etc) and company-specific (new product launch, modification requests, etc.) W4 BPM Suite provides an easy tool for modeling their processes and generate the presentation

layer (application) for both Java and .NET environments. It also offers managers reporting and supervision functionalities.

WORK MANAGEMENT EUROPE

Associate Member

www.wmeonline.com

Additional Workflow and BPM Resources

NON-PROFIT ASSOCIATIONS AND RELATED STANDARDS RESEARCH ONLINE

- AIIM (Association for Information and Image Management)
  http://www.aiim.org
- AIS Special Interest Group on Process Automation and
  Management (SIGPAM)
  http://www.sigpam.org
- BPM and Workflow online news, research, forums
  http://bpm.com
- BPM Research at Stevens Institute of Technology
  http://www.bpm-research.com
- Business Process Management Initiative
  http://www.bpmi.org *see* Object Management Group
- IEEE (Electrical and Electronics Engineers, Inc.)
  http://www.ieee.org
- Institute for Information Management (IIM)
  http://www.iim.org
- ISO (International Organization for Standardization)
  http://www.iso.ch
- Object Management Group
  http://www.omg.org
- Open Document Management Association
  http://nfocentrale.net/dmware
- Organization for the Advancement of Structured Information
  Standards
  http://www.oasis-open.org
- Society for Human Resource Management
  http://www.shrm.org
- Society for Information Management
  http://www.simnet.org
- Wesley J. Howe School of Technology Management
  http://howe.stevens.edu/research/research-centers/business-
  process-innovation
- Workflow And Reengineering International Association (WARIA)
  http://www.waria.com
- Workflow Management Coalition (WfMC)
  http://www.wfmc.org
- Workflow Portal
  http://www.e-workflow.org

2008 BPM & WORKFLOW HANDBOOK

Spotlight on Human-Centric BPM

Human-centric business process management (BPM) has become the product and service differentiator. The topic now captures substantial mindshare and market share in the human-centric BPM space as leading vendors have strengthened their human-centric business processes. Our spotlight this year examines challenges in human-driven workflow and its integration across the enterprise. **Retail $95.00**

2009 BPM & WORKFLOW HANDBOOK

Spotlight on BPM in Government

The question, "How can governments manage change organizationally and be agile operationally?" is answered in this special spotlight on BPM in Government with specific emphasis on the USA government where agencies, armed forces, states and cities are facing almost insurmountable challenges. **Retail $75.00**

BPM EXCELLENCE IN PRACTICE 2009

Innovation, Implementation and Impact

Award-winning Case Studies in Workflow and BPM

These companies focused on excelling in *innovation*, *implementation* and *impact* when installing BPM and workflow technologies. They recognized that implementing innovative technology is useless unless the organization has a successful approach that delivers—and even surpasses—the anticipated benefits. **$49.95**

BPMN MODELING AND REFERENCE GUIDE

Stephen A. White, PhD, Derek Miers

Understanding and Using BPMN
Develop rigorous yet understandable graphical representations of business processes

Business Process Modeling Notation (BPMN™) is a standard, graphical modeling representation for business processes. It provides an easy to use, flow-charting notation that is independent of the implementation environment. **Retail $39.95**

www.ingramcontent.com/pod-product-compliance
Lightning Source LLC
Chambersburg PA
CBHW080719220326
41520CB00056B/7150